Vegetarian Times Complete Cookbook

BY THE EDITORS OF VEGETARIAN TIMES AND LUCY MOLL

MACMILLAN - USA

MACMILLAN
A Simon & Schuster Macmillan Company
1633 Broadway
New York, NY 10019-6785

Library of Congress Cataloging-in-Publication Data
Vegetarian times complete cookbook / by the editors of vegetarian times and Lucy
Moll.
       p.   cm.
    Includes index.
    ISBN 0-02-621745-7
    1. Vegetarian cookery. I. Moll, Lucy. II. Vegetarian times.
  TX837.V427   1995
  641.5'636—dc20   95-30186
                                   CIP

Book design by Vertigo Design
Manufactured in the United States of America
10 9 8 7 6 5

Acknowledgments

THIS BOOK WOULD NOT BE IN YOUR HANDS if it weren't for Paul Obis, Jr., who founded *Vegetarian Times,* a magazine with a paid monthly circulation of more than 310,000, and counting. In the beginning, in the mid-1970s, Paul wanted to shout the good news of the vegetarian choice from the rooftops; instead, he chose a simple newsletter as his forum. He had a vision. He acted on it. And the dream lives on in a top-notch, four-color magazine.

A special thanks that defies words goes to all of the editors, past and present, who worked tirelessly throughout the years to edit recipes and text. Their insight and warmth—which come through in person and on the pages of *Vegetarian Times*—have proven invaluable to the success in reaching a wide audience and to my work.

I especially am indebted to Carol Wiley Lorente, food editor, who answered many of my food-related questions and who gave me support in completing this project, and to Terry Christofferson, editorial assistant, who helped me in little ways too numerous to count and who compiled a number of the nutritional breakdowns in this book at barely a moment's notice.

To Mary Carroll, Rema D'Alessandro, Lillian Kayte and Peggy Ramette, who together developed dozens of new recipes for this book, I say great work, great times.

My gratitude pours out to my word processors—my sister-in-law Mary Lee Moll, my cherished friend Laurie Hobson and my mom—and to Jan Gahala, a former *Vegetarian Times* copy editor, whose friendship warms my heart and whose unsurpassed skills in editing helped to ensure error-free recipes. Joe D'Alessandro got me out of a few mind-boggling computer jams—thanks, cousin.

Susan Sidler, former director of books and products at Cowles Magazines, was a wonderful companion and advisor during the early stages of the conception and writing of this book. Justin Schwartz, my editor at Macmillan, shared his insights and knowledge—invaluable. Steve Lehman and Toni Apgar of Cowles Magazines graciously contributed their wisdom whenever I asked for suggestions.

And whether several other special people—Jennifer, Wade, Wendy, Bob, Sue, Gene, Rich, Catie, Bill and Michelle (and Jim and John)—realize it, they helped make this book a reality by urging me to be all that I can be, through Him who empowers me. Thanks for walking beside me during an up-and-down yet joyful time in my life.

Most of all, I offer my thanks to my husband, Steve, and my daughter, Laura, who put up with my moods as well as my hours, which sometimes stretched into the wee hours of the morning. My Rock and my Precious: To both of you, my endless love.

Dedicated to the memory of my mother,
Carol G. Kuper, a lover of life, of Light. —L.M.

Contents

Introduction

Welcome, Friends

"CAN YOU HELP ME WITH A FOOD QUESTION?" asked the woman, who was calling long distance with the single-minded purpose of getting dinner on the table. "I want to cook one of your recipes, but it calls for dry beans and I don't have time to cook them from scratch. May I substitute canned beans?" The answer was an easy and emphatic "Yes." The long-distance caller and one of the *Vegetarian Times* editors worked together over the phone to calculate how many cans of beans she needed to make the recipe, and then she was off and cookin'.

The woman's call was no surprise and it made sense. She wanted a solution to her cooking dilemma and didn't mind spending a few quarters of phone time to get help. Similar requests for help, whether by phone, fax or mail, come in to our offices day after day. Around the holidays—when new cooks and veteran gourmets prepare extra-special meals—the phone calls and letters pour in. It seems that everyone needs a hand in the kitchen—or better yet, a knowledgeable friend.

This book, with its chapters on everything from why people are choosing to eat vegetarian meals to its practical information on how to plan menus to its more than 600 recipes, is that faithful friend. You can turn to it when you have specific questions about cooking or when you just want to curl up on the couch and read recipes for pleasure.

But before we go further, let's clear up one possible misconception. Yes, every recipe in these pages is vegetarian (containing no meat, poultry or fish). But this book isn't meant for vegetarians alone. As you know, people everywhere are cutting down on or cutting out meat and other animal foods. Even the conservative U.S. Department of Agriculture has gotten in on the act with its new Food Guide Pyramid, replacing the basic four food groups, two of which were animal-based. The Food Guide Pyramid is more on target with science, encouraging people to eat more grains, vegetables and fruits and less animal foods like meat, eggs and dairy products.

So whether you're a vegetarian or you simply want to update your recipe file and eat vegetarian meals some of the time (maybe your doctor suggested the change), this book will reinforce your choice to eat for good health and good taste. An entire chapter is devoted to why the vegetarian choice is healthful. By the way, seeking better health is the number-one reason people become vegetarians, so says the only comprehensive survey on the vegetarian choice (Yankelovich, Skelly & White/Clancy, Shulman, Inc., "The American Vegetarian: Coming of Age in the 90's." Clancy & Shulman, Inc., 1992). But other reasons—improving the environment and caring about animals, to name two of them—lead people to a healthier way of eating too.

The "whys" are important, but they wouldn't be complete without the "how." How do you make delicious vegetarian meals (with the emphasis on delicious)? Simple: Choose among the 63 sample menus we've provided, or devise your own menus by selecting from the 600-plus recipes in this book. The recipes have concise cooking instructions as well as useful tips. Don't know anything about an ingredient in a recipe? Check the glossary of less common foods in chapter 6. Want to learn what to do when the meat's off the plate? Read the section on menu planning in chapter 4. Are you interested in making low-fat substitutions for high-fat foods? Turn to our list of substitutions in chapter 8.

Most important, the recipes have been tested again and again by people like you. Nine out of ten recipes have appeared in *Vegetarian*

Times magazine during the last few years. The remainder are new; they were written by recipe developers just for this book. In addition to concise instructions, each recipe has a nutritional analysis. Again, our goal is to make it easy for you to eat wisely and enjoy cooking, savoring your meals and feeling good.

The one thing that the majority of the recipes lacks is lots of fat. Most weigh in low on this necessary yet easy-to-overeat macronutrient. That's a boon for anyone who's concerned about their health, including people who have high blood pressure or a high serum cholesterol level, or who have a few pounds to shed. In the majority of recipes, the calories that come from fat range from 20 to 25 percent of the total. (Though most health organizations recommend eating no more than 30 percent of calories from fat, many scientists say lower is better.) The rest of the recipes either have next to no fat or are dripping with fat. It's true: As long as your daily way of eating is healthful, there's no good reason not to splurge on a slice of Black Forest Cake (page 417) from time to time.

Eating ought to be celebratory. When you gather around the table with family and friends (or dine alone by candlelight), you're nourishing your whole being—body, mind and spirit. And when you do your body good by choosing healthful foods, you feel good. But it's not enough for food to be healthful; it has got to taste great, too. We know you'll find favorites among the recipes we selected. (It's all right if your book gets some food splatters on it. The more splatters, the more well-loved the recipes are shown to be, we think.)

You're getting your information from the source that *The New York Times* and CNN call when they want information about the vegetarian choice. *Vegetarian Times* magazine has celebrated its twentieth anniversary and still is going strong. As more people have opted for vegetarian meals—in fact, some twenty thousand people become vegetarians each week, surveys indicate—our emphasis is on letting people taste the difference for themselves by serving up dozens of recipes monthly.

We count you among our friends. Thank you for inviting us into your kitchen. We invite you to make yourself at home in these pages, put on a pot of soup or toss a salad (or, better yet, bake a cake) and stay awhile.

what is the vegetarian diet anyway?

1

THE VEGETARIAN STYLE OF EATING IS A CULINARY ADVENTURE. It's delicious, bountiful, gourmet or everyday, economical—and lovely. Yes, even a word like *lovely* comes to mind. But think about it for a moment: When you take care of yourself by eating the way that an increasing number of Americans—and scientists—are embracing (witness the countless studies on the benefits of vegetarian foods), you are taking a stand for better health—and not just for your personal health.

Choosing vegetarian foods—whether you eat meatless meals every day or only occasionally—makes a world of difference. This is no exaggeration. Among the effects of your vegetarian choice are a decrease in pollution (water, air and land) and other environmental ills, as well as the possibility for hungry people to be fed because the tons of grain given to livestock can instead go to families in want (although whether food gets to hungry people depends more on politics than on availability of food provided by relief agencies). For people in Third World countries, sticking with their traditional diets (which almost always are primarily vegetarian) is a better choice than adopting a rich, American-style fare, which puts a toll on their land, their economic stability and their personal health. (We'll get into the various health advantages of the vegetarian choice in the next two chapters.)

THE GREAT ADVENTURE

When you load up your shopping cart with produce, other vegetarian foods and possibly some dairy products and eggs—or when you order saffron-flavored Spanish paella (hold the meat) from a restaurant menu—you are walking into an exciting world that the average American has yet to truly explore. Yet, others have gone before you. In fact, the first vegetarians came to the United States in 1817. They were Bible-Christians, as they called themselves, who had broken ties with the Church of England. They believed that America's religious tolerance would be good for their church, which required members to be vegetarians. The Bible-Christians eventually disbanded, but their stance on the goodness of the vegetarian way influenced health reformers, including Sylvester Graham of graham cracker fame.

Before these vegetarians brought their recipes to our shores, meatless cuisine reigned humbly in many lands: India, China, Africa and the peasant sections of Europe, among others. When people ate meat, it was as a condiment or part of an out-of-the-ordinary meal.

Your own experience? Most likely, you tasted meat by the time you were one or two years old, learned about the four basic food groups in school (two of the four groups being centered squarely on animal foods) and ate dinners with meat in the middle of the plate and some sauced-up vegetables and buttered bread on the side. But you also have eaten meatless meals all your life: pasta with marinara sauce, cheese pizza, potato pancakes, chunky minestrone soup with crusty bread, hoppin' john (if you've spent time in the South), numerous traditional breakfast offerings, and so on.

Even so, as you set out on your culinary adventure, think of yourself as a treasure hunter. That goes for veteran vegetarians as well as for people new to preparing and eating vegetarian meals regularly or

GAINING NUMBERS

Just two or three decades ago, only 1 percent of Americans described themselves as vegetarian. Today the number is about 7 percent.

occasionally. We at *Vegetarian Times* find out something new about vegetarian foods nearly every day. For instance, we've learned that scientists are investigating how antioxidants (beta carotene and vitamins C and E, among others), which are abundant in certain vegetables and grains, may reduce your cancer risk and even may prove to reverse the disease; a number of top chefs are choosing vegetables grown without chemicals to make the best meals for their customers; and tennis legend Martina Navratilova has adopted the vegetarian choice for the taste of it.

Before you begin your journey, you'll need to get your bearings: a definition of vegetarian cuisine. Simply, vegetarian cuisine is resplendent with plant foods—vegetables, fruits, grains, legumes (including soyfoods such as tofu, also known as bean curd), soymilk and tempeh (savory, fermented soybean cakes), nuts and seeds—seasoned with a plethora of herbs, spices and various sauces and pastes such as tahini (sesame seed paste), and augmented with dairy products and eggs if desired. Nearly all U.S. vegetarians do eat dairy products and eggs; the most health-conscious among them limit their portions of these high-fat and cholesterol-laden foods.

You can combine these foods in so many ways that you need not eat the same meal twice in a year—so much for the myth that vegetarian meals are an endless march of salad greens. We know you won't cook a completely different meal every day; that's too much work for anyone. And the point of eating is to be kind to yourself and to celebrate as you try new taste sensations.

> **B.C. VEGETARIANS**
>
> Until 1847, vegetarians were known as Pythagoreans. The name came from the Greek philosopher Pythagoras (580–500 B.C.), whose writings on beans and cabbage made a case for vegetarianism in his day.

YOU'RE IN GOOD COMPANY

Without a doubt, you're not alone on your journey. The only comprehensive and representative survey of vegetarians (Yankelovich, Skelly & White/Clancy, Shulman, Inc., 1992) found that about 6.7 percent of the adult American population say they are vegetarian; that's about 12.5 million people. The market research firm of Bruskin Goldring Research came up with an almost identical figure. When these numbers are compared to findings of previous surveys, the results are remarkable: About 1 million

Americans each year are adopting the vegetarian choice. It's conceivable that some 25 million adult Americans will be trumpeting themselves as vegetarian by the year 2005.

"It seems that vegetarianism is breaking out of the health-food closet and onto more mainstream tables," says Linda Gilbert, president of HealthFocus, a marketing and consulting firm that conducted a survey of one thousand shoppers nationwide, asking questions about healthful eating. And there's no doubt, Gilbert says: "The trend toward eating less meat and smaller portions of meat is going to continue."

One of the most interesting findings of the Yankelovich survey was the number of people describing themselves as vegetarian though they may eat fish, chicken or meat several times a year or even a few times a week. This desire to identify oneself as vegetarian (in spite of Webster's definition, which echoes the definition we gave a moment ago) amazed us at first. Just a decade or two ago, words like *hippies, sprouts* and *Birkenstock sandals* were linked to vegetarians, and vegetarianism was seen as cultish to mainstream America. (By the way, Birkenstock footwear is now considered fashionable. Interesting, isn't it?)

Truth be told, people who regularly eat vegetarian food cannot be typified. They span all ages and socioeconomic scales: grandmas, CEOs, teens, pilots, military personnel, orchestra conductors, bikers, actors, ministers, physicians and a former Beatle and his wife. Some have been vegetarian for a few months, others for decades. According to the Yankelovich survey, about half of the vegetarians went "cold turkey," eating a hamburger one day and pledging the next day never to touch meat again; the other half gradually changed (or are changing) their diets. An unknown number were vegetarians in their teens or twenties, started eating meat again, and have returned to the vegetarian choice in their middle years.

Thankfully, vegetarian cuisine has come a long way since the days of the flower children. Science had branded the vegetarian diet as dangerous, and misguided vegetarian chefs—though laying the groundwork for today's scientific acceptance and culinary beauty—perpetuated the

---

WHY GO VEGETARIAN?

In the most comprehensive survey on the vegetarian choice, here's how interviewees answered the question, "What's your single most important reason for becoming a vegetarian?":

Health Reasons	46%
Not Sure/Other	18%
Animal Welfare	15%
Influence of Family and Friends	12%
Ethical Reasons	5%
Environment	4%

nutritional misconceptions with their oh-so-carefully designed recipes, lest someone should become ill. Nutrition—well, what was thought to be good nutrition—took precedence over taste.

Back then, the food seemed monotonously brown and as heavy as a brick. The flavor of the food was earthy—too earthy, many vegetarian chefs of those days have said in recent years. Wheat germ and nutritional yeast seemed to be sprinkled on everything. And, because these worry-warts feared they might court serious nutritional deficiencies on a vegetarian diet (the term *diet* fit back then, because it *was* restrictive), they snuck cheese, yogurt and eggs into nearly every meal.

Today, the vegetarian way of eating has an exceptional reputation for good nutrition *and* good taste. "By degrees, over the years, we loosened up and lightened up," says Carol Flinders, co-author of the celebrated *Laurel's Kitchen* (Ten Speed Press, 1976; a revised edition was published in 1986), who has cooked her way through more than two decades with vegetarian delight. "The more we learned about the value of whole foods...the more confident we felt that if we just avoided refined foods and embraced variety, we'd get all the nutrients we needed.

"This," she adds, "led to a lovely opening up."

The trend toward the vegetarian choice—or "lifestyle shift," to use the words of one social observer—has not gone unnoticed. The National Restaurant Association has encouraged its members to add creative vegetarian entrées to their menus because, based on the findings of one of its surveys, one-third of restaurant patrons would select a vegetarian entrée if one were offered; food manufacturers and fast-food chains have developed meatless products; and magazines and newspapers (*The New York Times* and *USA Today,* to name two) have published articles on the popularity of vegetarian cuisine.

Even baseball caught on. At San Francisco's Candlestick Park, a concession stand named The Natural opened in 1993, serving up vegetarian burgers, fruit salad, trail mix and other such goodies to fans who'd rather forgo hot dogs and beer for more healthful fare.

Looks like a home run to us.

SWEET TOOTH?

Myth: All vegetarians avoid sugar.

Reality: Some vegetarians skip junk foods, but many eat sugary treats occasionally. It depends on the individual's desire for sweets.

WHAT'S YOUR TYPE?

On one side of the ocean, Leo Tolstoy was writing *War and Peace*. Thousands of miles away, John Harvey Kellogg had perfected the cornflake. The connection? Both men were vegetarians, but their meals differed substantially. It is said that the writer liked his macaroni and cheese, while the cornflake pioneer was not the least bit fond of dairy foods.

Tolstoy, the ovo-lacto vegetarian. Kellogg, the aspiring vegan. Two men, two vegetarians, two styles of eating. Actually, the vegetarian choice has many variations. That's another reason why people who eat vegetarian meals cannot be lumped together and stereotyped: Two vegetarians' eating styles may be like night and day. It's impossible to say which style is right for you. So many factors come into play: your reason for eating vegetarian meals; the level of support from your family, friends and workplace; how comfortable you are with trying new tastes; and your love of various foods, among other factors.

Here, then, is a look at the major and some minor types of vegetarian styles of eating.

Ovo-Lacto Vegetarian

Most vegetarians in the Western world choose this style. Health is the number-one reason. (Forty-six percent of people describing themselves as vegetarian cite health as the top reason for their dietary preference, according to the Yankelovich survey.) This eating style is based on vegetables, fruits, grains, legumes, seeds and nuts, and includes eggs (ovo) and dairy products (lacto). The culinary possibilities are enormous: pizza, filled pasta, perogies, blintzes, omelets, stuffed vegetables, egg salad sandwiches, dessert of all sorts—almost anything except for foods that don't fit the definition of *vegetarian* (meat, poultry and fish).

Because the ovo-lacto choice allows for so many food possibilities, people who eat this way rarely have trouble finding food to eat on restaurant menus or while traveling, whether at home or abroad. It also is easy to find ample possibilities at a family buffet or at a business luncheon where a menu is provided.

I'M OK, YOU'RE OK

Myth: Vegetarians are food faddists.

Reality: Some vegetarians eat tofu, sprouts and granola regularly; others don't. Some vegetarians shop in natural food stores; the majority shop in supermarkets. Some vegetarians make their meals from scratch; few of us have the time. The upshot: What you eat is a matter of choice.

It's the easiest choice and a satisfying one. It's healthful, too, as long as you don't load up on eggs and dairy products to replace the meat you used to eat. We're happy to say that as people become more comfortable with their vegetarian choice and as they become better informed, they learn to avoid a common mistake of eating too much of these rich foods, research shows.

Etiquette tip: Occasionally, you'll find yourself in a situation in which you may feel the need to let out the word about your vegetarian choice. For instance, your boss invites you and your spouse over for a barbecue. What do you do? Your best bet is to be up front: Tell your boss. Depending on his or her response (she might say, "Really? My closest friend is a vegetarian, too. I'll put some vegetable kebabs on the grill. No trouble."), you might have a second helping of the vegetarian entrée, offer to bring a dish or eat a small meal before the party and pig out on the appetizers, salads and dessert.

In another scenario (you've been invited to a wedding or a school reunion held at a reception hall), you may choose to say nothing and eat around the meat entrée, or you could call the manager of the hall in advance and arrange for a vegetarian meal.

All in all, your best bet is to be gracious. Chances are that your host will be gracious too.

Lacto-Vegetarian

This choice is similar to ovo-lacto vegetarian except you skip the eggs. Two of the main reasons why Americans become lacto-vegetarians is to lower their cholesterol intake or avoid an allergic reaction. Others choose to eliminate eggs out of concern for laying chickens, whose factory farm conditions are known to be horrendous. Some people don't eat eggs for spiritual reasons: Hindus, for instance, consider an egg a potential life.

Again, the culinary possibilities are wonderfully abundant, thanks in part to Americans' growing concern about eating too much cholesterol. In fact, this eating style has the most popularity worldwide because it is the traditional East Indian diet. Outside India and countries with communities of Indians, where you need not concern yourself with finding ample food to your liking, you'll need to read product labels and ask restaurant staff

IN FLIGHT

Vegetarian meals are the most commonly requested special meal on airplanes.

whether a dish contains eggs—a minor inconvenience and a precious learning opportunity.

Some people go the other way, becoming ovo-vegetarians (still referred to as ovo-lacto vegetarians). This suits people who are allergic to milk products or have difficulty digesting them. A vegetarian who says no to dairy products can also take a stand against the milk industry, which employs some controversial practices. These practices include treating dairy cows with hormones to increase milk production; feeding antibiotics to cows whose udders have become infected, often due to unsanitary conditions; and taking calves away from their mothers and placing them in crates, where they are fed an anemic diet to keep their flesh as white as possible for the enjoyment of veal lovers.

Restaurant tip: If you want to circumvent the need to ask again and again at different restaurants about ingredients, make a list of your favorite dishes at various restaurants. When eating out, be the first in your group to suggest a few restaurants from your list. This way you know you'll be satisfied without a doubt.

Vegans

Okay, the word *vegan* (pronounced VEE-gun) sounds strange. It conjures up images of aliens with pointy ears. Nevertheless, it describes people who choose to eat no animal products whatsoever. About 4 percent of people who describe themselves as vegetarian are vegans. Some vegetarians dabble with the vegan choice, omitting eggs and dairy products from their diets for a while, then switching back when the urge for ice cream strikes. (We know of one vegan physician who sticks to his vegan choice every day of the year but one: Thanksgiving, when he joins his family for turkey dinner.)

Why go vegan? Most people cite ethical concerns. They do not want to contribute to the harming or killing of animals for any reason. (Some individual vegans may have exceptions, such as attending zoos that take good care of their animals.) The vegan choice sometimes is seen as the purest way to eat and live, because like theologian and Nobel Peace Prize winner Albert Schweitzer, who was careful where he stepped so not to kill a single insect, the vegan ethic is "reverence for life." This way of eating is healthful, too, though once in a while, you might hear that the vegan choice is seriously detrimental to health. But remain confident in your decision: Scientific studies on the whole debunk this charge. But please do keep in mind that it's all but impossible to be vegan.

Why? Think about it: Factory farms and ranches produce much more than the cellophane-wrapped packages that end up in the meat sections of supermarkets; the animals are used for their byproducts, too. The byproducts of meat production end up almost everywhere—and we mean everywhere. The video tape you rented the other day contains gelatin (from bone); shampoo may include collagen (found in bone, cartilage and connective tissue), placenta, and keratin (found in animal hair, nails and hooves); various byproducts are used in bricks, plaster, and home insulation materials; cement mix may contain dried ox blood and/or animal tallow (fat); and even your car contains animal byproducts. For instance, animal fat is used in the production of steel and to vulcanize rubber. Antifreeze and hydraulic brake fluid also contain animal fat. And that's only a part of the long list of how animal byproducts have found their way into nearly every aspect of our lives. Enough said.

The good news is vegan recipes aren't hard to find. This book has page after page of recipes with no dairy products or eggs. But eating out can be a little tricky. For breakfast, you can choose oatmeal, hashbrowns, toast, fruit and juice. When lunch and dinnertime arrives, think ethnic. Asian, Ethiopian and Middle Eastern cuisines are delicious options. Even pizza is a go—just order it without the cheese. In the *Vegetarian Times* office, the cheeseless pizzas are the first to disappear while the remainders of the cheesy ones end up in the refrigerator. But if you find yourself stuck in a steak house, your choices may be a salad and a baked potato (or two of each). Most vegans we know would rather eat at home, where they can delight in their creativity with gusto. One way or another, you'll be well fed.

Macrobiotics

Turning to lesser known variations of the vegetarian choice, let's start in the East, where macrobiotics was born. Although macrobiotics (*macro* meaning great and *bios* meaning life) includes dietary principles, it is more than a diet. It's a conscious way of living in harmony with the natural order of the universe. You may have heard of the terms *yin* and *yang*. These energetic concepts are used to describe every dimension of life from the spiritual to the physical. The goal is balancing yin and yang to achieve health in all senses of the word. If you're having trouble grasping what macrobiotics mean, join the crowd; most Westerners need to study macrobiotic principles before they understand them. According to macrobiotics, foods are classified as either yin or yang; the idea is to balance the foods so your diet is neither too yin or yang. A healthy balance, says the theory, is a diet in which whole grains make up about one half of the day's foods, vegetables make up one quarter to one third, legumes and sea vegetables make up 5 to 15 percent and the remainder is soup. Some people who follow a macrobiotic diet also eat fish.

Natural Hygiene

Food-combining principles are at the core of natural hygiene, a diet with the goal of aiding digestion by eating only foods that are compatible at any given meal. Compatibility is determined by the types of digestive enzymes needed to break down each food. When the enzymes are not harmonious, say natural hygienists, digestion runs less smoothly than is ideal, and mild to severe indigestion—even disease, they say—may result. (In general, scientists do not accept many of the principles of the natural hygiene diet.)

So which foods make great combos according to natural hygienists? Green and low-starch vegetables go well with either protein foods (such as legumes and dairy products) or starch foods (such as grains and potatoes), but eating protein and starch foods at the same meal is a definite no-no. Fruit is in a category by itself, and according to natural hygienists, it's best eaten alone because it digests so quickly.

A quick note: The food-combining principles of natural hygiene have nothing to do with protein complementarity, a theory that eating foods in certain combinations increases the protein content of the meal. Protein complementarity is discussed in detail in chapter 2.

LIMELIGHT VEGETARIANS (A NONINCLUSIVE LIST)

Hank Aaron (major league baseball home run champion), Grant Alexander (star of TV's *Guiding Light*), Bob Barker (TV personality), Kim Basinger (actress), Herbert Blomstedt (conductor of the San Francisco Symphony Orchestra), Surya Bonaly (Olympic medalist in ice skating), Boy George (rock vocalist), Berke Breathed (cartoonist), Andreas Cahling (champion bodybuilder), Chris Campbell (Olympic medalist in wrestling), Benjamin Carson, M.D. (prominent neurosurgeon), Peter Falk (actor), Sara Gilbert (actress), Elliot Gould (actor), Henry Heimlich, M.D. (inventor of Heimlich manuever), Dustin Hoffman (actor), Desmond Howard (Heisman trophy winner), Andrew Jacobs, Jr. (U.S. congressman), Billie Jean King (tennis champion), Tony LaRussa (pro-baseball manager), Cloris Leachman (actress), Marv Levy (pro-football head coach), Carl Lewis (Olympic runner), Steve Martin (comedian and actor), Coleman McCarthy (syndicated columnist), Paul and Linda McCartney (rock musicians), Natalie Merchant (rock vocalist), Edwin Moses (Olympic medalist in track), Olivia Newton-John (rock vocalist), Dean Ornish, M.D. (cardiologist and author), Raffi (children's musician), Phylicia Rashad (actress), Fred Rogers (TV's Mister Rogers), Boz Skaggs (rock musician), John Tesh (TV personality), Lindsay Wagner (actress), Vanessa Williams (actress and singer).

Ayurvedic

Ayurveda (pronounced I-ur-VAY-dah) is India's ancient system of healing, which regards both diet and medicine as important and complementary to wellness. A diet based on ayurvedic principles differs from person to person, depending on the individual's constitution—your physical makeup and temperament. An ayurvedic practitioner can determine your conditional type, or you can seek a book on the topic to make your own determination. Once you know your constitutional type—vata, pitta or kapha, or a combination—you can choose foods that suit you from an ayurvedic perspective. If you decide to try an ayurvedic diet, we suggest that you find out more about it. One source is *The Ayurvedic Cookbook* (Amadea Morningstar with Urmila Desai, Lotus Press, 1990).

Semi-Vegetarians

Some people like to say you can't be semi-vegetarian, because it's like being a little bit pregnant: You either are or aren't. But because we hear it all the time, we'll give a stab at a definition.

This term may refer to people who are vegetarian most of the time but occasionally eat fish, poultry or meat. Or it may describe people who eat fish and poultry regularly but skip meat. Theoretically, people who eat lots of vegetables could be called semi-vegetarians. The short of it is the term has no exact definition. So next time you hear someone use it, ask what he or she means. Their meaning may differ greatly from what you might imagine.

You never know: The person may be a crusto-vegetarian (eats shrimp, crab or other crustaceans), a mollo-vegetarian (eats clams, scallops, oysters or other mollusks), a porco-vegetarian (eats pigs), or even a repto-vegetarian (eats snakes and other reptiles) or an ento-vegetarian (eats insects). True, the definitions can get a little silly. And that's our point.

What's encouraging is how many people are moving in the direction of eating more vegetables, fruits, grains and legumes. Wherever you are along the path, we applaud you. You are doing something good for the Earth and the creatures that inhabit it as well as for yourself.

CELEBRATE!

The first of October is World Vegetarian Day.

the healthy choice

2

ONLY A DECADE OR TWO AGO, you might have thought that going vegetarian would jeopardize your health. Doctors, parents, scientists and well-meaning friends tried to scare aspiring vegetarians with dire health warnings and even predictions of death for those who opted for the vegetarian choice.

What an amazing turnabout: Scientists working in the field of nutrition now know the reassuring facts supporting the vegetarian choice. So do physicians who keep up with the latest findings on consuming meat versus eating vegetarian meals. Even the conservative American Dietetic Association jumped on the bandwagon with its strongly worded 1988 and 1993 position papers in favor of the vegetarian style of eating. And when the U.S. Department of Agriculture devised the Food Guide Pyramid, meat was put in a small trapezoid while grains, vegetables and fruits made up the most significant part of the pyramid. The case for choosing vegetarian foods is shut tight.

Once in a while, you may hear a news report suggesting that the vegetarian choice has its faults. But when you hear news about a person suffering ill health from a vegetarian diet, listen carefully. Often you'll discover that the person was subsisting on just one or two foods, or was in a state of malnutrition because he or she wasn't eating enough food. Sometimes the science methodology is faulty.

As you'll recall, our message is to go for the gastronomic gusto, eating a variety of vegetarian foods and taking in enough calories to satisfy your hunger drive. (A big plus for big eaters: You may eat more food when you opt for vegetarian foods, because most vegetarian meals are lower in fat and calories than meat-based meals.) And when you heed our delicious message, you'll stand a wonderful chance of becoming healthier—even to the point where some of your health problems may diminish or disappear. Many physicians promote the vegetarian choice in their practices and have seen successful results. Some of the more high-profile doctors include Dean Ornish, M.D., author of *Dr. Dean Ornish's Program for Reversing Heart Disease* (Ballantine Books, 1992); John McDougall, M.D., author of several books, including *The McDougall Program: 12 Days to Dynamic Health* (NAL/Dutton, 1990); and Christiane Northrup, M.D., a noted specialist in women's health in Yarmouth, Maine.

Case in point: At one time, physicians thought that reversing heart disease was a preposterous notion. Now Ornish, director of the Preventive Medicine Research Institute in San Francisco, California, has proven them wrong. In fact, his program of dietary therapy (in which patients follow a very low-fat vegetarian diet), stress management, meditation and exercise—a program costing about $4,000 per patient, less than one-tenth the cost of a typical bypass operation—has won respect from Mutual of Omaha. The insurance company announced in 1993 that it would reimburse policy holders for the cost of Ornish's services, marking the first time that an alternative therapy for heart disease has gotten the nod from a major insurance company. Why would Mutual of Omaha take this stand? Here's one probable answer: Ornish's published peer-reviewed clinical studies show that a high percentage of his patients get better and stay better, in stark contrast to half of all people undergoing bypass surgery, which often needs to be repeated after five years.

> **GREEN LIGHT**
>
> Now with a scientific green light for going green, it's no wonder that nearly half of adults who describe themselves as vegetarian cite health as their number-one reason for pushing aside the meat.

DIET DOWNPLAYED

But In the vast majority of medical offices, diet is given barely a passing thought—despite evidence that it plays a role in the development of six of the ten most common diseases: heart disease, cancer, stroke, diabetes mellitus, chronic liver disease and arteriosclerosis. This somber list, illustrating the prominent role lifestyle plays in health, has prompted some talk in government on preventing disease. Witness the new food product labels, which give more useful information on the nutrient value of the foods. The outdated labels focused on how to avoid deficiency diseases (such as scurvy), which are rare in the United States.

However, talk is just that: talk. In the debate over health care reform, there has been barely a mention of how to prevent disease in the first place. Prevention would save bundles of money (Americans already spend about a trillion dollars a year on health care) and ease inestimable pain for sufferers. Yet it's no wonder that many physicians give nutrition little emphasis: Only 20 to 25 percent of medical schools require that med students take nutrition courses, and there are no general nutrition questions on the national medical board exam, according to a 1993 report in the *American Journal of Clinical Nutrition.* Two reasons why nutrition gets little respect in medical schools are that it's considered a "soft" science and that because many doctors aren't knowledgeable about nutrition, the subject doesn't get taught.

To get a sense of the power of prevention, just look at these numbers, based on actual cases and provided by the Massachusetts Dietetic Association:

- A 56-year-old woman has diabetes. The cost of six nutrition counseling sessions tallies up to $260, and her blood sugar levels dropped from about 450 milligrams (mg) per deciliter (dl) to 108 mg/dl. She avoided admission to an emergency room and insulin therapy, which together would have cost $28,740.

- A 43-year-old man with high blood cholesterol attended three nutrition counseling sessions, costing a total of $105, and reduced his cholesterol level, avoiding a lifetime on

ALL THE WAY

You've made the decision to go vegetarian. Should you take the gradual approach, cutting back on nonvegetarian foods over time, or rid your home of meat, poultry and fish overnight? Either way is okay. Most important, pick the method that suits you (do you warm up slowly to new ideas or prefer to dive right in?), and experiment in the kitchen with new recipes, so you can share your good taste.

cholesterol-lowering drugs. The drugs would have stripped his wallet of $19,095.

- A 15-year-old girl had anorexia nervosa and lost 50 pounds in six months. She went to 20 nutrition counseling sessions, costing $800. She gained 34 pounds and avoided one month's hospitalization, with the hefty price tag of $10,835 to $19,150.

The good news is you, too, may experience an improvement in your health once you've started down the vegetarian path. You don't have to eat vegetarian meals every day to get some benefits; even if you're a part-time vegetarian, you likely will increase your intake of vitamins, minerals and fiber, and lower your consumption of fat and dietary cholesterol. And as you become accustomed to preparing vegetarian meals, you might find yourself eating meatless meals more often than not.

But before taking a closer look at some of the diseases that the vegetarian choice may help prevent, let's turn to three nutrition concerns you may have: fat, fiber and protein.

FAT: HOW LOW SHOULD YOU GO?

Top scientists are saying that the most healthful diets contain 10 to 25 percent fat calories in the overall diet. (No, you don't have to give up your favorite pigout food as long as you eat it in moderation. And it's okay to eat a high-fat lunch. Just be sure to go easy on fat at dinnertime.) Most important, how much fat you eat at one meal doesn't matter as much as how much fat you eat in a day or over a few days.

A little arithmetic makes it crystal clear that meat must take a back seat to vegetarian foods if you're going to eat the way that the nation's top scientists recommend. Just look: The average adult woman consuming 2,000 calories daily may eat 44 grams of fat when fat calories make up 20 percent of her daily diet. For example, this day's diet contains 44 grams: two cups of Wheaties topped with a sliced banana and skim milk for breakfast; a bean-and-cheese burrito, rice and salsa along with your favorite Snapple for lunch; two oatmeal-raisin cookies for a

---

LOW-FAT YOGURT SPECIAL

A sweet-tart dessert that's ready in just a minute is flavored nonfat yogurt combined with fresh fruit and spooned into stemmed glasses. Simply stir together the yogurt and the fruit. Some suggestions are peach yogurt with fresh raspberries, lemon or vanilla yogurt with blueberries, and strawberry yogurt with banana chunks.

pick-me-up snack; and second helpings of spaghetti with marinara sauce at dinner plus steamed asparagus, garlic bread, a glass of wine or sparkling grape juice and a dish of lemon sorbet or a blueberry turnover (or both).

The standard recommendation of most health organizations to keep the amount of fat calories to overall calories at 30 percent or less is a mistake, says Cornell University's T. Colin Campbell, a nutritional biochemist and a principal researcher of the massive, six-year China Health Project (and also a vegetarian). "I once thought that dietary recommendations for small changes, such as lowering dietary fat to 30 percent of calories, were fine," he says. "I no longer accept that strategy. It panders; it's arrogant. It seems to me that scientists must tell what they think is true, not what they think the public will accept." (More on fat—and how to make simple fat reductions—in chapter 8.)

FIBER: FILL 'ER UP

No, you don't have to eat prunes, though these wrinkled fruits are a sweet source of fiber (with nearly 2 grams of fiber in three medium prunes). But getting enough fiber is essential to good health. Even the experts at the National Cancer Institute and the U.S. Food and Drug Administration agree, recommending that Americans eat 25 to 30 grams of fiber a day. The average American gets less than half of the recommended amount.

Welcome news: The vegetarian diet (as long as it's not based on lots of junk food and refined foods) is full of fiber naturally. Here's an illustration, using two vegetarian staples: beans and rice. One-half cup of cooked kidney beans, for instance, has about 7 grams of fiber, and 1/2 cup of cooked lentils has a bit more than 5 grams of fiber. A 1-cup serving of cooked brown rice contains 5 grams of fiber. In contrast, an equal amount of white rice has only 1 gram of fiber. And meat? It has zilch.

Fiber, which only plant foods contain, comes in two types: water insoluble (often called "roughage") and water soluble. Insoluble fiber includes the peels of fruits and vegetables, and the husks of whole grains. Soluble fiber includes pectins, gums and musilages that are found in fruits and vegetables. Legumes and oat bran also contain soluble fiber.

A Dozen High-Fiber Foods

1/3 cup All Bran cereal	8.6 grams (g)
2/3 cup Post Bran flakes	5g
2/3 cup oatmeal	4.1g
1/2 cup cooked broccoli	2.4g
1 large carrot	2.3g
1 small apple	2.3g
3 dried figs	4.6g
1 small orange	2.9g
1/2 cup cooked brown rice	2.3g
1/3 cup oat bran	4g
2 1/2 tablespoons whole-wheat flour	2.1g
1/2 cup cooked legumes of all sorts	4 to 7g

These two types of fiber do a number of things. They keep food moving through your gastrointestinal plumbing and help reduce blood cholesterol levels. And because fiber is filling, you eat less fat. Among the results: Reduced risk for constipation, hemorrhoids, diverticular disease, colorectal cancer and heart disease.

How do you increase your fiber intake? Eat unrefined foods as close to their natural state as possible. That means an orange instead of orange juice, whole-grain bread instead of white bread, fruits and vegetables with their skins intact instead of peeled when it makes sense. (An unpeeled pineapple is an obvious no-go.) You get the idea. Take it easy as you increase your fiber intake. Doubling your fiber intake overnight might have some unpleasant, odoriferous consequences. Over time, you'll adapt to the increase because, scientists believe, your intestines will produce more or different beneficial bacteria.

One last word about fiber: You may have heard that eating more fiber interferes with the absorption of minerals. However, a 1993 study by researchers at the Beltsville Human Nutrition Research Center in Beltsville, Maryland, found that men in the study who ate a high-fiber, low-fat diet excreted more minerals than men who did not eat a high-fiber diet, but they also ate more minerals over all, so the losses balanced out.

PROTEIN: THE GREAT NON-ISSUE

Can you get enough protein on a vegetarian diet? One last time: Yes, yes, yes. The concept of protein complementarity, a theory proposed by sociologist Frances Moore Lappé in the first edition of *Diet for a Small Planet* (Ballantine Books, 1971; a revised edition was published in 1982) made the case that vegetarians can get just as much usable protein as meat eaters by combining protein from different types of foods (such as grains with legumes) to approximate the protein level in an egg. (Usable protein is absorbed by the body and used for various bodily functions.) She has since said—and the American Dietetic Association agrees—that protein complementarity is a non-issue because a vegetarian diet based on a variety of foods has ample usable protein. In fact, vegetarians—women, men and

---

PROTEIN: NO WORRY

The Recommended Dietary Allowance of protein for men is 56 grams. The average amount of protein consumed by a nonvegetarian male is typically 103 grams. For a vegetarian male, the figure is a surprising 105 grams.

The Recommended Dietary Allowance of protein for women is 44 grams. The average amount of protein consumed by a nonvegetarian female is 74 grams. For a vegetarian female, the amount is 65 grams.

children—generally surpass the Recommended Dietary Allowance for protein. So don't worry about it. Period.

"There's been a remarkable increase in interest [among researchers] in high-fiber, low-fat diets, and [healthful] vegetarian diets are by definition high-fiber and low-fat," says Suzanne Havala, a registered dietitian and co-author of the American Dietetic Association 1988 and 1993 position papers on vegetarianism. (She's a vegetarian, too). Only a few years ago, Campbell of Cornell University referred to humans as basically a vegetarian species and said that "animal foods, in general, are not really helpful and we need to get away from them."

His statements—and the American Dietetic Association's 1988 and 1993 position papers—merely confirmed what two decades of research collectively proved: The vegetarian choice is the healthy choice. Now let's look at some of the research embracing the vegetarian choice as a way to avoid disease and then we'll turn to why eating little or no meat reaps a harvest of benefits.

> **MEAT DOESN'T MAKE MUSCLE**
>
> Do you need meat for strength? No way, say vegetarian champion bodybuilders such as Bill Pearl, Andreas Cahling and Spice Williams. Protein from meat doesn't make muscle; exercise does.

HEART DISEASE

Numerous studies (many of them conducted with the cooperation of Seventh-Day Adventists, members of a Protestant denomination that promotes eating vegetarian foods as one way of taking proper care of one's body, the temple of the Holy Spirit) have found that vegetarians have lower risks of heart attacks, strokes and other types of circulatory illnesses. Even better, a low-fat vegetarian diet can actually reverse heart disease, Dean Ornish showed in his ground-breaking work. A decade ago, the medical community thought reversing heart disease was absolutely impossible.

But Ornish's research has shown that eating a very low-fat diet (10 percent of overall calories from fat), exercising and practicing meditation can unclog arteries and improve the efficiency of the heart. "[He] has given his program a very strong scientific basis and shown that you can have a marked effect on coronary health," says William C. Roberts, M.D., editor-in-chief of the *American Journal of Cardiology* and director of the

Baylor Cardiovascular Institute at the Baylor University Medical Center in Dallas.

Until Ornish's study was published, physicians clung to the belief that heart disease could only get worse over time and that the best ways to treat it were bypass surgery, angioplasty (a procedure in which a small balloon is inflated inside a blocked artery to widen the vessel) and a lifetime on cholesterol-lowering drugs. These treatments didn't cure patients; they only delayed the next heart attack. "One-third to one-half of angioplasties clog up again within four to six months," says Ornish, "and half of the bypasses have clogged up within five to seven years."

In his study, Ornish placed forty-eight subjects with severe heart disease on his program; the control group followed the usual advice of the American Heart Association to keep fat intake at no more than 30 percent of overall calories. After only one week, the experimental group showed a reduction in chest pain and depression and said they had more energy. Within a month, their blood cholesterol levels were markedly lower and their blood flow improved, allowing many in the experimental group to stop using antihypertensive and cardiac medications. After one year, 83 percent showed reversal of their arterial blockages by an average of 5.3 percent. In contrast, the people in the control group were worse off after a year, with more blockage in their arteries than before they had adopted the American Heart Association's diet for heart-disease patients.

Before heart disease strikes you, here are a few things you can do to help prevent it.

- Eat foods that are rich in vitamin E. Research has shown that a risk factor for dying from heart disease is a low blood level of vitamin E, an antioxidant nutrient. It is believed to protect low-density lipoproteins (so-called "bad cholesterol") from oxidizing in the bloodstream, thereby slowing or preventing the buildup of deposits on artery walls. This eventually restricts blood flow to the heart.

  The richest dietary sources of vitamin E include whole wheat, wheat germ, nuts and oils. But go easy on the nuts and oily foods because they are high in fat.

- Avoid saturated fats. It may be hard to believe, but research has shown that saturated fats (found in meat, eggs, dairy products and tropical oils)—not dietary cholesterol—have the strongest influence on blood cholesterol levels, followed by excess of total calories and then dietary cholesterol intake.

- Exercise regularly.

- Reduce stress in your life as much as possible and learn stress-management skills.

- Teach your kids good eating habits. In one study, research showed that of 1,532 autopsies of teenagers, the number that showed fatty patches in the aorta was 1,532.

CANCER

Worldwide, a population's incidence of breast, colon and prostate cancer reflects total fat intake, including saturated fats like butter and unsaturated fats like vegetable oil. The China Health Project—a joint research project of scientists from Cornell University in New York, Oxford University in England, the Chinese Academy of Preventive Medicine and the Chinese Academy of Medical Sciences—called for the gathering of detailed lifestyle and dietary habits of 6,500 Chinese (100 Chinese in each of 65 counties).

Many epidemiological studies—which analyze statistics of large groups to make links between disease and their causes—sometimes aren't exact enough to provide convincing results. China is different. Because the Chinese tend to stay in the same place and eat the same foods their entire lives, the effect of diet on health is apparent. Early conclusions from the research indicate that people living in counties where the diet is refined and high in protein and fat have a higher incidence of cancer than those in areas where a traditional grain-based diet is the norm. Also, fiber seems to protect against cancer, especially colon cancer, the second leading cause of cancer death in the United States.

Findings of the China Health Project also found that girls who eat a rich diet menstruate earlier than girls consuming a traditional Chinese

CANCER COUNTS

Estimates indicate that 30 to 70 percent of cancers in the United States may be diet-related. The two types with the strongest links to fat consumption are breast and colon cancers.

vegetarian choice is a great way to go—because you won't lack for food—willpower, maybe, but not food.

Try to avoid thinking of the vegetarian choice as a diet. People go on and off diets. But the vegetarian choice—even if you modify it by including small amounts of meat, poultry or fish—is for keeps. It becomes a way of life. It requires no calorie counting and no need for a food scale to weigh your portions. Just choose your foods wisely—and eat. (Please note that if you have an eating disorder, you may benefit from counseling to discover why you overeat. Also check with your doctor in case you have a medical condition that may be contributing to your weight problem.)

OSTEOPOROSIS

This disease, characterized by thinning bones that become brittle, debilitates more than 25 million Americans, most of them women. It results in more than 1.3 million bone fractures a year. What's the cost? Intense pain to those who suffer from osteoporosis and about $10 billion a year in medical care, some of which is picked up by Medicaid, which taxpayers fund.

If you know even a little bit about osteoporosis, you probably link it to calcium, and you're right to make the connection. But dealing with osteoporosis isn't a matter of guzzling several glasses of skim milk daily. The connection is more complex: When your body doesn't have enough calcium in its bloodstream to handle basic metabolic functions, your body starts to leach calcium from your bones. This is called reabsorption, and it's a normal part of aging. At about age forty, both men and women lose about 0.5 percent of their skeletons each year. When women reach menopause, their rate of bone loss increases to about 1 to 2 percent each year. Postmenopausal women are the most vulnerable to osteoporosis because their ovaries have stopped producing estrogen, which helps maintain bone mass. By age sixty, a woman may have lost 40 percent of her skeleton.

You can have strong bones in your later years by making good food choices—and the earlier you start, the better. Because you will lose bone mass as you age, a sound approach is to have as much bone mass

> ### BRITTLE BONES
> Risk factors for osteoporosis include cigarette smoking, a sedentary lifestyle, alcohol abuse, a slim physique, a long life and a history of low calcium intake and too much protein.

as possible before you reach your middle years. Taking in more calcium than you lose before your bones stop growing, at about age thirty-five, is important. After your bones stop growing, your goal is zero calcium balance—losing no more calcium than you take in.

You might think that milk products are the best sources of calcium. And, yes, many of them do contain significant amounts of this mineral, but they also are loaded with protein. So what? Well, it turns out that the more protein in the diet, the more the kidneys work overtime, and the more calcium is leached from the body. So eating high-calcium foods that are high in protein can backfire. What can you do? Eat plant sources of calcium (see "Calcium Countdown," at right). Greens like kale and bok choy are particularly strong contenders, despite pronouncements from some nutritionists that the oxalic acid in the vegetables inhibits calcium absorption, according to a study at Purdue and Creighton universities. In the study, the blood levels of calcium were higher in nine of the eleven subjects (all premenopausal women) when they ate kale than when they drank milk. In another study, researchers found that other vegetables—broccoli, bok choy and turnip, collard and mustard greens—contain calcium that's absorbed as readily as the calcium in kale.

And it turns out that the body is wonderfully made to absorb a higher percentage of calcium from food when overall calcium intake is relatively low; but eating tons of calcium-rich foods makes little difference, because your body will excrete what it doesn't need. To boost calcium absorption, go for vitamin D—either by eating egg yolks or vitamin D—enriched foods or by going outside to get some sun. The skin metabolizes vitamin D from sunlight, and the body stores the vitamin after exposure to sunlight for use during the cold months, when people tend to stay indoors.

Another tried-and-true way to increase bone mass is through weight-bearing exercise. Though there have been few studies on the long-term effects of exercise on the development of osteoporosis, current evidence indicates that weight-bearing exercise, such as jogging, aerobic dancing, weight lifting and racquet sports, help make your bones denser by putting stress on the skeleton.

What's out of your control is your genetics: Some people are more likely to develop osteoporosis. African-Americans, for example, in

CALCIUM COUNTDOWN

A glass of skim milk contains about 400 milligrams (mg) of calcium. That's about half the calcium an adult needs in a day, according to the Recommended Dietary Allowances. But dairy products aren't the only sources of calcium. Here are a few examples.

1 cup cooked collard greens	357mg
2 tablespoons blackstrap molasses	284mg
11 dried figs	269mg
4 ounces extra-firm tofu made with calcium salts	258mg
1 cup cooked spinach	244mg
1 stalk broccoli	205mg
1 tablespoon tahini	154mg
1/2 cup cooked amaranth	138mg
1 cup cooked, sliced okra	100mg
1/2 cup cooked white beans	81mg

general have denser skeletons than whites or Asians, so they are less likely to develop osteoporosis. Because you can't do anything about your genetics, focus on calcium-rich foods and exercise. And wait for more research on this disease. There's a lot left to learn.

DIABETES

For decades, physicians advised their diabetic patients to eat a high-fat, low-carbohydrate and low-fiber diet. That eating regimen would get loud hisses from doctors and diabetics today, but back then the common belief was that such a diet would help keep blood-sugar levels constant.

Research indicates that a high-carbohydrate diet improves blood-sugar control by enhancing insulin sensitivity. It can even head off the development of diabetes: In an important study of nearly 26,000 Seventh-Day Adventists several years ago, researchers found that vegetarians had significantly less risk of diabetes than the general population. The long-term studies by noted fiber researcher James Anderson, M.D., show that patients on his high-fiber, largely vegetarian diet are able to lower their insulin requirements, and that their blood cholesterol and blood pressure levels also are reduced. (High cholesterol and blood pressure levels are typical complications of diabetes.)

Before moving on to particulars about diet, here's some background about diabetes, the third leading cause of death in the United States. There are two types: Type I, insulin-dependent diabetes, and Type II, in which the body either produces very little insulin or does not use it properly. Type II is by far the most common form of diabetes, plaguing about nine times as many people as Type I. Type II, also known as adult-onset diabetes, often can be treated without drugs by following a proper diet and getting exercise. It makes sense. Eating too much food and the wrong type of food (particularly foods high in fat) are usually what cause Type II diabetes in the first place. So switching to a low-fat diet and losing weight sometimes are all that's needed to get the disease under control, though some Type II diabetics will need to take medication. People with Type I, sometimes referred to as juvenile diabetes, produce little or no insulin, a hormone that allows food to be converted into sugar by the body and used as fuel. Type I diabetics, who must inject insulin, may also be helped through dietary changes.

Diabetics are familiar with exchange lists developed by the American Diabetes Association; the lists are divided into groups of foods to ensure that diabetics get the "right" balance of nutrients.

Here's a list of some foods commonly eaten by vegetarians that may not show up on the lists:

Almond or cashew butter (2 teaspoons)	1 Meat Exchange
Bulgur (1/2 cup, cooked)	1 Bread Exchange
Brown rice (1/2 cup, cooked)	1 Bread Exchange
Kefir (1 cup)	1 Milk Exchange
Meatless burger (3 ounces)	3 Meat Exchanges
Meatless frank (1 ounce)	1 Meat Exchange
Miso (3 tablespoons)	1 Bread Exchange
Soybeans (1/3 cup, cooked)	1 Meat Exchange
Soymilk (1 cup)	1 Milk Exchange (because soymilk does not contain as many carbohydrates as cow's milk, you will need to consume an extra bread exchange with each cup of soymilk)
Tahini (2 teaspoons)	1 Meat Exchange
Tempeh (2 ounces, cooked)	1 Meat Exchange
Textured vegetable protein (reconstituted, 1/2 cup)	2 Meat Exchanges
Tofu (4 ounces)	1 Meat Exchange

Whether you, a family member or friend has diabetes, spread the message that a high-carbohydrate, low-fat, high-fiber diet (the vegetarian choice or something quite close to it) can help in the prevention and treatment of diabetes.

ET CETERA

The vegetarian style of eating has received applause in alleviating other conditions, including arthritis and anemia.

For example, in a Norwegian study of 27 rheumatoid arthritis sufferers, patients who fasted for seven to ten days—during which herbal teas, garlic and vegetable juices were among the only foods consumed, and then followed a year-long vegetarian diet—reported significant changes. Patients on the fasting-and-vegetarian-diet regimen had fewer tender joints, less pain, a shorter period of stiffness in the morning and improved grip strength compared to the arthritics in the control group who ate their usual daily fare.

And the myth that vegetarians are at greater risk for anemia is just that: a myth. In fact, women who are most susceptible to anemia—characterized by a reduction in the number of red blood cells or a reduction in hemoglobin—are more likely to be those who load up on junk food instead of whole foods, and they tend to have heavy menstrual periods. About 20 percent of American women (including nonvegetarians) have iron-deficiency anemia and 65 percent have low iron stores, says Susan Lark, M.D., who specializes in women's health in Los Altos, California. Though most people link iron deficiency to anemia, this condition also can result from too little B_{12} or folic acid in the body. If you suspect that you may have anemia, ask your doctor for a blood test.

A great way to overcome anemia is right in your kitchen. Here are a few suggestions:

- Go easy on dairy products, which can interfere with iron absorption.

- Eat iron-rich foods, including millet, kidney beans, chickpeas, pinto beans, spinach, Swiss chard and prunes.

- When you eat iron-rich foods, also take in some vitamin C, which helps in absorption.

- If you're low in folic acid, part of the B complex, replace high-fat foods with foods rich in folic acid. These include

Iron-Rich Foods— a Baker's Dozen

10 dried prunes	2.4 milligrams (mg)
1/2 cup raisins	1.7mg
1 cup cooked spinach	4mg
1 cup cooked Swiss chard	3.2mg
1 cup baked winter squash	1.4mg
1/2 cup cooked black-eyed peas	3.8mg
1/2 cup cooked lentils	3.4mg
1/2 cup cooked lima beans	2.9mg
1 cup cooked quinoa	5.3mg
1 cup cooked millet	2.2mg
1 tablespoon blackstrap molasses	2.3mg
1 tablespoon nutritional yeast	1.4mg
1/4 cup nori	5.6mg

cranberries, lentils, black-eyed peas, soybean flour, baby lima beans and black beans.

- B_{12}-deficiency anemia, called pernicious anemia, is caused by an absorption defect in the digestive tract. You may need B_{12} shots if your B_{12} stores are particularly low, but you might get along by increasing the amount of B_{12}-rich foods that you eat, including B_{12}-fortified cereals, cottage cheese and skim milk. (Check with your doctor.)

All in all, eating a low-fat, low-protein diet protects against cancer, heart disease, diabetes, osteoporosis and other illnesses. How reassuring—you can make a real difference in your own health.

GROWING INTERESTS
Pregnant Women

When a woman becomes pregnant, her need for certain nutrients (iron and calcium, for instance) increases. A vegan mom-to-be also requires a reliable source of vitamin B_{12} because this vitamin is in animal foods only. A pregnant woman also needs about 300 extra calories a day to help the baby grow. These dietary changes make sense: One body is building another, so more nutrients and calories are essential.

So is the vegetarian style of eating safe during pregnancy? That may be the question on your mind even if you've been a vegetarian for years. The answer: an unequivocable yes. Statistics compiled by midwives at a vegetarian community in Tennessee, for instance, showed that of the first one thousand births, the mother and babies had no nutritional problems. A 1989 study by the Centers for Disease Control showed that 404 vegetarian children raised at this Tennessee community grew just fine, too: There were no significant differences in height and weight when compared to children in the general population.

Here are a few specifics:

If you're a vegan mom-to-be or are nursing, it's wise to take a B_{12} supplement or to eat foods fortified with this vitamin. It's not known whether the fetus can absorb any of the mother's own B_{12} stores, says Neal

Barnard, M.D., president of Physicians Committee for Responsible Medicine in Washington, D.C., although the baby will get enough if the mother is taking in B_{12} through her diet. For a healthy vegetarian mom who eats dairy products or eggs, there is no need for B_{12} supplementation.

A woman deficient in iron may need supplementation. But a 1993 study in the *Journal of the American Medical Association* found little scientific evidence to suggest that routine iron supplementation during pregnancy is beneficial in improving outcomes for the mother, fetus or newborn. To check the iron level in your blood, ask your doctor for a ferritin test. Vegetarian foods have many iron winners among them, but because this mineral is necessary for the building of red blood cells and other cells in the baby's body, be sure you don't skimp on iron.

Equally important for pregnancy is calcium—and you don't have to drink milk. Calcium is plentiful in green leafy vegetables, some legumes and calcium-fortified orange juice. If you choose not to eat dairy products, be sure to eat ample amounts of these other calcium-rich foods. Also keep in mind that some experts believe that milk laced with growth hormones and drugs fed to dairy cows may be unsafe for drinking. The safety of cow's milk is under debate.

As for getting an extra 300 calories a day, no problem: three apples, an extra serving of beans and rice, a piece of chocolate cake—any of these will meet the need. About that piece of chocolate cake, you could choose this less-than-healthful goodie and get the extra calories you need, but by choosing a nutritious option, you'll be providing yourself and your baby with important nutrients for your health and hers (or his).

Children

As you no doubt know, the consensus is breast is best for babies. Breast milk has the all the nutrients a baby needs to grow and thrive. Store-bought formula is an adequate replacement for breast milk, but it's not the same. So make your choice for breast or bottles with care.

Until a child reaches two or three years of age and sees his or her playmates eating cut-up bologna, you have ultimate control over what your child eats—starting with first foods. Again, the best bets during weaning are pureed foods that are unrefined. Try one food at a time to watch

KID PLEASERS

"Yuck!" If you hear that word too often from your otherwise angelic child, listen up. You can turn *yuck* into *yum*—at least some of the time. First, if your child is old enough to help out with basic cooking techniques like stirring, enlist his help. He's less likely to turn down a dish he helped make. Better yet, get his ideas when you plan meals: The more he participates, the more successful your mealtime will be.

Second, be playful with food. A toddler or preschooler may go for a rice cake smeared with peanut butter with raisins in a smiley face design and chopped raw vegetables on the side. Older kids might like threading skewers (under your supervision) with tofu and various colored vegetables.

Third, keep nutritious nibbles on hand for snacking. Some ideas are whole-grain crackers, whole-grain pretzels, chopped raw vegetables, dried fruits and nuts. By offering healthful, tasty snacks, your child will get the nutrients he needs in the course of the day even when he barely touches his lunch.

for allergies. Continue trying different foods, introducing your older baby to many fruits, vegetables and grains. Hold off on hard-to-digest foods—such as legumes and dairy foods—until your baby is about one year old.

Once your baby is a pro at finger foods, he or she can eat what your family is eating. Just remember that few kids like mixed-up meals, such as casseroles. And keep in mind that pediatricians recommend that children under two get no less than 30 percent of the total calories from fat. After two years, children should eat a healthy diet low in fat and cholesterol to help prevent degenerative diseases in adulthood.

When your child goes into day care or grade school, you may have additional concerns because school lunches are notoriously high in fat and heavy on meat. You could speak with the day care personnel about arranging vegetarian lunches for your toddler or preschooler. If your child is in school, pack a lunch. But don't force foods that may get laughs from schoolmates. Listen to your child's concerns and compromise, or you may be in for a big fight with your gradeschooler. Some parents allow their children to eat meat outside the home at lunch, knowing that their homemade breakfasts and dinners are wholesome. Though your child may experiment with meat, you may see a turnabout sooner than later. Don't forget: By eating vegetarian meals, you're a persuasive role model—and you have science on your side. The overriding evidence shows that vegetarian children get all the nutrients they need as long as they eat enough calories and have a varied diet. If your child decides to eat meat regularly, a thoughtful and caring response ("You know I believe eating vegetarian foods is best, but I'll love you no matter what you eat") is the way to go. This sounds simple—and it is. But in some families, food can become a divisive, rather than a unifying, topic.

That also can happen in homes where the child announces to her meat-loving folks that she has become a vegetarian. Some parents view the announcement as an adolescent phase or even as an affront to the family's values. Other parents keep an open mind, asking questions and becoming informed about the vegetarian way. In either case—a child from a vegetarian background experimenting with meat or a child espousing vegetarian eating for the first time in her life—parents will have lines to draw. Here are some questions to consider: Is meat allowed at home where the

---

SCHOOL LUNCHES-F
The number of calories from fat in a typical meal from the U.S. government's school lunch program is a whopping 38 percent.

parents are vegetarian? If so, who prepares it? May the new vegetarian cook his or her food in the family kitchen? Will the family agree to try vegetarian recipes?

Foremost, think about the values you want to instill in your child—values such as respect, compassion and acceptance—and act with your heart. Then a potentially tricky situation won't seem so difficult.

Older Adults

Older vegetarians have a nutritional concern that a lot of adults over sixty-five share—getting enough nutrients. Sometimes low nutrient levels may be due to illness or poor food choices; other times, they result from not eating enough food. In the latter case, the solution is straightforward. It's a matter of eating calorie-dense, nutritional foods (such as legumes and dairy products). Moderate exercise (with your doctor's okay) is ideal, so that your weight remains at a healthful level.

A study published in the *Journal of the American Dietetic Association* has good news for vegetarians: It found that older vegetarian women eat better and have lower blood sugar and cholesterol levels than their nonvegetarian counterparts. Vegetarians have better nutritional profiles, too. But both vegetarians and nonvegetarians fell short of the Recommended Dietary Allowances in several nutrients. The researchers at Loma Linda University in Loma Linda, California, however, did not conclude that the vegetarian women were at nutritional risk.

More good news: An eleven-year study of 1,904 vegetarians in Germany found that mortality from all causes among vegetarians was one half that of the general population. And a study in a 1994 British medical journal found that, even after controlling for other variables that affect health (including smoking and weight), the 6,115 vegetarians had a 28 percent lower risk of dying from heart disease in any given year than meat eaters and a 39 percent lower risk of dying from cancer.

Place another candle on the birthday cake.

The bottom line is that the best diet known to us, based on the most reliable nutrition information available, is overflowing with grains, legumes, fruits and vegetables, with about 10 to 25 percent of fat calories and 25 to 30 grams of fiber in the overall diet. It also may contain limited portions of animal products, if it includes them at all. It keeps pesticide residues to a minimum too. (More on the environmental reasons to go vegetarian in the next chapter.) Most of all, the best diet tastes absolutely delicious—or why opt for the vegetarian style of eating?

It's your choice—your absolutely delicious choice.

more reasons to go vegetarian

3

FACT: RAISING ANIMALS FOR FOOD is the principal cause of topsoil loss. America is losing about 4 million acres of cropland each year due to soil erosion, and 85 percent of the topsoil loss is directly related to raising livestock, estimates indicate.

Fact: Shortly after birth, calves not destined to become milking cows are locked in crates so confining that the animals cannot turn around. They are fed an iron-poor diet to make them anemic. The purpose: to keep their flesh white, a favorite of veal gourmets.

Fact: Many Third World countries export crops to the West to satisfy the affluents' taste for exotic foods. The workers could be growing everyday food for their own hungry families, but instead the landowners ship fruits and vegetables to the highest bidder.

Fact: Many members of Eastern religions and a number of Christians and Jews believe that eating meat is a violent act. For spiritual reasons, they choose life.

The surge in interest in the vegetarian choice is led by Americans' admirable desire to eat better and feel better. Surveys are clear on this point. Yet the popularity of green cuisine goes beyond self. A patchwork of cultural phenomena sew together the various reasons that twenty thousand Americans from all walks of life become vegetarians each week.

And what's especially curious is that many people who become vegetarians for the health of it later adopt other reasons supporting their vegetarian choice. Call it a domino effect. As vegetarians and aspiring vegetarians learn more about their food choices, they want to know more. And as they know more, their reasons to be vegetarian multiply.

Let's consider the other reasons for savoring this taste-ful way of eating better.

SAVE THE PLANET

Supporting the environment is a win-win proposition. You feel better when you take action to help our Earth, and the planet benefits too. In fact, you'd have to travel far and wide to find a soul who says he or she wants to trash our Earth. But, unknowingly, people who sink their teeth in sirloin and other meats are harming the environment. Meat eating takes an enormous toll on land, water and air—resources that are becoming more dear to Americans as the environmental devastation hits home. According to fact sheets put out by the Humane Society of the United States, if U.S. agricultural practices were used to supply the typical American diet to the world, the world's oil reserves would run out in twelve years (assuming petroleum was the only source of energy for food production).

That's not all, says the Humane Society of the United States. Scientists from the Netherlands and Belgium have reported extensive damage to trees and vegetation near factory farms, which employ intensive husbandry systems; apparently, ammonia fumes from the animal wastes speed up the oxidation of sulfur dioxide, a key factor in the formation of acid rain. In addition, more than two thirds of Central America's forests are gone, and cattle ranching has played a major role in their disappearance. And in communities where hogs are raised in confinement systems, the

> ### CIRCLE OF POISON
> Banned pesticides are routinely sold to Third World countries, where they are used in growing food that is imported to the United States and ends up on our dinner plates.

waste is dumped into holding tanks, polluting the air, land and water. The examples could go on and on.

Says Alan Durning, former environmental researcher for Worldwatch Institute, a Washington, D.C.–based think tank:

> I can safely say that for the United States, livestock agriculture is by quite a bit the most environmentally damaging part of farming. It just jumps out: It's much more intensive in its use of resources, and it's much more polluting. Livestock played a very important role in the deforestation of Latin America. In Central America, 70 percent of deforested land ends up with cattle on it.

Among the first books to implicate meat eating as a nemesis of the environment was Frances Moore Lappé's *Diet for a Small Planet* (Ballantine Books, 1971). She argued—and few have disagreed—that meat eating wastes resources. In her book, she pointed out that 16 pounds of grain, soybeans and other plant foods are needed to make just 1 pound of beef. The exact number of pounds has been debated now and then, but without doubt, feeding food to cattle when it could be fed to far greater numbers of people is indeed wasteful.

The persuasive arguments continue to play to an eager audience. Witness the phenomenal success of John Robbins's *Diet for a New America* (Stillpoint, 1987). Robbins, a vegetarian who grew up eating ice cream (his dad helped to build the Baskin-Robbins ice cream empire), also spelled out the detrimental effects of meat eating on the planet. His book reads like one of novelist Stephen King's shockers—but Robbins's words are based on fact.

One of his statements receiving widespread attention pinpointed air pollution, specifically methane, one of the greenhouse gases. Robbins wrote that the world's 1.3 billion cattle produce nearly 100 million tons of methane, believed to be one of the gases responsible for the "greenhouse effect" (global warming). In response to Robbins's charge, researchers from Texas A&M University said in a report that methane represents only 18 percent of greenhouse gases and cattle account for about 7 percent of world

SOYBEANS VS. BEEF

Soybeans are 40 times more energy efficient than feedlot beef, says author John Robbins.

credo to reduce (consumption of beef), replace (the beef with grains, vegetables and fruits), and refine (the foods eaten by choosing organically grown items).

"The passing of the beef culture is the passing of a way of life," Rifkin writes. "We hope it is a passing toward a new vision."

But Rifkin and like-minded people are ready for their opposition. He says: "If I have to choose between the small, sustainable agriculture and saving the planet, we'll support the planet. If it's a choice between livestock farmers and preventing hunger, we'll go for [preventing] hunger, and nothing is going to stop us."

To sum up Rifkin's point, live and let most live—at the very least.

COMPASSION TOWARD ANIMALS

Most American children have heard the biblical story of Noah's ark and the animals brought aboard, a male and female of each species, before the rain came down. It's a warm account of love for all creation, including every type of animal on Earth. Even a major children's toy company sells a colorful plastic ark, with Noah and his wife, two sheep, two chickens, two elephants and two giraffes.

Now imagine a toddler playing with the ark during bath time, zooming it through bubbles and under a waterfall (from the faucet), then eating cut-up pieces of chicken—or ham or lunch meat—at noon the next day. Mixed messages? Some vegetarians respond with an emphatic yes. These vegetarians do not eat meat, poultry or fish because they believe animals have the right to live and be treated humanely. Animals don't belong on the plate, vegetarians favoring animal rights generally agree. Fifteen percent of the respondents to the Yankelovich survey cite animal welfare as their number-one reason to go vegetarian. Some of them also object to the wearing of fur and leather, scientific research on animals and even to animals' appearances in rodeos and circuses.

We could give you statistics on how many broilers (chickens grown for food) are packed into warehouses until they reach killing weight. Or on the widespread use of antibiotics and drugs among dairy cows and

THE ANIMAL RIGHTS "BIBLE"

Peter Singer's *Animal Liberation* (first published in 1975) is a serious discussion of the effects of man's domination of animals. He writes, "This tyranny [of human over nonhuman animals] has caused and today is still causing an amount of pain and suffering that can only be compared with that which resulted from the centuries of tyranny by white humans over black humans." The book is a good yet challenging read.

many other animals. Or on the numbers of pigs now in constraint systems to improve the economics of growing them for food.

But statistics are dry. And we refuse to print color photographs of the horrors of modern factory farming: Blood and food don't mix. But we will tell you that the way animals are grown today gives reason to pause.

The Humane Society of the United States—considered a moderate voice in the animal welfare arena—solidly objects to the systems of modern factory farming, which are abusive to animals. The vast majority of animals, and some animal rights advocates would say all animals, that are raised to feed people are exploited. At the top of the list are animals on modern factory farms, which are kept in overcrowded, unsanitary conditions, fed drugs and chemicals, subjected to painful procedures and slaughtered. Agribusiness does not see them as beings—no Elsies showing up on milk cartons here—but purely as economics. It is expected that some animals will die of disease or stress-related illness before slaughter; it's all a part of the economic equation.

A minuscule percentage of animals—those on family farms, which are quickly dwindling in numbers, or on organic meat farms (which avoid chemicals, antibiotics and drugs whenever possible)—do receive the type of treatment that resembles the image of Dorothy's Kansas farm, where animals see the outdoors and have names, and baby chicks are counted by Auntie Em to see that not a single one gets lost. But let's stick with the facts as they pertain to business as usual:

- Of all farm animals, laying hens endure the most restrictive life in factory farms. Three to five birds are kept in wire battery cages measuring approximately 10 inches by 12 inches by 14 inches; the cages are stacked on top of one another. The birds do not have room to spread their wings or to lay their eggs comfortably. They are routinely debeaked because they often exhibit cannabilistic behavior in their high-stress environment. About 95 percent of eggs are produced by factory-farmed laying hens.

- Broiler chickens (the type people eat) produced in factory farms have a better lot than laying hens, if only because they are slaughtered sooner. After hatching in an incubator, the

CHICKEN?

The chances of a shopper buying chicken infected with salmonella are greater than one in three. Salmonella poisons a great number of Americans each year: Two to four million people become ill, twenty thousand end up in the hospital, and about one thousand die from this disease.

chickens are transferred to enclosed sheds, which house thousands of birds. As they grow, stress becomes great because there is so little room to move. Some birds in the center of the mass die from suffocation. They reach market weight (3.5 pounds) in about four months.

- Many pigs are now being kept in confinement systems too, as hog farming has caught the attention of agribusiness. In the huge operations, thousands of hogs are bred with new genetic engineering to grow faster and are housed indoors in cubicles. Their diet often includes drugs. Sows have the toughest life; only a few weeks after the piglets are born, they are taken away. Then the sows are artificially inseminated again.

- Dairy cows raised in factory farms are selectively bred and fed growth hormones. About 50 percent of dairy cows develop udder infections. They are kept in small holding areas during part of the day and shuttled in and out of mechanized milk parlors, where their distended udders are hooked up to machines. When a cow gives birth, her calf is taken away. Many calves are sold to veal producers. The calves are fed an anemic diet to keep their flesh tender and white, and their crates are so small they cannot turn around. They are slaughtered at about 16 weeks of age.

- Relatively speaking, beef cattle enjoy the good life. Part of their life is spent on the range, the remainder in an often overcrowded feedlot, where they are fed a concentrated diet to ready them for market.

Uncomfortable? You're human. You have feelings. And scientists say animals have feelings, too. If you drink milk or eat meat, we encourage you to stay upbeat because you still can make a difference: Every time you cook up a vegetarian meal, you do.

Once aware of the animal welfare reasons to stop eating meat, some people choose to cut it out of their diets altogether. Others aren't ready for that step. Either way, when you eat the way that's healthiest for you, you're acting in the best interest of yourself and of animals.

A note is in order about animal rights groups: You may feel uneasy identifying animal rights as one reason you opt for vegetarian

---

A KLEENEX, PLEASE

Henry Spira, coordinator of Animal Rights International, said he tried to open a dialogue with Frank Perdue, head of a top chicken producer. (Perdue has appeared in homespun commercials touting the resort living of his chickens.) But Perdue wouldn't meet, Spira says. So, as a last resort, Spira took out full-page ads in major newspapers, asking, "Frank, are you telling the truth about your chickens?" Perdue was drawn with a Pinocchio-sized nose.

meals because of the bad press some animal rights groups have received. The groups range from very conservative (such as those involved in responsible sports hunting) to the radical fringe (such as groups that break into laboratories to liberate animals used in scientific experiments).

"Our movement used to be associated with weirdos and flakes, and that's no longer the case," says author Jim Mason. "Before a cause achieves popularity, average, normal people are afraid of it. [But now] the animal-rights movement seems to have attracted an increasing number of people who are normal and average. Instead of hard-core political types, they're plain, God-fearing people. It's a sign of the times."

IN THE NAME OF JUSTICE

A sudden insight flashed in the mind of author and sociologist Frances Moore Lappé (who was credited with helping vegetarians feel comfortable that they get ample nutrients without meat). The reason people go hungry isn't because the world cannot or does not produce enough food; rather, some governments get in the way of their citizens' receiving the food that relief agencies send to their countries.

This thinking changed the way Lappé looked at food (though she continues to believe the vegetarian choice is the best way to use the world's resources) and at how to feed starving masses. In the end, Lappé says, it's a political game.

Likewise, Joan Dye Gussow—professor of nutrition education at Columbia University Teachers College at New York City and author of *Chicken Little, Tomato Sauce and Agriculture* (The Bootstrap Press, 1992)—says people need to consider social justice when they shop for food. She says: "It is important for people to begin to think about where food comes from, who's growing it and where it's going."

She knows what she's talking about. In 1984, she became the first nutrition educator to serve on the Food and Nutrition Board of the highly respected National Academy of Sciences. She receives invitation after invitation to nutrition conferences in the United States and abroad. She and a

> **PASS THE POTATOES?**
>
> "The cause of hunger can be very simply described as the scarcity of democracy instead of the scarcity of food," says sociologist and author Frances Moore Lappé. "By democracy, I mean . . . structures of decision making that are participatory, fair and leave no one totally excluded and powerless."

colleague coined the phrase *sustainable diet* to describe her opinion of the best way to eat. In short, by *sustainable* she means organic, locally grown foods that are chosen with the world in mind. (Sorry, Northerners, no bananas in winter or anytime because bananas aren't grown in the North, but have your fill of apples, cherries and various berries when you're in the mood for fruit.)

Gussow says that when you select organic foods, you are making a statement against pesticide use. This has implications for the workers and the consumers of these foods. Workers who use pesticides put themselves at risk for illness, especially when they aren't dressed in protective clothes while using unregulated pesticides; consumers eat produce with residues (or the meat of livestock that have eaten pesticide-laced foods). Pesticide use also has serious repercussions for the Earth—see "Save the Planet," page 40.

And when you eat locally grown foods, you help to minimize the toll of packaging and transporting food on resource use. Just imagine how much fuel is used to fly a five-calorie strawberry from California to New York. Social costs come into play in Third World countries, where cash crops are grown to meet the First World's demand for off-season produce and exotic foods. Food corporations take advantage of the farmers' labor when the farmers might be better off growing traditional crops for their own use, Gussow argues.

Americans can learn much from Third World inhabitants who continue to eat whole foods. The overappreciation of refined foods in this country comes with social costs as well. For instance, most grain refining (making white rice into brown rice, for instance) profits middlemen, not the farmers. The refined grain may be turned into an amazing array of products that often contain more fat, salt and sugar than the grain itself. Estimates indicate that only about 10 percent of the retail cost of a processed food pays for the actual food. The rest pays for packaging, transportation, labor, fillers and additives.

The upshot: Eating vegetarian foods that are unrefined and locally grown without pesticides not only is nutritious but also is a just choice—because what you can eat has global implications. Think about it.

> ## OUT OF WHACK
> Half of the United States' farmland acreage is owned by less than 5 percent of the landowners. Food grown locally without the chemicals is sometimes hard to find.

ABBA, YAHWEH, GOD

Yes, even meditation—which goes far deeper than the simple chant of "Om"—has brought some people to greater awareness, including a clearer realization of what they're eating. Some people who meditate have opted for the vegetarian choice. One reason: spirituality.

Eastern spiritual practices in the United States date back to the 1960s and '70s, when philosophically minded people looked for meaning in their lives and found Hinduism and Buddhism. Concepts like karma became a part of their vocabulary, and so did vegetarianism. Followers of Eastern religions learned from their teachers that not eating meat is purer for body, mind and soul. These vegetarians of the hippie years were viewed as countercultural—for both their religious beliefs in a country founded on Judeo-Christian principles and for their diet, a perceived threat to mainstream America's meat-and-potatoes rituals.

Then it was quirky—is it smart today? It may be hard to believe, but conventional science is seeing the wisdom of combining a vegetarian diet with relaxation techniques (i.e., meditation in many cases) and exercise. Today's leading expert in this field is Dean Ornish, M.D. His research as well of the work of other scientists, which supports the idea of eating little if any meat as well as meditating, is so well accepted, in fact, that it no longer raises eyebrows. Rather, it attracts the dollars of average Americans who are willing to learn stress-management techniques for the sake of their health.

Hindus, Buddhists and others following Eastern spiritual paths aren't the only ones who became vegetarians out of a desire to know themselves and God. In the 1970s, some young Jews showed a growing interest in Jewish mysticism. "Mystical Judaism offered an alternative—what people were searching for—and [for many] that included vegetarianism," says Charles Stahler, one of the founders of the Jewish Vegetarian Society. These Jews found a spiritualism that was missing from the synagogues they knew as children, and they found expression for their beliefs in communalism and pacifism.

A small percentage of Christians, too, have chosen vegetarianism for spiritual reasons. Foremost among these Christians is the Seventh-Day

IN THE BEGINNING

The Bible-Christians, who were the first vegetarians in America, used Bible verses to support their chosen diet. A favorite: "And God said, Behold, I have given you every herb bearing seed, which is upon the face of all the earth, and every tree, in the which is the fruit of a tree yielding seed; to you it shall be for meat." (Genesis 1:29, King James Version)

Adventists, a Protestant denomination that encourages its members to be vegetarian. (About half of Adventists are vegetarian; most of the rest eat little meat and stay away from tobacco and alcohol.) The main reason Adventists are vegetarian is out of reverence of the Holy Spirit. Scripture says that the body is the temple of the Holy Spirit and that the body ought to be respected. As a verse in one of the Psalms says, "You are fearfully and wonderfully made" (Psalms 139:14, New International Version). (Fearfully, in this context, means respectfully.)

Other Christians—Protestants and Catholics—have adopted the vegetarian choice. They might believe that God made them stewards of the Earth and its creatures and ought not dominate the Earth without regard to how their choices affect God's gift of life. Some Christians believe that Jesus would not be pleased with modern factory farming—because it takes advantage of the weak—and do not support meat eating. Among Christians who follow a vegetarian diet is former Franciscan brother Ron Pickarski, whose culinary Olympic team has been awarded medals for their vegan creations; he hopes his message to live peacefully makes a difference in others' lives.

To shed perspective on the question of spirituality and the vegetarian choice, the Yankelovich survey found that 5 percent of self-described vegetarians selected "ethical reasons" as their top choice for becoming a vegetarian and 18 percent picked "not sure/other." Exactly how many of these vegetarians were thinking of spirituality when the interviewer asked, "What is your most important reason for becoming a vegetarian?" remains a mystery.

JUST BECAUSE

A final "other" reason why people say good-bye to meat, chicken and fish is simply because it feels good to be a vegetarian—in every way. The vegetarian choice is good for your health, the planet and its creatures, and in terms of social justice—and you may have spiritual reasons to go vegetarian, too.

The vegetarian choice is the feel-good choice. So the next time someone asks you why you are a vegetarian or are eating more vegetarian meals, make your answer simple. Say, "Just because . . . ," and you fill in the blank. Believe it or not, chances are that people who notice you're changing the food you eat will inquire why. The Yankelovich survey shows that the majority of people who opt for the vegetarian choice are seen as nutrition experts. That's right—most are asked questions about how to eat right.

So hey, expert (for whatever reason you've chosen to eat vegetarian meals), read on. In the next chapter, we get to the pleasures of menu planning.

meatless menu planning

4

IMAGINE THAT YOUR IN-LAWS FROM CATTLE COUNTRY are flying in for a week-long visit. They haven't seen their only grandson in two years. Back then, you ate vegetarian meals some of the time. Now you're committed to the vegetarian choice, and your toddler has yet to taste meat.

Your dilemma: What do you feed your husband's mom and dad to keep them satisfied? The food has to be delicious, smell great, look absolutely appetizing and taste like you chopped, stirred and seasoned all day, even though you didn't. (The last thing you want is static from your in-laws that their grandson is poorly fed when you know he's growing fine without meat.) You need a plan—specifically, a menu plan.

Let's start at a good, but not perfect, beginning: the Food Guide Pyramid. Unveiled by the U.S. Department of Agriculture in 1992, the pyramid is closer to what scientists are saying about nutrition than were the Four Basic Food Groups, which the pyramid replaces. You might remember those Four Basic Food Groups posters from grade school. The posters classified the foods we eat into these groups: dairy products, meat, breads, and fruits and vegetables. (Notice that two of the four groups highlighted animal foods, while fruits and vegetables were jammed into one group, and that the posters gave the impression that each group got equal weight. In fact, the serving suggestions emphasized meat and dairy products.)

The Food Guide Pyramid, though it has its faults, sends the message to eat lots of grains, vegetables and fruits and to limit dairy products, meats and fats and sweets. Grains make up the largest portion of the pyramid, with vegetables and fruits coming in second. Dairy products and meats are each allotted a small trapezoid, and fats and sweets fall in the tiniest section of the pyramid. At last, the U.S. Department of Agriculture let science get in a word against the powerful meat and dairy lobbies. (It cannot be forgotten that one of the department's main goals is to promote the consumption of meat and dairy products.)

So what are the pyramid's faults? We count at least two. First, and of less importance, if the pyramid were standing on its point, it might be a more accurate picture of how we ought to eat. You see, Americans' obsession with being at the top could muddle the message to cut down on fat, meat and dairy products because those foods are at the top of the pyramid. Second, dried beans (lentils, kidney beans, pintos and so on) are placed in the meat category. The reason? The U.S. Department of Agriculture says dried beans are a good alternative to meat because beans are rich in minerals and protein. The problem with the placement of dried beans in meat's small trapezoid is that Americans may get the wrong impression that they should limit their consumption of this wonderful, virtually fat-free food. Nothing could be further from the truth.

A sound vegetarian meal emphasizes fruits, vegetables and grains, includes a reasonable portion of protein (that doesn't exceed the Recommended Dietary Allowance for this macronutrient: 44 grams for women, 56 grams for men) and keeps fat, sugar and salt to a minimum. But that's only the nutrition part of the meal. Taste is equally important. In planning your meals, you'll need to consider some basics of menu planning: achieving the right texture, color, flavor, balance—even the right setting and ambiance. All of these determine whether your meal is well received or a flop. And you will have a few flops. We all do. Thankfully,

AND THE SURVEY SAYS...

In a 1993 survey published in *Vegetarian Times*, respondents shared some surprises when asked about their eating habits.

Answering the question, "How often do you eat breakfast cereal for snacks or for meals other than breakfast?" nearly half (47 percent) of the respondents said they eat cereal for a meal other than breakfast once or twice a week. There are even some die-hard cereal connoisseurs (3 percent) who eat cereal at a meal other than breakfast six or more times a week.

For a quick bite the majority (70 percent) want fast-food restaurants to serve veggie burgers. Some people (9 percent) preferred meatless hot dogs, the second most popular choice.

Even more amazing is the response to this question: "What vegetarian food, fresh or packaged, have you always wanted to try but don't know what to do with it or how to prepare it?" Though quite a few people want to learn more about preparing soyfoods (the first three picks), the fourth-place finisher was vegetables!

there are seven days in a week, giving you ample opportunities to perfect your menu-planning skills.

EATING FOR THE HEALTH OF IT

First, nutrition. We'll repeat our credo: As long as you're eating a variety of vegetarian foods and getting enough calories, you are eating just fine.

In keeping with the Food Guide Pyramid, carbohydrates ought to make up the bulk of your diet. Whole grains like brown rice, whole wheat (flour or bread), rolled oats, millet and barley are good choices. They are fiber-rich and contain significant amounts of B vitamins, vitamin E, and minerals, essential oils and protein. They contain almost no fat. Carbohydrates should make up about half of your daily calories. In planning menus, think rice pilafs, mushroom and barley soup, pasta, grain-based burgers and other sandwiches, stuffed vegetables and croquettes made with couscous.

Next come vegetables and fruits. These foods score high in vitamins and minerals. They are low in fat (with few exceptions, such as coconuts and avocados), rich in fiber and, face it, they're delicious. They also contain antioxidants that might prove important in fighting cancer and other diseases that compromise the immune system, scientists say. Try to work in at least five fruits and vegetables into each day. That's easier to do than you might realize: juice at breakfast, carrot salad and dried fruit at lunch, and a baked potato and sautéed greens at dinner (in addition to the other foods in your menu). Or have fruit for dessert instead of a second vegetable at lunch.

If possible, buy locally grown produce, which is fresher and more nutritious than fruits and vegetables trucked in from across the country or flown in from another nation. Also opt for organically grown produce, which is not treated with pesticides and other chemicals. (Be sure to look for produce that has been certified organic; the term has been misused at times.) And, lastly, avoid overcooking produce. The more it's cooked, the more nutrients that are lost.

Go easy on protein. That may sound blasphemous after hearing time and again in your childhood to finish your meat and drink your milk if you want to grow up strong and healthy. The idea of watching your protein intake also might sound strange if you bought into the concept of protein complementarity. This theory, first proposed in Lappé's *Diet for a Small Planet*, held that nonanimal foods lack one or more of the eight essential amino acids (building blocks of protein that cannot be synthesized by the body) and to have a "complete" protein, you must balance a meal by eating certain foods with others. An example of one of the three main combinations, based on the protein value of the foods in the given group, is grains and beans. The truth is that even vegetarians consume more protein than the Recommended Dietary Allowance, research shows. And it turns out that all vegetarian foods contain all eight essential amino acids in varying amounts.

The concern isn't protein deficiency, which may occur if you aren't eating enough food. It is consuming too much protein, possibly leading to certain diseases such as kidney stones, gout and osteoporosis, says John A. McDougall, M.D., author and advocate of vegetarian cooking.

Don't pig out on dairy products and eggs. These foods, with a few exceptions (such as skim milk and nonfat yogurt), are loaded with fat and cholesterol. If you're worried about getting enough calcium, don't: You can get plenty of calcium from broccoli, greens, acorn squash, soybeans, tofu that's coagulated with calcium salts and several other foods. Also note that taking in enough vitamin D (which the body can generate on its own with the help of sunshine) improves calcium absorption. We don't recommend eating a certain amount of dairy products and eggs; you can be healthy without them. But if you choose to eat no animal products whatsoever, please watch your vitamin B_{12} intake. This vitamin, found almost exclusively in animal foods, is critical for healthy red blood cells and nerves. To be on the safe side, take a B_{12} supplement or eat foods supplemented with B_{12}, such as fortified breakfast cereals.

Limit fats. Easier said than done, because fats (oils, butter and margarine) seem to find their way into everything and they make foods taste so good. Nearly all foods have at least a smidgen of fat, but though fat is essential for many body functions, it should make up only 10 to 25 percent of your caloric intake. (In the average American's diet, about 34 percent of the total calories come from fat.) Depending on your state of health and the doctor you consult, you might want to be lower or higher on the fat percentage range. Cardiologist Dean Ornish recommends the lower percentage, for example. If your blood cholesterol level is fine and you aren't overweight, you may be able to eat at the higher end of the fat percentage range and remain healthy.

The important thing is learning how much fat you eat and making substitutions where necessary. (See chapter 8 for substitution ideas.)

EATING FOR THE TASTE OF IT

Keeping our nutrition principles in mind, let's move on to the fun part: taste. Picture yourself in the kitchen. Before you've taken your seat at the table, you (and your in-laws) already have smelled savory and sweet aromas of a meal in progress, increasing the appetite for the good things to come. The table is set with care: a nubby, cotton tablecloth, earthenware dishes with a Southwestern design, a centerpiece of freshly cut daisies and candles of pinks and teals in brass holders, and jazz music playing softly in the background. You join your family in placing platters of tamales, apple-filled empañadas, rice and small bowls of salsa and sour cream on the table. Then all sit down and enjoy the conversation and the food with delight. After the table is cleared, out comes the chocolate mousse. A perfect finale.

Sounds wonderful, doesn't it? But there's no mystery to making a satisfying meal. You only need a few pointers. Here are six.

First, decide who will partake in the meal. Your immediate family? A significant other? Children celebrating a birthday? Your spouse's boss? Close friends? You and you alone? Then ask yourself whether your company is familiar with vegetarian food.

Your answers will say a lot. If you're making an everyday meal for your family, you might want to cook up a family favorite that even the pickiest eater will like. If you're entertaining a date, go elegant or casual in your meal planning, depending on your mood. Fun's the word for a kid's birthday. You get the idea.

If you suspect that some of your guests might be wary of vegetarian foods, select dishes that everyone will like: vegetable lasagna or other pasta dishes, an elegant risotto, vegetable kebabs with wild rice on the side, bean burritos, stuffed vegetables and the like. Go ahead and experiment with something a bit unusual, such as a side dish incorporating tofu, but be sure the main entrée and the other side dishes will go over well.

Second, consider flavor, texture and color. Compare a dinner of cauliflower, mashed potatoes and fettucine alfredo (all fairly bland, soft and white—boring!—served on white plates, no less) with a meal that excites the palate: winter pear salad in raspberry vinaigrette, rosemary-scented vegetable phyllo tart, Brussels sprouts and spiced carrot pudding. The second meal combines various flavors—sweet, sour, savory and spicy—various textures, and a palette of colors.

Third, keep in balance. Serve a savory entrée with a sweet salad and a spicy vegetable. If the entrée has some crunch, choose a side dish that's smooth in texture. Vary the colors of the dishes: a saucy tomato and cheese pasta with a green salad and crusty bread, for example. This principle extends to dessert, too. The last thing you want to do is top off a substantial supper with a filling chocolate cake, or else your diners may waddle from the table feeling bloated. Rather, go for the chocolate cake when the dinner is a light affair—perhaps a soup and salad. Opt for a light fruit dessert to follow three-bean chili, rice and tostadas.

The balancing theme applies to the seasons as well. In the middle of July, who wants to sit down to a hot, heavy meal? A pasta salad and fruit kebabs are a better selection. Save the heavy meal for a cold winter night. Timing of the meal also is important. Don't make a fancy dish when your family is in a hungry—and soon-to-be grumpy—mood. But go ahead and let your culinary skills shine when you've got the time to let loose.

Fourth, creativity is a must on your culinary adventure. Whether you follow the traditional salad-entrée—side dish theme, serve several smaller dishes at once in true Middle Eastern or Indian style, or opt for a classic combo (soup and salad, for instance), experiment to your heart's

SAY "FREEZE"

Remember frozen dinners? The meaty (and fatty) main dish took center stage, with a side dish in each triangular corner of the aluminum tray and a small square dessert, back and center.

Today frozen foods aren't so boring and they aren't necessarily laced with meat and dripping with fat. That's good news when you're really strapped for time. Among the offerings—many available in supermarkets—are vegetable pasta dishes of all sorts, stir-fries, spinach pizza and bean-and-cheese burritos. You even can find meatless patties and sausages in the breakfast section, but check labels: Many frozen foods are healthful, but some score high in fat and are best relegated to the once-in-a-while food category.

delight. As you gain confidence, you'll be ready to serve a party of twenty. And don't worry if things don't go as planned. Some of the most memorable meals are ones that have a surprise—such as the time the rice was burned and the beans undercooked so you and your friends made impromptu pizzas instead.

Fifth, think ahead, especially when entertaining. Advance preparation helps limit your time in the kitchen so you can be with your guests. Here are a few things you can do the night before.

- Arrange the seating and place settings. If you're going to have a buffet table, get it ready, too.

- Pull out your candlesticks and centerpiece and place them attractively on the tables. Select the background music you plan to play.

- Remember the serving utensils. Lay them out on your countertop so you don't have to fish for them on the big day.

- Prepare food garnishes and cover and refrigerate them.

- Prepare other dishes as necessary.

- Relax—you deserve it.

Note: For homes with babies on the move, toddlers and preschoolers, you might want to ask your spouse or a neighbor to care for your kids while you prepare the tables shortly before your party. For some reason, little ones just love to pull on tablecloths when you're not watching.

Finally, as you plan your menu, keep one word in mind: *celebrate.* That's what the vegetarian choice is all about. And a wonderful benefit of your example is that you're influencing others, research shows. It's not confrontation that convinces family, friends and acquaintances to try vegetarian foods; rather, the example of your good taste is the key.

UNDER-TWENTY-MINUTE DINNERS

Sometimes planning ahead means a quick glance in the pantry or refrigerator—and not a minute more. Here are ideas:

Spaghetti with prepared sauce

Pizzas made on English muffins and toasted in a toaster oven

Main-dish salad made with greens and cooked beans and grains

Precooked soyburgers grilled and served on buns with trimmings

Cheese-and-bean burritos topped with jarred salsa

Ramen noodles and crusty bread

Pancakes served with berries

Potatoes cooked in a microwave, split open and topped in myriad ways (tomato sauce and mozzarella; beans, salsa and cheddar; broccoli and pesto)

Grilled vegetables served over couscous

Leftover brown rice mixed with a can of vegetarian baked beans

CHAPTER 5

let's shop!

WE'VE CUSTOM-MADE A PANTRY LIST FOR YOU, with its foundation set squarely on staples, those foods at the heart of vegetarian cooking. When you make out your weekly shopping list, use the pantry list as a guide. Jot down any staples you need as well as other foods of your choosing. These optional foods will include perishables—fresh vegetables, fresh fruits, dairy products and soyfoods, for instance—and any out-of-the-ordinary foods you need for the week's meals. Also add snacks to your shopping list. (Go ahead, list frozen yogurt if that's your favorite munchie. The goal isn't denial; it's moderation.)

Depending on the recipes you select, you may need a side trip to an ethnic grocery or a natural foods store. If you live far from such specialty stores, go the mail-order route. (Some mail-order companies are listed in appendix B.)

Following the pantry list is a glossary of foods, with an explanation for each entry. We anticipate that you'll use this glossary often—not only to get acquainted with new or unusual foods but also to learn more about foods integral to vegetarian cooking. In the glossary, we've purpose-fully omitted some common foods, such as potatoes, lettuce and oranges. But we've included others. White rice, for example, appears in the glossary because we want you to know how it stacks up nutritionally against brown rice.

Once you peer inside a typical vegetarian pantry and learn about ingredients in the recipes that you'll be cooking, expect a confidence boost. You'll have a wealth of information and a clear sense of where your culinary adventure will lead.

The Very Basic Pantry

Whole-grain breadstuffs (such as bread, English muffins and tortillas)

Brown rice (conventional or quick-cooking)

Other whole grains of choice (such as barley, bulgur, millet, couscous and kasha)

Rolled oats

Pasta (preferably whole-grain)

Whole-grain cold cereal

Whole-grain flours, including whole-wheat flour, whole-wheat pastry flour and other favorites

Unbleached white flour

Legumes (dried or canned), including kidney beans, chickpeas, lentils and other favorites

Condiments of choice (such as soy sauce, miso, mustard, pickles, jellies and other favorites)

Sweeteners of choice (such as honey, brown rice syrup, granulated sugarcane juice, molasses and/or sugar)

Vanilla extract

Baking powder

Baking soda

Arrowroot, cornstarch or other thickener

Vinegars of choice

Vegetable oils of choice, including olive and canola

Salt

Peppercorns (for freshly ground pepper)

Herbs and spices of choice

Beverages

THE GLOSSARY

What's tempeh? How does white rice compare to brown rice? Is fructose better for you than table sugar? These are some of the questions that this glossary answers. The glossary focuses on foods that help define vegetarian cuisine. Definitions of many other foods—the likes of kohlrabi and phyllo, common in cuisines besides vegetarian—appear in the recipe section, not here. Check the index if you need help finding information on ingredients.

Breads and Grains

The staff of life? You bet. In every culture of the world, breads and grains are essentials: *chapatis* in India; *injera* in parts of Africa; scones and biscuits in the British isles; what we call French bread in France; rice in Asia; thick slices of peasant bread in the Ukraine; grits in Dixie; oatmeal in the North on cold winter mornings; and whole-grain bread all over America. Let's look at many of the flours from which breads and other baked goods are made, then the grains and pastas.

FLOURS

First we'll consider the champ of flours—wheat—then move on to some less common yet quite flavorful options. You may experiment with many of the other flours in your favorite whole-wheat bread recipe for a flavor change.

Whole-wheat flour: If you're baking bread, select "bread flour" made from hard red spring wheat (which makes the highest loaves) or red winter wheat. Bread flours are high in gluten, which helps make a structure that provides light, airy loaves. You may choose stone-ground flour or very finely ground flour. The latter will be lighter, but you might prefer the more robust flavor of stone-ground.

If you're not making baked goods—say, you need to thicken a gravy—any type of wheat flour will do.

Whole-wheat pastry flour: Milled from lower-protein flour (and therefore not a good choice for bread baking), whole-wheat pastry

---

KEEP FRESH

Whole-grain flours and cracked grains, such as bulgur, are susceptible to rancidity. Keep them covered in your refrigerator or freezer.

flour makes tender muffins, quick breads and pancakes. Other than protein content, this flour does not differ significantly from regular whole-wheat flour.

Unbleached white wheat flour: This flour loses the nutritional showdown against whole-wheat flour, with about half the calcium and one-fourth the iron, phosphorus, potassium and B vitamins. Yet it has its advantages. It's not quite so refined as bleached flour, and for people accustomed to white bread, mixing together unbleached white flour and whole-wheat flour while getting used to the stronger flavor of whole wheat is a gentle way to go.

Amaranth: This flour—if you can find it (you might have to make your own by grinding amaranth seeds)—has a distinctive flavor, so use it in small quantities. Add it to recipes for whole-wheat bread and other baked goods when you want a nutritional boost and a wonderfully unique taste.

Brown rice flour: For people with allergies to wheat, bread made from rice flour is a boon. Rice, however, contains no gluten, so bread made from rice flour won't rise. Your best bet is to choose a quick bread recipe made from rice flour and a binder to hold it together.

Buckwheat flour: This flour is very strongly flavored. Even 1/4 or 1/3 cup creates a robust loaf. It's a bread you'll love or detest.

Cornmeal: Cornmeal, whether yellow or white, has most of the fiber removed but not the germ, which contains protein and minerals. If you see the word *degerminated* on the package, then the germ has been removed, too. Manufacturers often enrich cornmeal, adding vitamins and minerals. You may use cornmeal to make bread, muffins and other baked goods.

Gluten flour: This refined wheat flour has a high content of gluten (protein) and a low content of starch for better rising.

Oat flour: You can make your own oat flour very simply—just place some rolled oats into a blender or food processor, and let 'em whirl. Use oat flour—which contains no gluten—in muffins, quick breads and cookies.

Rye flour: Rye flour makes great rye bread with little trouble at all. Replace about 1/2 cup of whole-wheat flour with rye flour, and follow your bread recipe as usual. If you desire, toss in some caraway seeds too, for an authentic taste and appearance.

Triticale flour: You may not have heard of triticale, yet it's simply a grain hybrid of rye and wheat. It has a hearty flavor and extra protein. Consider replacing half of the whole-wheat flour in your bread recipe with triticale flour for a protein boost.

GRAINS

Pilafs, muffins, puddings, casseroles, soups—a fantastic variety of foods, from main dishes to side dishes or desserts—may be made from humble grains and turned into everyday or gourmet meals. Each kernel of a whole grain has three parts: the germ, the endosperm and the bran. Whole grains are naturally low in fat and rich in nutrients, particularly the B vitamins, vitamin E, calcium and iron. They have lots of fiber, too.

Also, ancient grains, such as amaranth, spelt, kamut, quinoa and teff, are being rediscovered here in the United States, though their histories are amazing, dating back thousands of years. Spelt, for example, is believed to be among the most ancient of cultivated wheats. You'll find many of these grains incorporated in pastas sold in natural food stores and well-stocked supermarkets.

Barley: You may have eaten barley in a soup with mushrooms—delicious—and nowhere else. But this chewy, delicately flavored grain can have a place at nearly every meal, as a breakfast cereal, in a marinated salad or as a pilaf. Unrefined whole barley, sometimes called pot barley, has nutritional advantages over refined or "pearl" barley, which has had its hard outer layers removed. Whole barley is available in natural food stores.

Buckwheat: Buckwheat groats, or "kasha," as it's known, is an Eastern European favorite. You may want to cut kasha's strong flavor with other grains, such as cooked brown rice. Kasha is great to have on hand because it cooks quickly—a pot of it is ready in 30 minutes.

Bulgur: This quick-cooking grain—sometimes called bulgur wheat or cracked wheat—has a nutty flavor and a wonderful fluffy texture. Bulgur groats come in three sizes: small, medium and large. Many people favor the

BRAN FAN

Rice bran, oat bran and other types of bran add a bit of flavor and a lot of nutrients—most notably, fiber—to your meal. Bran is the outer layer of the grain. In various studies, the intake of bran has been shown to have positive health effects, such as lowering blood cholesterol levels and alleviating constipation.

large size. It works well in tabouli (a Middle Eastern salad), pilafs and as a base for chunky sauces and stews.

Corn: Many people believe corn is a vegetable, but it's a grain. Coarsely ground whole dried kernels produce corn grits, which you may turn into a tasty cereal.

Couscous: It's a pasta, technically speaking, but couscous seems so much like a grain that we've placed it in this category. It soaks up water like other grains and becomes light and fluffy. You may buy either whole-grain couscous or refined couscous. Either cooks up quickly.

Millet: Bird seed? That's right—the little yellow grains you put out for the birds is food for you, too. It cooks up quickly—just half an hour of simmering (a little more or less, depending on your preference)—and makes for tasty pilafs and stuffings. Try it in breads as well.

Quinoa: Pronounced KEEN-wa, this ancient grain hails from the Andes, where the Indian name for this food means "the mother grain." It has a distinctive flavor and a fluffy texture, which make it a tasty choice for pilafs and other dishes. Be sure to rinse quinoa before cooking to remove any bitterness.

Rice: Brown rice, the common term for unrefined rice, comes in three variations: short, medium and long grain. Short-grain rice is the sweetest and stickiest of the three and is just right for rice pudding. The longer variety makes delicious pilafs and a number of other dishes, including casseroles, muffins and other baked goods, croquettes and salads. Brown rice traditionally takes about 40 or so minutes to cook, but to the delight of cooks on the run, quick-cooking brown rice came on the market several years ago. Precooked, this version is ready in 10 minutes.

Nutritionally, brown rice is superior to white rice. Removing the bran and polishing rice strips it of its color and nutrients. To make up for the loss, some white rice is enriched; its surface is coated with vitamins and minerals. The coating may come off if rinsed. One cup of enriched instant cooked rice is about equal to brown rice in many nutrients except two: White rice has no potassium while brown rice has 137 milligrams of potassium, and white rice has 31 milligrams of phosphorus while brown rice has 142 milligrams. Most important, brown rice has far more fiber than white rice—4 grams versus 1 gram in a cup.

> **A TOAST**
>
> Toasting millet—with or without a little oil or butter—before cooking imparts a delicious nutlike flavor and helps keep the grains from becoming gummy and clumping together.

As a side note: Two special types of rice are basmati, a fragrant, nutty-flavored rice from India, and arborio, used to make Italian risottos in which the rice becomes creamy yet slightly chewy (and extra flavorful with various additions to the recipe).

And rice has even been processed into "ice cream" in a variety of flavors. It tastes creamy, just like the real thing. Look for rice-based frozen desserts in the frozen food section of natural food stores.

Teff: The tiniest of grains (several uncooked teff kernels fit on a pinhead) has a sweet and faintly chocolate flavor and an almost jellylike consistency when cooked. Around for thousands of years and popular in Ethiopia, where it's made into a flat bread called *injera*, teff has crossed the ocean and is being grown in Idaho. It comes in dark brown and white varieties. This ancient grain most commonly appears in baked goods and puddings.

Wild rice: Guess what? It isn't even a rice. It's the seed of a tall, aquatic grass native to North America. The price of it remains high, but consider cooking it with brown rice to make an elegant pilaf. Wild rice takes about 40 minutes to cook.

PASTA

The shapes and flavors are endless: shapes such as corkscrew, wagon wheels, flat noodles and linguine and flavors like spinach, herb and tomato. Pale yellow, forest green, light red, brown and speckled are among the colors pasta now comes in. And America used to believe pasta was synonymous with spaghetti. No more. As always, remember that pasta made from whole grains has more fiber and nutrients than refined pasta (though the latter oftentimes is enriched with some vitamins and minerals).

Here are some of the lesser known varieties that appear in vegetarian cooking.

Bean thread noodles: These chewy, transparent noodles (sometimes called cellophane noodles) are made from the starch of mung beans. Pair them with Thai food or other spicy Asian dishes. (The noodles have little taste on their own.) To prepare them, you need only soak them in hot water to soften them.

MOCHI MUNCHIES

Mochi is a traditional Japanese specialty is made from sweet, mashed brown rice, which is pressed into trays, and then dried, becoming hard and dense. You may prepare mochi several ways—baked, broiled, grilled, pan-fried and deep-fried. To bake mochi, preheat oven to 450°F. Separate cakes (along the marks if provided) and place them on a lightly oiled baking sheet. Bake until puffed and golden brown, about 10 minutes. Watch the mochi carefully because it may puff up more quickly. When done to perfection, it is crisp on the outside and pleasantly chewy on the inside. It may be filled with just about anything: peanut butter and honey, shredded cheese, soy sauce, honey and ginger, and so on. Look for this sweet treat in natural food stores and Asian markets.

Corn pasta: Are you allergic to wheat or simply looking for a flavor change? Pasta made from corn is a wise choice. Take care in cooking it. If cooked too long, it becomes pasty.

Ramen: You may have tried ramen—these squiggly noodles are common in packages on supermarket shelves, usually in the soup aisle. Some brands that come with a flavor packet, such as mushroom or chicken, are fried before packaging and are high in fat. Other brands have been baked, not fried, so their fat content is significantly lower. Check out natural food stores for the widest selections.

Rice noodles: These white noodles come in many shapes and are a breeze to prepare. They require only soaking in hot water to soften them. Add them to stir-fries and soups. Or fry them and they'll puff up, and serve them with a variety of dishes.

Soba: Most soba is a combination of buckwheat and wheat flours, though these long, thin, flat noodles are sometimes called "buckwheat" noodles. They are virtually fat free and relatively high in protein and other nutrients.

Udon: Here's another Asian noodle, with a sister named "somen." Both are made from whole-wheat flour or a mixture of whole-wheat and unbleached white flours (or sometimes refined white flour), but udon is thick and tubular while somen is thin, almost like angel-hair pasta.

Legumes

Whatever you call them—legumes or beans—many Americans have tasted legumes in only three ways: as baked beans, in minestrone soup and in three-bean salad (kidney beans, green beans and waxed beans drowned in oil and vinegar). The good news is you have an adventure ahead of you, because there are so many varieties of legumes to explore, from adzuki to rattlesnake beans. (Don't fear—they have nothing to do with snakes other than their name.)

Legumes are nutritious powerhouses with great taste. One cup has about 200 to 300 calories, next to no fat (except for soybeans), about one third the protein you need in a day and lots of fiber (6 to 9 grams).

So why is this vegetarian staple new to many Americans? Possibly cooks have thought that beans are difficult to make. Not true. The easy route is to buy cooked canned beans. But cooking from scratch is simple, too. Just rinse them, soak them, simmer and serve. Uncooked beans have a long shelf life: a year or so. But use them in a couple of months for the freshest flavor. Once cooked, store beans covered in your refrigerator for up to a week or in your freezer for up to six months.

Of the hundreds of legume varieties available, here are the most common.

Adzuki beans: Sometimes called aduki beans, these small reddish Japanese treasures aren't well known—unless you're familiar with macrobiotic diets. They are believed to be the most easily digested bean and have a flavor similar to red beans. You may substitute adzuki beans for pinto or red beans in Latin dishes, or add them to soups.

Black beans: These small oval-shaped beans make great soup and are integral to the Cuban classic black beans and rice. Also known as black turtle beans, they have a robust flavor that works well with strong herbs and spices.

Black-eyed peas: Popular in Southern and soul food cookery, these legumes are a creamy white with a black spot or "eye," as the name suggests. They have a fresh flavor that makes them great partners in salads made of strong-flavored greens such as collards. Also try Hoppin' John, page 275, a black-eyed pea favorite.

Chickpeas: These round, golden, nutty-tasting beans often are called garbanzos. Though they take quite some time to cook, these beans are well liked in salads or in Mediterranean favorites such as falafel.

Great northern beans: These large white beans make great stews, sandwich spreads and dips. You can mash them and use them to thicken soups. Quite versatile, they may be seasoned subtly or with boldness.

Kidney beans: These are related to red beans, which are smaller and rounder than kidney beans. They may be used in a variety of dishes—marinated salads, chili and Mexican dishes.

PICKY ABOUT BEANS

When buying dried legumes, look for beans with a vibrant color. Fading is a clear indication of long storage. The longer beans are stored, the less fresh they'll taste. And if their surface looks cloudy, they also may be moldy.

Lentils: These small, disk-shaped legumes come in different varieties: brown, green and red (the latter being a staple in India and gaining popularity in America). Lentils have the advantage of cooking quickly and having an earthy flavor. Perhaps that's why they make a popular soup. But you also can use lentils in pilafs or mash them into burgers, seasoned as you prefer.

Lima beans: You can find these favorites of the American South—also called butter beans—fresh (during certain times of the growing season), frozen, canned and dried. Small (baby) limas taste somewhat sweet, and large limas taste more beany. Either combines well with a variety of dishes.

Mung beans: You usually find these beans in their sprouted form, but small, dark green mung beans are tasty cooked up in a pot like any other bean. With a flavor similar to green split peas, mung beans combine well with garlic, tomatoes, ginger and chilies.

Navy beans: You find these beans in the old standby Boston baked beans. These small, mild white beans, which look like a miniature version of great northern beans, taste excellent in soups, pilafs and salads.

Pinto beans: This mild, pinkish bean cooks to a creamy texture, making it a perfect base for strong spices like chilies, garlic and others. A Hispanic staple, pinto beans show up in burritos, enchiladas and other dishes.

Red beans: These are related to the kidney beans. See page 69.

Soybeans: They taste bland, but soybeans are champs in nutrition. They are a rich source of protein, iron and vitamin E. Combine them with other beans and spice them as you like, and soybeans can taste as delicious as any other bean. You can buy them in bulk from natural food stores or through mail order (page 493). Or try one of the soybean spinoff products, such as tofu or soymilk (see pages 72 and 71). These are easier to digest than the whole bean.

Split peas: A smart introduction to people new to legumes, split peas make a tasty soup. (Feel free to make additions such as barley or rice.) You can also add them to stews, but because they become mushy, they don't work as well in other dishes as do other legumes.

Soyfoods

Talk about a food revolution: A decade or two ago, tofu was a curiosity; today it sits next to vegetables in the produce section of supermarkets. Other soyfoods have yet to taste tofu's fame, but many vegetarians continue to rely on them regularly. Soyfoods in general are a good source of protein and have been singled out in research as a possible immunity-booster. But soyfoods can be high in fat. Select "lite" versions when they're available.

Soybeans: See page 70.

Soy cheese: For people who pass up dairy foods, soy cheese is a big plus—a similar but not identical flavor to cow's milk cheese. Made from tofu or soymilk and a number of other ingredients, soy cheese is cholesterol-free but high in fat. (A word to the wise: Some soy cheese makers add casein to their products to make them melt when heated. Casein is a milk protein, and milk is the only place you'll find it naturally. There is no plant source for casein.) Some dairy-free soy cheeses are very soft, however, and are a fair imitation of dairy cheese.

Soymilk: Made primarily from soybeans and water, soymilk is a delicious alternative to cow's milk. Some brands taste more beany than other brands, so check out a few of them and select your favorite. And now with "lite" versions available, you may drink soymilk with little concern about fat. The original version of soymilk has 4 to 6 grams of fat per cup. It gives a protein boost, with 10 grams of this macronutrient per cup, and it contains some fiber as well (about 2 to 3 grams per cup).

Soy yogurt: Cultured from soymilk and available in many flavors, soy yogurt is lactose- and cholesterol-free.

Tempeh: Tempeh (TEM-pay) is a cultured food made from soybeans and sometimes grains. The grayish blocks are held together by a mold, but don't be shy to try this soyfood. Tempeh tastes similar to fresh mushrooms and you can serve it in many ways—on skewers, as burgers with all the trimmings, over grains.

Tempeh is sold fresh and frozen; store it in your refrigerator or freezer. There should be no sign of tempeh's culture at the time of purchase. As tempeh ages, you'll see white spots, which will turn black. It's

CASEIN DEFINED

Casein is found only in dairy products and is integral to cheese-making. It is necessary in cheese to make it melt. If you buy a casein-free cheese pizza, expect the cheese to get warm but not gooey.

okay to eat tempeh that has a few black spots. The older tempeh gets, the stronger its flavor. So, for starters, eat fresh tempeh, which tastes mild. Then, if you desire, you can experiment with older, more pungent tempeh.

Textured vegetable protein: The name of this meat substitute is quite a mouthful, which is why almost everyone refers to it as "TVP," a registered trademark of the American soy king, Archer Daniels Midland Company. It is basically a dehydrated soy product made from the flakes that remain after oil is extracted from soybeans. TVP is sold plain and flavored, and in mince, flakes and chunks. Reconstituted with water and added to casseroles, soups or stews, it lends a "meaty" texture. Meat replacers—many of which are fashioned from TVP—can taste so meatlike that some vegetarians won't touch them. Others—and especially new vegetarians who might have a craving for a meaty chili or sloppy joes—welcome meat replacers onto their dinner plates.

Meat replacers (or analogs, as they are known among manufacturers) come in many forms: burgers, sausages, hot dogs, chicken nuggets and fish fillets, to name a few. Unfortunately, most meat taste-alikes do not have a nutritional profile that far outshines meat. They can be rather high in fat and sodium. But when you (or your children) crave the taste of meat (or want to be one of the gang), meat replacers may do the trick.

Tofu: Tofu (TOE-foo), which also goes by the descriptive yet funny-sounding name "soybean curd," has become a household word, though perhaps not a regularly eaten food in most homes. Maybe the wiggly, white rectangular blocks of tofu scare some people, but they needn't. Dozens of cookbooks have been devoted to tofu, attesting to this Asian food's respectability and versatility. It doesn't have much flavor on its own—just a very mild cheeselike taste—but we've known a number of people to eat it straight from the carton.

Yet tofu cheerfully picks up the flavors of the foods and seasonings in which it's cooked. Tofu cooked in chili tastes like chili, and tofu cubes added to a stir-fry flavored by ginger, soy sauce and mirin have a zippy, salty and sweet taste. It can also be cubed and sautéed, then dipped into a variety of sauces. We could go on and on.

But most important, tofu is worth trying in a few different dishes. Though tofu is rich in protein, with about 10 grams in 4 ounces of the

A LOAD ON LECITHIN

When lecithin is listed as an ingredient in prepackaged foods, it is used as an emulsifier to keep the food from separating. (Lecithin almost invariably comes from soy because soy is the cheapest source of it.) Lecithin is also used in cosmetics and paints. However, the lecithin sold in stores or through mail order as a dietary nutrient is different. In fact, it improves overall health and the health of various body organs, according to makers of dietary lecithin. Other theories, in contrast, hold that because lecithin breaks down during digestion, it is not necessary to add it to your diet.

medium-firm variety, it's high in fat, too—about 50 percent of its total calories come from fat. But there's no need to remove it from your foods-to-eat list.

Tofu now comes in fat-reduced versions. One brand boasts that a 3-ounce slice of its extra-firm "lite" tofu has only 1 gram of fat and 35 calories. Another variation in tofu is firmness. You can buy it in three types: soft, firm and extra firm. In general, select soft tofu when making sauces, pie fillings, dips and puddings. Buy firm or extra-firm tofu for cubing, skewering or any preparation method in which you want the soyfood to hold its shape. Flavored tofu also is on the market. Try one when you're in the mood for a flavor change.

When you bring your tofu home, handle it one of two ways. If it's water-packed, store it in your refrigerator and change the water daily after opening the package. If it's vacuum (asceptically) packaged, you can store it in your pantry until you're ready to use it. Once opened, keep the package covered with water and refrigerated. In any case, buy tofu as far ahead of its expiration date as possible. If it becomes slimy, sour or otherwise unappetizing, throw it out.

Tofu-based desserts: If you've got a hankering for something cold and creamy, and do not want to eat dairy products, a tofu-based dessert may be the answer. But be advised that some tofu-based desserts are no more nutritious than many super-rich ice creams. Be sure to read the labels.

Sweeteners

Though refined white sugar can ruin teeth, few in the scientific community believe sugar causes illness. Yet desiring the least adulterated foods and hoping to avoid the infamous "sugar rush," many health-minded vegetarians prefer sweeteners other than sucrose (table sugar). The different types of sweeteners are surprisingly numerous. Look for them in supermarkets, specialty stores or natural food stores.

Barley malt syrup: Sometimes called malted barley syrup, this dark, thick sweetener—maltose being its principal sugar—is better tolerated by people with diabetes. It is prepared from sprouted, dried barley. It can replace honey or molasses in most baked goods.

Brown rice syrup: It's made by adding sprouted, dried barley or barley enzymes to cooked rice and allowing the mixture to ferment until it breaks down into sugars. This natural sweetener is mild-tasting and expensive.

Fructose: This sweetener is a boon to diabetics because fructose does not produce the highs and lows in blood-sugar levels that table sugar (sucrose) does. However—and this may come as a surprise—commercial fructose is more refined than table sugar. Though fructose is found naturally in fruit, commercial fructose is made from sucrose (which already has gone through a number of washings, filtering—sometimes with the use of animal bones—and bleachings) by using enzymes to isolate the fructose. It also is very sweet, almost twice as sweet as table sugar.

Granulated sugarcane juice: This sugar is made from sugarcane juice that is dehydrated by spinning it at a high temperature through a vacuum tunnel and then milled into a powder. Only the water is removed, leaving intact sugarcane's naturally occurring vitamins, minerals and trace elements. These nutrients are minimal.

Honey: The oldest known sweetener, honey is a product of busy bees that have collected the nectar of flowers and turned it into a golden syrup. You can buy various flavors, depending on the source of the nectar. In baking, use a lightly flavored honey, such as clover, so the honey doesn't overwhelm the flavor of your recipe's other ingredients. Honey contains few nutrients.

Maple syrup: It is made by boiling the sap from maple trees to about one-fortieth its original volume. It has only a minute amount of nutrients, but it is pure, unlike pancake syrup, which is mostly colored corn syrup.

Molasses: This dark, thick liquid remains after sucrose has been extracted from sugar cane or sugar beet juice. Unlike most other sugars, molasses can have a fair share of nutrients. Blackstrap molasses, for instance, has significant amounts of calcium and iron. A rule of thumb: the darker the molasses, the greater the nutritional value.

Sugar, brown sugar: Table sugar (sucrose) has been blamed for a host of diseases, but the only proven ailment it causes is tooth decay.

SWEET CORN?

The top three corn sweeteners that pop up on food labels with amazing frequency are dextrose, corn syrup and high-fructose corn syrup (HFCS). Highly refined, these three amount to empty calories. Dextrose is the powdered form of corn syrup, which is less expensive than sugar. Corn syrup is made from dextrose and fructose. HFCS varies in sweetness, depending on how much fructose it contains.

However, there have been questions regarding sugar's role in suppressing the immune system, which works to keep the body healthy. Brown sugar is simply white sugar that has a small amount of molasses added to it. In either case, sugar amounts to empty calories. It's smarter to skip the sugar—at least as much as possible and reasonable (many of us have sweet tooths, you know)—and fill up on whole foods.

Turbinado sugar: This refined, light brown sugar has not been bleached. It has no more nutrients that table sugar.

Condiments

Chilies: These immature pods of various peppers add heat and color to recipes. Of the most popular peppers in the United States, the ana-heim is the mildest and the habanero is the hottest. Well-known peppers like jalapeño and serrano are acceptably hot to a lot of people—just keep some milk, rice or bread nearby in case your tongue feels like fire. By the way, it's wise to handle peppers with gloves because they can burn your skin. And never touch your hands to your face or eyes when working with chilies. The seeds are the hottest part and can be removed to reduce the heat of most chilies.

Mirin: This sweet Japanese wine, made from rice, adds a special flavor to stir-fries and other dishes.

Miso: This salty paste is made from cooked, aged soybeans and sometimes grains. It's thick yet spreadable. It may be spread thinly on bread for a savory snack or used for flavoring in various dishes and as a soup base. Miso comes in many varieties. As a rule, the darker varieties are saltier and more strongly flavored than the lighter ones.

Tahini: Tahini is a smooth, thick paste similar to peanut butter, but is made from ground raw or toasted sesame seeds. Spread it on bread for sandwiches or use it in cooking as flavoring.

Tamari, shoyu: Tamari is a naturally brewed soy sauce with no sugar. By definition, it ought to be wheat-free but some brands contain wheat. Shoyu is made of soybeans and wheat that go through an age-old Japanese fermentation process resulting in a rich soy sauce. Regular soy sauce may replace tamari or shoyu in recipes.

Vinegars: A splash of vinegar can add that special something to a dish. But which one to choose? There's balsamic, the queen of vinegars; red wine vinegar; herbed vinegar; and run-of-the-mill white vinegar, among others. Here's a rundown:

Sold in supermarkets, balsamic vinegar has a mellow sweet-sour flavor. Integral to Italian cooking, it is aged for years in wooden barrels.

Rice vinegar, common in Chinese and Japanese cooking, is subtle and sweet. Another Asian vinegar is umeboshi, made from the pickled, slightly sour umeboshi plum. Look for it in well-stocked supermarkets or Asian markets.

Herb vinegars and fruit vinegars taste like their chosen flavorings but with a kick. Use them in dishes in which you want extra flavor.

Wine vinegars taste great on salads. Use white on light-colored foods, because red wine vinegar may turn them pinkish.

White, cider and malt vinegars are pungent and make good choices for pickling.

Worcestershire sauce: The common type contains anchovies. You can find vegetarian versions in natural food stores; they have as much zippy flavor as the original.

Seasonings and Spices

Most seasonings and spices (oregano, sage and cinnamon, for example) require little explanation because they're in almost everybody's pantry. Here are a few that you may not know.

Asafetida: This spice, also known as hing, has a garliclike flavor. You can find it in Indian grocery stores.

Ginger root: Ginger root has a thin, grayish skin and is usually found in the produce section of many supermarkets. When you get it home, store it in a container in your freezer. To use it, simply grate or slice it. It adds zip to recipes.

Liquid aminos: This flavoring tastes like soy sauce. You can find bottles of it in natural food stores.

Zest: It is scrapings from the outermost surface of citrus fruits and does not include the bitter white rind beneath it. Choose organic fruits, which have not been treated with dyes and pesticides, if possible.

And Everything Else . . .

From sauce thickeners to wild mushrooms, this category is a catch-all for miscellaneous ingredients that go hand in hand with vegetarian cuisine.

Agar-agar: This flavorless, freeze-dried sea vegetable works like gelatin, helping to set mixtures of food. You can find it in natural food stores and Asian markets. It is sold in powdered, flake or stick form.

Arrowroot: Derived from the root of a tropical American plant, this thickener makes shiny, transparent sauces. Mix arrowroot with cold water before adding it to your recipe. Bring it to boil. You can replace arrowroot with cornstarch measure for measure.

Carob: An acceptable replacement for chocolate, carob comes from the dried, roasted and ground pods of a Mediterranean evergreen known as the locust tree. If combined with sugar and other refined ingredients, carob is no more healthful than chocolate—save for the fact that it's caffeine-free.

Egg Replacer: This product is a combination of starches and leavening agents that bind and leaven cooked and baked foods. Egg Replacer is a boon for people who want to reduce dietary cholesterol or who object to the horrendous factory farm conditions laying hens endure. (For homemade egg substitutes, see chapter 8.)

Kudzu: Made from the root of the kudzu (pronounced KOOD-zoo) plant, this white starchy substance may be used to thicken soups, sauces and puddings.

Nutritional yeast: Unlike baker's yeast, which is fairly tasteless and used in baking, nutritional yeast is a good source of protein, iron and several B vitamins. It has an unusual flavor—a cross between meaty, cheesy and nutty—though it's made of yeast only. Some people like to sprinkle it on casseroles, soups, dips and even popcorn. It has been known to cause flatulence, so start out easy, just 1/4 teaspoon or so a day.

Seitan: Derived from wheat, this versatile food is gaining popularity for its healthfulness and its savory flavor, which varies according to the spices and herbs with which it's cooked. It's pronounced SAY-tan (see sidebar).

HOMEMADE SEITAN

To make your own seitan, start with 7 1/2 cups whole-wheat flour poured into a large bowl. Slowly stir in 6 cups of water, and keep stirring until the mixture forms a ball. Knead for 10 minutes to develop the gluten in the wheat. Remove the ball from the bowl and hold it under cold running water, stretching the dough repeatedly until the starch and bran wash away, about 10 minutes. Form the dough into a loaf, place it on cheesecloth and tie the ends. Then set it in a pot of boiling vegetable stock flavored to your liking and simmer 1 hour. Add more boiling water to the pot as necessary. Remove the loaf and let cool. Slice it or cube it for use in recipes where you want a meaty texture and flavor.

Sea vegetables: Call them seaweed if you must, but sea vegetables are worth trying at least once. Many people, including the Japanese and even the Irish (who make a soup out of dulse), eat sea vegetables frequently. Look for sea vegetables in well-stocked supermarkets, natural food stores or Asian markets. The common varieties are:

- *Kombu*—A member of the kelp family, kombu can add rich flavor to soup stock and even be cooked with legumes to help prevent flatulence.

- *Hijiki*—With a salty marine flavor and its black color, this sea vegetable tastes and looks best cooked with sweet vegetables like carrots and squash.

- *Wakame*—This mild-flavored vegetable is green, making it seem very much like leafy land vegetables. Try it in a variety of recipes.

- *Dulse*—The thin, purple sheets of dulse make an unusual, salty snack food.

- *Nori*—You can eat it as is, but many people prefer to toast it over an open flame before adding it to recipes, especially soups. It comes in thin, black sheets.

Mushrooms: Many varieties beside the common white button mushroom are in supermarkets now, and shiitake mushrooms have received the most attention by far. You can experiment in your cooking by substituting one type of mushroom for another and savor the flavor change.

- *Shiitake (she-TAH-kay)*—A regular in Japanese cuisine, shiitake mushrooms are dark brown and impart a complex and flavorful dimension to the dishes the appear in. They may be purchased fresh, or, in most cases, you'll find them dried, stored in sealed plastic bags. They can be reconstituted by soaking in hot water for about 20 minutes before using them in your recipe.

- *Porcini (por-CHEE-nee)*—An Italian favorite, porcini mushrooms taste a bit like hazelnuts. Available fresh in the fall, they have large caps and beige stems. They can be purchased

COW-ABUNGA!

Rennet is an enzyme in the lining of cows' stomachs and is used in the making of cheese. An animal byproduct, rennet is added to milk to speed up the curdling process. (The thin liquid that remains is known as whey.) After the curds form, they are pressed together and aged to make cheese. Rennetless cheese is available. Look for phrases like "rennetless," "made with vegetable rennet" or "contains no animal coagualent" on cheese packages if you don't want to eat cheese made with rennet.

dried in most Italian grocery stores and need to be reconstituted by soaking in hot water for about 20 minutes before using them in recipes.

- *Chanterelles (shan-tuh-REHLS)*—These trumpet-shaped mushrooms have a light flavor. They're relatively expensive, so save them for your most special dishes.

- *Enoki (e-NOH-kee)*—These long-stemmed mushrooms with tiny button tops lend a delicate flavor to various dishes. Common to Japanese cuisine, these mushrooms appear as garnishes.

- *Morel (moh-REL)*—These mushrooms, with tops that look like brown sponges, have a deep flavor. Be sure to clean them well to remove any insects hidden in the spongy cap.

ready-made menus

TONIGHT YOU NEED TO GET DINNER ON THE TABLE FAST. A quick menu is a must. On Saturday, you're entertaining out-of-town guests and plan an elegant evening. Next week is Halloween, and it's your turn to have the neighborhood kids over at your house for a party.

Then comes Thanksgiving, holiday parties, New Year's—and all of the meals year round. Sound overwhelming? Especially now as you update your old recipe file? To simplify your meal making and to really see how a vegetarian menu is put together, we've devised more than five dozen menus for every occasion. (Look for each menu's recipe suggestions in the recipe section, which begins on page 117.)

FORMAL DINNERS

When you're entertaining, treat your guests to spectacular recipes that delight the senses. Keep in mind the extra touches: place settings, lighting (candles are romantic), your centerpiece (such as fresh or dried flowers, a collection of small statues or items from nature arranged attractively) and background music. Also remember that formal doesn't have to mean fussy. You can have your special dinner outdoors, weather permitting, in front of a fireplace or on a porch. Basically, the trick to success is planning on the unexpected and enjoying yourself and your guests.

Menu 1.

Spinach and Pea Soup

Olive-Tomato Crostini

Marinated Vegetable Salad

Saffron Risotto Timbales with Grilled Tomato Sauce

Roasted Potatoes with Thyme

Quince, Pear and Persimmon Compote

Almond Cooler

Menu 2.

Green Pea and Artichoke Terrine

Chilled Ginger Borscht with Mushrooms

Mixed Vegetable Salad

Braised Seitan Roll with Apricots

Strawberry-Banana Glace in Lacy Maple Cups

Menu 3.

Garlic Toasts with Sun-Dried Tomato Sauce

Green Pea Mousse with Carrot Garnish

Mushroom Bourguignonne in a Whole Pumpkin

Pears in Raspberry Sauce

Chocolate-Espresso Cake with Espresso Sauce

EVERY DAY

Here are a week's worth of menus, followed by some extra-quick ones.

Menu 1.

Cabbage Rolls with Seasoned Rice

Cinnamon-Glazed Carrots

Low-Fat Chocolate Mousse

Menu 2.

Roasted Asparagus Salad

Vegetable Provençal Soup with Hazelnut Pistou

Couscous Pilaf with Saffron Cream

Menu 3.

Stuffed Shells

Garlicky Greens Sauté

crusty bread

Menu 4.

Twenty-Minute Minestrone with Fennel

Macaroni and Cheese

Black Forest Cake

Menu 5.

Potato Medley

Stir-Fried Collards

Pears in Raspberry Sauce

Menu 6.

Good Shepherd's Pie

Herb-Roasted Corn

Baked Apples

Menu 7.

Golden "Chicken" Patties

Baked Sweet Lima Beans

Summer Peaches with Raspberries

Under Thirty Minutes

Menu 1.

Peanut Butter Spirals

Vegetables with Far East Flair

Menu 2.

Simple Seasoned Black Beans

Greens with Avocado and Pear

Menu 3.

Tofu with Fermented Black Beans and Ginger

Sesame Broccoli

SEASONAL

These menus show how different recipes work best in warmer or cooler seasons. But make exceptions. On a cabin-fever day in late January, have a picnic in your living room, complete with picnic blanket, lemonade, sandwiches and salads—but no ants, thank you very much. Sometimes being adventuresome makes the meal.

Spring

Menu 1.

Sesame-Crusted Tempeh with Fruited Barbecue Sauce

Roasted Asparagus with Sesame Seeds

Banana-Raspberry Ice Cream Pie

Menu 2.

Asparagus and Carrots with Pasta

Mushrooms with Wild Rice

One-Rise Bread Sticks

Summer
Menu 1.

Pickled Vegetable Appetizer

Farfalle with Carrot, Sage and Scallions

Orange-Scented Asparagus with Sweet Red Pepper and Kiwifruit

Lemon Pudding Updated

Menu 2.

Better than Sloppy Joes

Coleslaw with Pineapple Dressing

Strawberry Bars

Autumn
Menu 1.

Vegetarian Pot Pie with Basic Biscuit Crust

Skinny French Fries

Apple Tart

Menu 2.

Rutabagas, Chickpeas and Greens

brown rice

Baked Apples Filled with Chestnut Purée

Winter

Menu 1.

Easy Borscht

Cheesy Pasta Wedges with Vegetable Sauce

Sesame Broccoli

Pumpkin Freeze

Menu 2.

Spinach Salad with Saffron Rice

Oven-Crisp Tofu Sticks with Ketchup Sauce

Paprika Mashed Potatoes

Warm Pear Charlotte

TABLE FOR ONE

When you're eating alone, preparing dinner may not seem worth the effort. Actually, cooking for yourself can be more enjoyable than cooking for a group. That's because the only person you have to please is yourself. So do it right: Use your finest dishes, light the candles and enjoy.

Menu 1.

Pasta with Dill and Tomatoes

Steamed Broccoli with Garlic

Pear Cobbler

Menu 2.

Chickpea Sauté with Garlic and Olives

Sautéed Peppers and Squash

Parslied Bulgur Pilaf

MAIN-DISH SALADS

Menu 1.

Mandarin Salad with Tempeh

crusty bread

Not Too Rich Brownies

Menu 2.

Spicy Black Bean and Lentil Salad

Lemony Orange Slices

ETHNIC

Menus based on the world's various cuisines present a spectrum of flavors. Feel free to try other cuisines not included among these menus; these include Thai and Ethiopian (a favorite because utensils are off limits).

Hispanic

Menu 1.

Three-Bean Chili

Flame Toasted Whole-Wheat Tortillas

Spring Lettuce with Avocado, Radish and Orange

Menu 2.

Black Bean Medley

Simple Tortillas

Savory Apple Empanada

Indian

Indian Vegetable Stew

Vegetable Samosas

basmati rice

Stir-Fried Kale with Ginger

Mango Chutney

Simple Chapatis

Italian

Menu 1.

Bulgur-Herb Crostini

Creamy Pea Soup

Eggplant Parmesan

Lima Beans with Fennel Seeds

Key Lime Italian Ice

Menu 2.

Creamy Spinach Lasagna

mixed green salad with **Mustard Dressing**

garlic bread

Banana-Blueberry Crisp

Japanese

Sukiyaki

brown rice

Vegetables with Far East Flair

Eastern European

White Radish Salad

Sweet and Sour Cabbage Rolls with Sauerkraut

Golden Potato-Rutabaga Whip

Braised Green Peas with Scallions

Cran-Raspberry Crisp

Greek

Spanakopita

Roasted Vegetables

Fresh Fruit with Honey-Lime Dressing

Honey-Yogurt Cake with Syrup

Middle Eastern

Falafel-Stuffed Wrappers

Middle Eastern Rice with Lentils

Marinated Vegetable Salad

Rice Pudding with Dates

French Bistro

Potato-Leek Soup

Chickpea-Couscous Croquettes

Sauce Bourguignonne

Braised Red Cabbage with Currants

Ring of Rice with Parsley

Glazed Onions

Pear Tart with Almond Crust

Down Home Dixie

Ambrosia Fruit Salad

Fried Green Tomatoes

Southern Crookneck Squash

Tofu with Key West Barbecue Sauce

Hoppin' John

Feather-Bed Biscuits

Peach Yogurt Freeze

BARBECUE

Who says vegetarian foods don't belong on a grill? Each of these menus include at least one grilled item. If you plan on barbecuing regularly, we suggest that you purchase a small screen for your grill to keep smaller items, such as cut vegetables, from falling through the openings into the fire. These screens are available at gourmet specialty shops and many department stores.

Menu 1.

Pacific Rim Brochettes
Thai Noodle Salad
Teriyaki Grilled Corn
Banana-Pineapple Kabobs

Menu 2.

Tandoori Tofu Brochettes
Cumin Nan
Pineapple-Cucumber Chutney

Menu 3.

Italian Brochettes with Angel-Hair Pasta
Cannellini Salad in Butter Lettuce Cups
Grilled Angel Food Cake with Nectarines and Blueberries

BREAKFAST

Menu 1.

Good Grains Pancakes
Blueberry Sauce

Fruity Bran Muffins

juice

Menu 2.

Oat Muesli with Dried Peaches

Tropical Yogurt Smoothie

Menu 3.

Cherry Clafouti

Carrot and Tofu Scramble

juice

SUNDAY BRUNCH

Menu 1.

Cantaloupe Soup

Yogurt-Cheese Blintzes with Raspberries

Almost-Classic Quiche with Broccoli

Blueberry Buttermilk Coffeecake

Whole-Wheat Apple Bread

juice

tea

Menu 2.

Baked Vegetable Frittata

Potato-Apple Torten

Nutty Blintzes

Orange-Almond Scones

juice

tea

LUNCH

Menu 1.

"Egg" Salad Sandwich

Skinny Potato Chips

carrot sticks

juice

Menu 2.

Cream Cheese Sandwich

celery sticks

Cinnamon Oatmeal-Apple Cookies

juice

Menu 3.

Submarine Sandwich

Not Too Rich Brownies

SPECIAL OCCASIONS

Those special days in the calendar year are all the more festive with food.

New Year's Day Brunch

Orange Sunrise

Better than Champagne

Spiced Tomato Sunset

Soufflé Roulade with Herbed Cheese

Garlic Toasts with Black Olive Tapenade

Sautéed Peppers and Squash

Sweet Stuffed Japanese Eggplants

Hot Corn Sticks

Salade de Mesclun

Super Bowl Party

Chile-Mole Popcorn

Orange-Honey-Sesame Popcorn

Sloppy Joes

Dilly Dip (with raw vegetables)

No-Toll Cookies

Valentine's Day

Artichokes with Light Lemon Dipping Sauce

Pasta in Southwestern Sauce

Orange-Scented Asparagus with Sweet Red Pepper and Kiwifruit

Papaya-and-Watercress Salad with Lime

Grape Ice

St. Patrick's Day

St. Patrick's Day Stew

Scalloped Potatoes

Orange-Almond Scones

Shamrock Torte

Easter

This holiday, celebrating the resurrection of Jesus Christ, brings together Christian families for the most glorious spiritual event of the year. Easter bunnies, baskets filled with treats, egg hunts and new spring clothes go hand in hand with this celebration of life. So does a flavorful feast.

Cream of Parsley Soup

Roasted Squash with Fruited Couscous

Potato Logs

Roasted Asparagus with Sesame Seeds

Cherry Tomatoes with Tomato Cream

Cherry Heart Tartlets

Passover

Garlic-Marinated Tofu with Olives and Tomato Fans

Fragrant Broth with Herbed Matzoh Dumplings

Vegetable-Stuffed Potato Kugel

Sauté of Spaghetti Squash, Carrot and Daikon

Fresh Fruit with Honey-Lime Dressing

Mother's Day

Pasta with Asparagus and Strawberries

Cheese Muffins

Layered Berry Parfaits in Champagne Glasses

Fruity Spritzer

Picnic

To transport the food to your picnic site, simply store the items in containers and serve them on sturdy, unbreakable plates with utensils on a festive tablecloth. If you're in a romantic mood, bring along candles and flowers in a vase.

Mixed Olives with Herbs

Herbed White Bean and Cucumber Sandwiches

Apple-Carrot-Pineapple Salad

Fruity Bran Muffins

Fourth of July

Here's a fairly standard menu for any Fourth of July celebration. A note about the Lentil Burgers: You may bake them (as the recipe instructs) or grill them. To grill them, place the burgers on a small screen made for grills (available in gourmet specialty shops or department stores) and cook until crispy.

Baked Beans
Macaroni Salad
Lentil Burgers
Very Berry Good Treats

Rosh Hashanah

Rosh Hashanah, the Jewish New Year, is both solemn and celebratory as Jews gather in synagogues to admit their failings and ask for
forgiveness, while pledging to do better in the coming year. This menu
includes favorite Jewish dishes.

Noodle-Currant Latkes with Mock Sour Cream
Tzimmes with Potato Dumplings
Baked Sweet Lima Beans
Orange-and-Tomato Salad
Challah
Potato-Pumpkin Soup
Simple Honey Cake
Dried Fruit Compote

Thanksgiving

Thanksgiving with no turkey? You got that right. And the results
are downright delicious. At this autumn feast celebrating the bounty of the
land, plates are overflowing with stuffing, mashed potatoes and other family favorites. In this menu, savory stuffed pumpkins take center stage, com-
plemented with other lower-fat dishes that leave guests satisfied but with
no need to loosen their belts.

Cilantro Dip
raw vegetables (for dipping)
Olive-Tomato Crostini

Stuffed Pumpkins with Herbs and Bread Crumbs

Pesto Mashed Potatoes

Greens with Avocado and Pear

Sweet-Tart Cranberry Muffins

Tofu-Pumpkin Pie

Christmas Buffet

Unlike Thanksgiving, Christmas dinner has no set formula. That's great for innovative cooks. This menu combines a variety of dishes to fit anyone's particular holiday craving.

Winter Pear Salad in Raspberry Vinaigrette

Straw and Hay Pasta

Herb-Stuffed Grape Leaves with Minty Yogurt Sauce

Rosemary-Scented Vegetable Phyllo Tart

Honey-Glazed Onions

Brussels Sprouts à la Grecque

Three Kings Bread

Easy Holiday Fruitcake

Hibiscus Cooler

Kwanzaa Feast

Kwanzaa (meaning "first of the fruits") is a holiday celebrated in late December by African-Americans. With spiritual and social significance, this holiday grew out of the 1960s civil rights movement. Its purpose is to celebrate and promote bonds among all Americans of African heritage, including Puerto Rican, Caribbean and South American peoples. The feast includes traditional dishes of Africa and is rich in symbolism.

Grilled Plantains

Grilled Green Bean–and-Eggplant Salad

Jolof Rice

Teff Cakes with Groundnut Sauce

Banana Condiment

Fluffy Mashed Sweet Potatoes

Braised Greens with Vinegar and Sesame Seeds

Berry-Pecan Cornbread

Caribbean Bananas

Hors D'Oeuvres Party

Finger foods are fun to make and eat. Just provide napkins, beverages and some music, and dance the night away.

Pears with Spicy Lime, Chile and Peanut Chutney

Cucumber Logs Filled with Black and Gold Hummus

Pan-Fried Vegetable Wontons with Sesame Dip

Snow Peas with Radish Cream

Bermuda Onion Toasts

Skewered Cheese Tortellini with Garlic-Parmesan Sauce

Mushroom Caps Stuffed with Basil, Sun-Dried Tomatoes and
    Parmesan

Radicchio Leaves Filled with Pineapple-Pecan Salad

Walnut-Stuffed Baby Red Potatoes

Kid's Birthday Party

Make your child's party special by serving well-loved foods centered around a theme. (You can let older kids make their own pizzas or tostadas—just have various toppings already chopped.) Possible themes include Teddy Bears, Tea Party, Dinosaurs, Space Adventure and a Treasure Hunt. The party may take place indoors or out, depending on weather. Just be sure to fashion invitations and decorate the party area according to the theme. Party games (such as tape the tail on the teddy bear) and crafts (such as painting T-shirts) keep the party running smoothly. Books at your library are full of ideas. And don't forget loot bags filled with items that fit the party's theme.

Pita Pizzas
Six-Fruit Kabobs with Strawberry-Yogurt Dip
Spiced Popcorn Balls
Chocolate Layer Cake
Melon-Lime Refresher

Wedding

If you have been searching for the perfect recipes for your big day, take a breather. This lineup is lovely, elegant and satisfying. You may give the recipes to caterers or turn them over to family and friends if they have offered to prepare the food. All of the recipes (except the dessert) serve six. You can increase the amount of food for a larger party by multiplying the ingredients to accommodate the number in the group. Please note that we've omitted a wedding cake on purpose. We figured that you might prefer to ask your baker to prepare the cake of your dreams.

Mixed Olives with Herbs
Focaccia with Coarse Salt and Fennel
Tomato-and-Rosemary Tartlets
Artichokes with Green Herb Sauce
Spinach Roulade with Red Pepper Sauce
Cherry Heart Tartlets

kitchen techniques

7

COOKING IS A BLEND OF ART AND SCIENCE. The science requires the knowledge of cooking basics; the art builds on the fundamentals, allowing you to tinker with recipes, substituting one ingredient for another or turning a stew into a pot pie crowned with a golden crust.

As your confidence grows, you become an adventuresome culinary artist. Then cooking is pure joy. Let's forge ahead into the specifics of cooking grains and legumes, staples in vegetarian cuisine. Then we'll look at cooking methods you need to know.

COOKING GRAINS

Rice, barley, couscous (pronounced KOOZ-KOOZ) and kasha—these are but four grains common in vegetarian cuisine. (For definitions, see the glossary in chapter 5.) As you try out recipes, you'll become accustomed to their flavors and textures: mild, nutty, robust, chewy, tender—you name it. But first, a cooking lesson.

Simmering is by far the most common way to cook grains. The grains swell and absorb moisture as they cook, while a tight-fitting lid traps the steam. Choose the boiling water method or the cold water method. For the boiling water method, bring a pot of water or vegetable broth to a boil and sprinkle in the grain (using the measurements below). Cover the pot and reduce the heat to a simmer. This method causes the grains to swell quickly and keep separate. For the cold water method, rinse the grain through a sieve under cool running water. Place the grain in a pot, add cold water, cover and bring to a boil. Reduce the heat to a simmer.

Your grains will be fluffier if you don't stir them while they simmer. Also, after the cooking time is up, leave the lid in place a few minutes longer; the grains will continue to cook.

RICE COOKER

One time-saving device (sort of) is an electric rice cooker. It still takes about 45 minutes to cook rice, but you can leave your home to run some errands and the appliance will turn itself off when the rice has finished cooking. It also will keep it warm (if you have a warmer on your unit). We know people who say they couldn't do without their rice cooker: The pot of rice is perfect every time. There are many manufacturers of rice cookers and various sizes, so shop around.

Grain	Water per cup of dry grain	Cooking time (covered)	Yield (approx.)
Whole Barley (presoaked)	2 1/2 to 3 cups	1 hour	3 cups
Bulgur	1 1/2 cups	15 min.	2 1/2 cups
Corn grits	4 cups	15 min.	3 to 4 cups
Couscous (whole grain)	2 cups	5 min.	4 cups
(refined)	1 1/2 cups	5 min.	4 cups
Kasha	1 3/4 cups	30 min.	4 cups
Millet	2 cups	30 min.	3 to 4 cups
Brown rice	1 3/4 cups	45 min.	3 to 4 cups
Quinoa	1 1/2 cups	15 min.	4 cups
Teff	3 cups	15 min.	3 cups
Wild rice	2 1/2 cups	35 min.	3 cups

Note: Some grains—whole barley, millet and brown rice—may be prepared in a pressure cooker. Use a little less water and cut the cooking time by one third to one half. Check your pressure cooker manual for specifics.

COOKING LEGUMES

You may cook legumes in a few different ways. Pick the one that suits your time schedule.

Traditional method: After rinsing the beans and picking out any debris, such as tiny stones (usually there isn't anything to pick out), place the beans in a large pot with three to four times their volume of water. Cover them and soak overnight or for about 8 hours. (In warm weather, soak beans in your refrigerator to prevent fermentation.) Bring the water and beans to a boil, lower heat to a gentle simmer and cook until done. Please note that lentils, split peas and mung beans do not require soaking.

Quick-soak method: Here's a way to speed up preparation. Instead of soaking beans overnight, place them in a large pot with three to four times their volume of water. Bring to a boil, remove from heat and let stand, covered, for an hour. Then cook the beans.

Pressure-cooker method: Soak the beans by either the traditional or quick-soak method. Follow the cooker's manufacturer's instructions and make sure that the vents on the cooker don't get clogged with foam. One way to reduce foam is to fill your cooker no more than one-third full with water and beans; also add a tablespoon of oil. Cook according to the manufacturer's instructions.

Slow-cooker method: After soaking by either the traditional or quick-soak method, place beans with four times their volume of water in your slow cooker. Cover and cook for 6 to 8 hours. If you wish, you may add onion, garlic and herbs to the beans before cooking to produce a delicious broth.

Cooking Times for Legumes

The times will vary depending on the type of bean, simmering temperature, the soaking time and the age of the beans. You can tell that they are cooked when you bite into one and it is tender but not mushy. You'll end up with 2 1/4 to 2 1/2 cups of cooked beans for every cup of dry beans.

Legumes	Presoak	Cooking Time
Adzuki Beans	yes	45 to 60 min.
Black Beans	yes	1 to 1 1/2 hours
Black-Eyed Peas	yes	1 to 1 1/4 hours
Chickpeas	yes	2 1/2 to 3 hours
Great Northern Beans	yes	1 1/2 to 2 hours
Kidney Beans	yes	1 1/2 to 2 1/2 hours
Lentils	no	30 to 45 min.
Lima Beans (small)	yes	45 to 75 min.
Lima Beans (large)	yes	1 to 1 1/2 hours
Mung Beans	no	45 to 60 min.
Navy Beans	yes	1 to 2 hours
Pinto Beans	yes	1 1/2 to 2 1/2 hours
Red Beans	yes	1 1/2 to 2 1/2 hours
Soybeans	yes	3 or more hours
Split Peas	no	45 to 60 min.

Many varieties of beans are available jarred or canned in supermarkets. Unless a recipe says differently, be sure to rinse the legumes to reduce salt and sugar that may have been added during processing.

Psst: If you're new to eating legumes regularly and want to avoid odoriferous consequences while your body adjusts to your greater fiber intake, try replacing the soaking water with fresh water before cooking. This removes some of the sugars that cause flatulence.

GENERAL COOKING METHODS

Baking: When you bake more than one thing at a time, stagger the dishes so the air may circulate. Also keep in mind that few ovens accurately reflect the temperature at which they're set. Some ovens run hot, others cool. A good way to learn about your oven is to note whether your dishes seem to cook more or less quickly than the time listed in your recipe. If

BASIC EQUIPMENT

To make most recipes, Here's what you'll need:

Pots and pans with lids

Steamer

Griddle

Baking pans and cookie sheets

Wooden cooking spoons and other utensils

Hand-held shredder

Measuring cups and spoons

A vegetable peeler (wash and dry it after use to prevent rusting)

A large colander

Small- and medium-size strainers with fine sieves

Kitchen scissors

your dishes bake less quickly, you probably have a cool oven (and vice versa). Compensate by adjusting the oven dial. Or, simply measure the oven's temperature with an oven thermometer.

Blanching: Quickly boiling or steaming vegetables and then cooling in water for a few seconds readies vegetables and some fruits for freezing. You also may blanch nuts—but skip the cold water dunk—to ease the removal of their skins. To remove the skins, rub the nuts with your fingertips.

Braising: This traditional French method of cooking vegetables in a little butter (or oil) and liquid in a covered pot over low heat makes for richly flavored side dishes (with extra fat calories).

Broiling: Simply turn your oven dial to "broil" and place your ovenproof dish or pan on the broiling rack at the height called for in your recipe. In vegetarian cooking, broiling is used primarily for melting cheese on casseroles or for top browning. Say good-bye to grease buildup.

Grilling: A handy item you may have packed away when you decided to cut down on or cut out meat is the all-American barbecue. But meat doesn't have sole rights to the grill; vegetables (and not only potatoes and corn) and other nonmeat foods belong on the barbie, too. You'll just need a few accessories to get you started.

First, buy a screen attachment (sometimes called a grilling rack) for your grill. What could be more frustrating than watching your veggie burger fall into the flames, then break apart while you try to extract it—all while your stomach is grumbling? A screen attachment, available at gourmet kitchen stores and many department stores, prevents such fiascoes. It sits on top of the grill and keeps food from falling through.

When you invest $15 or $25 for the attachment, remember that another reason you need it is because veggie and beans burgers have less fat and fall apart more easily than meat burgers. Likewise, vegetables lightly brushed with a marinade have a home on a grill, and so do kabobs (which usually don't need the screen) and even fruit. Grilling gives nonmeat food that great taste that no other cooking method can—so heat the coals and enjoy.

Microwaving: This method of cooking depends on invisible microwaves, which affect only electrically unbalanced polar molecules

> **HAUTE!**
>
> When grilling, try flavor-enhancing woods, such as mesquite or hickory, or drop some fresh herbs into the flames and cover the grill to jazz up your dinner.

(i.e., water) to heat food. That's why microwave ovens work best on foods that are moist or are cooked in water. Certain foods, such as pasta, rice and legumes, cook just as quickly the conventional way. But vegetables, fruits, eggs (never cook an egg in its shell in your microwave; it might explode) and many other foods are ready in a few minutes when microwaved. To microwave a specific dish, follow the instructions in the recipe you've selected, paying close attention to cooking times and power setting for the best results.

A health advantage of microwaving is you do not need as much fat (and often no fat) to fix a dish that would require fat on the stove. Concerns about the safety of microwave ovens linger, but today's models with their multi-safety features are considered safe when used properly. Be sure to keep your microwave oven clean and in good repair. A practical advantage is microwaves don't heat up your kitchen. But sometimes the food containers become hot because they are warmed by their hot contents, so keep oven gloves nearby.

Pressure cooking: When you're pinched for time, a pressure cooker can rescue you. Most vegetables cook in seconds, and grains and beans can be ready in less than half their stovetop cooking time. Today's pressure cookers have safety features that make accidents quite unlikely. Be sure to read your manual.

Puréeing: Puréeing means to turn something—vegetables or fruits, for instance—into a smooth, thick liquid. Think soup, sauces, frothy fruit smoothies. You may use a food mill, blender or food processor to purée. Keep in mind that puréeing in a blender requires special attention if the food is hot. Hot liquids can crack glass and plastic, and cause burns if the blender contents spill. Fill the blender no more than half full and hold the cover in place with a thick towel.

Sautéing: Sautéing sounds like a nicer way to say "frying." But there's a difference: Sautéing traditionally uses far less butter or oil than frying, so you benefit by consuming far fewer fat calories. To sauté, heat your fat (or a mixture of fat and a liquid such as vegetable broth, or a liquid alone) over high heat and add your food, taking care not to overcrowd. If you are sautéing with only liquid, you probably will need to replenish it periodically.

PARCHED

Another flavorful but under-used cooking method is cooking with parchment paper. Food is placed on individual sheets of parchment, which are folded over to seal in the food and its juices. The parchment packets are then baked until the food is cooked to your liking. Transfer the packets to dinner plates and fold back the parchment to expose the wonderful edibles.

Simmering: This is a very slow boil in which only small bubbles come to the surface.

Steaming: Steaming vegetables makes them tender-crisp, assuming you don't overcook them. Just bring about an inch of water to a boil in a covered pot. Meanwhile, place your rinsed vegetables in a collapsible steamer basket (sold in supermarkets and stores with kitchen gadgets). Set the basket in the pot, allowing the flowerlike petals of the basket to expand to the size of the pot. Reduce the heat to a simmer. Let cook until desired tenderness is achieved. Time varies depending on the vegetable, but often just a few minutes suffice. The big plus: Because the vegetables do not touch the water, most vitamins and minerals remain intact.

Stir-frying: Stir-frying is a method of quick cooking in which you constantly stir the ingredients over high heat. You may use a wok, but a skillet or other pan works fine, too. A wok has a flat or rounded bottom, where the heat is the hottest, and sloping sides, which remain cooler. The differences in heat allow you to cook the ingredients evenly by rearranging the food. For stirring, you may use a wooden spoon, but a Chinese-style spatula is best.

Traditionally, heated oil is used to stir-fry onions, garlic, vegetables, tofu and other foods, but you may use wine, broth or water instead of oil if you wish. (You'll save some calories and fat grams when foregoing the oil.) The flavor will change slightly depending on the liquid you use.

Before cooking, have your ingredients prepared as directed in your recipe and lined up in order. The oil (or other liquid) will sear the vegetables, locking in their juices. This takes a minute or two, and sometimes only seconds, depending on the ingredient. The final product ought to be tender-crisp and taste fresh. It's the healthy answer to fast food.

MORE KITCHEN TECHNIQUES

Preparing food involves more than cooking. Here are some extra tips to give you a hand in the kitchen.

Seeding tomatoes: To peel and seed tomatoes, cut an X on the bottom of each one. Then drop them into a small pot of boiling water for

THE ANCIENT BLENDER

From high-tech to ancient times, a mortar and pestle is just right for crushing seeds and garlic, grinding fresh herbs, and mixing together small quantities of various pastes. A mortar looks like a simple bowl; you can find them in beautiful wood. A pestle is similar to a stick but with a rounder, fatter end, which is used to do the work, with a bit of your muscle power. Mortars and pestles, available in gourmet kitchen shops, predate biblical times.

THE WOK ROCK?

To keep a round-bottomed wok from rocking, be sure to use a metal ring stand underneath.

1 to 2 minutes, until the skins begin to loosen. Drain and rinse under cold water. The skins will easily slip off. Slice the tomatoes in half crosswise, then squeeze to remove the seeds.

Roasting bell peppers: To roast bell peppers, place them under your broiler until the skin is charred, turning frequently, about 8 to 12 minutes. Remove the peppers from the broiler, place them in a paper bag and close the top. Let stand about 10 minutes. Remove the peppers from the bag and peel off the charred skin. Slice the peppers into strips and remove the seeds.

Making bread crumbs: You can make your own bread crumbs by cutting fresh bread into cubes. Then place them on a baking sheet and bake at 350°F until crisp, about 15 to 20 minutes. Process the cubes in a blender or food processor until finely ground.

Toasting seeds and nuts: To toast nuts, bake at 350°F for about 10 minutes on a baking sheet.

To toast pumpkin seeds, rinse them thoroughly and remove all strings and pulp. Allow them to dry, then toss with 1 1/2 tablespoons oil and salt to taste. Place them on a baking sheet. Bake at 350°F for 20 to 30 minutes, stirring every 5 minutes, until the seeds are golden brown.

For mustard seeds, a dry skillet with a lid is best. When they heat up, they pop—all over your kitchen if you've forgotten the lid. Lightly shake the contents as they pop. Remove them from the heat when the popping slows down.

Other seeds, such as sesame and sunflower seeds, may be toasted in a dry skillet until lightly brown. Stir frequently to prevent burning.

Making yogurt cheese: To make yogurt cheese, line a colander with a large cloth napkin or paper towels. Place the colander over a bowl. Spoon two cups plain yogurt into the colander. Let the yogurt drain in your refrigerator for several hours or overnight. The yogurt will become thicker like cheese.

Handling tofu I: Depending on your recipe, you may want to make your tofu firmer by pressing out some of its water. For instance, if you want cubes that'll hold their shape in your stir-fry, press the block of

---

MAKING THE MOST

If you own a food processor, use it to speed up preparation time. Set aside an hour every week or two to chop up lots of food, and pack and store it. For instance, you could chop several onions, bell peppers and bread crumbs, wiping out the work bowl between foods; then grind nuts and hard cheeses, and shred cheddar, mozzarella and other favorites (one at a time, transferring each food to a zipper-type baggie). Label and store in your freezer. If you're an expert planner, you can purée soup on your "food processor" day as well.

tofu before cutting it. Otherwise, you might end up with crumbled tofu when you stir-fry. But if you're making scrambled tofu, don't bother with pressing unless your recipe gives that instruction.

To press tofu, wrap it in a cloth towel or several paper towels. Place a breadboard on top of the tofu, and if you wish, set a pot of water or several books on the breadboard. (Be careful not to place too much weight on top; the block of tofu might smoosh down irrevocably.) Let it sit for 25 or 30 minutes. Check the tofu. Still too water-logged? Then replace the breadboard and the weight, and allow the tofu to drain another 15 minutes. Now you're ready to use it in your recipe.

Handling tofu II: When you freeze then thaw tofu, it transforms into a chewier, more "meaty" food, making it a satisfying meat substitute in many dishes, such as sloppy joes, spaghetti sauce and casseroles.

To freeze tofu, wrap the block in plastic wrap and place it in the freezer until it is frozen solid, at least 24 hours. Thawing takes longer, all day or overnight in the refrigerator. If you didn't leave enough time in your schedule for a complete thaw, you may place the frozen block in a bowl and pour boiling water over it several times until thawed. Or try microwaving the frozen block on high power a minute at a time. When it's thawed, squeeze out excess water by hand.

If you thaw more tofu than you can use, it's fine to refreeze the unused portion. The refrozen tofu will become chewier the next time you thaw it.

Freezing: Freezing is an excellent way to preserve food. You may freeze leftovers, of course, or you may plan ahead and freeze food for those busy days when you barely have time to set the table.

Either way, freeze and store food properly. For fresh vegetables, blanch them first. Most vegetables may be frozen, but salad vegetables such as lettuce become mushy when thawed. For fruits, peel and slice them before freezing them in a thick sweet liquid; berries may be flash-frozen on baking sheets then transferred to plastic bags and sealed. Breads, cooked legumes and cooked grains may be placed in plastic bags or in tightly covered containers and frozen.

WHAT'S A BOUQUET GARNI?

A *bouquet garni* is indispensable to French cooks. It imparts a subtle herb flavor to stews and other dishes. To make a basic *bouquet garni*, place 3 bay leaves, 12 peppercorns, 10 to 12 parsley stems, 1 sprig of fresh thyme (or 1 teaspoon of dried) and 2 to 3 whole cloves of garlic in the center of a 12-inch square of cheesecloth, then tie the ends together.

In general, use your frozen foods in about three to six months. And don't forget to label and date your food, or you may be in for a big surprise.

Juicing: From a nutritional standpoint, whole fruits contain more vitamins and minerals than juices. But many juicers are made to extract as much of the fruit as possible. When comparing fresh juice to the store-bought variety, fresh tastes, well, fresher and its nutrients are more potent.

The easiest way to juice is to use a juicer. You'll need to do a bit of shopping before you choose one, because juicers of various qualities and prices fill store shelves. Bigger machines have bigger motors and tend to be noisy and expensive (several hundred dollars), but they can do big jobs well and without overheating. A smaller juicer takes up less room; however, you may have to endure the noise longer when juicing several small batches. Look for multiple-task capabilities. At least one juicer can grind flour, knead bread dough and whip up nut butters.

Now you know nearly everything you need to prepare a meal. In the next chapter, we'll look at substituting one food for another (that's art) for a sound reason—to get rid of the "F" word: *fat*.

how to lower your fat intake

JEAN LAWRENCE, WHOSE NAME HAS BEEN CHANGED for the sake of privacy, knows the health reasons to cut back on fat—and that's one reason she was determined to lose the 34 pounds she had put on her 5-foot-9-inch frame while coping with the stress of divorce and single motherhood.

Years later and remarried, Jean has lost weight because she returned to eating a sensible vegetarian diet, allowing herself treats occasionally. She exercises regularly, too. To her credit, Jean avoided the mistake that so many people make when they decide to lose weight: She didn't diet.

People who are overweight are at risk for a number of ailments, including high blood pressure, adult-onset diabetes, diverticular disease, cancer (especially cancer of the breast and colon), stroke and heart disease. The good news is that research shows that vegetarians on the whole are thinner than people who eat meat.

THE VEGETARIAN CHOICE

You have every reason to make a commitment to celebrate the vegetarian choice: Most meatless meals—especially traditional ethnic fare—are low in fat, but others nearly drip with fat. There's nothing wrong with eating a high-fat meal or snack now and then, as long as your everyday diet is low in fat. In our selection of recipes, we've included some rich recipes for special occasions and for those times when you're in the mood for indulgence.

If you've picked up the habit of swearing off recipes that appear high in fat because the fat measurement in a given portion is higher than you like, may we suggest that you consider an alternative. Don't look at any one recipe's fat grams and say no. Consider a day's worth of fat grams or even the number of fat grams eaten over several days.

As a general guideline, a person eating 2,700 total calories a day (the typical amount for a 154-pound man) who wants to consume no more than 20 percent of calories from fat would eat about 60 fat grams. Similarly, at 2,000 total daily calories (the typical amount for a 120-pound woman), the person would eat about 44 fat grams. At 1,500 total calories, the allotment would be about 33 fat grams. To do your own figuring, follow this formula: First, multiply the number of total calories by your desired percentage of fat calories. In each case above, it was .20. Then divide that number by 9. (Each gram of fat has nine calories.) The resulting figure tells you how many fat grams you may consume in a day and stay at your desired percentage of fat calories.

So you see, if you have a hankering for a 1/2-cup serving of notoriously high-fat cheese-and-broccoli sauce (160 total calories; 9 grams of fat; 50 percent of calories from fat) over 2 cups of pasta (320 total calories; 1 gram of fat; 0 percent of calories from fat), the percentage of fat calories for the entire dish is 19 percent. Not bad. Add some steamed zucchini and a plate of orange slices and strawberries, and the percentage of fat calories for the meal inches lower.

The point is, avoid the trap of bypassing a higher-fat recipe. Rather, think in broader terms. What did you eat for breakfast? A bowl of oatmeal and a banana, both of which have a trace of fat. And for lunch? An

NO DEPRIVATION

The point of eating healthful foods is not to deprive yourself. And you won't. Switching to lower-fat foods allows you to eat more (because fat calories are more fattening than protein calories or carbohydrate calories). Don't forget to allow yourself treats occasionally: In fact, planning on them may help you stick to a lower-fat diet because you won't feel deprived.

open-face French bread pizza, topped with tomato sauce, mushrooms and onions, sprinkled with about 2 ounces of cheese. You ate perhaps 20 grams of fat, depending on your appetite. So, having eaten a moderate amount of fat throughout the day, dinner can be higher in fat and guilt-free.

Please, don't let fat math boggle you down. When you choose a variety of healthful vegetarian foods that meet your caloric needs, you're set: You have a life plan for better health. It's that simple.

TIPS FOR SUCCESS

Going vegetarian, all or part of the time, sets the stage for hunger-free weight loss. In fact, vegetarians wanting to slim down often find out that they can eat more food—not less—when they make the switch from meat meals to vegetarian meals. Most meats also contain significant amounts of fat. A single 3 1/2-ounce beef patty, for instance, contains 27 grams of fat. So if you're serious about losing weight, cut out or significantly cut down on the amount of meat you eat, and—this is important—don't replace the meat with high-fat vegetarian foods like cheese, potato chips and other fried foods. Also, rethink the way you cook and how you can make substitutions to further lower your fat intake.

Here are some tips that you can use in your favorite recipes:

- *Opt for fat-reduced foods.* Today you can buy shopping bagfuls of slimmed-down versions of old favorites. They include tofu, chips, sour cream, cheese, margarine, ice cream and frozen foods. Look at the label to be sure the number of fat grams is lower than the original version of the food.

- *Lower the fat of rich-tasting sauces.* Creamy sauces, usually based on the French roux (a mixture of butter and flour thickened with stock or milk), are delicious but fatty. One way to make a lower-fat sauce is to replace the butter with sherry or vegetable broth. (Use 3 parts sherry or vegetable broth to 1 part butter.) Add flour, a little at a time, to make a paste; pour in warm skim milk very slowly, while stirring, until the sauce thickens.

SPICE SAVER

When you cook meals that are low in fat, spices take on greater importance because they add flavor that had been provided by the fat. For a pungent touch, try horseradish, ginger, cayenne pepper or mustard. Aromatic spices like anise, cumin and coriander add exotic flavor, and cinnamon, cloves, allspice and nutmeg add sweetness.

Another method (with a nondairy option) is to dry-roast flour in a heavy pan over low heat until aromatic. Transfer the flour to a blender and pour in warm skim milk or water (equal to the amount of flour), and blend until creamy. Add more milk or water, blending until smooth; then transfer the mixture to the pan and heat until thickened.

A third possibility is to replace butter with a mixture of a little less than a teaspoon of vegetable oil and water to equal 3 tablespoons, plus seasonings of your choice. Heat this mixture in a saucepan over medium heat. Stir in 1/4 cup of flour. A little at a time, add about 1 1/2 cups of warm skim milk, stirring constantly. Cook another few minutes until the sauce is the consistency of thick cream. If you wish, you may add reduced-fat cheese at this point to make a cheese sauce.

For vegetable sauces, sauté a few tablespoons of red wine, sherry or vegetable broth with onions, garlic and vegetables of your choice over medium heat until soft. Then purée half of the mixture in a blender, return it to the pan and let it thicken.

- *If you have a taste for something meaty, you have a number of options.* If the dish is thick and rich in the first place (chili, for instance), you might be satisfied going heavy-handed on the spices and skipping the meat—simple, and it's doubtful you'll miss the meat. Or, depending on your appetite, you could use crumbled tofu or diced tempeh in place of ground beef in a number of recipes, including spaghetti sauce, sloppy joes and stir-fries. (Both tofu and tempeh contain fat—about 3 grams per 2-ounce serving of tofu, and about 2 grams per 2-ounce serving of tempeh—but no saturated fat or cholesterol.) Cubed tofu tastes great skewered along with various vegetables, marinated, then grilled. Tofu may also be fashioned into burgers. So can various legumes, which have barely a trace of fat, except for soybeans. Add a binder (such as nut butter or egg—see page 115) and season to your liking; heat in a pan or grill on a grilling rack. Legumes can also take the place in other meaty recipes. Just use your imagination.

- *Textured vegetable protein—it's the super meat replacer.* Known by the acronym TVP, it is made from the flakes that remain after oil is extracted from soybeans. The soybean

---

KIDS' FAT WORRIES

Researchers interviewed about 500 fourth graders in rural Iowa a few years ago to find out how worried the preteens were about their weight. About 60 percent said they wished they were thinner and that they weighed themselves nearly every day. But only 20 percent were overweight, according to body-mass index figures.

flakes are ground into defatted soy flour, which is blended
with water and sometimes other flavorings, then whipped,
extruded and dried into granules, flakes or chunks. The
description of how TVP is made may not have you salivating,
but the number of the flavorful dishes this food can make
will. Rehydrated in water, TVP can be used to make burgers,
stews, stroganoff and many other main courses. (Fat gram
count per ounce: zero.)

- *When you're adding cheese (or sugar, for that matter) to a
  dish, sprinkle it on top.* The flavor of the cheese will be
  stronger, so it's more likely you'll use less.

- *When ordering a salad at a restaurant, ask for the salad
  dressing on the side.* Then you may lightly dip your fork into
  the dressing before you spear a lettuce leaf and have just
  enough dressing for taste but not so much that you take in
  loads of calories. As you know, many commercial salad dressings are almost pure fat. You'll find recipes for homemade
  low- and no-fat dressings starting on page 211.

- *Instead of sautéing foods in butter or oil, substitute
  water, wine or vegetable broth.* Because these nonfat liquids
  evaporate quickly, use twice as much of your chosen substitution than the amount of butter or oil listed in the recipe. Stir
  frequently.

- *When you can avoid frying, especially deep frying, in
  which food is immersed in fat at high temperature, do so.*
  Frying is the most fattening method of cooking. Frying food
  occasionally is acceptable, but avoid making it a habit. Case
  in point: A regular serving (about three ounces) of deep-fried
  french fries contains 14 grams of fat. In contrast, an equal
  amount of Skinny French Fries, page 374, which are lightly
  brushed with oil before baking, has only 2 grams of fat.
      When eating in restaurants, ask how a given dish is
  cooked. You might be surprised that egg rolls, blintzes, hash
  browns, tortillas and many other foods are fried. Find out if a
  pan-fried food can be cooked in a very small amount of butter or oil. Or, skip the dish.

- *Bake to your heart's desire.* If you assumed that cakes and
  cookies were off the okay-to-eat list when you opted for the

TEN 'MUST' HERBS

Herbs get high billing in low-
fat dishes for adding depth to
dishes. Here are ten to have on
hand.

Basil

Bay leaf

Dill

Oregano

Paprika

Parsley (fresh)

Rosemary

Sage

Tarragon

Thyme

vegetarian choice, listen up: We'll share some baking secrets that lower fat yet accentuate taste. The good news is you can make low-fat cookies. The not-so-good news is they won't taste like Mrs. Fields'. That's because the fat in a cookie is what makes a cookie a cookie. But we do have a few tricks up our sleeves.

Traditionally, fat has performed two roles in baking: adding flavor and lightening baked goods by holding in place tiny air bubbles in the batter.

One easy method is to replace part or all of the butter or other fat with an equal amount of a thick liquid. Good bets are mashed bananas, yogurt, tofu and applesauce. For cookie recipes, replace the amount of fat you've removed with a sweet liquid (or semi-liquid) that fits the flavor of your recipe. For instance, applesauce works well with oatmeal cookies. Puréed prunes—no joke—go nicely with chocolate cookies. Chopped dried fruit adds moistness to fruity cookies.

These ingredients may also replace egg yolks in your recipe. Use about 1/8 cup (2 tablespoons) of your chosen thick liquid to replace each yolk. Or use two egg whites for each yolk. For the easiest choice, use a commercial egg substitute intended to replace the leavening and binding properties of eggs in baked goods. (More on egg substitutions in a moment.)

When you lighten a cookie recipe, try adding stiffly beaten egg whites to the batter. This helps make the cookies flatter and crispier. Otherwise, your cookies may not spread, and they'll end up cakelike. Be sure not to overmix the batter.

Another help is to use lighter flour, such as whole-wheat pastry flour or unbleached white flour, in place of heavier flour like whole-wheat regular flour. These lighter flours have a lower gluten content; gluten can toughen unyeasted baked goods.

Also, when cutting down on the fat in a recipe, feel free to use a heavy hand with spices. Extra spices and flavorings will help compensate for any flavor loss due to a lesser amount of fat.

Be gentle with your batter. The more gingerly you stir the batter, the lighter your creation. When you stir lightly, the gluten in the flour is less likely to become tough. (If your recipe calls for mixing the batter with an eggbeater or

---

WHIP IT

To lighten an eggless or fat-reduced batter, cream together the sweetener and the fat very well before adding the dry ingredients.

mixer, do so. The beating action incorporates air into the batter.)

Act fast. As soon as wet and dry ingredients are combined, the leavening action of baking powder starts. So get your filled cake pans, muffin tins or quick-bread loaf pans into your preheated oven right away. Baking powder helps trap those most welcome tiny air bubbles, which lighten your baked goods.

Keep an eye on your goodies while they bake. Low-fat baked goods tend to bake more quickly than their richer counterparts. Once your cookies or muffins cool, try one. If they taste great, marvelous. Your experiment paid off. If not, try again. Or, if you wish to be on the safe side, try the low-fat cookies on page 414.

- *Replacing eggs.* Notoriously high in cholesterol, eggs are fat demons. There are nearly 6 grams of fat in one large egg. People who are allergic to eggs or who choose to eat no animal products also want to say good-bye to eggs. But how?

Figure out the function of the egg you're replacing. If it's for leavening in baked goods, see the previous page. But if you're looking for egg's binding power—in foods such as pancake mix, lentil loaf, veggie burger or a casserole—you have at least two ways to go. You can use a commercial egg substitute or try 2 ounces of mashed tofu per egg.

You'll never be able to make a decent angel-food cake without eggs. But you can whip up a double-fudge cake, pumpkin pie and even quiche.

A DELIGHTFUL DESTINY

Having selected the naturally low-fat vegetarian choice, you're destined to lose weight. Just don't forget to eat a favorite food now and again. Most important, celebrate your decision to be good to yourself and to your planet and its creatures—with such good taste. Look to these recipes in upcoming chapters as examples of dishes that you can eat with gusto: Grilled Vegetable Pizza, Three-Fruit Sorbet, Pasta with Asparagus and Strawberries, Not Too Rich Brownies, Banana Cake with Chocolate Glaze, Mock Meatballs, Herbed Grape Leaves with Minty Yogurt Sauce, Cabbage Rolls with Seasoned Rice, No-Toll Cookies. Mmmm . . .

[the recipes]

ABOUT OUR RECIPES

PLACING A PREMIUM ON TASTE AND NUTRITION, we present to you the delicious results of the culinary adventure you've begun. You'll have expert guides along the way: the veteran cooks who developed the recipes and 1 million reader-cooks of *Vegetarian Times,* the monthly food and lifestyle magazine in which most of these recipes first appeared.

The recipes cover the food spectrum—simple fruit and vegetable dishes to elaborate meals fit for . . . you. And for whomever you'd like to invite to your table to savor the flavorful and satisfying tastes of vegetarian cuisine. It's a treasure that multiplies with every bite.

We've included nutrition analyses for you to use. (See the "Nutritional Abbreviations" chart for abbreviations used. Note also that the nutrition analyses are figured on the first ingredient when more than one choice is given and that optional ingredients are not included in the calculation.) Our hope is that you'll see not only how low in fat and calories most meatless meals are but also why it's perfectly all right for you to splurge now and then. As long as your usual eating style is in line with the recommendations of most scientists in the know (see chapter 2), a piece of pie won't matter.

What matters is you—your health, your enjoyment. We have only two requests: The first is to please write us with suggestions and comments so we can incorporate them in future recipes. (Write to Comments, Vegetarian Times Complete Cookbook, P.O. Box 570, Oak Park, IL 60303.)

And the second? Celebrate.

Living life to its fullest is at the heart of the vegetarian choice.

NUTRITIONAL ABBREVIATIONS	
Cal.	Calories
Prot.	Protein
Carb.	Carbohydrates
Chol.	Cholesterol
Sod.	Sodium
g	Grams
mg	Milligrams

9

appetizers and snacks

APPETIZERS ARE A DELICIOUS START TO A MEAL—as long as you don't eat too many of them and ruin your appetite. And it's easy to overindulge; appetizers look so little and so appealing. The great news is that most of these recipes take nutrition into account, so you can munch on several appetizers with pure contentment. Here's an idea: When you're in the mood for an out-of-the-ordinary dinner, prepare several appetizers and snacks, and throw a little party for your family and friends (or just for yourself).

Snow Peas with Radish Cream

m a k e s   24   •   s e r v e s   12

Crunchy snow peas are filled with a spicy pink radish cream—a real treat for the senses.

> 24 snow peas, trimmed
> 6 ounces low-fat cream cheese, at room temperature
> 3/4 cup sliced red radishes
> 1 tablespoon prepared horseradish
> Salt and freshly ground black pepper to taste

BLANCH the snow peas in boiling water for 1 minute. Immediately cool in ice water and pat dry. Slit open one side of each snow pea. Set aside. Purée the remaining ingredients in a food processor or blender.

PIPE the radish cream into the snow peas with a pastry tube, or spoon it in by hand. Arrange the filled snow peas decoratively on a serving platter.

Helpful hints:

- Radish cream may be prepared up to a week in advance. Snow peas may be filled several hours in advance; cover with plastic wrap.
- The snow peas look especially beautiful presented in a fan shape over deep red radicchio leaves or red-leaf lettuce and garnished with radish sprouts.

> **PER APPETIZER:**
> 22 Cal.; 1g Prot.; 1g Fat; 2g Carb.;
> 4mg Chol.; 86mg Sod.; 0.3g Fiber.

Skewered Cheese Tortellini with Garlic-Parmesan Sauce

m a k e s   24   •   s e r v e s   8

This fail-proof recipe takes a minimal amount of effort to prepare. Just purchase ready-made tortellini, cook and thread on skewers.

> 72 cheese tortellini
> 6 tablespoons minced fresh parsley
> 1/2 cup virgin olive oil
> 1/2 cup grated Parmesan cheese
> 1/3 cup fresh lemon juice
> 3 cloves garlic, pressed or minced
> Salt and freshly ground black pepper to taste

PREPARE the tortellini according to the package directions. Add a little fresh water to the cooked tortellini to keep them from sticking together. Thread twenty-four 4-inch skewers with 3 tortellini each. Arrange the skewers on a platter and sprinkle with 2 tablespoons of the parsley.

IN A SMALL mixing bowl, mix together the remaining parsley, oil, Parmesan, lemon juice, garlic, salt and pepper. If desired, purée the sauce in a blender for 1 minute. With a pastry brush, brush the sauce on the tortellini. Reserve the remaining sauce to dip the skewers into when serving.

Variation:

Substitute fresh spinach and egg tortellini for the cheese tortellini.

Helpful hints:

- If you don't have skewers, place the tortellini on a large serving plate with a supply of toothpicks.

- The sauce may be made up to a week in advance. The skewers may be prepared several hours in advance.

PER SKEWER:
93 Cal.; 4g Prot.; 3g Fat; 12g Carb.;
1mg Chol.; 44mg Sod.; 0g Fiber.

Mock Meatballs

makes 24 • serves 8

| 2 cups uncooked bulgur
| 1 tablespoon minced onion
| 1 egg, beaten
| Dried oregano to taste
| Freshly ground black pepper to taste
| 1 to 3 tablespoons virgin olive oil
| 1 cup tomato juice (plus extra if needed)

MIX together the bulgur, onion and egg. Season with oregano and pepper. Form into walnut-sized balls.

LIGHTLY COAT a large skillet with oil and place over medium-high heat. Add the balls and cook until browned. Add the tomato juice; cover and simmer until the bulgur softens, about 5 minutes. (Add extra juice if the skillet becomes dry.) Serve the balls in a shallow serving dish with cocktail forks or toothpicks.

PER BALL:
61 Cal.; 2g Prot.; 1g Fat; 11g Carb.;
9mg Chol.; 4mg Sod.; 1g Fiber.

Mushroom Caps Stuffed with Basil, Sun-Dried Tomatoes and Parmesan

makes 24 • serves 12

Stuffed white button mushrooms are a party favorite. This update has an intensely flavored pesto filling.

| 24 large white button mushrooms
| 15 sun-dried tomatoes (not packed in oil)
| 2 cups loosely packed fresh basil leaves
| 1/4 to 1/3 cup virgin olive oil
| 1 to 2 tablespoons water
| 1/3 to 1/2 cup grated Parmesan cheese
| 1/2 cup dry bread crumbs
| 4 cloves garlic, pressed or minced
| Salt and freshly ground black pepper to taste

REMOVE the mushroom stems and reserve them for another use. Hollow out each mushroom cap and set aside. Soak the tomatoes in very hot water until soft and pliable, about 15 minutes; drain. Cut into slivers.

PREHEAT the oven to 325°F. In a food processor or blender, purée the tomatoes, basil, oil, water, Parmesan, bread crumbs, garlic, salt and pepper. Fill the mushroom caps with the stuffing and place on a baking sheet. Bake in the lower half of an oven until the mushrooms are just beginning to release their juices, about 12 minutes.

PER APPETIZER:
62 Cal.; 2g Prot.; 3g Fat; 7g Carb.;
1mg Chol.; 89mg Sod.; 0.4g Fiber.

DIP: Process the dip ingredients in a food processor or blender until smooth. Transfer to a bowl, cover and refrigerate until ready to serve.

KABOBS: Thread chunks of the fruit onto toothpicks, bamboo skewers or plastic swizzle sticks. (Remove the pointed ends if you're serving the kabobs to children.) Serve the kabobs with the dip.

Note:

The tropical kiwifruit has a fuzzy brown skin and a beautiful green interior. For the sweetest flavor, look for kiwi that is somewhat soft but not mushy when you gently press the skin. (Unripe kiwi tastes sour.) To prepare kiwi, peel then slice it. You may arrange the slices on a platter. The effect is dramatic: The emerald green is offset by edible black seeds. Or, add kiwi to a vegetable or fruit salad just before the salad is lightly tossed. Too much tossing may break up the kiwi.

> **PER SERVING WITH 1/4 CUP DIP:**
> 139 Cal.; 2g Prot.; 7g Fat; 17g Carb.;
> 7mg Chol.; 144mg Sod.; 2g Fiber.

Cucumber Logs Filled with Black and Gold Hummus

makes 12 • serves 6

Crunchy and creamy, these cucumber logs will prove popular on your buffet. They look beautiful resting on lettuce leaves arranged on a serving tray.

2 cucumbers

One 15-ounce can chickpeas, rinsed

1 tablespoon virgin olive oil

1 tablespoon water

1/3 cup fresh lemon juice

1 teaspoon salt

1/4 cup diced black olives

CUT OFF the ends of the cucumbers. Cut each cucumber crosswise into 6 rounds and turn the pieces so they are flat. Using a melon baller or grapefruit spoon, gently scoop out some flesh from the top of each cucumber round.

IN A FOOD PROCESSOR or blender, make the hummus by combining the chickpeas, oil, water, lemon juice and salt. Purée, adding more water if needed for creaminess. Stir in the black olives. Spoon the mixture into the hollowed out part of each cucumber round. Arrange on a serving tray.

Helpful hint:

Hummus may be made up to a week in advance. Filled rounds may be prepared up to two days in advance but are best assembled before serving.

> **PER APPETIZER:**
> 58 Cal.; 2g Prot.; 2g Fat; 8g Carb.;
> 0mg Chol.; 193mg Sod.; 1g Fiber.

Herb-Stuffed Grape Leaves with Minty Yogurt Sauce

makes 40 • serves 20

These grape leaves are stuffed with a refreshing combination of rice, dill, mint, parsley and currants.

FILLING

- 40 grape leaves (a 16-ounce jar contains about 50 leaves)
- 1 cup uncooked basmati rice
- One 14 1/2-ounce can vegetable broth, plus enough water to make 2 cups liquid
- 2 medium onions, minced
- 4 cloves garlic, pressed or minced
- 1/4 cup chopped fresh dillweed (or 2 tablespoons dried)
- 1/4 cup chopped fresh mint leaves (or 2 tablespoons dried)
- 1/4 cup chopped fresh Italian flat-leaf parsley (or 2 tablespoons dried)
- 1/2 cup dried currants, soaked in hot water until softened, then drained
- 2 teaspoons freshly ground black pepper
- 2 cups water

SAUCE

- 2 cups plain nonfat yogurt
- 1/4 cup chopped fresh mint leaves (or 2 tablespoons dried)
- 1 clove garlic, minced
- 1 teaspoon salt
- 4 scallions (green and white parts), minced

FILLING: In a mixing bowl, pour boiling water to cover the grape leaves and let them soak 1 hour. Meanwhile, in a saucepan, combine the rice and broth-water mixture. Cover, bring to a boil, lower the heat and simmer 10 minutes. Stir in the onions and garlic, cover and simmer until all of the liquid has been absorbed, about 10 minutes more. Remove the saucepan from the heat. Stir in the herbs, currants and pepper with a fork while fluffing the rice.

DRAIN the grape leaves and pat them dry with a paper towel. Remove the stems. Lay a grape leaf vein side up with stem end toward you on a flat surface. Place a heaping tablespoon of the filling in the center. Fold in the sides, then roll up the leaf from bottom to tip. Repeat with the remaining grape leaves and filling.

LINE the bottom of a large saucepan with extra grape leaves to prevent the stuffed grape leaves from sticking to the pan. Place the filled grape leaves in the saucepan seam side down in layers. Pour 2 cups water over the leaves, cover and simmer until the leaves are tender, about 30 to 45 minutes. (It may be necessary to add an additional 1/3 to 1/2 cup water during cooking to keep the leaves from sticking.) Let cool.

SAUCE: Combine all the sauce ingredients in a bowl and stir together. Serve the sauce on the side.

PER SERVING:
80 Cal.; 3g Prot.; 0.3g Fat; 15g Carb.;
0.5mg Chol.; 164mg Sod.; 2g Fiber.

Mushroom and Rice–Stuffed Grape Leaves

makes 36 · serves 12

Every Persian family has its own recipe for stuffed grape leaves. Here's one with an authentic taste and not too many calories.

| 1 to 2 tablespoons virgin olive oil
| 1 medium onion, chopped finely
| 5 cups chopped white button mushrooms
| 1 tablespoon chopped fresh parsley, or to taste
| 1/4 teaspoon freshly ground black pepper, or to taste
| 1/8 teaspoon cayenne pepper, or to taste
| 1/4 teaspoon turmeric, or to taste
| 1 cup cooked yellow split peas
| 2 cups cooked white rice
| One 16-ounce jar grape leaves
| 1 cup water

IN A SKILLET, heat the oil and sauté the onion and mushrooms until soft. Add the parsley and spices. Transfer the mixture to a bowl. Mix in the peas and rice.

PREHEAT oven to 350°F. Line a 3-quart baking dish with a few grape leaves to keep the stuffed leaves from sticking and burning. Place 1 heaping tablespoon of the rice mixture (more or less, depending on the size of the leaf) in the center of a grape leaf. Fold in the sides, then roll the leaf from stem to tip. Place the stuffed grape leaf in the baking dish. Repeat procedure with the remaining grape leaves until the rice mixture is used up. Pour water in the bottom of the dish (to prevent sticking and drying out). Bake 25 minutes.

> **PER SERVING:**
> 91 Cal.; 3g Prot.; 2g Fat; 14g Carb.;
> 0mg Chol.; 94mg Sod.; 3g Fiber.

Pickled Vegetable Appetizer

makes 8

| 1 cup sliced red or white radishes
| 1/2 cup sliced cucumber
| 1/2 cup diagonally sliced carrot
| 1/2 teaspoon salt
| 2 tablespoons umeboshi vinegar (see Note) or white vinegar
| 6 tablespoons water
| 6 to 8 lettuce leaves, for garnish

IN A MEDIUM BOWL, toss together the radishes, cucumber, carrot and salt. Let sit at room temperature for 2 hours. Press the vegetables gently in a colander to drain off liquid. Return the vegetables to the bowl.

IN A SAUCEPAN, bring the vinegar and water to a boil. Remove from the heat at once and let cool. Pour over the vegetables. Cover the bowl and refrigerate for 24 hours. To serve, place the lettuce leaves on a large platter and arrange the chilled vegetables on top.

Note:

Umeboshi vinegar is made from umeboshi plums, a Japanese favorite. Look for it in Asian markets.

> **PER APPETIZER:**
> 7 Cal.; 0g Prot.; 0g Fat; 2g Carb.;
> 0mg Chol.; 142mg Sod.; 1g Fiber.

Vegetable Samosas

makes 18

Samosas, a North Indian wrapped food, are a savory treat, whether served as appetizers or as a meal. Traditionally, samosas are fried; this version is baked, so its fat content plummets.

> **5 large potatoes, peeled and diced**
>
> **1 cup frozen peas**
>
> **3 tablespoons vegetable oil**
>
> **2 medium onions, chopped finely**
>
> **1-inch piece fresh ginger root, peeled and minced**
>
> **2 cloves garlic, minced**
>
> **2 teaspoons garam masala or curry powder**
>
> **1/8 teaspoon cayenne pepper (optional)**
>
> **2 teaspoons ground coriander**
>
> **1/8 teaspoon ground turmeric (optional)**
>
> **1/8 teaspoon ground cumin (optional)**
>
> **Salt to taste**
>
> **One 17 1/4-ounce package thawed puff pastry shells**
>
> **1/4 cup all-purpose flour, for dusting**

BOIL the potatoes in a large pot until very tender and crumbly. Place the frozen peas in a colander and drain the potatoes on top. Set aside.

MEANWHILE, in a large skillet, heat the oil over medium heat. Cook the onions, ginger and garlic, stirring, until the onions are translucent. Add spices. Raise the heat and fry for 5 minutes to release the flavors. In a large bowl, mix together the onion-spice mixture with the potatoes and peas. Add the salt. Set aside.

PREHEAT the oven to 350°F. To prepare the pastry, cut each piece of dough into 3 equal panels, then cut each panel into two 1/4-inch squares; you will have 18 squares. Dust your work surface with flour. Roll out the dough pieces to twice their size. (The dough pieces do not have to be exact square shapes.) If necessary, use your fingers to spread the dough into shape. Place a heaping tablespoon of the vegetable mixture in the center of each square, and fold over one corner to make a triangle. Pinch the sides to enclose the mixture.

PLACE the samosas 2 inches apart on a baking sheet. Bake until golden, about 25 minutes. Serve hot.

Helpful hint:

Uncooked samosas may be frozen. Before cooking, allow the frozen samosas to sit at room temperature for 20 minutes. Bake as directed until golden, about 30 minutes. Serve hot.

PER SAMOSA:
171 Cal.; 2g Prot.; 8g Fat; 17g Carb.;
2mg Chol.; 111mg Sod.; 2g Fiber.

Savory Sunflower Paté

makes 2 loaves • serves 24

> 1/2 cup warm water
>
> 1/2 cup virgin olive oil
>
> 1 onion, peeled and chopped coarsely
>
> 1/4 cup soy sauce
>
> 1 large potato, peeled and diced
>
> 1 cup raw, shelled sunflower seeds
>
> 1/2 cup whole-wheat flour
>
> 1/2 cup nutritional yeast
>
> 1 or 2 cloves garlic
>
> 1 1/2 teaspoons dried herbs of choice: sage, basil, oregano or marjoram

PREHEAT the oven to 350˚F. Process all the ingredients in a food processor or blender until very smooth. Pour the mixture into two greased 6 × 3-inch fruitcake loaf pans. Bake until set, about 1 hour. Cool the patés thoroughly. Loosen the loaves from the pans with a table knife, then remove them carefully. Wrap them well in plastic. Store in the refrigerator for up to 2 weeks or in the freezer for up to 3 months.

Variations:

- Use 1 tablespoon chopped fresh herbs in place of the dried herbs.
- Before baking, cover the top of the patés with coarsely ground black pepper and just a sprinkling of dried whole rosemary leaves.

> **PER 1/2-INCH SLICE:**
> 92 Cal.; 3g Prot.; 7g Fat; 5g Carb.;
> 0mg Chol.; 175mg Sod.; 0.6g Fiber.

Sun-Dried Tomato Paté

serves 8

The tart flavors of goat cheese and sun-dried tomatoes blend tastefully.

> 1/4 cup low-fat cottage cheese
>
> 2 ounces creamy goat cheese
>
> 3 ounces oil-packed sun-dried tomatoes, drained and chopped
>
> 1/8 teaspoon dried thyme
>
> 8 large slices French bread
>
> 2 teaspoons minced fresh parsley

DRAIN the cottage cheese and purée until smooth in a blender. In a medium bowl, mash together the cottage cheese, goat cheese, tomatoes and thyme. Lightly toast French bread and spread the slices with the cheese-tomato mixture. Top with parsley and serve.

> **PER SERVING:**
> 147 Cal.; 6g Prot.; 3g Fat; 21g Carb.;
> 3mg Chol.; 262mg Sod.; 0.4g Fiber.

Green Pea and Artichoke Terrine

serves 12

This exquisite appetizer has two layers of contrasting green shades.

4 fresh artichokes (see Helpful hint)

1/2 cup vegetable stock (page 178)

2 cups fresh or frozen green peas

3 medium potatoes, peeled and diced

1/4 teaspoon ground nutmeg

Salt and freshly ground black pepper to taste

WITH A SHARP KNIFE, cut off the tops of the artichokes. Remove the thorns on the outer leaves and tiny outer leaves. Steam the artichokes upside-down in a steamer basket or in a saucepan with an inch of water for 30 to 60 minutes. The artichokes are done when the outer leaves come off easily. Let cool.

MEANWHILE, bring the stock to a boil in a saucepan. Add the peas and potatoes. Lower the heat and simmer until the potatoes are tender, about 15 minutes. Let cool. Add the nutmeg, salt and pepper. Purée in a blender or food processor. Set aside.

WHEN THE ARTICHOKES ARE COOL, gently remove the outer leaves and scrape off the tender flesh with a spoon. The middle leaves will come off together; chop the tender portion. Spoon out the fuzzy choke from the center and discard. Dice the heart, which is directly beneath the choke. You should have 2 cups total. Purée in a blender or food processor. Set aside.

POUR the pea-potato purée into a terrine pan or a 5-cup loaf pan. Spread the artichoke purée on top. Refrigerate overnight. Just before serving, run a thin knife along the perimeter of the pan to loosen the terrine. Place an inverted serving platter over the pan and carefully turn it over to unmold the terrine.

Helpful hint:

If fresh artichokes are unavailable, substitute 2 cups chopped canned artichoke hearts (not packed in oil).

> **PER SERVING:**
> 71 Cal.; 3g Prot.; 0g Fat; 15g Carb.;
> 0mg Chol.; 54mg Sod.; 5g Fiber.

Orange and Gold Millet Terrine

serves 8

The layers of pale gold millet and puréed carrots make this elegant terrine worth the extra work. Arrange it on a bed of lettuce and serve it with crackers.

3 cups sliced carrots

1/2 teaspoon ground cardamom

1 tablespoon honey

1 teaspoon vegetable oil

1/4 cup white wine or vegetable broth

2 scallions (green and white parts), chopped (see Note)

1/2 cup minced onion

2 cups chopped white button mushrooms

3 cloves garlic, minced

1/4 teaspoon ground coriander

1/4 teaspoon dried basil

1/4 teaspoon dried thyme

3 cups cooked millet

2 eggs (or equivalent egg substitute), lightly beaten

1/2 cup chopped fresh parsley

1/2 cup plain nonfat yogurt

1/2 cup soft whole-wheat bread crumbs

1 1/2 teaspoons salt

2 tablespoons low-sodium soy sauce

1/4 teaspoon cayenne pepper

8 to 10 lettuce leaves

PREHEAT the oven to 350°F. Lightly oil a 9 × 5-inch loaf pan. In a saucepan fitted with a steamer, steam the carrots until soft, about 5 minutes, and drain. Purée the carrots in a blender with the cardamom and honey. Set aside.

IN A LARGE SKILLET over medium-high heat, heat the oil and wine or broth until bubbling. Add the scallions and onion. Cook, stirring, until limp, about 3 minutes. Add the mushrooms, garlic, coriander, basil and thyme. Cook, stirring, until the mushrooms release moisture, about 5 minutes. Remove from the heat and stir in the remaining ingredients except the lettuce.

SPREAD half of the carrot purée into the bottom of the prepared loaf pan, smoothing with a spoon. Top with all of the millet mixture, again smoothing the layer. Then spread on the remaining carrot purée. Place the loaf pan in a 9 × 13-inch shallow baking dish. Add 1 inch of water to the baking dish (the steaming water will prevent the paté from browning as it cooks). Bake until firm, about 1 hour. Cut the terrine into 1-inch slices and serve on lettuce.

Note:

Whether you call them scallions or green onions, these long green vegetables with a small white bulb add zest to recipes. You may sauté them or chop them and use them as a garnish. In most recipes, you may substitute onions, leeks or shallots for scallions.

PER SERVING:
151 Cal.; 5g Prot.; 3g Fat; 24g Carb.;
54mg Chol.; 579mg Sod.; 7g Fiber.

Grilled Polenta with Mushroom Topping

serves 6

Polenta is cornmeal that is simmered in water, then cooled and sliced. It may be eaten plain or made fancy with an elegant topping like this one.

4 cups water
1/2 teaspoon salt
1/2 teaspoon freshly ground black pepper
1 cup cornmeal, preferably coarsely ground
1/4 cup virgin olive oil
1 pound white button mushrooms, sliced thinly
1/2 small onion, minced
4 cloves garlic, minced
1 tablespoon dried basil
1 tablespoon minced fresh parsley

IN A HEAVY SAUCEPAN over high heat, combine the water, salt and pepper. When the water boils, add the cornmeal in a steady thin stream, stirring constantly with a wooden spoon. Lower the heat to low and continue cooking for 20 minutes, stirring frequently. The polenta will become very thick.

SPOON the polenta onto a sheet of waxed paper. With a wet spatula, spread the polenta until it is 1/2 inch thick. While it cools, heat the oil over high heat in a skillet and cook the mushrooms, onion, garlic and herbs, stirring, until the mushrooms are soft. Set aside and keep warm.

CUT the polenta into 6 large or 12 small squares, and place them on a lightly oiled baking sheet. Broil on both sides until golden-brown spots appear. Top with the mushroom sauce. Serve at once.

Bean-and-Greens Crostini

serves 6

Italian crostini, literally "toast," should be made with a peasant-style bread that is firm and crusty around the edges and chewy in the middle. Any combination of greens and beans may be used for this delicious appetizer or light supper.

Olive oil cooking spray or oil for brushing

Twelve 1/2-inch slices of bread

1 tablespoon virgin olive oil

1/4 teaspoon cayenne pepper

1/2 teaspoon dried rosemary, crumbled

2 pounds fresh broccoli rabe or spinach, trimmed and chopped (see Note)

2 1/2 cups cooked cannellini or white beans

3 to 4 tablespoons water

1/4 teaspoon salt

Freshly ground black pepper to taste

1/4 cup finely chopped fresh Italian flat-leaf parsley

1/4 cup chopped oil-packed sun-dried tomatoes or pitted olives

PREHEAT the oven to 400°F. Spray or dribble oil over the bread and bake until lightly browned, turning once, about 15 minutes. In a large skillet, heat 1/2 tablespoon oil over medium heat. Add the cayenne, rosemary, and broccoli rabe or spinach. Cover and cook 10 minutes for broccoli rabe or 3 to 4 minutes for spinach.

MEANWHILE, in a medium saucepan, combine the beans and water. Season with salt and pepper, and cook over low heat for 10 minutes. Coarsely mash the beans with a spoon and add to the greens. Mix in the parsley and sun-dried tomatoes or olives. Spoon this mixture over the bread and drizzle with the remaining 1/2 tablespoon oil.

Note:

Greens (including spinach, mustard greens, collard greens, beet greens, kale and chard) sometimes are sandy and dirty, so rinse them well in a basin of cold water, lest you chomp into a piece of something you cannot identify. Dry well with towels. Use the greens in salads or cook them as your recipe directs.

Olive-Tomato Crostini

makes 16 • serves 8

OLIVE PASTE

- 1 cup kalamata or Niçoise olives, pitted
- 2 tablespoons chopped shallot or onion (see Note)
- 2 tablespoons capers, rinsed (optional—see Note)
- 1/4 teaspoon dried thyme
- 2 tablespoons virgin olive oil
- 2 to 3 teaspoons fresh lemon juice or red wine vinegar, or to taste

CROSTINI

- 16 thin slices of bread
- 1 to 2 cloves garlic, cut in half
- 16 small ripe, firm tomatoes (red and yellow if possible), sliced (see Note)
- Fresh basil leaves
- Freshly ground black pepper

PASTE: Rinse the olives to remove excess salt. Combine the olives, shallot or onion, capers, thyme and olive oil in a food processor. Process to make a smooth or textured paste, whichever you prefer. Stir in the lemon juice or vinegar. Set aside.

CROSTINI: Toast the bread on both sides and immediately rub with garlic. Spread a thin layer of olive paste on the bread and top with a few slices of tomato. Put a few basil leaves between the tomatoes. Sprinkle with a generous amount of pepper. Serve at once.

Notes:

- The shallot, a mild-flavored bulb, has an oniony flavor. You can find it in the produce sections of supermarkets. Feel free to substitute onion, leeks or scallions for shallots in most recipes.

- Capers, the flower buds of a Mediterranean shrub, are picked before they blossom, then packed in salt or brine. They are used to flavor a number of dishes.

- Most tomatoes in supermarkets are hideous versions of their freshly grown, tender sisters. So if you can't get your hands on truly delicious tomatoes, make your sauce or stew or whatever from canned tomatoes, which are more flavorful.

> **PER CROSTINI:**
> 97 Cal.; 3g Prot.; 3g Fat; 15g Carb.;
> 0mg Chol.; 166mg Sod.; 1g Fiber.

Bulgur-Herb Crostini

serves 6

Bulgur, a quick-cooking grain with a nutty flavor, is an unusual yet delicious topping for crostini.

- 1/3 cup uncooked bulgur
- 2/3 cup plus 1 1/3 tablespoons water or tomato-vegetable juice
- 2 tablespoons chopped fresh Italian flat-leaf parsley
- 2 tablespoons chopped fresh basil leaves
- 1/2 cup Sicilian or kalamata olives, pitted
- 2 tablespoons capers (optional)
- 1 teaspoon coarsely chopped fresh ginger root
- 2 teaspoons fresh lemon juice
- 1 1/2 tablespoons virgin olive oil
- 1 loaf whole-wheat bread or Italian bread

TOAST the bulgur in a dry saucepan until it darkens slightly. Add 2/3 cup water or juice and bring to a boil. Remove from the heat, cover and let sit until the liquid is absorbed, about 10 minutes.

IN A FOOD PROCESSOR, combine the remaining 1 1/3 tablespoons water or juice, herbs, olives, capers and ginger. Process to a smooth paste, scraping down the sides of the work bowl as necessary. Transfer to a mixing bowl. Drain any excess liquid from the bulgur and stir the bulgur into the olive mixture. Mix in the lemon juice and oil.

PREHEAT the oven to 400°F. Cut 12 slices of bread 1/2 inch thick on the diagonal. Bake on a baking sheet until lightly browned on both sides, about 15 minutes. Spread the bulgur-herb mixture on top. Serve at once.

> ### PER SERVING:
> 175 Cal.; 6g Prot.; 6g Fat; 21g Carb.;
> 0mg Chol.; 306mg Sod.; 6g Fiber.

Gingered Crostini and Pepper Spread

makes 24 • serves 12

PEPPER SPREAD

- 1/2 tablespoon virgin olive oil
- 1 small jalapeño pepper, minced
- 1 teaspoon mustard seeds
- 1 ounce sun-dried tomatoes (not packed in oil), chopped
- 1/2 cup water
- 2 roasted red bell peppers, chopped
- 3 tablespoons chopped fresh basil leaves (or 1 teaspoon dried)
- 2 tablespoons chopped fresh parsley
- Salt and freshly ground black pepper to taste

TO FINISH THE DISH

- One 9-ounce loaf rustic-style bread or baguette
- 2 tablespoons finely grated fresh ginger root
- 1/2 cup minced fresh parsley
- Salt (optional)
- Olive oil cooking spray or virgin olive oil

PEPPER SPREAD: Heat the oil in a saucepan and add the jalapeño and mustard seeds. Cover and toast the seeds until they pop. Add the dried tomatoes and water. Cover and cook until the tomatoes are plump, about 2 to 3 minutes. Remove from heat.

IN A FOOD PROCESSOR, process the roasted peppers to a chunky purée. Add the tomato mixture and process until smooth. Season with basil, parsley, salt and pepper. Set aside.

TO FINISH THE DISH: Preheat the oven to 375°F. Cut the bread into 24 slices and place on a baking sheet. Mix together the ginger and parsley; season with salt. Sprinkle the ginger mixture evenly over the bread slices. Lightly drizzle olive oil on top. Bake the crostini until lightly toasted, about 8 to 10 minutes. Serve topped with a dollop of the pepper spread.

> ### PER SERVING:
> 217 Cal.; 6g Prot.; 6g Fat; 33g Carb.;
> 0mg Chol.; 288mg Sod.; 4g Fiber.

Garlic Toasts with Sun-Dried Tomato Sauce

serves 12

SAUCE

- 10 sun-dried tomatoes
- 1 1/2 cups boiling water
- 2 cloves garlic, chopped coarsely
- 2 teaspoons drained and rinsed capers (optional)
- 1 tablespoon fresh lime or lemon juice
- 1/4 to 1/2 cup virgin olive oil
- Salt and freshly ground black pepper to taste (optional)

TO FINISH THE DISH

- 1 loaf baguette or Italian bread
- Virgin olive oil for brushing (optional)
- 1 to 2 large cloves garlic

SAUCE: Pour 1 1/2 cups boiling water over the sun-dried tomatoes and soak until softened, about 5 to 15 minutes. (The timing will vary depending on the brand.) Drain, reserving the liquid.

IN A BLENDER, combine the soaked tomatoes, 1/4 cup soaking liquid, garlic, capers and lime or lemon juice. Process until smooth. Uncover the blender jar and with the machine running, pour in the oil a drop at a time at first, until the mixture starts to thicken; then pour the oil in a steady stream (use the smaller amount of oil to keep the fat content low). Transfer to a bowl. Add salt and pepper.

TO FINISH THE DISH: Preheat the oven to 450°F. Just before serving, slice the bread into 12 thick pieces and brush with the olive oil. Rub with garlic. Toast in oven or under the broiler. Spread the sauce lightly over the bread and serve.

> **PER SLICE:**
> 157 Cal.; 4g Prot.; 6g Fat; 21g Carb.;
> 0mg Chol.; 223mg Sod.; 1g Fiber.

Garlic Toasts with Black Olive Tapenade

makes 12 • serves 6

Tapenade is a flexible dish that can vary according to individual taste. The only absolutes are black olives, garlic and capers.

- 4 ounces pitted black olives, drained
- 4 ounces oil-cured Greek olives, pitted and drained
- 1/3 cup capers, drained
- 2 cloves garlic, minced
- 1/4 teaspoon dried thyme
- 1 tablespoon Dijon mustard
- Fresh lemon juice
- Freshly ground black pepper to taste
- 3 tablespoons minced fresh parsley
- 1 baguette, sliced on the diagonal into 12 slices, rubbed lightly with garlic and toasted

IN A BLENDER or food processor, purée the olives. Add the capers, garlic, thyme and mustard; purée until smooth. Transfer the mixture to a mixing bowl. Add the lemon juice and pepper. Stir in the parsley. Serve the tapenade surrounded by garlic toasts.

> **PER SERVING:**
> 161 Cal.; 4g Prot.; 7g Fat; 19g Carb.;
> 0mg Chol.; 832mg Sod.; 2g Fiber.

Bermuda Onion Toasts

makes 24 • serves 12

A takeoff on bruschetta, these pieces of toast are topped with an intensely flavored onion sauce that's a beautiful deep burgundy color. The recipe seems to call for an astonishing quantity of onions, but their bulk is reduced during the long, slow cooking.

I loaf French bread, sliced diagonally into 24 slices

2 to 4 tablespoons virgin olive oil

1 to 3 tablespoons water, as needed

3 pounds Bermuda onions, peeled and sliced thinly

4 cloves garlic, pressed or minced

1 teaspoon dried sage, crumbled

1 teaspoon dried thyme, crumbled

1 cup dry red wine

Salt and freshly ground black pepper to taste

1 clove garlic, sliced in half

24 fresh sage leaves, for garnish (optional)

PREHEAT the oven to 350°F. Place the bread slices on a baking sheet and toast them until lightly crisp, about 5 minutes. In a skillet, heat the oil and water over medium heat. Add the onions, garlic, sage and thyme. Sauté, stirring frequently, for 15 minutes. Don't let the onions brown. Add the wine, salt and pepper, and simmer 15 minutes more. The onion mixture should be thick and soft. If the skillet becomes too dry, add more wine and lower the heat.

MEANWHILE, rub one side of each toasted bread slice with the cut side of the garlic. Spread the onion mixture on top of each slice and place on a serving tray. Garnish with fresh sage leaves.

Helpful hint:

The onion mixture may be prepared up to a week in advance. Warm it slightly before spreading on toast.

> **PER SLICE:**
> 85 Cal.; 2g Prot.; 2g Fat; 13g Carb.;
> 0mg Chol.; 155mg Sod.; 2g Fiber.

Pita Crisps with Spinach, Red Pepper and Feta

serves 8

This appetizer is pretty and delicious. And with the help of a microwave, it's quick to make, too.

- 4 whole-wheat pita rounds
- 2 large cloves garlic, cut in half
- 4 cups fresh spinach leaves
- 1/2 cup roasted red pepper strips
- 3 tablespoons crumbled feta cheese

SPLIT the pita rounds in half crosswise. Toast under a conventional broiler or in a toaster. Rub each toasted pita half with garlic. Set aside. Place the spinach in a 1 1/2-quart casserole dish. Microwave at high power until the leaves begin to wilt, about 1 to 2 minutes. Arrange the toasted pita halves on a serving platter. Top them evenly with the spinach, red pepper strips and feta cheese. Microwave at high power until the cheese begins to melt, about 1 1/2 to 2 minutes, rotating the platter once.

PER SERVING:
82 Cal.; 3g Prot.; 2g Fat; 16g Carb.;
0mg Chol.; 197mg Sod.; 3g Fiber.

Tomato and Rosemary Tartlets

serves 6

- 1 package active dry yeast
- 1/2 cup lukewarm water
- 1/4 cup virgin olive oil
- 2 cups all-purpose flour, plus extra flour for kneading
- 1/2 teaspoon salt
- 2 tablespoons finely chopped fresh rosemary leaves
- 2 tablespoons grated Parmesan cheese
- 1 pound tomatoes, thinly sliced
- 18 Niçoise olives or 9 kalamata olives, pitted and quartered
- 1 tablespoon virgin olive oil
- Salt and freshly ground black pepper to taste
- Fresh rosemary sprigs or blossoms, for garnish

STIR the yeast into the water and set aside until foamy, about 10 minutes. Stir in the oil. Combine 2 cups flour and salt in a large bowl. Make a well in the center and pour in the yeast mixture. Stir together to make a dough.

TURN the dough out onto a lightly floured surface and knead just until smooth, about 2 to 3 minutes. Add extra flour as needed to keep the dough from sticking to the surface. Place the dough in a lightly oiled bowl, cover with a damp dishcloth or plastic wrap and set aside until doubled in bulk, about 1 hour.

DEFLATE the dough and divide it into 6 equal pieces. Shape each piece into a smooth ball, cover with the cloth or plastic and let rest 15 minutes. Then roll each piece into a 5- to 6-inch circle about 1/8 inch thick; place the circles on a baking sheet.

SPRINKLE 1/2 teaspoon rosemary over each circle and press into the dough. Scatter 1 teaspoon cheese on top of each circle. Overlap 5 or 6 tomato slices on each circle, leaving a border at least 1 inch wide around the edge. Divide the olives among the circles, and sprinkle the remaining 1 tablespoon rosemary on top. Drizzle with 1/2 tablespoon virgin olive oil and season with salt and pepper. Fold the edge of the dough over tomatoes, creasing every inch or so. Brush the dough with the remaining 1/2 tablespoon oil.

PREHEAT the oven to 400°F. Bake the tarts on the lower rack of your oven until the crust is browned, about 20 minutes. Remove to a cooling rack and serve warm, garnished with fresh rosemary sprigs.

Helpful hints:

- The tarts are best if baked just before serving, but you may bake them a few hours ahead of time—be sure to cool on a rack—and reheat them in a 400°F oven for 10 minutes.
- For additional color, use a combination of red and yellow gourmet tomatoes.

> **PER TART:**
> 274 Cal.; 5g Prot.; 15g Fat; 31g Carb.;
> 1mg Chol.; 460mg Sod.; 3g Fiber.

Far East Spring Rolls

makes 16

- 2 large carrots
- 1/2 red bell pepper, julienned
- 2 tablespoons chopped scallion (green and white parts)
- 1 tablespoon virgin olive oil
- 1 tablespoon minced fresh cilantro leaves
- 1/4 teaspoon freshly ground black pepper
- 16 rice-paper rounds, 6 inches in diameter
- 2 cups cooked bean-thread noodles (6 ounces dried), or rice noodles

USING a vegetable peeler, shave off thin slices of carrot. Place the carrot shavings, red bell pepper, scallion, olive oil, cilantro and black pepper in a large bowl. Let sit for 1 hour.

FILL a bowl with warm water, then dip each rice-paper round in the water until softened and translucent, about 10 seconds. Let the round drain briefly on a dishcloth.

PLACE 2 tablespoons cooked noodles plus a few tablespoons of the carrot-pepper mixture about 1 inch from the lower edge of a piece of rice paper. Fold the bottom of the paper over the filling, fold both sides over the filling, then roll into a cylinder shape. Repeat with the remaining noodles, carrot-pepper mixture and rice-paper rounds. Place the spring rolls on a plate and cover with plastic wrap. Chill for 30 minutes. Serve cold.

> **PER SPRING ROLL:**
> 31 Cal.; 0.8g Prot.; 0.9g Fat; 5g Carb.;
> 0mg Chol.; 3mg Sod.; 0g Fiber.

Pan-Fried Vegetable Wontons with Sesame Dip

makes 24

You may make these wontons fiery hot or quite mild by adjusting the amount of cayenne pepper you use.

DIP

- 1/3 cup rice vinegar
- 1/3 cup soy sauce
- 1/3 cup water
- 2 tablespoons sesame oil
- 1 teaspoon chili oil (or 1/2 teaspoon cayenne pepper)

TO FINISH THE DISH

- 1/2 cup shredded cabbage
- 1/3 cup shredded carrots
- 3 scallions (green and white parts), minced
- 4 tablespoons chopped fresh cilantro leaves
- 3 cloves garlic, minced
- 1/4 teaspoon cayenne pepper, or to taste
- 1 tablespoon soy sauce
- 1 tablespoon sesame oil
- 24 wonton wrappers
- 1 to 3 tablespoons vegetable oil
- 1/8 cup water

DIP: Combine all the dip ingredients in a small serving bowl. Place it in the center of a serving platter.

TO FINISH THE DISH: In a bowl, combine the cabbage, carrots, scallions, cilantro, garlic, cayenne, soy sauce and sesame oil. Mix well. Put a small spoonful of this mixture on a wonton wrapper. Fold corner-to-corner to make a triangle, then fold in the sides, like an envelope. Repeat with the remaining cabbage mixture and wontons.

COAT the bottom of a nonstick skillet with oil and heat over medium-high heat until hot. Gently place the filled wontons in the skillet and let cook until the bottoms are golden and crusty, about 3 minutes. Then pour water into the skillet, cover and let wontons steam for 2 minutes. Arrange them on a platter.

PER WONTON:
38 Cal.; 1g Prot.; 1g Fat; 6g Carb.;
0mg Chol.; 130mg Sod.; 0.2g Fiber.

Crispy Baked Egg Rolls

makes 24

- 1/4 cup water
- 1 cup diced onion
- 1 tablespoon minced fresh ginger root
- 4 cloves garlic, minced
- 2 cups diced celery
- 1/2 cup diced fresh shiitake mushrooms
- 1/2 cup diced white button mushrooms
- 3 cups diced green cabbage
- 1 cup diced, drained bamboo shoots
- 1 cup diced, drained water chestnuts
- 2 tablespoons low-sodium soy sauce
- 1 tablespoon rice wine or mirin
- 1 tablespoon honey
- 24 egg roll wrappers
- 2 tablespoons dark sesame oil, warmed

PREHEAT the oven to 400°F. Heat the water in a wok until simmering. Stir-fry the onion, ginger and garlic until the onion is soft but not browned, about 5 minutes. Add the celery, all mushrooms, cabbage, bamboo shoots and water chestnuts and stir-fry until the vegetables soften, about 5 to 8 minutes. Remove from the heat. Add the soy sauce, rice wine or mirin and honey; toss well. Place the mixture in a colander over a bowl; let sit 10 minutes to drain off excess moisture.

BE SURE your counter or tabletop is dry for egg roll wrapping. Stack the egg roll wrappers with one corner pointing away from you. Have a small bowl of water ready. Spoon 1/4 cup drained filling into the center of each wrapper. Lightly brush the edges of the wrapper with water.

FOLD the side corners to the center, covering the filling. Next bring the bottom corner to the center; tuck slightly under the filling and continue to roll the wrapper into a cylinder, sealing the top corner by moistening it slightly with water and pressing it down.

PLACE the egg rolls seam side down on two nonstick baking sheets. Do not crowd. Lightly brush with a little sesame oil. Bake in the center of your oven, turning once, until golden and crispy, about 15 to 20 minutes. Serve at once.

> **PER EGG ROLL:**
> 80 Cal.; 3g Prot.; 1g Fat; 14g Carb.;
> 0mg Chol.; 57mg Sod.; 1g Fiber.

Pot Stickers

makes 28 • serves 14

The combination of pan frying and steaming makes these little dumplings both crunchy and juicy. Dip them into small bowls filled with soy sauce, rice vinegar or chili oil.

FILLING

- 5 dried shiitake mushrooms (or use fresh, but do not soak)
- 2 scallions (green and white parts), chopped finely
- 1 1/2 cups finely shredded napa or other Chinese cabbage
- 1 cup finely chopped carrots
- 1 tablespoon soy sauce
- 1 tablespoon rice wine or dry sherry
- 1 tablespoon cornstarch
- 2 teaspoons sesame oil
- 1 teaspoon grated fresh ginger root
- 1/2 teaspoon sugar

DOUGH

- 3 cups all-purpose flour
- 1 1/3 cups boiling water
- 2 tablespoons vegetable oil for frying
- 2/3 cup vegetable stock (page 178) for steaming

FILLING: Soak the mushrooms in warm water for 30 minutes; drain. Cut off and discard the stems, and finely chop the caps. Combine the mushrooms with the remaining filling ingredients in a medium bowl, mixing well. Set aside.

DOUGH: Measure the flour into a large bowl. Mix in the boiling water, stirring with chopsticks or a fork until the dough is evenly moistened. Cover and let sit for 30 minutes. On a lightly floured surface, knead the dough until smooth and elastic, about 5 minutes. Divide the dough in half. Roll each half into a 14-inch-long cylinder, then cut crosswise into 1-inch pieces. Shape each piece into a ball and cover with a damp dishcloth.

TO SHAPE each pot sticker, flatten 1 ball of dough with a rolling pin to make a 3-inch circle. Keep the remaining dough covered to prevent it from drying. Place 1 heaping teaspoon of the filling in the center of the circle. Lightly moisten the edges on the circle with water. Fold the circle in half to form a semicircle. Starting at one end, pinch the curved edges together to make 4 to 6 pleats along the edge. Press to seal securely. Place the pot sticker seam side up. Cover with a damp dishcloth while you shape the remaining pot stickers.

PLACE a large nonstick skillet over high heat until hot. Add 1 tablespoon of oil, swirling to coat the sides. Set half of the pot stickers seam-side-up in the skillet. Cook until the bottoms are golden brown, about 2 to 3 minutes, gently swirling the skillet occasionally. Drain excess oil and lower the heat to medium. Pour in 1/3 cup stock, cover and cook until the liquid has evaporated, about 5 to 6 minutes, swirling the skillet occasionally. Transfer the pot stickers to a serving platter and keep them warm in a 200°F oven. Cook the remaining pot stickers with the remaining oil and remaining stock. Serve hot.

PER POT STICKER:
63 Cal.: 2g Prot.; 2g Fat; 11g Carb.;
0mg Chol.; 39mg Sod.; 1g Fiber.

Baba Ganoujh

serves 4

This much-revered Middle Eastern eggplant purée gets its name by way of a devoted son who set out to prepare something wonderful that his very old and toothless father could eat. For an authentic smokey taste, grill or broil the eggplant first.

> **2 pounds purple eggplant, cut in half lengthwise, flesh side scored deeply in a crosshatch pattern (see Note)**
> **1 tablespoon virgin olive oil**
> **Lemon juice from 1 to 2 lemons, or to taste**
> **2 small cloves garlic, finely minced**
> **4 tablespoons plain low-fat or nonfat yogurt**
> **4 tablespoons tahini (sesame paste)**
> **1 teaspoon salt, or more to taste**
> **Minced fresh parsley**
> **Assorted raw vegetables, at least 3: red bell pepper strips, green bell pepper strips, carrot sticks, celery sticks, cucumber spears, jicama sticks, fennel slices (see Note)**

IF YOU'RE USING A GRILL, maintain heat at a medium-low temperature. If you're using a broiler, preheat first and then turn it down to the lowest possible temperature.

BRUSH the eggplant halves with olive oil and place, flesh-side down if using a grill, flesh-side up if using a broiler, and cook until charred and very soft, turning once, about 40 minutes. Set the eggplant to drain in a colander in your sink until it's no longer warm to the touch.

SCOOP the flesh into a food processor or food mill, discarding skin. Process the eggplant with a few off-on pulses or force it through a food mill into a mixing bowl. Stir in the lemon juice, garlic, yogurt, tahini and salt. Place the mixture in a serving dish and sprinkle the top with parsley. Chill well. Serve as a dip with raw vegetables.

Variation:

Serve baba ganoujh with wedges of pita or with crackers.

Notes:

- The dark purple eggplant makes an acceptable—some people would say great—replacement for meat in many recipes. When choosing an eggplant, look for a firm, glossy skin. When you press the skin, it should give and bounce back. If it doesn't, check another one. If you want an eggplant with minimal seeds, look at the small scar opposite the stem end. If the scar is round, you've found a not-so-seedy "male." If the scar is oval, expect seeds from this "female."

  Because eggplants are spongelike, they soak up the juices or oils with which they are cooked. When cooking eggplant, avoid excessive amounts of oil, or you'll have a high-fat food on your hands. (That's why traditional eggplant Parmesan is a nightmare for the fat-conscious.)

  The easiest way to prepare eggplant is to cut it in half lengthwise and bake it face down on a lightly greased nonstick baking sheet at 350°F until tender, about 30 minutes. Let it cool and chop or slice it, or scoop out the center and stuff it.

  Tip: Before cooking an eggplant, especially if you are frying it and want to remove some of the liquid and bitterness, you may slice and salt the eggplant and let it drain for an hour, rinse if desired, then cook.

- Fennel is a crazy-looking vegetable, with long, light green, treelike stalks and a white bulb, and a licorice flavor that becomes less pronounced when cooked. To prepare fennel, wash, dry and trim the stalks level with the bulb tops. Trim the root end, too, but keep enough of the vegetable intact to hold the bulb together. Cut the bulk in quarters and slice. Cook as directed in your recipe. If necessary, substitute

celery for fennel, but the flavor of your dish will lack the licorice touch.

> **PER SERVING:**
> 225 Cal.; 5g Prot.; 9g Fat; 28g Carb.;
> 1mg Chol.; 611mg Sod.; 8g Fiber.

Garlic-Marinated Tofu with Olives and Tomato Fans

serves 6

Here's a variation of a traditional dish on Israeli breakfast menus.

> 1 1/2 pounds extra-firm tofu, pressed for at least 1 hour and cut into 1/2-inch cubes
> 3 tablespoons rice wine vinegar
> 2 medium cloves garlic, puréed or minced
> 1 teaspoon Dijon mustard
> Minced fresh parsley or fresh cilantro leaves
> 1/4 teaspoon dried tarragon
> 1/4 teaspoon dried marjoram
> Salt and freshly ground black pepper to taste
> 1/3 cup virgin olive oil
> Boston or bibb lettuce leaves
> 20 black olives, for garnish
> 6 medium plum tomatoes, sliced vertically from bottom to stem and fanned out, for garnish
> 6 sprigs of fresh parsley or fresh cilantro, for garnish

PLACE the tofu in a medium mixing bowl. In a second bowl, combine the vinegar, garlic, mustard, herbs, salt and pepper. Whisk in the olive oil. Pour this mixture over cubed tofu and toss gently.

JUST BEFORE SERVING, line 6 salad plates with lettuce leaves and divide the marinated tofu among them. Garnish each with 4 black olives, a tomato fan, and a sprig of fresh parsley or cilantro.

> **PER SERVING:**
> 239 Cal.; 16g Prot.; 14g Fat; 11g Carb.;
> 0mg Chol.; 252mg Sod.; 3g Fiber.

Baked Samosa Logs

serves 8

This baked version of fried samosas makes use of a time-saving shortcut: ready-made whole wheat chapatis. Serve them with a sweet chutney.

    5 cups diced cauliflower
    1 1/3 cups baby peas (fresh or thawed frozen)
    1 1/2 tablespoons unsweetened coconut flakes
    1 teaspoon curry powder
    1/8 teaspoon cayenne pepper or 1/2 teaspoon paprika
    2 tablespoons chopped fresh cilantro
    1 1/2 tablespoons fresh lemon juice
    1/2 teaspoon salt
    12 whole-wheat chapatis (see Helpful hints)
    Olive oil cooking spray or virgin olive oil for brushing

IN A LARGE SAUCEPAN fitted with a steamer, steam the cauliflower for 10 minutes. Add the peas and steam 3 minutes more. Transfer the cauliflower and peas to a bowl, and add the coconut, curry powder, cayenne or paprika, cilantro, lemon juice and salt. Toss to mix. Allow the mixture to cool slightly and divide it into 12 portions, about 1/2 cup each.

PLACE 1 chapati on a work surface and brush it lightly with water. With your hands, shape a portion of the vegetable mixture into a log. Place it about 1 1/2 inches from the bottom edge of the chapati. Roll the chapati halfway, fold in the sides, then finish rolling into a log. Place it on a baking sheet, seam-side-down. Repeat with the remaining vegetable mixture and chapatis.

PREHEAT the oven to 375°F. Spray or brush the samosas lightly with oil. Bake until crisp and golden, about 15 to 20 minutes. Cut each samosa in half.

Helpful hints:

- Samosas may be made a day ahead of time and baked just before serving.

- If you can't find ready-made chapatis, substitute flour tortillas (either white or whole wheat).

> **PER SERVING:**
> 174 Cal.; 6g Prot.; 3g Fat; 30g Carb.;
> 0mg Chol.; 321mg Sod.; 4g Fiber.

Almost-Sushi Appetizer Crepes

serves 8

    1 to 2 avocados
    1 to 2 cucumbers
    1 to 2 carrots
    8 Basic or No-Cholesterol Dinner Crepes (see page 441),
        cut in half
    2 to 4 sheets nori (page 78) (optional)
    Several leaves red leaf lettuce (optional)

DIPPING SAUCE

| 1/3 cup soy sauce
| 1/3 cup rice vinegar
| 2 to 3 tablespoons mirin (or 2 tablespoons sherry and
| 1 tablespoon honey)
| 1/2 teaspoon chili oil
| 3 tablespoons chopped fresh cilantro

CUT the vegetables into thin sticks about 1 1/2 to 2 inches long. Cut the nori sheets in quarters. On half a crepe, lay down the nori and lettuce. Place a small bundle of vegetable sticks at one end and roll up the crepe into a cone. Repeat this method with the remaining vegetables and crepes.

COMBINE all the sauce ingredients in a small dish and mix well. Place the dish in the center of a platter and surround with rolled-up crepes.

> **PER SERVING:**
> 230 Cal.; 11g Prot.; 9g Fat; 28g Carb.;
> 73mg Chol.; 817mg Sod.; 3g Fiber.

Mixed Olives with Herbs

serves 6

| 2 cups mixed green and black pitted olives (such as
| calamata, Niçoise, nyon or Sicilian)
| 10 sprigs fresh thyme
| 4 bay leaves
| 1 large clove garlic, sliced thinly
| 1/4 teaspoon fennel seeds
| Several strips orange peel
| 2 tablespoons virgin olive oil

COMBINE the ingredients in a covered container. Serve at room temperature. Store in the refrigerator for up to 4 days.

Note:

If you're using oil-cured olives, add them just before serving because they may stain the green ones black.

> **PER SERVING:**
> 46 Cal.; 2g Prot.; 4g Fat; 0.9g Carb.;
> 0mg Chol.; 307mg Sod.; 1g Fiber.

Skinny Potato Chips

serves 10

In this oil-free recipe, paper-thin slices of potatoes are baked until the moisture evaporates and the potatoes become crisp chips.

| Nonstick cooking spray
| 1 pound red potatoes
| Salt and freshly ground black pepper to taste

PREHEAT the oven to 450°F. Lightly spray a baking sheet with nonstick cooking spray. Using a food processor fitted with a slicing blade or a sharp knife, slice the potatoes very thinly. Toss gently with salt and pepper. Spread the slices on the baking sheet in a single layer. Bake until lightly browned and crisp, about 15 minutes. Then turn over the chips and bake 10 minutes more.

> **PER SERVING:**
> 132 Cal.; 3g Prot.; 0.1g Fat; 31g Carb.;
> 0mg Chol.; 115mg Sod.; 1g Fiber.

Chili-Mole Popcorn

serves 4

These exotic flavors carry with them the savory chili-chocolate charm found in a classic Mexican mole sauce.

  1 tablespoon chili powder

  1 teaspoon unsweetened cocoa powder

  1 teaspoon vegetable seasoning

  1 teaspoon salt (optional)

  1/4 teaspoon freshly ground black pepper

  Butter-flavored nonstick cooking spray

  8 cups hot air-popped popcorn

IN A CUP OR SMALL BOWL, combine the chili, cocoa, vegetable seasoning, salt and pepper. Set aside.

LIGHTLY SPRAY a large serving bowl on all sides with butter-flavored spray. Add 2 or 3 cups of hot popcorn, spray lightly and sprinkle evenly with a heaping teaspoon of mixed seasonings. Add another layer of the popcorn, spray and seasoning mixture. Add a final layer of the popcorn and spray, and sprinkle the remaining seasoning over all. Serve at once without tossing.

> **PER SERVING:**
> 71 Cal.; 2g Prot.; 2g Fat; 13g Carb.;
> 0mg Chol.; 20mg Sod.; 2g Fiber.

Caribbean Spice Popcorn

serves 4

All of the fiery taste of the islands is here, so proceed with caution. If fire isn't your style, neither is this popcorn.

  2 teaspoons vegetable seasoning

  1 teaspoon lemon zest

  1 teaspoon best-quality curry powder

  1 teaspoon salt (optional)

  Pinch cayenne pepper, or to taste

  Nonstick cooking spray

  8 cups hot air-popped popcorn

IN A SMALL BOWL, combine the vegetable seasoning, lemon zest, curry powder, salt and cayenne.

SPRAY a large serving bowl on all sides lightly with butter-flavored spray. Add 2 or 3 cups of hot popcorn, spray lightly and sprinkle evenly with a heaping teaspoon of mixed seasonings. Add another layer of the popcorn, spray and seasoning mixture. Add a final layer of the popcorn and spray, and sprinkle the remaining seasoning over all. Serve at once without tossing.

> **PER SERVING:**
> 69 Cal.; 2g Prot.; 2g Fat; 13g Carb.;
> 0mg Chol.; 3mg Sod.; 2g Fiber.

Orange-Honey-Sesame Popcorn

serves 4

Sweet enough to pinch-hit for dessert, this seasoned popcorn is a combination of flavors that will be a winner with everyone, so be prepared to make a second batch on demand.

2 tablespoons margarine

3 tablespoons orange blossom honey

1 teaspoon fresh orange zest

8 cups hot air-popped popcorn

3 tablespoons pan-toasted sesame seeds (page 106)

IN A SMALL SAUCEPAN, melt the margarine over low heat. Stir in the honey and orange zest.

PUT the popcorn into a large serving bowl, pour the honey mixture over it and toss lightly to combine. Sprinkle with sesame seeds and serve at once.

> **PER SERVING:**
> 184 Cal.; 3g Prot.; 7g Fat; 26g Carb.;
> 0mg Chol.; 38mg Sod.; 3g Fiber.

Hot Broccoli Dip with Roasted Red Peppers and Pine Nuts

serves 16

The microwave speeds up the preparation of this savory dip. Serve it with soft breadsticks or crackers.

1 tablespoon pine nuts

One 9-ounce package frozen chopped broccoli

4 ounces light cream cheese

One 10 1/4-ounce package soft tofu, divided (reserve half for another use)

2 tablespoons chopped roasted red pepper

1 clove garlic, minced

1/2 teaspoon vegetarian Worcestershire sauce

1/8 teaspoon cayenne pepper (optional)

TOAST the pine nuts in a nonstick skillet over medium heat, stirring frequently, until golden brown. Set aside. Unwrap broccoli and place in a 1-quart casserole dish. Cover and microwave at high power until defrosted, about 2 to 4 minutes. Drain, pressing to remove excess moisture. Return the broccoli to the casserole. Set aside.

PLACE the cream cheese in a small mixing bowl. Microwave at high power until softened, about 30 to 45 seconds. Add the tofu and stir until the mixture is smooth. Add the tofu mixture and the remaining ingredients except the pine nuts to the broccoli, mixing well. Cover and microwave at medium power (50 percent) until warm, about 2 to 4 minutes, stirring once. Sprinkle with the pine nuts.

> **PER SERVING:**
> 32 Cal.; 2g Prot.; 2g Fat; 1g Carb.;
> 4mg Chol.; 43mg Sod.; 6g Fiber.

Dilly Dip

makes 3 cups

This tasty dip is a natural with raw vegetables.

> 21 ounces (2 packages) firm tofu
> 1/4 cup fresh lemon juice
> 1/2 to 1 teaspoon salt
> 1 teaspoon sugar
> 2 teaspoons dried dillweed (or 2 tablespoons fresh)
> 1/2 teaspoon onion powder
> 1/2 teaspoon garlic powder
> 2 teaspoons dried basil (or 2 tablespoons fresh)

PLACE all the ingredients in a blender or food processor. Blend until smooth. Spoon the dip into serving bowls, cover and refrigerate until serving time.

Helpful hint:

This dip may be made several days ahead of time and stored in your refrigerator.

> **PER TABLESPOON:**
> 18 Cal.; 2g Prot.; 0.9g Fat; 0.8g Carb.;
> 0mg Chol.; 24mg Sod.; 0.1g Fiber.

Lemony Chickpea Dip

makes 2 cups

If allowed to sit, this dip thickens. Add a small amount of water as needed. Spoon into pocket bread or dip vegetables into it.

> 1 1/2 cups cooked or canned chickpeas
> 3 cloves garlic
> 3 tablespoons tahini (sesame paste)
> 5 tablespoons water
> 3 tablespoons fresh lemon or lime juice

PLACE all the ingredients into a blender or food processor and process until smooth.

Variation:

Add 1 tablespoon chopped fresh cilantro leaves or fresh parsley before blending.

> **PER 1/2 CUP:**
> 176 Cal.; 8g Prot.; 8g Fat; 21g Carb.;
> 0mg Chol.; 11mg Sod.; 4g Fiber.

Cilantro Dip

makes 1 1/2 cups

Serve this dip with raw vegetables or crackers.

> 1/4 cup scallions (green and white parts), chopped
>
> 1/2 cup fresh cilantro leaves, chopped
>
> 1/4 cup fresh parsley, chopped
>
> 2 to 3 cloves garlic, minced
>
> 2 tablespoons virgin olive oil
>
> 1/4 cup fresh lemon juice
>
> 2 tablespoons mayonnaise
>
> 2 tablespoons water
>
> 1 cup crumbled tofu
>
> Salt and freshly ground black pepper to taste

COMBINE the scallions, cilantro, parsley, garlic, oil, lemon juice and mayonnaise in a blender and blend 30 seconds. Add the water and half of the tofu, and blend 1 minute. Add the remaining tofu, salt and pepper, and blend 1 minute more.

> **PER TABLESPOON:**
> 21 Cal.; 0.6g Prot.; 2g Fat; 0.6g Carb.;
> 1mg Chol.; 40mg Sod.; 0g Fiber.

Broccomole

makes 1 1/2 cups

With 30 grams of fat per avocado, guacamole is out for anyone who wants to go easy on fat. Here's a fat-free version using broccoli. Try it with Mexican dishes or serve it as a dip for tortilla chips.

> 1 1/2 cups well-cooked broccoli stems
>
> 1 1/2 tablespoons fresh lemon juice
>
> 1/4 teaspoon cumin
>
> 1/8 teaspoon garlic powder
>
> 1/2 tomato, diced
>
> 1 scallion, sliced
>
> 1 green chili pepper, chopped

PLACE the broccoli stems, lemon juice, cumin and garlic powder in a blender or food processor and purée until smooth. Transfer to a bowl. Add the remaining ingredients and mix well. For the best flavor, chill before serving.

> **PER 3-TABLESPOON SERVING:**
> 14 Cal.; 1g Prot.; 0.1g Fat; 3g Carb.;
> 0mg Chol.; 5mg Sod.; 2g Fiber.

Spiced Popcorn Balls

makes 12

| 8 cups popped corn
| 1 cup roasted almonds, chopped coarsely (optional)
| 1/2 cup butter or margarine
| 1/2 cup honey or maple syrup
| 1 tablespoon orange extract
| 1/4 teaspoon ground cinnamon
| 1/4 teaspoon ground nutmeg

PREHEAT the oven to 350°F. In an 11 × 17-inch roaster pan, mix together the popcorn and almonds. Set aside. Melt the butter or margarine in a small pot. Add the honey or maple syrup, orange extract and spices. Boil gently over medium heat, stirring, for 1 minute. Drizzle over the popcorn mixture and stir well.

BAKE for 15 to 20 minutes, stirring every 5 minutes. Remove the pan from the oven. With gloved hands, shape the hot mixture into 12 balls. Cool thoroughly. Wrap in plastic wrap until serving time.

> **PER BALL:**
> 132 Cal.; 0.8g Prot.; 8g Fat; 15g Carb.;
> 20mg Chol.; 77mg Sod.; 1g Fiber.

Stress-Reducing Trail Mix

makes 16 cups

Remember trail mix? Here's one packed with fiber, potassium and B vitamins. Store double-wrapped in your freezer.

| 2 cups chopped walnuts
| 2 cups chopped peanuts
| 2 cups almonds
| 2 cups sunflower seeds
| 2 cups toasted pumpkin seeds (page 106)
| 2 cups chopped dried apricots
| 2 cups raisins
| 2 cups chopped dried figs

PREHEAT the oven to 300°F. On a baking sheet, spread the walnuts, peanuts, almonds, sunflower seeds and pumpkin seeds. Toast for 30 minutes, stirring occasionally. Cool. Toss with the remaining ingredients.

> **PER 1/2-CUP SERVING:**
> 353 Cal.; 10g Prot.; 22g Fat; 26g Carb.;
> 0mg Chol.; 8mg Sod.; 7g Fiber.

CHAPTER 10

drinks

FEW PEOPLE BOTHER TO CONCOCT THEIR OWN BEVERAGES. That's a shame: Homemade drinks are more creative and delicious than beverages you find in the store. Your own drinks generally fare better nutritionally than store-bought varieties, too. If you're not accustomed to making your own drinks (save for a pot of coffee or tea), we invite you to try a few of these recipes—just for the fun of it. You might find that making your own beverages is worth the minimal time and effort they require because they taste so good. An added bonus: Many of these drinks mimic alcoholic beverages but won't leave you with a buzz.

149

Spiced Tomato Sunset

serves 8

An acceptably delicious substitute for a Bloody Mary, this spicy drink has plenty of kick.

- 1 large can vegetable or tomato juice
- 2 teaspoons prepared horseradish
- 1 tablespoon vegetarian Worcestershire sauce
- 1 small lemon, sliced thinly
- Hot pepper sauce to taste
- Freshly ground black pepper to taste

IN A PITCHER, stir together all the ingredients. Cover and chill. Serve cold over lots of ice, or heat the beverage and serve hot in mugs.

> **PER SERVING:**
> 29 Cal.; 0.8g Prot.; 0g Fat; 7g Carb.;
> 0mg Chol.; 59mg Sod.; 1g Fiber.

Orange Sunrise

serves 6

- 1 quart orange juice
- One 10-ounce package frozen strawberries in syrup, thawed

PROCESS the orange juice and strawberries in a blender until smooth. Strain if desired. Chill. Serve over chipped ice.

> **PER SERVING:**
> 104 Cal.; 1g Prot.; 0.1g Fat; 28g Carb.;
> 0mg Chol.; 3mg Sod.; 1g Fiber.

Better than Champagne

serves 8

This drink tastes amazingly like the real thing. If you prefer pink champagne, add a tablespoon or two of grenadine or cranberry juice.

- One 32-ounce bottle club soda or seltzer
- Two 6-ounce cans frozen white grape juice concentrate, thawed

GENTLY stir together the club soda or seltzer and the thawed grape juice concentrate. Pour into 2 soda bottles. Cap tightly and chill. Serve in champagne glasses.

> **PER SERVING:**
> 30 Cal.; 0g Prot.; 0g Fat; 7g Carb.;
> 0mg Chol.; 29mg Sod.; 0g Fiber.

Almond Cooler

serves 4

This creamy-white almond milk is sweetened just a little with honey and flavored with orange-flower water. With 11 grams of fat in a cup, it's best to make this drink an occasional treat.

- 4 cups cold water
- 3/4 cup blanched almonds
- 1/4 cup honey
- 2 drops almond extract
- 1 or 2 tablespoons orange-flower water, or to taste (see Note)
- 4 sprigs fresh mint, for garnish
- Additional water or seltzer (optional)

POUR the water into a blender. With the blender on high speed, gradually add the almonds, processing until well pulverized, about 5 minutes. Set a strainer lined with cheesecloth over a medium saucepan. Pour the liquid through the strainer; then twist the cheesecloth to squeeze out all of the liquid. Stir in the honey. Bring the mixture to a boil, lower the heat and simmer 2 minutes. Let cool. Stir in the almond extract and orange-flower water. Transfer the almond milk to a covered container and refrigerate. To serve, pour the almond milk into glasses with ice and garnish with mint. (If the drink is too thick, dilute it with cold water or seltzer.)

Note:

Orange-flower water, extracted from the blossoms of orange trees, has a citrus flavor. It is available in Greek and Middle Eastern groceries. You may omit it or use a drop of orange extract.

> **PER SERVING:**
> 189 Cal.; 5g Prot.; 11g Fat; 22g Carb.;
> 0mg Chol.; 3mg Sod.; 3g Fiber.

Fruity Spritzer

serves 8

This bubbly drink takes on the color and the nutritional value of the fruit concentrate you choose.

| 1/2 cup thawed frozen fruit concentrate
| 16 ice cubes
| 3 cups sparkling water, chilled

PLACE 1 tablespoon thawed fruit concentrate in each of eight 4- or 5-ounce glasses. Divide the ice cubes among the glasses and stir in sparkling water.

> **PER SERVING:**
> 50 Cal.; 0 Prot.; 0g Fat; 12g Carb.;
> 0mg Chol.; 2mg Sod.; 0g Fiber.

Cranberry Sparkler

serves 8

| 16 ice cubes
| 2 cups cranberry juice, chilled
| 8 cups sparkling water, chilled

DIVIDE the ice cubes among 8 glasses. Add 1/4 cup juice to each glass, then fill the glasses with sparkling water.

> **PER SERVING:**
> 36 Cal.; 0g Prot.; 0g Fat; 9g Carb.;
> 0mg Chol.; 4mg Sod.; 0g Fiber.

Hibiscus Cooler

serves 12

This refreshing beverage simulates the rose-colored iced drinks at Caribbean street carnivals in Manhattan. For best results, make the tea the night or morning before serving.

| 8 tea bags (Red Zinger or other tea containing hibiscus flowers)
| 4 cups boiling water
| 1 quart chilled pineapple juice
| 1 quart chilled sparkling water
| 1 to 2 cups orange juice (optional)
| 1 sliced lime, lemon or orange, for garnish

STEEP the tea bags in the boiling water for 30 minutes. Remove and discard the tea bags. Refrigerate about 4 hours or overnight. Combine the tea with the pineapple juice, sparkling water and orange juice. Stir. Add more or less juice or water to taste. Garnish with lime, lemon or orange slices.

Variations:
- Add a cinnamon stick to the tea as it brews.
- Add 1 to 2 teaspoons fresh ginger juice just before serving.

> **PER SERVING:**
> 48 Cal.; 0g Prot.; 0g Fat; 12g Carb.;
> 0mg Chol.; 3mg Sod.; 0g Fiber.

Melon-Lime Refresher

serves 8

> 5 1/2 cups chopped cantaloupe or
>   watermelon pieces (seeds removed)
> 1/2 cup sugar
> 1/2 cup fresh lime juice
> 4 cups water

IN A BLENDER, process the melon, sugar and lime juice. Strain the melon mixture through a fine sieve into a large bowl and stir in the water. Rub the sieve with the back of a spoon to push through any remaining fruit liquid; discard the pulp.

PLACE the fruit-water mixture in a gallon jar or 2 large pitchers. Cover and chill. Before serving, mix well and pour over ice into glasses.

> **PER SERVING:**
> 88 Cal.; 0.8g Prot.; 0.1g Fat; 21g Carb.;
> 0mg Chol.; 10mg Sod.; 1g Fiber.

Frothy Fruit Shake

serves 2

Here's a beverage that you can make at home or on the trail.

> 1 teaspoon unsweetened powdered fruit drink mix
>   (like Kool-Aid)
> 1/2 cup instant nonfat powdered milk
> 4 tablespoons sugar
> 3 cups water

AT HOME, mix together the drink mix, powdered milk and sugar. Store in a sealed plastic bag.

ON THE TRAIL, transfer the mixture to a quart-size plastic bottle and add the water; screw on the top. Shake vigorously to make the liquid frothy. (If this drink is allowed to sit and the creamy part separates, just shake again.)

> **PER SERVING:**
> 194 Cal.; 6g Prot.; 0.1g Fat; 44g Carb.;
> 3mg Chol.; 101mg Sod.; 0g Fiber.

Mango-Citrus Cocktail

serves 4

> 2 mangoes, peeled and sliced
> 1 to 2 tablespoons sugar
> 2 cups fresh orange juice
> 2 limes, juiced
> 8 ice cubes plus additional cubes for glasses
> 2 cups sparkling water or to taste
> Mint sprigs (optional)

IN A BLENDER, blend the mangoes, sugar, orange juice, lime juice and 8 ice cubes for 1 minute. Pour the mixture into a pitcher and refrigerate. When you're ready to serve the cocktails, thin the mixture with sparkling water and stir. Pour into 4 glasses filled with ice cubes. Garnish with mint.

> **PER SERVING:**
> 138 Cal.; 2g Prot.; 0.7g Fat; 35g Carb.;
> 0mg Chol.; 3mg Sod.; 2g Fiber.

Supreme Green Pasta

page 345

Photo by Bob Skalkowski

Bulgur-Herb Crostini

page 132

Photo by Bob Skalkowski

Wild Rice Crepes

page 288

page 169

Chickpea-and-Cabbage Soup

Eggplant Pita Sandwiches

page 468

Photo by Bob Skalkowski

soups

DEPENDING ON YOUR MOOD, the season and your dinner plans, a soup can be a first course, an elaborate meal, or a simple bowlful of delicious warmth that needs only crusty bread to satisfy your hunger. Soup is so versatile it may even be chilled. And the ingredients? Vegetables, fruits, noodles, legumes, nuts—almost anything and everything has a place in soup. Please note: Many of these recipes call for vegetable stock. You may prepare one of our stock recipes or use a vegetable bouillon cube dissolved in very hot water.

Moroccan Vegetable Soup

serves 8

Cumin, coriander and turmeric give this hearty Middle Eastern soup its unique flavor.

| 1 large onion, chopped coarsely
| 2 teaspoons ground cumin
| 1 teaspoon ground coriander
| 1 teaspoon turmeric
| 2 tablespoons canola oil
| One 28-ounce can whole tomatoes (with juice), chopped coarsely
| 6 cups vegetable stock (page 178)
| 2 cups cooked or canned chickpeas
| 2 large red or green bell peppers, chopped
| 1/4 teaspoon freshly ground black pepper
| 2 small zucchini, diced
| 4 ounces seitan, diced finely
| 8 ounces uncooked vermicelli or thin spaghetti, broken into 1-inch pieces
| 1 tablespoon nutritional yeast

IN A LARGE POT. sauté the onion, cumin, coriander and turmeric in the oil until the onion is soft. Add the tomatoes with juice, stock, chickpeas, bell peppers and black pepper; simmer, uncovered, 1 hour. Add the zucchini, seitan and vermicelli or spaghetti. Cook until the pasta is just tender, about 10 minutes. Stir in the nutritional yeast and serve.

> **PER SERVING:**
> 205 Cal.; 7g Prot.; 4g Fat; 32g Carb.;
> 0mg Chol.; 407mg Sod.; 5g Fiber.

Any Vegetable Soup

serves 8

| 8 cups assorted chopped vegetables, cooked or raw: cabbage, lettuce, potatoes, leeks, onions, tomatoes fresh or canned), green beans, peas (fresh or frozen), zucchini or summer squash, turnips, spinach
| 8 cups vegetable stock (page 178) or water
| 1 1/2 teaspoons salt
| Herb of choice: 1 teaspoon basil, oregano or marjoram; 1/4 teaspoon rosemary; or 1 bay leaf
| Cayenne pepper or freshly ground black pepper to taste

PLACE all the ingredients in a soup pot. Bring to a boil, cover and simmer until the vegetables are tender, about 20 minutes. Serve hot.

Optional additions:

- 1/2 cup uncooked macaroni, or 1 cup cooked macaroni or grain (If you're using uncooked macaroni, add it when the vegetables are still crunchy; simmer, stirring occasionally, until tender. If you're using cooked macaroni or grains, add them during the last 5 minutes of cooking time.)

- chunks of tofu (Add during last 10 minutes of cooking.)

Variation:

Purée soup. (Stir in additions as desired after puréeing soup.)

> **PER SERVING:**
> 69 Cal.; 3g Prot.; 0.2g Fat; 15g Carb.;
> 0mg Chol.; 430mg Sod.; 4g Fiber.

Almost-Classic French Onion Soup

serves 4

The traditional version calls for beef stock, but here the full-bodied flavor is imparted by herbs. Serve it with croutons or garlic toast.

> One *bouquet garni* (page 107), with additional herbs of choice (1 sprig fresh or 1 teaspoon dried): rosemary, marjoram, dill, coriander seeds, celery seeds
>
> 4 to 6 cups thinly sliced onions
>
> 2 teaspoons virgin olive oil
>
> Pinch salt
>
> 6 cups water or vegetable stock (page 178)
>
> Salt, soy sauce or light miso to taste (optional)
>
> Sliced scallions (green and white parts) or minced fresh parsley, for garnish

ADD your herbs of choice to the *garni's* basic ingredients and retie. Set aside. In a large pot, sauté the onions in the oil over medium-low heat. Add salt to help prevent sticking, and stir frequently. Cover the pot, leaving the lid slightly ajar. The onions should sauté 30 minutes to 1 hour. They will reduce to about one third of their original volume and become sweet and golden.

ADD the water or stock along with the *bouquet garni*. Simmer at least 30 minutes. Remove the *bouquet garni*. Season with extra salt, soy sauce or miso. Garnish with scallions or fresh parsley.

> **PER SERVING:**
> 71 Cal.; 1g Prot.; 3g Fat; 10g Carb.;
> 0mg Chol.; 69mg Sod.; 2g Fiber.

African Peanut Soup

serves 8

Traditionally, the peanuts in this West African soup are hand-ground with a pestle and mortar. To simulate the flavor and simplify the process, use a smooth peanut butter that has no salt or sugar added.

> 2 medium onions, chopped
>
> 2 large green or red bell peppers
>
> 4 medium cloves garlic, mashed
>
> 2 tablespoons canola oil
>
> One 28-ounce can whole tomatoes (with juice), chopped coarsely
>
> 8 cups vegetable stock (page 178)
>
> 1/4 teaspoon freshly ground black pepper
>
> 1/4 teaspoon crushed red chili peppers
>
> 1/2 cup uncooked short-grain brown rice
>
> 2/3 cup no-salt, no-sugar smooth peanut butter

IN A LARGE SOUP POT. sauté the onions, bell peppers and garlic in the oil until the onions just begin to brown. Add the tomatoes with juice, stock, black pepper and chili peppers. Simmer, uncovered, over low heat for 30 minutes. Add the rice, cover and simmer 15 minutes more. Stir in the peanut butter until dissolved and smooth. Heat to a simmer and serve.

> **PER SERVING:**
> 251 Cal.; 8g Prot.; 15g Fat; 21g Carb.;
> 0mg Chol.; 209mg Sod.; 4g Fiber.

Fragrant Broth with Herbed Matzoh Dumplings

serves 6

The infamous chicken soup cure of Jewish lore (in New York, it's called "penicillin") doesn't suffer one bit from this fowl-free translation. Add fluffy herb-scented matzoh dumplings, and it's even better.

BROTH

1 large carrot

4 stalks celery (with leaves)

1 large onion, washed but not peeled

2 medium parsnips, peeled

4 cups pea pods (or one 16-ounce bag frozen peas)

1 bunch fresh parsley stems (reserve leaves for dumplings)

1 small beet, peeled

1/4 head cabbage, chopped

6 whole allspice

6 whole peppercorns

2 bay leaves

3 quarts fresh cold water

Salt to taste

DUMPLINGS

2/3 cup finely minced fresh parsley

2 large eggs, well beaten

1/4 cup parsley liquid (see directions) or vegetable soup stock

1/2 cup matzoh meal

Up to 1 teaspoon salt (optional)

1/4 teaspoon freshly ground black pepper

2 tablespoons canola oil

2 quarts water

BROTH: Combine all the broth ingredients in a large pot. Cover and simmer 2 to 3 hours. Strain through a colander set over a large bowl and discard the solids.

DUMPLINGS: Place the parsley inside a cloth and twist tightly over a small bowl to extract as much liquid as possible. Add the water or stock to the parsley liquid to measure 1/4 cup liquid. (The leaves should now measure 1/2 cup.) In a medium bowl, combine the parsley, eggs, liquid, matzoh meal, salt, pepper and oil. Blend well, cover and refrigerate at least 20 minutes to firm the mixture.

BRING 2 quarts water to a boil. Shape the matzoh meal mixture into 20 walnut-size balls or 10 larger ones. Place them into the boiling water, lower the heat and boil gently, covered, for 30 minutes. The dumplings will double in volume. Remove the dumplings with a slotted spoon, place them in a single layer, cover and let cool. (You may skip the cooling step if you're in a hurry, but cooling the dumplings achieves a more intense flavor and fluffier texture.) To serve, place the dumplings in the soup and reheat for 10 minutes.

> **PER SERVING:**
> 211 Cal.; 7g Prot.; 7g Fat; 30g Carb.;
> 71mg Chol.; 780mg Sod.; 9g Fiber.

French Garlic Panade Soup

serves 6

A *panade* is a paste made by combining liquid and bread to form a smooth purée. It is found in many French dishes. Here, the *panade* provides the soup with a satisfying texture.

> 3 tablespoons canola oil
>
> 2 medium onions, chopped
>
> 6 shallots, chopped
>
> 3 leeks (white and light green parts only), chopped (see Note)
>
> 3 cloves garlic, minced
>
> Six 1/2-inch-thick slices stale French bread, crusts removed
>
> 2/3 cup milk or skim milk
>
> 6 cups vegetable stock (page 178) or water
>
> 1 teaspoon light miso, or to taste
>
> *Bouquet garni* (1 piece celery tied with 1 bay leaf, 1 sprig of thyme and 6 fresh parsley stems, page 107)
>
> 1 cup evaporated skim milk
>
> Salt and white pepper to taste
>
> 1/2 cup chopped watercress or fresh parsley (see Note)
>
> 1 tablespoon chopped fresh chives

IN A LARGE POT, heat the oil over medium heat and sauté the onions, shallots, leeks and garlic until the onions begin to turn golden.

MEANWHILE, crumble the bread into a medium bowl. Heat the milk to barely boiling and pour over the bread; mix well to form the *panade*. Add the *panade* and stock or water to the pot. Bring to a boil. Stir in the miso and *bouquet garni*. (Tie the string to the pot handle for easy retrieval.) Simmer, uncovered, for 30 minutes. Discard the *bouquet garni*. Pour enough of the soup into a blender to fill it only half full, and blend until smooth. Repeat with the remaining soup. Add the condensed skim milk and reheat gently. Do not allow the soup to boil.

A FEW MINUTES before serving, warm the soup and season with salt and white pepper. Stir in watercress or parsley and chives. Serve at once.

Notes:

- Leeks are in the onion family and look like large scallions. They grow underground in sandy soil, so you must take care to wash them well. You can eat only the white base and a little of the tender greens above the base. First trim the long green leaves above the base, then, using a sharp knife, cut deeply into the leek but not all the way through. Fan open the layers and rinse the leek under running water to remove the sand and any dirt. Finish preparing the leek as your recipe directs. In most recipes, you may replace the leeks with onions, scallions or shallots.

- Watercress is one of the oldest edible plants known to humans, but when was the last time you ate this spicy, pungent green? To prepare it, trim any very thick stems and wilted leaves. Rinse under running water and pat dry.

> **PER SERVING:**
> 348 Cal.; 13g Prot.; 11g Fat; 46g Carb.;
> 5mg Chol.; 615mg Sod.; 5g Fiber.

Twenty-Minute Minestrone with Fennel

serves 12

Italian vegetable soup is probably as old as Italy itself, and in traditional kitchens, it sometimes simmers on the back of the stove all day. This modern version is geared to a faster-paced world.

5 quarts cold water

Three 16-ounce cans white or pink beans
  (great northern, cannelini or pinto), rinsed

2 large russet potatoes, peeled if desired, and diced

1 carrot, sliced

3 bay leaves

4 cloves garlic, minced

1/4 cup virgin olive oil

1 cup chopped canned or fresh plum tomatoes

3 quarts water

1 pound spinach, trimmed and sliced

1 pound Swiss chard, trimmed and sliced

10 ounces whole-kernel corn (fresh or frozen)

10 ounces green peas (fresh or frozen)

1 pound fennel bulb, diced

Salt and freshly ground black pepper to taste

IN A LARGE POT, combine the 5 quarts water, beans, potatoes, carrot and bay leaves, and bring to a boil. In a skillet over medium heat, lightly sauté the garlic in the olive oil until light golden. Add the tomatoes and sauté 10 minutes longer. Add to the pot.

MEANWHILE, in a large skillet, bring the 3 quarts water to a boil and add the spinach, Swiss chard, corn, peas and fennel. Cook 10 minutes, drain and set aside.

WITH A POTATO MASHER, mash down the vegetables in the pot, then add the vegetables from the skillet. Simmer another 10 minutes, uncovered, stirring occasionally. Remove and discard the bay leaves. Add salt and pepper. Let cool uncovered. Before serving, reheat slightly if necessary. Serve warm.

> **PER SERVING:**
> 258 Cal.; 11g Prot.; 5g Fat; 41g Carb.;
> 0mg Chol.; 201mg Sod.; 12g Fiber.

Classic Minestrone

serves 8

| 1 teaspoon virgin olive oil
| 1/4 cup water
| 1 large onion, chopped
| 4 cloves garlic, minced
| 2 leeks, chopped
| 1 carrot, chopped
| 2 celery stalks, chopped
| 1 bay leaf
| 1 tablespoon dried basil
| 1 teaspoon dried oregano
| 1/2 teaspoon dried rosemary
| 1/4 teaspoon freshly ground black pepper
| 3/4 pound fresh mushrooms, sliced
| 1/2 cup dry red wine or vegetable stock (page 178)
| 1/2 small head of green cabbage
| 2 1/2 cups (20 ounces) canned tomatoes, chopped
| 2 cups cooked white beans
| 6 cups water
| 1 cup trimmed green beans (fresh or frozen)
| Salt to taste
| Freshly grated Parmesan cheese (optional)

HEAT the oil and water in a large soup pot and sauté the onion until translucent. Add the garlic, leeks, carrot and celery and sauté until soft, about 10 minutes. Add the herbs and pepper and cook, stirring, briefly; then add the mushrooms. When the mushrooms are soft and have released most of their liquid, about 10 minutes, add the wine or stock and boil until the liquid is reduced by half, about 45 minutes.

SHRED the cabbage and add to the soup along with tomatoes and white beans. Add the water and simmer until the vegetables are tender. Then add the green beans and cook just until they turn bright green. Add salt. Serve with Parmesan cheese (about 1 teaspoon per bowl).

> **PER SERVING:**
> 121 Cal.; 6g Prot.; 1g Fat; 21g Carb.;
> 0mg Chol.; 168mg Sod.; 8g Fiber.

Potato-Leek Soup

serves 6

A simple and satisfying first course, this soup is creamy without the addition of cream. The secret? White rice.

| 6 cups chopped leeks (white part only)
| 1 cup diced celery
| 4 cups peeled and cubed potatoes
| 1 teaspoon virgin olive oil
| 6 cups water
| 1/3 cup uncooked white rice or basmati rice
| 1/4 teaspoon white pepper
| 1 teaspoon dried dill (optional)
| 1/2 teaspoon salt, or to taste
| Splash wine vinegar (optional)
| 1/2 cup watercress, for garnish

IN A LARGE POT over medium heat, sauté the leeks, celery and potatoes in the olive oil for 5 to 7 minutes. Add the water, rice, white pepper, dill and salt. Bring to a boil, lower the heat and simmer until the rice is cooked and the potatoes are very soft, about 15 minutes. Purée the soup 2 to 3 cups at a time in a blender or food processor until smooth. Return the mixture to the pot. Stir in the vinegar. Add the watercress 5 minutes before serving.

> **PER SERVING:**
> 203 Cal.; 3g Prot.; 0.8g Fat; 45g Carb.;
> 0mg Chol.; 222mg Sod.; 6g Fiber.

Carrot Soup with Cilantro

serves 6

- 1 tablespoon unsalted butter or corn oil
- 1/2 teaspoon fennel seeds
- 1 apple, peeled, cored and diced
- 1 1/2 pounds carrots, sliced
- 1/2 pound sweet potatoes, peeled and cubed
- 2 tablespoons white or brown basmati rice or regular long-grain rice
- 1/4 teaspoon turmeric or curry powder
- 5 1/2 cups vegetable stock (page 178) or water
- 1 bay leaf
- Salt and freshly ground black pepper to taste
- Fresh lemon juice to taste (optional)
- 2 tablespoons minced fresh cilantro or fresh parsley

IN A LARGE POT, heat 1/2 tablespoon butter or oil over medium heat. Toast the fennel seeds until darkened, about 2 to 3 minutes. Add the apple, carrots and sweet potatoes, and cook 5 minutes, stirring occasionally. Add the rice, turmeric or curry powder, vegetable stock or water, and bay leaf. Bring to a boil, lower the heat, cover and simmer until the rice and vegetables are tender, about 30 minutes. Drain, reserving broth. Remove and discard the bay leaf.

TRANSFER the mixture and small amounts of the reserved broth in batches to a food processor and purée until smooth. Return the puréed soup and any remaining reserved broth to the soup pot. Simmer 5 minutes. Season with salt, pepper and lemon juice. To serve, drizzle the soup with the remaining melted butter or oil and sprinkle with cilantro or fresh parsley.

> **PER SERVING:**
> 211 Cal.; 4g Prot.; 2g Fat; 44g Carb.
> 6mg Chol.; 234mg Sod.; 4g Fiber.

Creamy Spinach Soup

serves 4

Puréed potatoes give this soup a rich taste and texture.

- 1 large onion, chopped coarsely
- 6 cups water
- 3 potatoes, peeled and chopped
- 3 zucchini, sliced thickly
- 1 tablespoon low-sodium soy sauce
- 2 cups tightly packed fresh spinach leaves
- Freshly ground black pepper to taste
- 1/3 cup trimmed enoki mushrooms (optional)

PLACE the onion in a large pot with 1/2 cup water. Cook and stir over medium-high heat until the onion softens, about 3 minutes. Add the remaining 5 1/2 cups water, the potatoes, zucchini and soy sauce. Bring to a boil. Lower heat, cover and simmer 35 minutes. Add the spinach and pepper, and cook 2 minutes more. Remove from the heat. Purée the soup in batches in a blender. Return to the pot. Stir in the mushrooms. Heat gently for 5 minutes. Serve hot.

PER SERVING:
123 Cal.; 3g Prot.; 0.1g Fat; 27g Carb.;
0mg Chol.; 181mg Sod.; 5g Fiber.

Creamy Pea Soup

serves 6

| 1 tablespoon virgin olive oil
| 2 1/2 cups fresh or frozen peas, or chopped sugar snap peas
| 1 potato, peeled and cubed
| 1 small head butter lettuce (such as bibb or Boston), chopped
| 6 cups water or vegetable stock (page 178)
| Salt and freshly ground black pepper to taste
| Shredded fresh mint, marjoram or basil leaves, for garnish

PLACE 1/2 tablespoon oil, the peas, potato and lettuce in a large pot and cook over medium-low heat for 5 minutes. Add the water or stock and bring to a boil. Lower the heat, cover and simmer until the vegetables are very tender, about 20 minutes.

IN A FOOD PROCESSOR or blender, purée the soup until creamy. Return to the pot and reheat slowly. Season with salt and pepper. Serve in shallow soup bowls, garnished with the remaining 1/2 tablespoon oil and herbs.

PER SERVING:
100 Cal.; 4g Prot.; 2g Fat; 16g Carb.;
0mg Chol.; 183mg Sod.; 4g Fiber.

Cream of Parsley Soup

serves 8

Quick and super-easy, this starter course has everything going for it, including an appealing fresh spring-green color.

| 8 cups vegetable stock (page 178)
| 2 cups packed, chopped fresh parsley leaves
| 1 pound soft tofu
| Salt to taste
| White pepper to taste
| 8 sprigs of fresh parsley, for garnish

IN A LARGE POT, combine the vegetable stock and parsley. Bring to a boil, lower the heat, cover and barely simmer, 5 minutes only. Remove from the heat. Pour the stock and solids through a wire mesh strainer into a large bowl; set aside.

IN A FOOD PROCESSOR fitted with a steel blade, process the drained parsley, tofu and 2 cups of the stock until the parsley is very finely chopped. Return to the pot. Stir in the reserved broth, salt and white pepper, and reheat gently. (Do not boil.) Ladle the soup into 8 bowls. Garnish each bowl with parsley.

PER SERVING:
60 Cal.; 5g Prot.; 3g Fat; 3g Carb.;
0mg Chol.; 322mg Sod.; 1g Fiber.

Gingered Green Soup

serves 6

I cup chopped onions

I cup peeled, chopped celery or fennel

I cup peeled, cubed potatoes

I small zucchini, chopped

1/3 cup uncooked basmati or other white rice

1/8 teaspoon white pepper

I bay leaf

Pinch dried thyme

Pinch dried basil

7 to 8 cups water

4 cups chopped string beans

1/4 cup chopped fresh parsley

One 3-inch piece ginger root

1/2 teaspoon salt, or to taste

1/4 teaspoon freshly ground black pepper, or to taste

2 to 3 tablespoons garnish of choice: Chopped fresh
chives, mint, cilantro, scallions (green and white
parts), basil leaves

COMBINE the onions, celery or fennel, potatoes, zucchini, rice, white pepper, bay leaf, herbs and water in a large pot. Bring to a boil, lower the heat and simmer until the potatoes are tender, about 15 minutes. Add the string beans and simmer, uncovered, until tender, about 10 minutes. Add the parsley. Remove and discard the bay leaf.

PURÉE the soup in batches until smooth, adding water if necessary. Peel the ginger root, grate and press out the ginger juice through a strainer into a small bowl. Add 2 to 3 teaspoons of the juice to the soup. Add salt, pepper and garnish of choice. Serve hot or cold.

> **PER SERVING:**
> 98 Cal.; 3g Prot.; 0.4g Fat; 21g Carb.;
> 0mg Chol.; 200mg Sod.; 5g Fiber.

Kabocha Squash Soup

serves 8

Kabocha is a sweet Japanese squash. It's round and dark green. Look for it in a well-stocked supermarket or Asian grocer.

3 leeks, sliced thinly

2 tablespoons vegetable oil

3 green apples, peeled, cored and diced

I kabocha squash, peeled, seeded and diced

4 cups vegetable stock (page 178)

One 12-ounce can evaporated milk or evaporated skim
milk

3 cups cooked short-grain brown rice

1/4 teaspoon ground ginger

Salt to taste

IN A LARGE POT, cook the leeks in the oil over low heat for 10 minutes, stirring occasionally. Add the apples, squash and stock. Bring to a boil, lower the heat, cover and simmer for 10 minutes. Add the milk, rice, ginger and salt. Heat through.

> **PER SERVING:**
> 270 Cal.; 8g Prot.; 5g Fat; 51g Carb.;
> 2mg Chol.; 197mg Sod.; 8g Fiber.

Russian Bean-and-Potato Soup

serves 4

| 1 tablespoon vegetable oil
| 1 large onion, sliced thinly
| 3 russet potatoes, cubed
| 1/2 pound green beans, cut into 1-inch pieces
| 5 cups vegetable stock (page 178)
| 2 tablespoons whole-wheat pastry flour
| 1/3 cup low-fat sour cream
| 3/4 cup prepared sauerkraut (with juice)
| 1 tablespoon dried dill weed
| Salt and white pepper to taste

IN A LARGE POT over medium-high heat, heat the oil and sauté the onion until limp, about 5 minutes. Add the potatoes and green beans, and cook 3 minutes more, stirring frequently. Add the stock as needed by tablespoonfuls to keep the potatoes from scorching; then add the remaining stock. Lower heat, cover and cook for 1 hour on your stovetop or 3 hours in a slow cooker.

COMBINE the flour and sour cream in a small bowl. Add to the hot stew by spoonfuls, stirring to blend. Add the sauerkraut and dill. Let cook 15 more minutes on stovetop or 30 minutes in the slow cooker. Season with salt and white pepper.

> **PER SERVING:**
> 182 Cal.; 4g Prot.; 5g Fat; 26g Carb.;
> 0mg Chol.; 323mg Sod.; 15g Fiber.

Savory Custard Soup

serves 4

Considered a delicacy in Japan, this soup gets an update: tofu takes the place of eggs.

| 1 pound soft tofu
| 1 cup vegetable stock (preferably made from kombu or shiitake mushrooms; see page 178)
| 2 tablespoons soy sauce
| 3 tablespoons sake, white wine or dry sherry
| 4 to 8 spears asparagus
| 4 large white button mushrooms or shiitake mushrooms (either fresh or reconstituted), cut in half or quartered
| 8 to 12 ginkgo nuts, shelled (optional)
| 2 scallions (green and white parts), minced or sliced

IN A FOOD PROCESSOR or blender, process the tofu, stock, soy sauce, and sake, wine or sherry until well blended. Cut the asparagus into 1/2-inch lengths and steam until barely tender, about 2 to 3 minutes.

DISTRIBUTE the asparagus, mushrooms and ginkgo nuts equally in the bottom of 4 heat-resistant ceramic coffee mugs. Fill the mugs three-quarters full with the tofu mixture. Cover each mug with aluminum foil, and place the mugs in a large pot. Fill the pot with water so the bottom half of the mugs are covered. Cover the pot, bring to a boil, lower the heat and simmer until the custard has risen and set, about 40 minutes. Top each mug with scallions and serve at once.

> **PER SERVING:**
> 98 Cal.; 10g Prot.; 4g Fat; 6g Carb.;
> 0mg Chol.; 524mg Sod.; 2g Fiber.

Caribbean Black Bean Soup

serves 6

1 1/3 cups dry black beans, soaked overnight in water to cover

7 to 8 cups vegetable stock (page 178) or water

1/2 cup flat beer or nonalcoholic beer

1/4 cup dark rum, additional vegetable stock or water

4 cloves garlic, minced

2 medium onions, sliced

2 tablespoons butter or vegetable oil

1 cup finely chopped celery

1 green bell pepper, seeded and diced

1 red bell pepper, seeded and diced

1 chili pepper, seeded and minced

2 large carrots, peeled and diced

1/2 cup canned crushed tomatoes

1 1/2 tablespoons ground cumin

1/2 tablespoon chili powder

1 teaspoon red pepper sauce

1/2 teaspoon freshly ground black pepper

1/2 teaspoon salt

1/4 teaspoon cayenne pepper

1 tablespoon minced fresh cilantro

Yogurt or sour cream (optional)

DRAIN the beans. Place in a large pot with the stock or water, beer, rum or additional liquid, garlic and half of the onions. Simmer, uncovered, for 1 to 2 hours, stirring occasionally. (If the stock evaporates too quickly, lower the heat, add up to 2 cups of hot water and continue simmering.)

HEAT the butter or oil in a saucepan. Sauté the remaining onions, celery, peppers and carrots over medium heat until the vegetables are soft, about 5 to 7 minutes. Set aside.

WHEN the beans are soft, purée half of the bean mixture in a food processor fitted with a steel blade. Return the purée to the pot and add the sautéed vegetables, crushed tomatoes and seasonings. Bring to a simmer and cook 15 minutes, stirring occasionally. Add a little more hot water or rum if soup is too thick, or continue to simmer if it is too thin. Serve with a dollop of yogurt or sour cream.

> **PER SERVING:**
> 139 Cal.; 5g Prot.; 4g Fat; 20g Carb.;
> 10mg Chol.; 281mg Sod.; 5g Fiber.

Spinach and Pea Soup

serves 6

This easy-to-make soup is a vivid green.

| 1/2 tablespoon virgin olive oil
| 1/2 tablespoon butter
| 2 medium leeks (white part only), sliced
| 1 medium onion, sliced
| 3 medium carrots, sliced
| 1 stalk celery, chopped
| 10 sprigs fresh parsley, chopped
| 1/4 teaspoon dried marjoram (or 1 teaspoon fresh marjoram)
| 1 teaspoon salt
| 5 1/2 cups water
| 1 cup fresh or frozen peas
| 1 large bunch spinach, stems removed
| Freshly ground black pepper to taste
| 1 to 2 teaspoons fresh lemon juice or white wine vinegar
| Garnishes: Calendula, borage blossoms or croutons (optional)

HEAT the oil and butter in a large pot over medium-high heat. Add the leeks, onion, carrots, celery, parsley, marjoram, salt and 1/2 cup water. Stir well and cook 1 or 2 minutes, then add the remaining 5 cups water. Bring to a boil, lower the heat, cover and simmer until the vegetables are tender, about 25 minutes.

STIR the peas and spinach leaves into the soup until they wilt and turn bright green. Remove from the heat. In a food processor or blender, process the soup in batches at high speed until smooth. Return to the pot.

SEASON with pepper, and stir in enough lemon juice or vinegar to enhance the flavor. Garnish and serve at once.

PER SERVING:
83 Cal.; 5g Prot.; 2g Fat; 13g Carb.
3mg Chol.; 453mg Sod.; 5g Fiber.

Calabasa Soup with Lima Beans

serves 4

Calabasa is a favorite squash in Central and South America. It's large and round with orange and green coloring on the outside and an orange-yellow, mild-flavored flesh. Another uncommon ingredient—red miso—is an easy find in natural food stores. This condiment, made from soybeans, comes in various flavors, from light and mellow to dark and quite salty. Red miso is among the salty varieties; you may substitute another salty miso if desired.

| 1 cup dry lima beans, soaked overnight in water to cover
| 4 to 5 cups fresh water
| 4 to 5 cups peeled and cubed calabasa
| 2 bay leaves
| 5 cups water
| 1 to 2 tablespoons red miso dissolved in 1/2 cup water (or salt to taste)

DRAIN and rinse the beans. In a large pot, bring to a boil in fresh water. Add the calabasa, bay leaves and water. Simmer until the beans are soft and the calabasa "melts" into the soup, about 1 hour. Remove 1 cup of the soup and process in a blender until smooth, then return it to the pot. Add the dissolved miso or salt. Remove and discard the bay leaves. Serve hot.

Spicy Thai Soup

serves 4

This dish calls for traditional Thai ingredients such as lemon grass, an herb that lends a subtle, lemony perfume to the soup, and kaffir lime leaves, which impart a citrus flavor. Both are available in Asian markets. If you prefer, opt for the suggested substitutes.

- 1 quart vegetable stock (page 178) or water
- 1 teaspoon shredded fresh ginger root and a few slivers lime zest
- 5 cloves garlic, crushed
- 1 lemon grass bulb, cut in 1-inch pieces (or 1/2 teaspoon lime zest)
- 4 shallots, sliced thinly
- 3 or more small fresh chili peppers (with seeds), chopped
- 2 tablespoons soy sauce
- One 15-ounce can straw mushrooms, drained
- 4 kaffir lime leaves (or 1 teaspoon lime zest)
- 1/8 cup fresh lime juice
- 1/2 teaspoon freshly ground black pepper
- 1/3 cup chopped fresh cilantro

IN A LARGE POT, bring the stock or water, ginger, garlic, lemon grass or lime zest, shallots, chilies, soy sauce, mushrooms and kaffir lime leaves or zest to a boil. Lower the heat and simmer 15 minutes. Remove the pot from the heat, and add the remaining ingredients. Remove and discard the lemon grass and lime leaves before serving. Serve at once.

Cabbage Soup with Dumplings

serves 6

This variation of cabbage with egg dumplings has a buttery taste without butter. The trick? Using unrefined, cold-pressed corn oil, available in natural food stores and gourmet specialty shops.

DUMPLINGS
- 1 egg and 1 tablespoon water (or 1/4 pound firm tofu and 4 tablespoons water)
- 1 cup sifted whole-wheat pastry flour or barley flour
- 1/8 teaspoon freshly ground black pepper (optional)
- 1/4 teaspoon salt

SOUP
- 1/2 head cabbage
- 1/4 cup water plus 1 teaspoon unrefined, cold-pressed corn oil
- 6 to 8 cups boiling water
- 1 bay leaf
- 1 tablespoon soy sauce, or to taste
- Chopped scallions (green and white parts), for garnish

DUMPLINGS: Beat together the egg and water, or blend the tofu with the water in a blender until smooth. Sift together the dry ingredients. Stir in the egg or blended tofu. Knead 1 minute, then form into 1/2-inch balls. Set aside.

SOUP: Mince the core of the cabbage and shred the leaves finely. Heat the water-oil mixture in a large pot. Add the cabbage and sauté over medium heat until golden. Add the water and bay leaf, and return to a boil. Drop the dumplings into the boiling soup. Bring to a boil again, cover and simmer until the cabbage is very soft and the dumplings float to the top, about 15 to 20 minutes. Remove and discard the bay leaf. Add the soy sauce to the soup and simmer 5 minutes more. Pour into 6 soup bowls. Garnish with scallions.

> **PER SERVING:**
> 94 Cal.; 4g Prot.; 2g Fat; 16g Carb.;
> 36mg Chol.; 277mg Sod.; 1g Fiber.

White Bean and Greens Soup

serves 4

1 cup dry white beans

8 cups water

1 bay leaf

1 medium onion

1/2 cup chopped celery

1/4 cup water

Water or vegetable stock (optional)

3/4 teaspoons salt, or to taste

2 to 3 tablespoons wine vinegar

1 quart chopped Swiss chard leaves

IN A SOUP POT, combine the beans with water and bay leaf. Bring to a boil, lower the heat and simmer, with the lid ajar, until the beans are tender, about 1 1/2 hours. Meanwhile, in a skillet, sauté the onion and celery in 1/4 cup water until soft; add to the beans. If necessary, add the water or stock to bring the soup's volume to 6 cups. Add the salt, vinegar and chard. Cook until the chard is tender but still bright green, about 5 minutes. Remove and discard the bay leaf. Serve at once.

> **PER SERVING:**
> 207 Cal.; 14g Prot.; 1g Fat; 37g Carb.;
> 0mg Chol.; 738mg Sod.; 14g Fiber.

Chickpea-and-Cabbage Soup

serves 4

1/2 onion, chopped

1 clove garlic, crushed

1/4 cup water

1 tomato, peeled and diced

2 cups finely shredded cabbage

1 small potato, diced

4 cups vegetable stock (page 178) or water

2 cups cooked chickpeas

Juice of 1/2 lemon

1 teaspoon paprika

1/2 cup minced fresh parsley

1 teaspoon salt (less if stock is salty)

Water or vegetable stock (optional)

IN A MEDIUM SKILLET, sauté the onion and garlic in water until soft. Stir in the tomato and cabbage. Cover and simmer until the cabbage is cooked, about 10 minutes. Set aside.

IN A LARGE SOUP POT, cook the potato in stock or water until tender, about 15 minutes. Strain off 2 cups of the liquid, and purée in a blender with 1 cup of the chickpeas until smooth. Add the puréed chickpeas and the sautéed vegetables to the soup pot. Stir in the 1 cup remaining chickpeas, lemon juice, paprika, parsley and salt. Thin the soup with additional stock or water to reach desired consistency.

> **PER SERVING:**
> 176 Cal.; 9g Prot.; 2g Fat; 32g Carb.;
> 0mg Chol.; 551mg Sod.; 8g Fiber.

Nostalgic Noodle Soup

serves 6

Tempeh is a savory food made from fermented soybeans. Look for it in natural food stores.

- 8 cups strained vegetable stock (page 178), carrots reserved
- 4 ounces tempeh, cubed, shredded or sliced finely
- Pinch dried tarragon, crumbled
- 1 tablespoon fresh lemon juice
- Handful minced fresh parsley
- 6 ounces vermicelli or spaghetti, broken into 3-inch pieces

POUR the vegetable stock and reserved carrots into a large saucepan. Add the tempeh, tarragon and lemon juice. Bring to a boil. Toss in the parsley and pasta. Lower the heat and simmer until the pasta is *al dente*. Serve at once.

> **PER SERVING:**
> 130 Cal.; 7g Prot.; 2g Fat; 19g Carb.;
> 0mg Chol.; 290mg Sod.; 1g Fiber.

Kreplach in Vegetable Broth

serves 6

Kreplach are filled dumplings that are served in soup or sautéed for a side dish.

PÂTÉ

- 1 tablespoon water
- 3/4 cup egg substitute (or 3 hard-cooked eggs, chopped)
- 2 medium onions, sliced
- 2 medium stalks celery, sliced
- 1/3 cup chopped walnuts
- 2 tablespoons creamy or chunky peanut butter
- 10 ounces fresh green beans, French-cut and cooked until tender-crisp (or one 10-ounce package frozen French-style green beans, thawed and cooked until tender-crisp)
- 2 tablespoons chopped fresh parsley
- 1/2 teaspoon salt, or to taste
- 1/4 teaspoon freshly ground black pepper

WRAPPERS AND BROTH

- 36 wonton wrappers
- 6 cups vegetable stock (page 178)
- Minced fresh parsley, for garnish

PÂTÉ: Spray a small skillet with nonstick cooking spray and add 1 tablespoon water. If you're using egg substitute, scramble it. Remove from the skillet and reserve. Add more spray and water if necessary and sauté the onions and celery until tender, about 5 minutes. Return the egg substitute to the skillet (or add chopped hard-cooked eggs), and cook 1 or 2 minutes. Remove from the heat and let cool. Combine the egg-vegetable mixture and remaining pâté ingredients in a food processor fitted with a steel blade. Pulse on and off until finely chopped but still chunky. (Do not overprocess.) Chill the pâté at least 6 hours to blend the flavors.

WRAPPERS AND BROTH: Put a teaspoon of the pâté filling near one corner of each wonton wrapper, moisten the edges with a drop of water and fold the wrapper over to form a triangle. Press the edges together firmly to seal. Repeat with the remaining wontons. Cook in a large pot of salted boiling water just until they float to the surface and are tender, about 2 minutes. Remove from the water with a slotted spoon and drain. Heat the vegetable stock until steaming, and serve the kreplach in the broth. Garnish with parsley.

> **PER SERVING:**
> 304 Cal.; 14g Prot.; 9g Fat; 36g Carb.;
> 3mg Chol.; 538mg Sod.; 8g Fiber.

Potato-Pumpkin Soup

serves 6

- 8- to 10-pound pumpkin
- 2 medium potatoes, peeled and chopped
- 2 medium white onions, chopped
- 6 cups water
- 1 teaspoon salt, or to taste
- White pepper to taste
- 1 teaspoon dried thyme
- 1/2 cup condensed skim milk
- 2 tablespoons minced fresh parsley, for garnish
- Toasted pumpkin seeds, for garnish (optional)

WITH A HEAVY KNIFE, cut off the top third of the pumpkin. Scoop out the seeds and strings. (Reserve the seeds.) Using a heavy spoon, scoop out the pumpkin flesh, leaving a 1-inch wall inside. Refrigerate the shell and top.

IN A LARGE POT, combine the potatoes, onions, 2 cups pumpkin flesh and water. Add the salt, white pepper and thyme. Bring to a boil, cover and cook over medium heat until the vegetables are fork-tender, about 20 minutes. Meanwhile, preheat oven to 200°F. Place the pumpkin shell and top on a baking tray and place in your oven to warm.

WITH A SLOTTED SPOON, remove the vegetables from the cooking water. Purée the vegetables in a food processor fitted with a steel blade, or mash by hand until no lumps remain. Return the purée to the cooking water. Stir in the condensed milk, adding more if necessary to create desired consistency. Heat gently over low heat until hot. (Do not boil.)

TO SERVE, place the pumpkin shell on a large serving tray. Pour in the hot soup and sprinkle with parsley and toasted pumpkin seeds. Cover with the lid to keep warm.

> **PER SERVING:**
> 103 Cal.; 3g Prot.; 0.1g Fat; 22g Carb.;
> 1mg Chol.; 386mg Sod.; 4g Fiber.

Squash-and-White Bean Soup

serves 8

- 2 tablespoons oil
- 4 cups chopped calabasa, butternut squash or acorn squash
- 2 cloves garlic, minced
- 1 medium onion, sliced
- 1 cup sliced celery
- 1/2 scotch bonnet pepper (or 1 jalapeño pepper), seeded and minced
- 1 tablespoon minced fresh ginger root
- 6 cups vegetable stock (page 178) or water
- 1 tablespoon minced fresh parsley
- 1 tablespoon fresh thyme leaves (or 1 teaspoon dried)
- 1 tablespoon curry powder
- 1 teaspoon ground cumin
- 1/2 teaspoon salt
- 1/2 teaspoon ground allspice
- 1 cup finely chopped kale
- 1 cup cooked white beans

IN A LARGE POT, combine the oil, calabasa or squash, garlic, onion, celery, pepper and ginger. Sauté over medium

heat until soft, about 7 to 10 minutes. Add the vegetable stock or water and seasonings, and simmer 20 minutes, stirring occasionally. Add the kale and beans, and cook 5 to 10 minutes more. Serve at once.

> **PER SERVING:**
> 126 Cal.; 4g Prot.; 3g Fat; 20g Carb.;
> 0mg Chol.; 156mg Sod.; 6g Fiber.

Classic Borscht

serves 8

- 2 tablespoons vegetable oil
- 2 medium onions, chopped
- 1 large carrot, chopped
- 2 stalks celery, chopped
- 1/4 teaspoon freshly ground black pepper
- 1 cup tomato purée
- 1 teaspoon dill weed
- 1 pound beets, peeled and grated
- 1/2 pound potatoes, peeled and grated
- 1/2 small head cabbage, shredded
- 8 cups water
- Juice of 1 lemon
- Tamari or salt to taste
- Yogurt or sour cream (optional)
- Fresh dill, for garnish

HEAT THE OIL in a large pot and sauté the onions until translucent. Add the carrot, celery and pepper, and sauté until the vegetables are soft, about 15 minutes. Add the tomato purée and dill. Simmer 10 minutes. Then add the beets, potatoes, cabbage and water. Bring to a boil, lower the heat and simmer until the vegetables are tender. Add the lemon juice and tamari or salt to taste. Top with a dollop of yogurt or sour cream and garnish with dill.

> **PER SERVING:**
> 107 Cal.; 2g Prot.; 4g Fat; 17g Carb.;
> 0mg Chol.; 102mg Sod.; 4g Fiber.

Potato-Mushroom Soup with Apple

serves 6

This hearty autumn soup combines the earthy flavors of potatoes, mushrooms, onions and scallions. The diced apple provides a sweet, crunchy contrast to the savory broth.

> 6 scallions (green and white parts), sliced thinly
> 1 small onion, finely chopped
> 1 1/2 tablespoons margarine
> 1 tablespoon vegetable oil
> 3 cups peeled and thinly sliced potatoes
> 1 1/2 cups sliced white button mushrooms
> 6 cups vegetable stock (page 178)
> 1 to 2 tablespoons soy sauce
> 1/4 teaspoon freshly ground black pepper
> 1/2 teaspoon dried thyme
> 3 tablespoons chopped fresh Italian flat-leaf parsley
> 1 Rome beauty apple, cored and diced finely

IN A LARGE POT, sauté the scallions and onion in the margarine and oil over medium-high heat for 2 minutes. Add

the potatoes and mushrooms, and sauté 5 minutes, stirring frequently. Add the stock, soy sauce and pepper. Cover and simmer until the potatoes are tender, about 15 minutes more. Stir in the thyme. Before serving, add parsley and apple.

> **PER SERVING:**
> 111 Cal.; 2g Prot.; 5g Fat; 15g Carb.;
> 0mg Chol.; 212mg Sod.; 2g Fiber.

Italian Chickpea Soup

serves 6

This classic Italian soup is a cinch to make when you use canned chickpeas. It freezes well, so make it in quantity for quick and easy suppers.

> 1 medium onion, diced
> 2 large cloves garlic, minced
> 1 small bay leaf
> 1/2 teaspoon dried thyme
> 4 vegetable bouillon cubes
> 4 cups water
> Two 16-ounce cans chickpeas, rinsed
> 1 large sweet potato, peeled and cut in 1-inch cubes
> 3 large carrots, cut in 1-inch cubes
> 1 stalk celery, diced finely
> 1 tablespoon prepared yellow mustard
> 1/3 cup minced fresh parsley leaves
> Freshly ground black pepper to taste

IN A LARGE POT, combine the onion, garlic, bay leaf, thyme, bouillon and water. Bring to a boil and simmer 5 minutes. Add the chickpeas, sweet potato, carrots, celery and mustard; simmer until the vegetables are very soft, about 10 to 12 minutes.

WITH A POTATO MASHER, mash the vegetables and chick-peas to a chunky purée. (The chickpeas will remain mostly whole.) Stir in parsley and pepper.

> ## PER SERVING:
> 286 Cal.; 9g Prot.; 2g Fat; 57g Carb.;
> 0mg Chol.; 574mg Sod.; 10g Fiber.

Bean-and-Dumpling Soup

serves 8

With the use of a pressure cooker, this soup is ready in less than an hour, but it tastes like you slaved all day.

SOUP

- 2 cups dry navy beans or great northern beans
- 2 quarts water
- 2 teaspoons minced garlic, or to taste
- 1 large onion, sliced
- 1 leek, sliced thickly
- 1 tablespoon caraway seeds, crushed in a mortar and pestle
- 1 large bell pepper, sliced
- 2 Hungarian peppers or other mildly hot peppers, chopped (see Note)
- 4 stalks celery, cut into bite-sized chunks
- 1 tablespoon corn or peanut oil

DUMPLINGS

- 1 cup biscuit mix
- 2 eggs
- 1/4 to 1/3 cup soymilk or low-fat milk, depending on desired moistness

SOUP: Soak the beans overnight in water to cover. Add the beans, 2 quarts water, garlic, onion, leek and caraway to your pressure cooker. Bring to pressure, then lower heat to medium-low. Cook for 10 minutes under pressure. Let the pressure drop naturally. Remove the lid and add the remaining soup ingredients.

DUMPLINGS: Mix together all the dumpling ingredients. Drop the mixture by the tablespoonful into the soup. Bring the soup back to a boil. Cook, uncovered, until the dumplings are cooked and the vegetables are tender, about 15 minutes.

Note:

Instead of the Hungarian pepper, you may use 1 poblano pepper or 1/4 teaspoon hot paprika.

> ## PER SERVING:
> 318 Cal.; 17g Prot.; 4g Fat; 53g Carb.;
> 54mg Chol.; 217mg Sod.; 8g Fiber.

Gazpacho

serves 10

Gazpacho is traditionally served uncooked, but it needs to sit for several hours for the flavors to blend.

> 4 cups tomato juice
> 2 cups peeled, seeded and chopped tomatoes (fresh or canned)
> 1 cup chopped cucumber
> 1/2 cup chopped red onion
> 1/2 cup chopped celery
> 1/2 cup whole-kernel corn
> 1/2 cup chopped green bell peppers
> 1/4 cup chopped scallions (green and white parts)
> 1/4 cup chopped zucchini
> 1/4 cup chopped green chilies
> 1/4 cup chopped fresh parsley
> 1/4 cup chopped fresh cilantro (optional)
> 1 to 2 cloves garlic, minced
> 2 tablespoons red wine vinegar
> 2 tablespoons fresh lime juice

COMBINE all the ingredients in a large bowl. Cover and chill for several hours before serving.

> **PER SERVING:**
> 39 Cal.; 2g Prot.; 0.1g Fat; 9g Carb.;
> 0mg Chol.; 18mg Sod.; 2g Fiber.

Chilled Ginger Borscht with Mushrooms

serves 6

This cold soup is elegantly offbeat. It has zip and a nice balance of savory and sweet flavors.

> 2 1/2 pounds beets, trimmed
> 2 quarts vegetable stock (page 178)
> 1/2 cup dry red wine
> 2 to 4 tablespoons soy sauce
> Juice of 1 lemon
> 3 to 4 tablespoons finely slivered fresh ginger root
> 8 ounces white button mushrooms, sliced
> Freshly ground black pepper to taste
> 1 vegetable bouillon cube (optional)

IN A LARGE POT, boil the beets in the stock until tender, about 30 to 45 minutes. Remove the beets with a slotted spoon, and cool them slightly under running water; slip off their skins. Add the remaining ingredients to the beet water. Slice the beets into thin slivers or matchsticks and return them to the soup. Simmer gently for 30 minutes. Chill at least 3 hours before serving.

> **PER SERVING:**
> 88 Cal.; 2g Prot.; 0g Fat; 16g Carb.;
> 0mg Chol.; 437mg Sod.; 5g Fiber.

Jackson's Soup

serves 4

This soup combines Jackson wonder beans, a relative of the kidney bean, with vegetables in a rich broth.

| 1 cup dry Jackson wonder beans or red kidney beans
| 1 1/2 cups sliced white button mushrooms
| 6 cups vegetable stock (page 178)
| 3 scallions (green and white parts), sliced thinly
| 1 stalk celery, diced finely
| 1/2 medium turnip, diced finely
| 1/4 teaspoon freshly ground black pepper
| Chopped fresh parsley, for garnish

COVER the beans with 2 inches of water in a large pot. Bring to a boil and simmer 10 minutes; remove from the heat, cover and let sit 1 hour. (Or soak overnight in water.) Drain and rinse. Return the beans to the pot, and add all the remaining ingredients except the parsley. Bring to a boil, lower the heat, cover and simmer until the beans are tender, about 45 minutes. (If you're using red kidney beans, cook about 1 1/2 hours.)

> **PER SERVING:**
> 129 Cal.; 7g Prot.; 0.3g Fat; 24g Carb.;
> 0mg Chol.; 431mg Sod.; 6g Fiber.

Cantaloupe Soup

serves 4

A bowlful of this sweet soup provides your day's requirement of betacarotene and vitamin C.

| 1 medium cantaloupe
| 1 cup fresh orange juice
| 2 teaspoons fresh lime juice
| 1 cup plain yogurt
| Fresh mint leaves, cut into strips (optional)
| Slivers of melon, for garnish

QUARTER the cantaloupe, remove and discard the seeds and cut the fruit from the rind. Dice the fruit and place it in a food processor or blender. Add the orange and lime juices, and purée until smooth. Place the yogurt in a glass mixing bowl and beat it with a whisk until it's light and smooth. Whisk in the melon mixture.

COVER the bowl and refrigerate until chilled, at least 3 hours. Serve cold, sprinkled with fresh mint leaves. Garnish with slivers of melon.

> **PER SERVING:**
> 110 Cal.; 5g Prot.; 0.2g Fat; 21g Carb.;
> 1mg Chol.; 61mg Sod.; 1g Fiber.

Souper Salad

serves 8

This chilled soup has lots of crunchy vegetables.

> One 46-ounce can tomato juice
> 1 small red onion, chopped finely
> 1 clove garlic, minced
> 1/4 cup water
> 1/2 cup whole-kernel corn (fresh or frozen)
> One 15-ounce can black beans, rinsed
> 1 cucumber, seeded and chopped finely
> 1 red bell pepper, seeded and chopped finely
> 1 green bell pepper, seeded and chopped finely
> 1 zucchini, chopped finely
> 1 stalk celery, chopped finely
> 4 scallions (green and white parts), chopped finely
> One 4-ounce can diced green chilies
> 1 cup finely chopped jicama
> 1/4 cup chopped fresh cilantro or fresh parsley
> 2 tablespoons red wine vinegar
> 2 tablespoons fresh lime juice
> Hot pepper sauce to taste
> 1 teaspoon prepared horseradish
> Freshly ground black pepper to taste
> 16 melba rounds, for garnish

POUR the tomato juice into a large bowl. Set aside. Place the onion, garlic and water in a small saucepan. Cook and stir until the onion softens slightly, about 2 minutes.

ADD the onion-garlic mixture and the remaining ingredients except the melba rounds to the tomato juice. Stir well. Cover and refrigerate several hours to allow flavors to blend. Stir well and pour into soup bowls. Serve with the melba rounds.

> **PER SERVING:**
> 143 Cal.; 6g Prot.; 0.3g Fat; 28g Carb.;
> 0mg Chol.; 774mg Sod.; 6g Fiber.

Easy Creamy Berry Soup

serves 4

This soup makes a tantalizing start or a refreshing finish to a summer meal.

> 2 pints blueberries
> 1 2/3 cups water
> 1/2 cup honey
> 1 cup plain yogurt
> Pinch ground cinnamon (optional)

IN A MEDIUM SAUCEPAN, combine the berries, water and honey, and heat to a gentle simmer. Cook until the fruit breaks down and softens, about 20 minutes. Purée the fruit mixture in a food processor or blender. Transfer to a mixing bowl and stir in the yogurt. Season with cinnamon. Cover and refrigerate until chilled, at least 3 hours.

> **PER SERVING:**
> 247 Cal.; 5g Prot.; 0.2g Fat; 56g Carb.;
> 1mg Chol.; 59mg Sod.; 3g Fiber.

Vegetable Stock

makes 8 cups

4 large carrots, sliced

1 large yellow onion, sliced thinly

1 large bulb fennel (including leaves), chopped coarsely
    (or 4 large stalks celery, chopped)

4 cloves garlic, crushed

2 medium red potatoes, quartered

1 bay leaf

2 tablespoons fresh minced oregano leaves
    (or 2 teaspoons dried)

2 tablespoons fresh minced basil leaves
    (or 2 teaspoons dried)

2 tablespoons fresh minced thyme leaves
    (or 2 teaspoons dried)

Salt and freshly ground black pepper to taste

10 cups water

IN A LARGE SOUP POT, combine all the ingredients. Bring to
a boil, cover, lower heat and simmer for 1 1/2 hours.
Remove and discard the bay leaf. Line a colander with
cheesecloth, set it over a bowl, and strain the broth.
Either discard the vegetables or purée half of them with
the broth for a thicker stock. Store the broth in your
refrigerator for up to 3 days or in your freezer for up to
3 months.

> **PER CUP (STRAINED):**
> 22 Cal.; 0.6g Prot.; 0g Fat; 5g Carb.;
> 0mg Chol.; 288mg Sod.; 1g Fiber.

Quick Stock

makes 5 1/2 cups

2 cups chopped leeks, green part only (or 1 cup chopped
    onion)

2 carrots, peeled and chopped

1 celery stalk (including leaves), chopped

1 bay leaf

10 large sprigs fresh parsley, chopped

1 large clove garlic, sliced

1/4 teaspoon dried marjoram

Pinch dried thyme

1 teaspoon salt

7 cups cold water

COMBINE all the ingredients in a large pot. Bring to a boil,
lower heat and simmer gently for 25 minutes. Strain in a
colander set over a bowl.

> **PER CUP (STRAINED):**
> 12 Cal.; 0 Prot.; 0g Fat; 1g Carb.;
> 0mg Chol.; 406mg Sod.; 0g Fiber.

salads

CALL IT RABBIT FOOD IF YOU MUST, but these salads are anything but boring. With intriguing combinations of vegetables, fruits, pasta, grains, legumes and soyfoods, they run the gamut from the simple to the complex. We've included remakes of high-fat classics, and we've chosen some innovative salads, too. The variety is simply remarkable. If you thought salad meant iceberg lettuce topped with some carrot slices and tomato wedges, you're in for a pleasant surprise.

Antipasto Platter

serves 8

This beautiful platter makes great party fare.

   2 cups whole white button mushrooms

   1 cup canned artichoke hearts (not marinated), drained
     and quartered

   1 tablespoon virgin olive oil

   1 cup balsamic vinegar

   2 tablespoons red wine (optional)

   1 teaspoon dried basil

   1 teaspoon dried oregano

   1 teaspoon salt

   1/2 teaspoon freshly ground black pepper

   1 head romaine lettuce, chopped coarsely

   1 cucumber, sliced thinly

   2 stalks celery, julienned

   4 large tomatoes, cut into eighths

   4 scallions (green and white parts), trimmed and cut in
     half lengthwise

   1/2 cup quartered radishes

   Whites from 3 hard-cooked eggs, chopped coarsely
     (optional)

IN A LARGE BOWL, combine the mushrooms, artichoke hearts, oil, vinegar, wine, basil, oregano, salt and pepper. Toss well. Let marinate at room temperature for 30 minutes.

ARRANGE the lettuce on a large platter. Strain the mushrooms and artichokes from the marinade and place them in the center of the platter. Arrange the remaining vegetables and egg whites around the center. Drizzle the remaining marinade over the antipasto.

PER SERVING:
69 Cal.; 3g Prot.; 2g Fat; 9g Carb.;
0mg Chol.; 320mg Sod.; 4g Fiber.

Simple Salad

serves 8

This mild salad complements rather than competes with any entrée.

   2 heads Boston or bibb lettuce

   8 to 10 plum tomatoes

   Salt and freshly ground black pepper to taste

   3 tablespoons minced fresh parsley

   1 lemon

ARRANGE the lettuce leaves attractively on a large platter. Slice the tomatoes thinly on the diagonal, and arrange the slices on the lettuce. Sprinkle with salt and pepper. Scatter the parsley evenly on top.

CUT the lemon in half lengthwise. Squeeze the juice from 1 lemon half over the salad. Bring the other half to the table in case a diner wants more lemon on his or her portion.

PER SERVING:
33 Cal.; 0.3 Prot.; 0.1g Fat; 6g Carb.;
0mg Chol.; 148mg Sod.; 3g Fiber.

Vibrant Vegetable Salad

serves 6

Here's an opportunity to be extravagant with color and to showcase many beautiful vegetables, including scarlet pickled onions, bright green beans or broccoli, and yellow and purple peppers.

> 3 cups trimmed green beans or chopped broccoli
> 2 tablespoons virgin olive oil
> 2 teaspoons chopped fresh marjoram, tarragon or basil
> Salt to taste
> 2 to 3 red beets
> 1 purple bell pepper
> 2 yellow roasted peppers (page 106)
> 1 recipe Roasted Potatoes with Thyme (page 371)
> 2 medium orange or yellow tomatoes
> 3/4 cup pickled onions (page 365)
> 12 deep-red lettuce leaves
> Blue or purple blossoms, such as borage, rosemary or hyssop (optional)
> 6 lemon wedges

IN A SAUCEPAN fitted with a steamer, steam the beans or broccoli until tender but still firm. Spread on a plate and let cool. Toss with 2 teaspoons oil, herbs and salt.

PREHEAT oven to 350°F. Place the beets in a baking pan with about 1/4 inch water. Cover with foil and bake until tender-firm when pierced with a knife, about 25 minutes. Slip off the skins and slice the beets into rounds or wedges.

CUT the purple pepper in half and remove seeds and membranes, then slice thinly. Cut the roasted peppers into 1/2-inch strips. Slice the potatoes in half or cut into rounds. Cut the tomatoes into wedges or slices.

ARRANGE all of the vegetables on a large platter. Drizzle with the remaining 1 1/3 tablespoons oil, and garnish with lettuce leaves. Top with the blossoms and serve with lemon.

> **PER SERVING:**
> 208 Cal.; 5g Prot.; 7g Fat; 27g Carb.;
> 0mg Chol.; 451mg Sod.; 7g Fiber.

Mixed Vegetable Salad

serves 6

> 1 cup whole-kernel corn (fresh or frozen)
> 1 cup julienned green beans
> 1 cup julienned carrots
> 1 cup julienned zucchini
> 1 cup julienned yellow squash
> 1 cup julienned red bell pepper
> 1/2 cup thinly sliced mild onion
> 1 cup oil-free salad dressing
> Freshly ground black pepper to taste

BRING a pot of water to a boil. Drop in the corn, beans and carrots, and cook 3 minutes. Drain the vegetables and plunge them into cold water. Drain again and place in a large bowl. Add the remaining ingredients and toss well. Refrigerate for 1 hour to blend the flavors.

> **PER SERVING:**
> 79 Cal.; 2g Prot.; 0.1g Fat; 14g Carb.;
> 0mg Chol.; 98mg Sod.; 4g Fiber.

Gazpacho Salad

serves 6

Instead of a spicy and cold soup, gazpacho is creatively transformed into a salad. It's colorful, crunchy and piquant—plus it's easy to make.

> One 16-ounce can tomatoes, drained and chopped
>
> 2 cucumbers, diced
>
> 2 green bell peppers, slivered
>
> 1 onion, chopped
>
> 6 to 8 black olives, pitted (or 2 tablespoons drained capers) (optional)
>
> 2 cloves garlic, minced
>
> Pinch cumin
>
> 1/4 cup red wine vinegar
>
> 1 to 3 tablespoons virgin olive oil
>
> 1 tablespoon minced fresh parsley
>
> 1 tablespoon minced shallots

LAYER the tomatoes, cucumbers, bell peppers, onion and olives or capers in a bowl in that order. In a separate small bowl, mix the remaining ingredients. Pour over the layered vegetables, cover and refrigerate for at least 2 hours. Toss before serving.

> **PER SERVING:**
> 65 Cal.; 1g Prot.; 4g Fat; 9g Carb;
> 0mg Chol.; 127mg Sod.; 3g Fiber.

Roasted Asparagus Salad

serves 6

Fresh orange and lime juices give this light salad plenty of citrus flavor.

SALAD
> 1 pound asparagus, trimmed and cut diagonally into 1/2-inch pieces
>
> Olive oil cooking spray
>
> Salt to taste

DRESSING
> 1/2 cup fresh orange juice
>
> 1 tablespoon fresh lime juice
>
> 2 tablespoons orange marmalade
>
> 1/2 teaspoon grated fresh ginger root
>
> 1 to 2 tablespoons virgin olive oil
>
> 7 cups chopped romaine lettuce
>
> 3 tablespoons toasted pine nuts or slivered almonds, for garnish (page 106)

SALAD: Preheat the oven to 450°F. Spread the asparagus on a baking sheet in a single layer and mist lightly with olive oil cooking spray. Roast until the asparagus is tender when pierced with a knife, about 10 to 12 minutes. Season with salt. Set aside.

DRESSING: In a small blender or bowl, whisk together orange and lime juices, marmalade, ginger and olive oil. Just before serving, arrange the romaine on 6 plates or a platter and top with the asparagus. Pour on the dressing, and garnish with nuts.

> **PER SERVING:**
> 101 Cal.; 3g Prot.; 4g Fat; 8g Carb.;
> 0mg Chol.; 9mg Sod.; 3g Fiber.

Spring Lettuce with Avocado, Radish and Orange

serves 6

You may prepare and refrigerate the vegetables and dressing up to 3 hours in advance, but don't cut the avocado or dress the salad until you're ready to serve it.

DRESSING

> 2 tablespoons fresh lime juice
>
> 2 tablespoons fresh orange juice
>
> 1 to 3 tablespoons fruit-sweetened apricot jam
>
> 1 to 3 tablespoons avocado oil or virgin olive oil
>
> Salt and freshly ground black pepper to taste
>
> 2 tablespoons hot water

SALAD

> 8 cups torn mixed lettuce (such as bibb, looseleaf, romaine, red oakleaf or buttercrunch)
>
> 12 red radishes, sliced thinly
>
> 2 seedless oranges, peeled and sliced thinly
>
> 1 avocado

DRESSING: In a blender, process the lime and orange juices, jam, oil, salt and pepper until smooth. With the machine running, slowly add the water and process until creamy. Set aside.

SALAD: Line a large shallow bowl with lettuce. Alternate rounds of radish and orange slices on top. Cover and refrigerate until serving time.

AT SERVING TIME, peel, pit and dice the avocado into 1/2-inch cubes. Place on top of the salad and drizzle with dressing. Toss if desired and serve at once.

> **PER SERVING:**
> 137 Cal.; 2g Prot.; 7g Fat; 11g Carb.;
> 0mg Chol.; 103mg Sod.; 3g Fiber.

Papaya-and-Watercress Salad with Lime

serves 2

SALAD

> 1/2 cup watercress leaves
>
> 1 cup peeled, seeded and thinly sliced papaya
>
> 1/2 cup canned hearts of palm, drained and sliced
>
> 1/2 cup thinly sliced tomato

DRESSING

> 1 tablespoon fresh lime juice
>
> 1 tablespoon chopped fresh cilantro leaves
>
> 1/4 teaspoon salt
>
> Pinch ground coriander
>
> Pinch allspice

ARRANGE the watercress on 2 small salad plates. Top with layers of papaya, hearts of palm and tomato. Combine the dressing ingredients and drizzle over the salads. Let sit for 30 minutes before serving.

> **PER SERVING:**
> 90 Cal.; 3g Prot.; 0.1g Fat; 19g Carb.;
> 0mg Chol.; 354mg Sod.; 5g Fiber.

Salade à la Niçoise

serves 6

- 2 red onions, sliced thinly
- 2 stalks celery, sliced
- 1/4 cup minced fresh parsley
- 2 or more cloves garlic, minced
- 1 tablespoon virgin olive oil
- 1 to 2 tablespoons red wine vinegar
- 1/2 teaspoon dried basil
- 1/2 teaspoon dried oregano
- 1/4 to 1/2 cup black olives, whole or pitted
- 2 to 3 cups string beans, trimmed
- 1 to 2 cups yellow wax beans
- 4 to 5 new potatoes (or 1/2 small cauliflower)
- Red leaf lettuce, radicchio or Boston lettuce
- Additional ingredients of choice: 1 cup cooked white beans (or 1/2 pound fried tempeh); 2 to 3 hard-boiled eggs, quartered; cherry tomatoes; sliced avocado

COMBINE the onions, celery, parsley, garlic, oil, vinegar, basil, oregano and olives in a dish. Set aside to marinate. Slice the beans on the diagonal or leave whole. Steam or blanch until very bright and just tender. Quarter the potatoes, bring to a boil in water to cover and simmer until tender, about 10 minutes; drain. (If you're using cauliflower, slice it into bite-sized florets and steam until just tender.)

AN HOUR or so before serving, combine the bean-potato mixture with the marinated vegetables. Serve on a bed of lettuce and top with one or more additional ingredients.

> **PER SERVING**
> **(WITHOUT ADDITIONS):**
> 131 Cal.; 3g Prot.; 4g Fat;23g Carb.;
> 0mg Chol.; 53mg Sod.; 5g Fiber.

Moroccan Eggplant Salad

serves 4

North African food has a Mediterranean influence. Tomatoes, olive oil and hot pepper are characteristic.

- 2 medium eggplants, peeled and cubed
- 2 large tomatoes, chopped
- 2 teaspoons cayenne pepper
- 1 teaspoon salt
- 1 tablespoon virgin olive oil
- 1 tablespoon tomato juice

BOIL the eggplant in water to cover for 30 minutes; drain. Squeeze out excess moisture. In a large skillet over medium heat, sauté the eggplant, tomatoes, cayenne and salt in oil and tomato juice for 5 minutes, mashing the ingredients with a fork until somewhat smooth. Chill before serving.

> **PER SERVING:**
> 86 Cal.; 1g Prot.; 3g Fat; 12g Carb.;
> 0mg Chol.; 561mg Sod.; 4g Fiber.

Marinated Vegetable Salad

serves 12

  6 carrots, grated

  1 cup French-cut green beans, steamed

  1 cup shredded cabbage

  1 cucumber, grated coarsely

  1 cup bean sprouts

  2 cloves garlic, minced

  1/2 teaspoon to 2 teaspoons sambal or cayenne pepper

  3 tablespoons brown sugar

  3 tablespoons rice vinegar or cider vinegar

  1 tablespoon fresh lime or lemon juice

  1 to 2 teaspoons turmeric (optional)

PLACE the vegetables in a large bowl. Mix together the remaining ingredients. (The turmeric will give the dish a lovely yellow color.) Pour this mixture over the vegetables. Toss well, cover and chill for at least 4 hours. Serve cold or at room temperature.

> **PER SERVING:**
> 39 Cal.; 1g Prot.; 0.1g Fat; 9g Carb.;
> 0mg Chol.; 17mg Sod.; 3g Fiber.

Winter Green Salad with Olives

serves 6

This salad's flavor depends on the kind of olives you use: Kalamatas, Sicilians and tiny black olives all work well.

VINAIGRETTE

  1/3 cup fresh orange juice

  3 tablespoons fresh lemon juice

  2 tablespoons virgin olive oil

  1 tablespoon chopped, drained capers (see Note)

  1/2 teaspoon dried oregano

  Salt and freshly ground black pepper to taste

SALAD

  6 cups mixed winter greens

  1/2 cup pomegranate cells

  3 tablespoons chopped pitted green or black olives

  2 tablespoons toasted pine nuts (page 106)

VINAIGRETTE: Combine all the ingredients except the salt and pepper in a jar. Cover and shake well. Season with salt and pepper.

SALAD: Combine the greens, pomegranate cells, olives and vinaigrette in a large bowl. Sprinkle with pine nuts.

> **PER SERVING:**
> 78 Cal.; 1g Prot.; 6g Fat; 4g Carb.;
> 0mg Chol.; 128mg Sod.; 1g Fiber.

Apple-Walnut Salad with Watercress

serves 4

Served with a loaf of crusty bread, this colorful salad makes a satisfying light lunch.

DRESSING

- 2 tablespoons fresh lemon juice
- 2 tablespoons vegetable stock (page 178)
- 1 1/2 tablespoons vegetable oil
- 1/2 teaspoon salt (or 1 teaspoon soy sauce)
- 1/4 teaspoon freshly ground black pepper

SALAD

- 1 large bunch watercress, tough stems removed
- 1 large carrot, shredded
- 1 red Delicious apple, cored and shredded
- 2 tablespoons fresh lemon juice
- 1/4 to 1/2 cup chopped walnuts

DRESSING: In a small bowl, whisk together the dressing ingredients.

SALAD: Arrange the watercress around the outside edge of a large platter. Scatter the carrot next to the watercress. In a small bowl, toss the apple with lemon juice. Spoon the apple into the center of the platter. Scatter the nuts on the top of the apples. Drizzle the dressing over the salad. Serve at once.

PER SERVING:
159 Cal.; 2g Prot.; 10g Fat; 17g Carb.;
0mg Chol.; 300mg Sod.; 2g Fiber.

Fennel-and-Red Onion Salad

serves 4

- 1 bulb fennel
- 1 medium red onion
- 1 small head of Boston or bibb lettuce
- 1 tablespoon finely chopped fresh cilantro leaves or fresh parsley
- Salt and white pepper to taste
- 1 to 2 tablespoons virgin olive oil
- Juice of 1 lemon

SEPARATE the fennel bulb from its stem, trimming away the root end and any dark spots. Thinly slice lengthwise, making slivers that resemble the petals of a blossom. Slice the red onion lengthwise in slivers.

ARRANGE the lettuce on 4 individual plates. Top with the fennel, red onion and cilantro or parsley. Sprinkle with salt and pepper. Drizzle with the oil and lemon juice. Serve at once.

PER SERVING:
104 Cal.; 1g Prot.; 3g Fat; 14g Carb.;
0mg Chol.; 151mg Sod.; 3g Fiber.

Thai Salad with Peanut Dressing

serves 4

This salad has a bit of crunch and lots of flavor.

SALAD

- 1 head lettuce (preferably butter lettuce), torn into bite-sized pieces
- 1/2 cucumber, sliced
- 1 carrot, sliced or slivered
- Orange slices, for garnish
- 2 tablespoons chopped fresh cilantro leaves, for garnish

DRESSING

- 1/4 cup low-salt, low-sugar peanut butter
- 4 tablespoons water
- One thin slice fresh ginger root, peeled and minced (or 1/2 teaspoon ground ginger)
- 1 tablespoon soy sauce
- 1/4 cup fresh lime juice
- 1 teaspoon sugar
- 1/2 small clove garlic, minced (optional)
- Dash hot chili paste (optional)
- 2 tablespoons chopped unsalted dry-roasted peanuts, for garnish (optional)

LINE a large platter with the lettuce. Arrange the cucumber and carrot on top of the lettuce, and garnish with orange and cilantro. In a bowl, stir together the dressing ingredients except the peanuts and drizzle over salad. Sprinkle with peanuts.

Variations:

- If you prefer a sweeter dressing, add another 1 or 2 teaspoons of sugar or reduce the amount of lime juice.
- Use the peanut dressing as dipping sauce for vegetables or cubes of tofu, or toss it with cooked noodles.

> **PER SERVING WITH**
> **1 TABLESPOON DRESSING:**
> 66 Cal.; 3g Prot.; 3g Fat; 6g Carb.;
> 0mg Chol.; 117mg Sod.; 3g Fiber.

Spinach-and-Mushroom Salad

serves 4

- Bowl of fresh spinach leaves
- 3/4 cup thinly sliced white button mushrooms
- 1/3 cup nonfat yogurt
- 1 1/2 teaspoons vegetable oil
- 1/4 cup fresh parsley, fresh basil or cilantro leaves
- 1 teaspoon chopped fresh chives
- 2 teaspoons fresh lemon juice
- 1/4 teaspoon salt
- 1 clove garlic, pressed or minced (optional)

TOSS together the spinach and mushrooms in a serving bowl. In a blender, combine the remaining ingredients to make a dressing. Drizzle over the salad just before serving.

> **PER SERVING:**
> 84 Cal.; 4g Prot.; 6g Fat; 6g Carb.;
> 2mg Chol.; 192mg Sod.; 5g Fiber.

Grilled Green Bean-and-Eggplant Salad

serves 6

Use long, thin Japanese eggplants for this salad because they grill faster than the plump variety.

    2 Japanese eggplants
    1/2 pound fresh green beans, trimmed but left whole
    1/4 cup balsamic vinegar
    2 large red bell peppers, seeded and julienned
    2 cups mixed greens
    1 to 2 tablespoons minced red onion
    1 tablespoon virgin olive oil
    2 tablespoons fresh lemon juice
    2 tablespoons balsamic vinegar
    Salt and freshly ground black pepper to taste

PREPARE your grill. Slice the eggplants into rounds about 1/4 inch thick. In a bowl, toss the eggplants and green beans with 1/4 cup balsamic vinegar. Place the vegetables on a grill rack, and grill until lightly browned and tender, about 8 to 10 minutes, turning frequently.

IN A LARGE salad bowl, toss together the bell peppers, greens, onion, oil, lemon juice, balsamic vinegar, salt and black pepper. Arrange the grilled vegetables on top. Serve at once.

Helpful hint:

To prevent your vegetables from falling into the flames, use a grilling rack, which looks like a baking sheet with holes in it. The racks are available at gourmet cookware stores.

> **PER SERVING:**
> 82 Cal.; 2g Prot.; 3g Fat; 44g Carb.;
> 0mg Chol.; 276mg Sod.; 3g Fiber.

Oriental Green Salad

serves 4

SALAD
    1 cup torn lettuce
    1 cup torn Chinese cabbage
    1 cup mung bean sprouts
    1/2 cup trimmed snow peas
    1/2 cup canned sliced bamboo shoots
    1/4 cup thinly sliced carrots
    1/4 cup thinly sliced celery
    1/4 cup chopped broccoli

DRESSING
    3 tablespoons low-sodium soy sauce
    3 tablespoons rice vinegar
    2 tablespoons water
    1/4 teaspoon minced fresh garlic
    1/4 teaspoon minced fresh ginger root

SALAD: Combine all the vegetables in a large bowl. Toss to mix. Set aside.

DRESSING: Combine all the dressing ingredients in a blender or a small jar. Process briefly or shake well to combine the ingredients. Pour over the salad and toss to coat. Serve at once.

> **PER SERVING:**
> 42 Cal.; 3g Prot.; 0.1g Fat; 7g Carb.;
> 0mg Chol.; 464mg Sod.; 3g Fiber.

Salade de Mesclun

serves 8

Mesclun is a wonderful mix of wild field lettuces. If you can't find it, combine equal amounts of mild and peppery lettuces.

> 2 pounds mesclun or mixture of greens
>
> 3 tablespoons canola oil
>
> 2 tablespoons walnut oil
>
> 1/4 cup red wine vinegar
>
> 1 1/2 tablespoons raspberry preserves
>
> 1/2 tablespoon Dijon mustard
>
> Salt to taste
>
> Freshly ground pepper to taste
>
> 1 cup Parmesan cheese (optional)

ARRANGE the greens in a large serving bowl. Combine the remaining ingredients except the Parmesan in a jar. Shake well. Pour over the greens. Sprinkle with Parmesan and serve at once.

> **PER SERVING:**
> 86 Cal.; 0 Prot.; 6g Fat; 13g Carb.;
> 0mg Chol.; 28mg Sod.; 1g Fiber.

Tangy Cucumber Salad

serves 4

Served with wedges of pita bread, this salad makes a cool, light lunch or a delicious appetizer.

> 2 1/2 cups plain yogurt
>
> 1/2 teaspoon minced garlic, or to taste
>
> 1/2 teaspoon dried dillweed
>
> 1/2 teaspoon dried mint
>
> 1 large Kirby cucumber or regular cucumber, grated

MIX together all the ingredients. Refrigerate 1 hour before serving.

> **PER SERVING:**
> 87 Cal.; 8g Prot.; 0.3g Fat; 12g Carb.;
> 3mg Chol.; 111mg Sod.; 0.5g Fiber.

Spicy Cucumber Salad

serves 4

This Thai classic is often served as a condiment to accompany satay (skewered food dipped in peanut sauce).

> 2 cucumbers, peeled
>
> 1/2 small red onion, chopped
>
> 1 to 2 fresh green chilies, seeded and minced
>
> 3 tablespoons fresh lime juice
>
> 1 tablespoon soy sauce
>
> 1 tablespoon sugar
>
> 1 tablespoon sesame oil
>
> 1/4 cup chopped, unsalted dry-roasted peanuts, for garnish (optional)

CUT the cucumbers in half lengthwise, remove the seeds and slice the cucumbers thinly. Place the slices, onion and chilies in a bowl. Combine the remaining ingredients except the peanuts and drizzle over the salad. Toss well. Garnish with the peanuts and serve at once.

> **PER SERVING:**
> 74 Cal.; 1g Prot.; 3g Fat; 7g Carb.;
> 0mg Chol.; 260mg Sod.; 2g Fiber.

Minted Cucumber Salad

serves 4

This cool, minty salad complements a spicy main dish. It also can be added as a garnish to sandwiches and burgers.

> 3 to 4 Kirby cucumbers, peeled and sliced (see Note)
>
> 3 to 4 tablespoons chopped fresh mint leaves
>
> 3 to 4 tablespoons chopped fresh parsley (optional)
>
> 1 tablespoon fresh lime or lemon juice, or more to taste
>
> Pinch salt
>
> Drizzle of virgin olive oil (optional)

SLICE the cucumbers in half lengthwise, then slice diagonally to make 1/4-inch-thick slices. Toss with the remaining ingredients. The salad keeps for 2 days in your refrigerator.

Variations:

- Add chopped tomatoes, lettuce, olives, onions or sliced radishes.
- For a quick Mediterranean meal, toss in some chickpeas and cooked rice, couscous or pasta.

Note:

If you can't find Kirby cucumbers, you may use the regular kind. Be sure to peel them, cut them in half lengthwise and scoop out the seeds before slicing.

> **PER SERVING:**
> 12 Cal.; 0 Prot.; 0g Fat; 3g Carb.;
> 0mg Chol.; 36mg Sod.; 1g Fiber.

Pickled Cucumber Salad

serves 4

| 3 medium cucumbers, peeled, halved and seeded
| 1/3 cup distilled white vinegar
| 1 1/4 teaspoons sugar
| 1/4 teaspoon cayenne pepper, or to taste
| 1 tablespoon chopped fresh cilantro

SLICE the cucumber 1/2 inch thick, and place in a medium serving bowl. Add the remaining ingredients and toss gently. Cover and refrigerate at least 1 hour before serving.

PER SERVING:
29 Cal.; 0.1g Prot.; 0g Fat; 6g Carb.;
0mg Chol.; 3mg Sod.; 1g Fiber.

Chinese Radish Salad

serves 4

The tang of radishes awakens this combination.

| 1/2 cup thinly sliced radishes
| 1 carrot, sliced thinly
| 1 tablespoon soy sauce
| 1 tablespoon rice wine vinegar
| 1 teaspoon honey
| 1 teaspoon peanut oil
| 1/2 teaspoon hot pepper sauce (optional)
| 2 cups alfalfa sprouts

COMBINE the radishes and carrot in a shallow container. In a small bowl, whisk together the soy sauce, vinegar, honey, oil and hot pepper sauce. Pour over the radishes and carrot. Cover and marinate in your refrigerator for at least 1 hour. Just before serving, place the alfalfa sprouts on a small serving dish and arrange the radishes and carrots on top.

PER SERVING:
34 Cal.; 1g Prot.; 1g Fat; 5g Carb.;
0mg Chol.; 267mg Sod.; 1g Fiber.

White Radish Salad

serves 6

This traditional Eastern European salad is made even better with a flavorful oil, such as walnut or hazelnut. If icicle radishes aren't available, use daikon radish (see Note).

| 1/2 pound white radishes, preferably icicle radishes
| 1/2 teaspoon salt
| 4 tablespoons walnut or hazelnut oil, preferably unprocessed
| 1/4 teaspoon freshly ground white pepper
| Boston or bibb lettuce leaves
| 3 tablespoons finely minced fresh parsley
| 6 tomato roses, for garnish (see Note)

USING a food processor fitted with the smallest grater disc, grate the radishes into long, thin shreds. Set a non-reactive colander (such as one made from stainless steel or enamel) in your sink, add the radishes and sprinkle with salt. Let drain for 15 minutes.

TRANSFER the radishes to a dishcloth and bring the ends of the cloth together, twisting to extract excess liquid. Place the radishes in a medium mixing bowl; add the oil and white pepper. Toss well.

LINE 6 small salad plates with lettuce leaves. Divide the radishes equally among them in small mounds. Sprinkle with minced parsley and garnish with tomato roses.

Notes:

- The long, white Japanese radish known as the daikon, which often weighs 3 to 5 pounds, has a sweet, pungent flavor. Scrub and peel before use. Eat daikon raw in salads or cooked in stir-fries. You may substitute red radishes if you can't find daikon.

- To make tomato roses, cut the skin away from each tomato in long spiral, then coil tightly.

> **PER SERVING:**
> 87 Cal.; 0.5g Prot.; 9g Fat; 1g Carb.;
> 0mg Chol.; 185mg Sod.; 1g Fiber.

Spaghetti Squash Salad

serves 4

> 1 spaghetti squash
>
> 8 cherry tomatoes, quartered
>
> 1 green bell pepper, chopped
>
> 4 scallions (green and white parts), sliced
>
> 2 cloves garlic, minced
>
> 1 tablespoon capers (optional)
>
> 2 tablespoons virgin olive oil
>
> 2 tablespoons red wine vinegar
>
> Salt and freshly ground black pepper to taste

PREHEAT oven to 350°F. Prick the squash with a fork and bake until it's easy to make an indentation in the shell with a spoon, about 45 to 60 minutes. (Or, pierce the skin in several places with a fork and microwave on high power for 10 to 15 minutes.) Cut the squash in half and remove the seeds and stringy flesh. Using a fork, gently scrape remaining flesh to remove the spaghetti-like strands of squash.

IN A LARGE salad bowl, combine the strands of squash, tomatoes, green bell pepper, scallions, garlic and capers. Toss with the oil and vinegar. Season with salt and pepper. Serve at once.

> **PER SERVING:**
> 179 Cal.; 4g Prot.; 7g Fat; 25g Carb.;
> 0mg Chol.; 146mg Sod.; 7g Fiber.

Greens with Avocado and Pear

serves 6

This simple salad needs little in the way of dressing. Try a splash of lemon juice, balsamic vinegar or your favorite vinaigrette.

> 1 pear, cored and diced
>
> 1 avocado, peeled, pitted and diced
>
> 1/2 cucumber, peeled and sliced
>
> 4 cups chopped romaine or red leaf lettuce, or a combination

COMBINE the pear, avocado and cucumber in a salad bowl. Add lettuce and toss gently.

Variation:

You may substitute diced apple or jícama for the pear, or add chopped fresh cilantro to the combination of chopped greens.

> **PER SERVING**
> **(WITHOUT DRESSING):**
> 79 Cal.; 1g Prot.; 5g Fat; 7g Carb.;
> 0mg Chol.; 7mg Sod.; 3g Fiber.

Corn-Olive Salad

serves 6

| One 16-ounce package frozen whole-kernel corn, thawed
| 1 red or green bell pepper, cut into 1-inch strips
| 1/4 cup black olives, chopped coarsely
| 1/4 cup green olives, chopped coarsely
| 1 celery stalk, diced
| 1 scallion (green and white parts), chopped finely
| 1 tablespoon virgin olive oil
| 3 tablespoons apple cider vinegar
| 1 teaspoon honey
| 1/2 teaspoon dried dillweed
| Freshly ground black pepper to taste

COMBINE all the ingredients in a large bowl and mix thoroughly. Place in your refrigerator until ready to serve.

> **PER SERVING:**
> 107 Cal.; 2g Prot.; 4g Fat; 16g Carb.;
> 0mg Chol.; 156mg Sod.; 5g Fiber.

Coleslaw with Vinaigrette

serves 6

VINAIGRETTE

| 2 tablespoons balsamic vinegar
| 6 tablespoons cider vinegar
| 2 tablespoons Dijon mustard
| 1 tablespoon low-sodium soy sauce
| 2 teaspoons honey
| 1/2 teaspoon celery seed
| 1/2 teaspoon caraway seed
| 1/4 teaspoon freshly ground black pepper

SALAD

| 2 cups shredded green cabbage
| 2 cups shredded red cabbage
| 1 carrot, julienned
| 1 red bell pepper, julienned
| 1 yellow bell pepper, julienned
| 1/4 cup scallions (green and white parts), chopped finely
| 1/4 cup minced fresh parsley

VINAIGRETTE: Mix the vinaigrette ingredients together in a small jar. Set aside.

SALAD: Combine the vegetables in a large bowl. Pour the vinaigrette over the vegetables and toss well. Refrigerate at least 1 hour to blend the flavors.

> **PER SERVING:**
> 38 Cal.; 1g Prot.; 0.8g Fat; 6g Carb.;
> 0mg Chol.; 130mg Sod.; 1g Fiber.

Coleslaw with Pineapple Dressing

serves 8

This vitamin-rich classic needs no high-fat mayo.

COLESLAW

- 1/2 head green cabbage, shredded
- 1/8 head purple cabbage, shredded
- 1 cup shredded carrots
- 1 cup crushed pineapple, drained

DRESSING

- 3 tablespoons cornstarch
- 2 cups water
- 1/2 cup unsweetened pineapple juice
- 3 tablespoons fresh lemon juice
- 1 teaspoon vanilla extract
- 1 tablespoon sugar
- 1 tablespoon vinegar
- 1/2 teaspoon salt

COLESLAW: Combine the vegetables and pineapple in a serving bowl. Set aside.

DRESSING: In a saucepan, dissolve the cornstarch in 1/2 cup water. Stir in the remaining 1 1/2 cups water. Bring the mixture to a boil, stirring constantly until thickened. Remove from the heat. Add the juices and vanilla. Chill. Stir 3/4 cup of the dressing into the coleslaw. Chill thoroughly before serving. Pass the remainder at table.

> **PER SERVING:**
> 87 Cal.; 1g Prot.; 0.1g Fat; 21g Carb.;
> 0mg Chol.; 17mg Sod.; 2g Fiber.

Roasted Red Pepper-and-Potato Salad

serves 8

DRESSING

- 1/2 cup virgin olive oil
- 1/4 cup raspberry vinegar or red wine vinegar
- 1 1/2 teaspoons Dijon mustard
- Salt and white pepper to taste

SALAD

- 2 pounds new potatoes (about 20 to 24)
- 6 to 8 red bell peppers, roasted, peeled and sliced
- 2 to 4 ounces feta cheese

DRESSING: Combine the oil and vinegar in a jar, cap the jar and shake. Add the mustard, salt and pepper, and shake again. Set aside.

SALAD: Cut the potatoes into 1-inch cubes, and steam until tender, about 15 to 20 minutes. Place the potatoes and roasted pepper slices in a large bowl, and add the dressing. Stir gently and refrigerate until serving time. To serve, remove the peppers with a slotted spoon and arrange on a large platter like the spokes of a wheel. Remove the potatoes with a slotted spoon and place between the peppers. Crumble the feta cheese over the salad.

> **PER SERVING:**
> 262 Cal.; 6g Prot.; 7g Fat; 44g Carb.;
> 6mg Chol.; 159mg Sod.; 3g Fiber.

Hot Potato Salad

serves 8

German-style hot potato salad is delicious with yellow potatoes, but red spuds will do.

- 6 to 8 medium yellow potatoes, such as Yukon Gold or Yellow Finn
- 1 teaspoon virgin olive oil
- 1/4 cup chopped onion
- 1/4 cup chopped celery
- 1 tablespoon minced dill pickle
- 1/4 cup diced red bell pepper
- 1/4 cup water
- 1/2 cup apple cider vinegar
- 1 teaspoon honey
- 1/4 teaspoon dry mustard
- Salt and freshly ground black pepper to taste

BOIL the whole, unpeeled potatoes until tender when pierced with a fork, about 20 minutes. Drain and let cool slightly. Cut into bite-sized pieces and transfer to a large bowl. Drizzle with the oil and toss well. Stir in the onion, celery, pickle and bell pepper.

IN A SMALL saucepan, combine the water, vinegar, honey and mustard. Bring to a boil, lower the heat and simmer 2 minutes. Pour over the potato salad and toss well. Serve at once.

> **PER SERVING:**
> 102 Cal.; 1g Prot.; 0.7g Fat; 22g Carb.;
> 0mg Chol.; 171mg Sod.; 2g Fiber.

Summer Rice Salad

serves 4

This crunchy, vegetable-studded rice salad may be made up to 24 hours ahead of time. Add the red pepper garnish just before serving.

- 2 cups cooked short-grain brown rice
- 1/4 cup minced scallion (green and white parts)
- 1/4 cup minced green bell pepper
- 2 tablespoons minced fresh parsley
- 1/2 cup peeled and diced jicama or sliced red radishes
- 1/4 cup minced celery
- 1/4 cup low-calorie, eggless mayonnaise
- 1 teaspoon low-sodium soy sauce
- 1 tablespoon fresh lemon juice
- 1/4 teaspoon cayenne pepper
- 1 red bell pepper, seeded and cut into strips, for garnish

IN A BOWL, combine all the ingredients except the red bell pepper and toss well. Garnish with the red bell pepper just before serving.

> **PER SERVING:**
> 163 Cal.; 3g Prot.; 4g Fat; 29g Carb.;
> 0mg Chol.; 106mg Sod.; 3g Fiber.

Chilled Couscous Salad with Mango

serves 4

A ripe mango is a great salad ingredient. Choose one that gives slightly when you press it and smells faintly sweet. Avoid mangoes that are too hard because they often ripen unevenly at home.

> 1 cup water
>
> 2/3 cup uncooked couscous
>
> 1 tablespoon tahini (sesame paste)
>
> 2 tablespoons fresh orange juice
>
> 1 cup plain yogurt or soft tofu
>
> 1/2 teaspoon ground cumin
>
> Pinch ground ginger
>
> 1/2 cup cooked chickpeas
>
> 1 large mango, peeled and diced
>
> 1/4 cup golden raisins
>
> 1/4 cup minced fresh cilantro leaves
>
> 1/2 cup assorted diced dried fruits (optional):
>   pineapple, papaya, orange

BRING THE WATER to a boil in a saucepan. Stir in the couscous, return to a boil, cover and remove from heat. Let sit (without lifting the lid) until the water has been absorbed, about 5 minutes.

MEANWHILE, stir together the tahini and orange juice to make a smooth paste. Place the yogurt or tofu in a large mixing bowl and whisk until light and smooth. Whisk in the tahini mixture, cumin and ginger. Stir in the chickpeas, mango and raisins.

FLUFF the couscous with a fork to break up any lumps. Stir it into the mango mixture. Add the cilantro and dried fruits; stir until blended. Cover and refrigerate until chilled, about 3 hours.

> **PER SERVING:**
> 246 Cal.; 10g Prot.; 2g Fat; 47g Carb.;
> 1mg Chol.; 61mg Sod.; 6g Fiber.

Marinated Kidney Bean Salad

serves 4

> 2 cups cooked kidney beans
>
> 1/3 cup prepared no-oil Italian-style dressing
>
> 1 small onion, cut into rings
>
> 1/3 cup chopped celery
>
> 1/4 cup chopped sweet pickles
>
> 4 lettuce leaves
>
> Chopped hard-boiled egg, for garnish

PLACE the kidney beans in a medium bowl and top with dressing. Let marinate in your refrigerator at least 2 hours. Just before serving, stir in the onion, celery and pickles. Serve the salad on 4 small plates lined with lettuce. Garnish with hard-boiled egg.

> **PER SERVING:**
> 142 Cal.; 9g Prot.; 2g Fat; 22g Carb.;
> 69mg Chol.; 505mg Sod.; 11g Fiber.

Two-Rice Salad with Almonds and Ginger

serves 8

If you can't find quick-cooking wild rice, cook up a pot of wild rice and measure 1 1/2 to 2 cups for the salad.

- 1 1/2 cups uncooked quick-cooking brown rice
- 1 cup uncooked quick-cooking wild rice
- One 10-ounce package frozen green peas, thawed
- 1/2 cup scallions (green and white parts), sliced thinly
- 1/4 cup chopped red bell pepper
- 1/4 to 1/3 cup canola oil
- 1/4 cup tarragon vinegar
- 2 tablespoons Dijon mustard
- 1 tablespoon freshly grated fresh ginger root
- 1/2 teaspoon salt (optional)
- 1 teaspoon freshly ground black pepper
- 2/3 cup sliced almonds, toasted (page 106)
- Lettuce, for garnish (optional)

PREPARE the rices in separate pans according to the package directions. Combine in a large bowl and let cool. Add the peas, scallions and bell pepper.

In a small bowl, whisk together the oil, vinegar, mustard, ginger, salt and black pepper. Stir into the rice mixture, add the almonds and toss well. Serve in a lettuce-lined bowl or on individual plates.

> **PER SERVING:**
> 226 Cal.; 5g Prot.; 10g Fat; 28g Carb.;
> 0mg Chol.; 197mg Sod.; 4g Fiber.

Amaranth, Fig and Arugula Salad with Dressing

serves 6

Amaranth, with a flavor redolent of buckwheat, is an outstanding source of calcium and protein.

AMARANTH

- 1/2 tablespoon virgin olive oil
- 1 teaspoon mustard seeds
- 2 tablespoons sesame seeds
- 1 1/2 cups uncooked amaranth
- 2 1/4 cups vegetable stock (page 178) or water
- 2 cups cooked beans (such as white beans or kidney beans)
- 10 dried Calmyrna figs, chopped (or other dried figs)
- 1/3 cup minced fresh parsley
- 1/2 teaspoon salt
- Freshly ground black pepper to taste
- 1 tablespoon toasted sesame seeds, for garnish (page 106)

SALAD AND DRESSING

- 1/4 cup tahini (sesame paste)
- 1/2 cup fresh orange juice
- 1/2 to 2/3 cup water
- Salt to taste
- 8 cups shredded, mixed salad greens or romaine lettuce
- 1 cup chopped arugula

AMARANTH: Warm the oil in a saucepan over medium heat. Add the mustard and sesame seeds, cover with the lid ajar and toast until the sesame seeds darken a shade or two, about 30 seconds. Stir in the amaranth to coat the grains with oil. Add the stock or water and bring to a boil. Lower the heat and simmer until the grains are tender and the liquid has been absorbed, about 20 minutes. Fold in the beans and figs, cover and set aside for 5 minutes. Stir in the parsley, and season with salt and pepper.

SALAD AND DRESSING: In a blender, blend the tahini, orange juice, water and salt until smooth.

TO SERVE, mound the amaranth mixture on 6 plates. Surround with the salad greens, and garnish with the sesame seeds. Drizzle with the dressing.

> **PER SERVING:**
> 482 Cal.; 17g Prot.; 11g Fat; 77g Carb.;
> 0mg Chol.; 385mg Sod.; 13g Fiber.

Cannellini Salad in Butter Lettuce Cups

serves 6

- One 15-ounce can cannellini beans (or other white beans), rinsed
- Grated zest of 1 lemon
- Juice of 1 lemon
- 1 bunch fresh parsley, chopped
- 3 cloves garlic, minced
- 2 teaspoons minced fresh rosemary
- 2 to 3 fresh sage leaves, chopped (optional)
- 1 to 2 tablespoons Niçoise olives, pitted and chopped (optional)
- Salt and freshly ground black pepper to taste
- 6 leaves butter lettuce

IN A BOWL, combine all the ingredients except the lettuce. Toss well. Chill for at least 1 hour. To serve, place a lettuce leaf on each of 6 plates and spoon a portion of cannellini salad on each lettuce leaf.

> **PER SERVING:**
> 91 Cal.; 5g Prot.; 0.1g Fat; 18g Carb.;
> 0mg Chol.; 185mg Sod.; 3g Fiber.

Moroccan Salad

serves 8

This colorful salad also makes a wonderful stuffing for red or yellow bell peppers.

- 1 cup dry European soldier beans or other beans, rinsed
- 6 cups boiling water
- 1 1/2 cups vegetable stock (page 178)
- 1/4 to 1/2 cup virgin olive oil
- 1 cup uncooked couscous
- 3 tablespoons white wine vinegar
- 1/2 teaspoon ground cumin
- 1/4 teaspoon freshly ground black pepper
- 1 teaspoon grated lemon zest
- 2 medium cloves garlic, minced finely
- 1/2 green bell pepper, diced finely
- 1/2 red bell pepper, diced finely
- 2 slices red onion, diced finely

PLACE the beans in a large saucepan. Pour boiling water over the beans, cover and let soak 1 hour or overnight. Drain and rinse the beans, then add fresh water to cover by 1 inch. Simmer until tender but not mushy, about 45 minutes; drain.

IN A SMALL saucepan, heat the vegetable stock with 1 teaspoon oil until simmering. Remove from the heat and stir in the couscous. Cover and let sit until the liquid is absorbed, about 5 minutes. In a large bowl, whisk together the remaining oil, vinegar, cumin, black pepper, lemon zest and garlic. Add the bell peppers and onion. Stir in the cooled couscous and beans, and toss lightly.

> **PER SERVING:**
> 162 Cal.; 5g Prot.; 7g Fat; 21g Carb.;
> 0mg Chol.; 4mg Sod.; 4g Fiber.

Bean-and-Basmati Salad

serves 4

DRESSING

- 1 clove garlic, minced finely
- 1 shallot, minced
- 2 1/2 tablespoons balsamic vinegar
- 2 1/2 tablespoons virgin olive oil
- 2 tablespoons chopped fresh basil leaves
- 1/4 teaspoon freshly ground black pepper

SALAD

- 1 cup dry rattlesnake beans or red kidney beans, rinsed
- 6 cups boiling water
- 1 cup cooked basmati rice
- 1/2 cup diced celery
- 1/2 cup diced jícama
- 1/2 cup diced green or yellow bell pepper
- 2 scallions (green and white parts), sliced
- 1 hard-boiled egg, chopped (optional)

DRESSING: Combine all the dressing ingredients in a small bowl. Set aside.

SALAD: Place the beans in a large pot. Pour in the boiling water, cover and let soak for 1 hour or overnight. Drain and rinse, then add fresh water to cover by 1 inch. Bring to a boil and simmer gently until tender but not mushy, about 45 minutes.

DRAIN the beans and place in a medium bowl. Add the dressing while the beans are still warm and toss gently. Let cool to room temperature. Gently stir in the cooked rice, celery, jícama, bell pepper, scallions and egg.

> **PER SERVING:**
> 249 Cal.; 8g Prot.; 8g Fat; 34g Carb.;
> 0mg Chol.; 17mg Sod.; 6g Fiber.

PASTA SALADS

Asparagus and Carrots with Pasta

serves 4

This recipe calls for fresh asparagus, which makes a wonderful salad in the spring. During other seasons, choose cauliflower, broccoli or very tender green beans.

DRESSING

| 1 tablespoon virgin olive oil
| 2 tablespoons balsamic vinegar
| 1 to 2 teaspoons Dijon mustard
| 1/2 teaspoon salt
| Freshly ground black pepper to taste

SALAD

| 1/2 pound uncooked whole-wheat pasta of choice: spirals, shells or elbows
| 1 tablespoon virgin olive oil
| 1/4 pound fresh asparagus
| 1/4 pound carrots, julienned
| 2 tablespoons capers (optional)
| 1/4 cup chopped fresh parsley

DRESSING: Whisk together all the ingredients.

SALAD: Prepare the pasta according to the package directions; drain. Stir the oil into the pasta to prevent sticking. Let cool. Meanwhile, slice the asparagus lengthwise into quarters, then across into 1 1/2-inch pieces. Steam or blanch the asparagus and carrots for a few minutes, then combine with the pasta, capers and parsley. Drizzle the dressing over the salad. Serve at room temperature.

> **PER SERVING:**
> 297 Cal.; 9g Prot.; 7g Fat; 48g Carb.;
> 0mg Chol.; 304mg Sod.; 6g Fiber.

Macaroni Salad

serves 4

What would a picnic be without macaroni salad? This combination of macaroni, corn, tomatoes and a mayonnaise-free dressing is creamy and delicious.

| 1 pound uncooked small macaroni
| 1/2 cup nonfat cottage cheese
| 2 teaspoons apple cider vinegar
| 2 tablespoons virgin olive oil
| 1/4 cup nonfat plain yogurt
| Salt and freshly ground black pepper to taste
| 2 cups halved cherry tomatoes
| 1 1/2 cups whole-kernel corn
| 1 tablespoon minced fresh basil leaves

PREPARE the macaroni according to the package directions; drain. Purée the cottage cheese in a blender or food processor until smooth. In a large bowl, combine the cottage cheese purée, vinegar, oil, yogurt, salt and pepper; whisk to blend. Add the macaroni and toss well. Let sit 30 minutes. Before serving, add the tomatoes, corn and basil, and toss well.

> **PER SERVING:**
> 471 Cal.; 17g Prot.; 9g Fat; 82g Carb.;
> 3mg Chol.; 269mg Sod.; 4g Fiber.

Apple-Fennel Salad with Fusilli

serves 4

The flavor of fresh fennel gives this pasta salad a lovely twist.

DRESSING

> 1/4 cup red wine vinegar
>
> 1 1/2 tablespoons virgin olive oil
>
> 1 tablespoon frozen apple juice concentrate, thawed
>
> 1 1/2 teaspoons dried thyme
>
> 1/2 teaspoon salt
>
> 1/4 teaspoon freshly ground black pepper

SALAD

> 8 ounces uncooked fusilli pasta
>
> 3 McIntosh apples, cored and diced
>
> 2 tablespoons fresh lemon juice
>
> 1/2 pound fennel, trimmed and sliced thinly
>
> 1 small head of Boston lettuce

DRESSING: In a small bowl, whisk together the dressing ingredients.

SALAD: Prepare the pasta according to the package directions until *al dente*; drain. In a medium bowl, toss together the apples and lemon juice. Stir in the fennel. Add the pasta and dressing and toss well. Serve on a bed of lettuce.

> **PER SERVING:**
> 288 Cal.; 5g Prot.; 7g Fat; 53g Carb.;
> 0mg Chol.; 341mg Sod.; 6g Fiber.

Twenty-Minute Pasta Salad

serves 4

Make this quick and colorful salad for your next get-together. Just multiply the ingredients as needed to accommodate the number of guests.

> 2 cups uncooked pasta of various shapes (rotini, elbows, shells)
>
> 1 1/2 cups sliced carrots
>
> 2 1/2 cups broccoli florets
>
> 1/2 large red bell pepper, diced
>
> 1/4 cup minced red onion
>
> Half of a 7-ounce can whole-kernel corn, drained
>
> 2 tablespoons virgin olive oil
>
> 1 teaspoon red wine vinegar
>
> 3 cloves garlic, minced
>
> 1 teaspoon dried basil
>
> Salt and freshly ground black pepper to taste

PREPARE the pasta according to the package directions; drain. Meanwhile, steam the carrots and broccoli just until tender, about 4 to 5 minutes. Place the vegetables in a large bowl along with the bell pepper, onion and corn. Add the remaining ingredients and mix well. Add the pasta to the bowl and toss lightly.

> **PER SERVING:**
> 305 Cal.; 10g Prot.; 8g Fat; 50g Carb.;
> 0mg Chol.; 163mg Sod.; 8g Fiber.

Summer Squash-and-Bow Tie Salad

serves 8

SALAD

| 1 pound bow tie pasta

| 2 to 3 tablespoons virgin olive oil

| 1 tablespoon minced garlic (or 1 bunch scallions, sliced)

| 2 large carrots, grated

| Pinch salt

| Pinch freshly ground black pepper

| 1 large or 2 medium zucchini, shredded into long pieces

| 1 large or 2 medium yellow squash, shredded into long pieces

DRESSING

| 1/2 cup bottled oil-and-vinegar salad dressing

| 2 to 3 teaspoons prepared mustard or horseradish

| 2 tablespoons fresh lemon juice

| Optional garnish: Broccoli, fresh peas, sliced red peppers or olives

SALAD: Prepare the pasta according to the package directions; drain and rinse with cool water. In a large skillet or wok, heat the oil, and sauté the garlic or scallions for 1 minute. Add the carrots, sprinkle with salt and pepper and stir frequently until the carrots wilt slightly. Add the zucchini and yellow squash and cook, stirring constantly, about 1 minute. Transfer to a large mixing bowl and spread out the vegetables to cool. Add the pasta to the vegetables.

DRESSING: Combine the dressing ingredients in a small bowl. Stir well and pour over the pasta-vegetable mixture. Toss lightly. Add garnish if desired.

PER SERVING:
298 Cal.; 7g Prot.; 13g Fat; 40g Carb.;
0mg Chol.; 92mg Sod.; 3g Fiber.

Vegetable-Pasta Salad

serves 12

Vary the vegetables in this fat-free salad to suit the season and your appetite.

| 4 cups cooked pasta

| 1 cup broccoli or cauliflower florets

| 1 cup slivered carrots

| 20 whole, fresh snow peas, trimmed

| 1/2 pound white button mushrooms, sliced

| 1 cup cherry tomatoes, cut in halves

| 2 scallions (green and white parts), chopped

| One 2 1/2-ounce can black olives, sliced (optional)

| One 2-ounce jar chopped pimiento

| 1/2 cup prepared oil-free Italian dressing

| Freshly ground black pepper (optional)

PREPARE the pasta according to the package directions. Drain and rinse under cool water. Set aside. In a saucepan fitted with a steamer, steam the broccoli or cauliflower, carrots and snow peas for about 5 minutes. Combine the steamed vegetables in a large bowl with the pasta and remaining ingredients. Refrigerate 2 or more hours before serving.

PER SERVING:
234 Cal.; 9g Prot.; 0.3g Fat; 47g Carb.;
0mg Chol.; 98mg Sod.; 3g Fiber.

Thai Noodle Salad

serves 4

3 1/2 ounces dried thin rice noodles

2 carrots

1/2 medium napa cabbage

4 cloves garlic, minced

1 tablespoon minced fresh ginger root

3 scallions (green and white parts), chopped

1/2 to 1 teaspoon toasted sesame oil

1 to 2 tablespoons brown sugar

Juice of 1 lime

2 tablespoons low-sodium soy sauce

2 teaspoons chili powder

1 tablespoon tomato paste

2 teaspoons chopped peanuts (optional)

2 tablespoons chopped fresh basil, mint or cilantro
leaves (optional)

PLACE the rice noodles in a heat-proof bowl. Pour the boiling water over them to cover completely. Let the noodles soak 7 minutes; drain.

GRATE the carrots and finely shred the cabbage into a large bowl. Set aside. In a large saucepan, sauté the garlic, ginger and scallions in sesame oil, tossing frequently, for about 2 minutes. Whisk in the brown sugar, lime juice, soy sauce, chili powder and tomato paste. Bring to a boil, then lower heat and simmer 2 minutes. Add the drained noodles to the sauce and toss for about 4 minutes. Remove from heat and let cool to room temperature.

ADD the noodles and sauce to the carrot-cabbage mixture. Toss well and place on a serving platter. Garnish with peanuts and basil, mint or cilantro leaves.

> **PER SERVING:**
> 174 Cal.; 3g Prot.; 4g Fat; 30g Carb.;
> 0mg Chol.; 706mg Sod.; 2g Fiber.

FRUIT SALADS

Ambrosia Fruit Salad

serves 6

Here's a modern version of an old Southern classic. Tropical fruits are dressed with a special sweet and sour sauce, then finished with a sprinkling of coconut and a sprig of mint. Scarlett definitely would have approved.

SALAD

- 1 small ripe pineapple
- 1 ripe mango or papaya
- 2 seedless navel oranges, peeled
- 3 kiwifruit, peeled
- 1/2 pound seedless red grapes
- 2 ripe bananas
- 1 to 2 teaspoons fresh lemon juice
- 1 pint fresh strawberries
- 1/2 pint fresh raspberries
- 1/2 cup dried unsweetened coconut
- Fresh mint sprigs, for garnish

DRESSING

- 1/2 cup fresh lemon juice
- 1/2 cup honey
- 1 tablespoon mango or apricot chutney, mashed
- 1/2 teaspoon curry powder
- 1/2 cup plain low-fat yogurt or soy yogurt
- Pinch salt

SALAD: Slice off the top and bottom of the pineapple, then stand the fruit on one end and cut off the thick rind by slicing down in wide strips all around the fruit. Cut the peeled pineapple in half lengthwise, then cut each half lengthwise again to make 4 spears. Cut away the core of each spear, then cut each one in half again to make 8 spears. Cut each spear in half crosswise. Set aside.

PEEL the mango or papaya with a small sharp knife, and cut the fruit from the pit and slice. Set aside. Slice the oranges and kiwis into rounds. Set aside. Remove the grapes from their stems. Set aside. Peel the bananas, slice on the diagonal and brush with lemon juice. Set aside. Place the strawberries and raspberries in a small strainer and gently rinse with cold water; drain. Transfer to a dishcloth to dry.

DRESSING: In a small bowl, whisk together all ingredients.

TO ASSEMBLE. arrange all of the fruits except raspberries in an attractive pattern on each of 6 serving plates. Dribble 2 to 3 tablespoons of the dressing over each salad, then sprinkle coconut on top. Place the raspberries in a random pattern on top of the coconut, tuck a sprig of mint to one side and serve.

Variation:

Combine all of the fruits in a large, decorative bowl. Drizzle the dressing on top and add garnishes.

> **PER SERVING:**
> 319 Cal.; 3g Prot.; 3g Fat; 45g Carb.;
> 1mg Chol.; 85mg Sod.; 6g Fiber.

Winter Pear Salad in Raspberry Vinaigrette

serves 15

This crunchy salad contains a wonderful melange of flavors. Serve it on individual salad plates or arrange it on a large, round tray at your buffet table.

SALAD

- 8 cups torn radicchio
- 10 bosc pears, cored and sliced thinly
- 1 cup gorgonzola, crumbled feta or grated Parmesan cheese
- 2 cups chopped, toasted walnuts (page 106)
- 1/2 cup chopped fresh Italian flat-leaf parsley
- 1 cup fresh raspberries (optional)

VINAIGRETTE

- 1/2 cup raspberry vinegar
- 1/2 cup virgin olive oil
- 1 teaspoon salt
- 1 teaspoon freshly ground black pepper

SALAD: Make an attractive bed of torn radicchio leaves on salad plates or a large platter. Arrange the pear slices on the radicchio in fan shapes. Thinly slice or crumble the cheese over the pears. Sprinkle the walnuts, parsley and raspberries if desired over the salad.

VINAIGRETTE: Place all the ingredients in a jar and shake to combine. Just before serving, drizzle the vinaigrette over the salad.

PER SERVING
279 Cal.; 5g Prot.; 19g Fat; 20g Carb.; 13mg Chol ; 328mg Sod.; 4g Fiber.

Star Fruit Salad

serves 4

Star fruit (known as carambola) has a juicy, citrus flavor, looks exactly like a star and is a beautiful yellow color when sliced in this composed salad.

- 4 large red leaf lettuce leaves
- 1 star fruit, sliced 1/4 inch thick
- One 14-ounce can artichoke hearts, drained
- 1/2 red pepper, seeded and cut into thin strips
- 1/4 cup fresh lime juice
- 2 teaspoons honey
- 1/8 teaspoon salt
- Parsley sprigs, for garnish

ARRANGE the lettuce on 4 salad plates. Divide the star fruit slices among the plates, overlapping them slightly. Divide the artichoke hearts among the plates on the side of the star fruit. Place the red pepper strips over each plate in a crisscross pattern. Combine the lime juice, honey and salt in a small bowl; drizzle over the salads. Garnish each plate with a parsley sprig.

PER SERVING:
73 Cal.; 2g Prot.; 0.1g Fat; 13g Carb.; 0mg Chol.; 134mg Sod.; 4g Fiber.

Ensalada de Naranjas

serves 12

Translated as "orange salad," this Hispanic dish has just a touch of spiciness.

SALAD
- 8 navel oranges
- 1 medium pineapple
- 24 romaine lettuce leaves
- 1 large red bell pepper, sliced thinly
- 1 large green bell pepper, sliced thinly

DRESSING
- 2 cloves garlic
- 2 tablespoons canola oil
- 6 tablespoons vinegar
- 1 cup fresh orange juice
- 1/2 teaspoon chili powder
- 1/4 teaspoon dry mustard

SALAD: Peel the oranges and remove as much white pith as possible. Slice into rounds. Cut the pineapple crosswise into 1/2-inch-thick slices, then cut each slice in half. Remove the cores and skin and slice thinly.

PLACE the lettuce leaves on 1 large or 2 small platters. Arrange the fruit and bell peppers attractively on top. Cover with plastic wrap and refrigerate.

DRESSING: In a blender, blend all the ingredients for 30 seconds. Just before serving, drizzle the dressing over the salad. Pour any unused dressing in a serving bowl and pass at the table.

PER SERVING:
96 Cal.; 1g Prot.; 1g Fat; 19g Carb.;
0mg Chol.; 4mg Sod.; 4g Fiber.

Orange-and-Tomato Salad

serves 6

- 6 large ripe plum tomatoes, peeled
- 3 medium navel oranges
- 1 small red onion, peeled
- 1 head Boston or bibb lettuce
- 2 teaspoons Dijon mustard
- 2 tablespoons fresh orange juice
- 2 tablespoons walnut oil

CUT each tomato into 6 to 8 wedges. Drain the wedges, seed side down, on paper towels to remove excess moisture. Set aside.

PEEL the oranges and remove as much white pith as possible; slice thinly. Slice the onion into paper-thin rounds. Set the orange and onion aside. Arrange the lettuce leaves on 6 chilled salad plates; arrange the tomato wedges, orange slices and red onion on top.

IN A SMALL BOWL, whisk together the mustard, orange juice and walnut oil. Dribble 2 teaspoons dressing over each salad.

PER SERVING:
100 Cal.; 1g Prot.; 5g Fat; 13g Carb.;
0mg Chol.; 54mg Sod.; 3g Fiber.

Apple-Carrot-Pineapple Salad

serves 2

Here's a simply sweet salad that's nearly fat free.

- 1 apple, shredded
- 1 carrot, grated finely
- 1/2 cup unsweetened pineapple chunks
- 2 tablespoons plain nonfat yogurt
- Dash ground cinnamon

COMBINE all the ingredients. Chill before serving.

PER SERVING:
109 Cal.; 2g Prot.; 1g Fat; 27g Carb.;
0mg Chol.; 25mg Sod.; 5g Fiber.

MAIN-DISH SALADS

Curried Couscous Salad

serves 4

Couscous, a staple of North African dishes, adds an exotic touch to main-dish salads. This one takes less than 30 minutes to prepare.

COUSCOUS
- 1 cup vegetable stock (page 178)
- 1 tablespoon mild curry powder
- 1 cup uncooked couscous
- 1/3 cup golden raisins

SALAD AND DRESSING
- 2 cups torn leaf lettuce
- 2 large plum tomatoes, chopped
- 1/4 cup minced red onion
- 1/3 cup chopped tart apple
- 1 large yellow bell pepper, seeded and chopped
- 1 tablespoon virgin olive oil
- 1/4 cup nonfat plain yogurt
- 3 tablespoons rice vinegar or fresh lemon juice
- Sprigs of fresh cilantro, for garnish

COUSCOUS: In a medium saucepan, bring the stock and curry powder to a boil. Remove from the heat. Stir in the couscous and raisins. Cover and let sit until all the liquid has been absorbed, about 15 minutes. Transfer to a bowl and let cool.

SALAD AND DRESSING: In a large salad bowl, combine the lettuce, tomatoes, onion, apple and bell pepper. In a small bowl, whisk together the oil, yogurt and vinegar or lemon juice; pour over the salad. Toss gently to combine. Arrange the dressed salad on 4 salad plates, top with the couscous mixture and garnish with cilantro.

PER SERVING:
200 Cal.; 5g Prot.; 3g Fat; 37g Carb.;
0.1mg Chol.; 25mg Sod.; 6g Fiber.

Rice Noodle-and-Chickpea Salad

serves 4

| One 14-ounce package rice noodles
| 4 cups boiling water
| One 15-ounce can chickpeas, rinsed
| 1/4 cup fat-free Italian salad dressing
| 1 bunch watercress
| 1/2 cup chopped roasted red pepper

PLACE the noodles in a large pot or heat-proof bowl. Pour boiling water over them, cover and let sit 7 to 10 minutes. Place the chickpeas in a small bowl. Add the salad dressing to the chickpeas and let marinate at least 10 minutes.

MEANWHILE, wash and dry the watercress. Remove the stems and discard. Slice the watercress into 2- to 3-inch lengths and transfer to a large bowl. Drain the noodles, rinse with cool water and drain again. Add the noodles, marinated chickpeas and red pepper to the watercress and toss well.

Variations:

Instead of rice noodles, use 3 cups cooked pasta or rice. Instead of watercress, use arugula.

PER SERVING:
303 Cal.; 13g Prot.; 2g Fat; 66g Carb.;
0mg Chol.; 363mg Sod.; 7g Fiber.

Mandarin Salad with Tempeh

serves 6

The sour flavor of tempeh, a fermented soyfood available in natural food stores, contrasts with the sweetness of mandarin oranges.

MARINADE
| 2 tablespoons low-sugar orange marmalade
| 1 teaspoon minced fresh ginger root
| 1 teaspoon minced garlic
| 1/4 cup fresh lemon juice
| 1/4 cup rice vinegar
| 1/4 cup low-sodium soy sauce
| 1/3 cup fresh orange juice
| 1/4 to 1/2 teaspoon cayenne pepper, or to taste

SALAD
| 1 pound tempeh
| 4 cups mixed fresh greens (such as curly endive, radicchio and leaf lettuce)
| 1 medium carrot, grated coarsely
| 1 cup thinly sliced fresh white button mushrooms
| 1 cup canned mandarin orange slices, drained
| 1/3 to 1/2 cup nonfat plain yogurt

MARINADE: Combine the marinade ingredients in a shallow pan. Set aside.

SALAD: Cut the tempeh into strips about 2 inches long and 1/2 inch wide. In a saucepan fitted with a steamer, steam the tempeh for 20 minutes; drain and add to the marinade. Cover and marinate in your refrigerator at least 2 hours or overnight, basting the tempeh with the marinade occasionally.

IN A LARGE SALAD BOWL, toss together the greens, carrot, mushrooms and orange slices. Strain the marinade from the tempeh into a separate bowl. Toss the tempeh with the salad. Stir the yogurt into the marinade, adding the greater amount for a creamier texture. Toss together the dressing and salad.

Variation:

For a lovely presentation, garnish the perimeter of the serving dish with slices of cooked beets.

PER SERVING:
235 Cal.; 15g Prot.; 5g Fat; 31g Carb.;
0.1mg Chol.; 428mg Sod.; 6g Fiber.

Spicy Black Bean and Lentil Salad

serves 8

Properly seasoned, black beans and red lentils lend tremendous flavor and depth to main-dish salads. Marinate them separately so the colors don't blend.

2 cups cooked black beans
2 cups cooked red lentils
1 teaspoon dry mustard
3 tablespoons minced garlic
1 tablespoon minced fresh parsley
1 tablespoon minced fresh cilantro leaves
1/2 cup rice vinegar
Juice from 1 lemon
1 teaspoon salt, or to taste
2 to 3 tablespoons virgin olive oil
1 teaspoon cayenne pepper
1 small head butterleaf lettuce, washed and torn
2 large red bell peppers, cut into 8 rings each
2 large red potatoes, cooked and sliced thinly
1/2 cup grated carrots or raw beets

PLACE the black beans in one bowl and lentils in another. In a third bowl, whisk together the mustard, garlic, parsley, cilantro, vinegar, lemon juice, salt, oil and cayenne. Divide the mixture equally between the beans and lentils, cover with plastic wrap and marinate 1 hour in your refrigerator.

LINE 8 salad plates with the lettuce leaves, then top with rings of bell pepper. Arrange small piles of potatoes, carrots or beets, beans and lentils on each plate, then drizzle the remaining marinade over all. Serve at once.

PER SERVING:
205 Cal.; 8g Prot.; 4g Fat; 33g Carb.;
0mg Chol.; 277mg Sod.; 5g Fiber.

Southwestern Salad

serves 6

Fans of Hispanic food will enjoy this vegetarian taco salad.

1 cup crumbled firm tofu

2 teaspoons ground cumin

2 tablespoons chopped fresh cilantro leaves

1/2 teaspoon chili powder, or to taste

1 teaspoon salt

1/4 teaspoon freshly ground black pepper

Nonstick cooking spray

1 teaspoon canola oil

6 corn tortillas

3 cups torn romaine lettuce

4 large tomatoes, chopped coarsely

1 cup whole-kernel corn

2 large carrots, grated coarsely

1/2 cup minced red onion

1 cup seeded and diced cucumber

1/2 cup salsa

1/2 cup grated part-skim mozzarella cheese (optional)

PREHEAT oven to 400°F. In a bowl, combine the tofu, cumin, cilantro, chili powder, salt and pepper. Lightly spray a nonstick skillet with nonstick cooking spray and place over medium heat. Add the oil and cook the tofu mixture for 10 minutes. Let cool. Using a pair of scissors, cut the tortillas into wedges and place them on a nonstick baking sheet. Bake until crisp, about 15 minutes.

PLACE the lettuce in a large salad bowl and spoon the tofu mixture into the center. Arrange the tomatoes, corn, carrots, onion and cucumber on top, then sprinkle with salsa and cheese. Garnish with the baked tortilla wedges.

> **PER SERVING:**
> 208 Cal.; 10g Prot.; 5g Fat; 29g Carb.;
> 0mg Chol.; 672mg Sod.; 5g Fiber.

salad dressings

HOMEMADE DRESSINGS HAVE A BIG ADVANTAGE over their commercial counterparts: The ones you make taste fresher and they can be seasoned to your liking. These dressings—from simple vinaigrettes to concoctions with unusual (and unusually good) ingredient combinations—aren't meant for salads only. They may be tossed with pasta, used as marinades or spooned over cooked vegetables. Another plus: Most of the dressings go very easy on fat.

211

Balsamic Vinaigrette

makes 1 cup

Toss this dressing with a mixture of fresh greens or cooked pasta. If you prefer a sweeter vinaigrette, add a spoonful of honey to the other ingredients.

1/3 cup balsamic vinegar

1/4 cup apple cider

1/4 cup water

1 tablespoon Dijon mustard

1 tablespoon minced garlic

1 tablespoon virgin olive oil

1 tablespoon minced fresh parsley

1/2 teaspoon apple juice concentrate (optional)

IN A SMALL BOWL, whisk together all the ingredients.

> **PER TABLESPOON:**
> 13 Cal.; 0 Prot.; 1g Fat; 1g Carb.;
> 0mg Chol.; 12mg Sod.; 0g Fiber.

Tomato Vinaigrette

makes 2/3 cup

This vinaigrette is great for marinating cooked pasta and vegetables for a quick supper. Or use it simply as a salad dressing. Miso is a soyfood condiment that comes in mild (or light) and stronger, saltier flavors; you'll find it in natural food stores.

1 teaspoon Dijon mustard

2 tablespoons minced garlic

1/4 cup apple cider vinegar

2 tablespoons fresh lemon juice

1 tablespoon virgin olive oil

3 tablespoons tomato juice

1/2 teaspoon honey

1 teaspoon light miso (or salt to taste)

1/4 teaspoon freshly ground black pepper

PLACE all the ingredients in a blender or food processor; purée until frothy.

> **PER TABLESPOON:**
> 23 Cal.; 0 Prot.; 1g Fat; 2g Carb.;
> 0mg Chol.; 24mg Sod.; 0g Fiber.

Garlicky Caesar Dressing

makes 1/3 cup

Say good-bye to anchovies and egg: An excellent Caesar dressing may be made without them. Pour over romaine lettuce and top with croutons.

4 to 5 cloves garlic, or to taste

1 teaspoon virgin olive oil

1 teaspoon red wine vinegar

2 teaspoons balsamic vinegar

Juice of 1 lemon

1 teaspoon water

1/2 teaspoon dry mustard

1 to 2 drops hot pepper sauce

WITH A FORK, mash garlic in olive oil. Whisk in the remaining ingredients. Let the dressing sit overnight in your refrigerator if you want a stronger garlic flavor.

> **PER TABLESPOON:**
> 16 Cal.; 0g Prot.; 1g Fat; 2g Carb.;
> 0mg Chol.; 27mg Sod.; 0g Fiber.

Orange-and-Tahini Dressing

makes 1 cup

Orange sweetens this creamy dressing. Try it with grilled vegetables, couscous and tofu.

- 2 teaspoons tahini (sesame paste)
- 1 tablespoon fresh lemon juice
- 2 tablespoons balsamic vinegar
- 1/2 cup water
- 1 medium orange, peeled, sectioned and seeded
- 1/2 teaspoon dry mustard
- 2 teaspoons honey, or to taste
- Pinch cayenne pepper
- Pinch ground cumin

PLACE all the ingredients in a blender or food processor; purée until smooth.

> **PER TABLESPOON:**
> 11 Cal.; 0.3g Prot.; 0.1g Fat; 1g Carb.;
> 0mg Chol.; 1mg Sod.; 0g Fiber.

Sweet Sesame Dressing

makes 1/2 cup

- 2/3 cup fresh pineapple juice
- 1 tablespoon sesame seeds, lightly toasted (page 106)
- 1 teaspoon grated ginger root
- 1 teaspoon minced garlic
- 1 teaspoon brown sugar
- Splash soy sauce
- Splash brown rice vinegar or cider vinegar

IN A SMALL SAUCEPAN, combine all the ingredients. Bring to a simmer over low heat, stirring occasionally, until the liquid has thickened and reduced in volume, about 7 minutes. Remove from the heat and let cool.

> **PER TABLESPOON:**
> 21 Cal.; 0.5g Prot.; 0.5g Fat; 4g Carb.;
> 0mg Chol.; 31mg Sod.; 0g Fiber.

Mango Chutney-and-Yogurt Dressing

makes 1 1/4 cups

The unexpected combination of yogurt and mango chutney creates a wonderful dressing.

> 1/2 cup nonfat plain yogurt
> 1/2 cup low-fat vanilla yogurt
> 1/4 cup mango chutney
> 1 teaspoon Dijon mustard
> 1/4 cup peeled, chopped apple

PLACE all the ingredients in a blender or food processor; purée until smooth.

> **PER TABLESPOON:**
> 21 Cal.; 0.8g Prot.; 0.1g Fat; 2g Carb.;
> 0.1mg Chol.; 12mg Sod.; 0g Fiber.

Creamy Green Dressing

makes 1 cup

Here's a low-fat replacement for ranch-style dressing.

> 3/4 cup part-skim ricotta cheese
> 1/4 cup skim milk
> 2 cloves garlic, minced
> 1/4 cup minced fresh parsley
> 1 teaspoon dried basil
> Salt and freshly ground black pepper to taste

PLACE all the ingredients in a blender or food processor; purée until smooth.

> **PER TABLESPOON:**
> 19 Cal.; 2g Prot.; 1g Fat; 1g Carb.;
> 4mg Chol.; 4mg Sod.; 0g Fiber.

Buttermilk-Blue Cheese Dressing

makes 1 1/4 cups

> 1/2 cup soft tofu
> 1/2 cup low-fat buttermilk
> 3 tablespoons white wine vinegar
> 1 tablespoon canola oil
> 1 clove garlic, minced
> 2 tablespoons sharp blue cheese

IN A BLENDER or food processor, purée the tofu, buttermilk, vinegar, oil, garlic and 1 tablespoon blue cheese. Stir in the remaining blue cheese.

> **PER TABLESPOON:**
> 17 Cal.; 1g Prot.; 1g Fat; 0.5g Carb.;
> 1mg Chol.; 9mg Sod.; 0g Fiber.

Mustard Dressing

makes 1 cup

- 1 tablespoon Dijon mustard
- 1/2 cup vegetable broth
- 3 tablespoons virgin olive oil
- 2 cloves garlic, minced
- 1/4 cup red wine vinegar or fresh lemon juice
- 1/4 teaspoon salt
- 1/4 teaspoon freshly ground black pepper
- 1/2 teaspoon dried herbs of choice

IN A MEDIUM BOWL, whisk together the mustard and broth. Slowly add the oil while whisking. Add the garlic and vinegar or lemon juice, and whisk again. Season with salt, pepper and herbs.

> **PER TABLESPOON:**
> 25 Cal.; 0 Prot.; 2g Fat; 0 Carb.;
> 0mg Chol.; 60mg Sod.; 0g Fiber.

Green Goddess Dressing

makes 2/3 cup

This tofu-based salad dressing is a low-fat takeoff on the high-fat original.

- 1/4 pound soft tofu, crumbled
- 1 teaspoon Dijon mustard
- 2 tablespoons coarsely chopped fresh parsley
- 1 scallion (green and white parts), sliced
- 1 tablespoon fresh lemon juice
- 1 tablespoon vinegar
- 1/2 teaspoon salt
- 1 clove garlic, minced (optional)

THOROUGHLY BLEND all the ingredients in a blender.

> **PER 2-TABLESPOON SERVING:**
> 20 Cal.; 2g Prot.; 1g Fat; 1g Carb.;
> 0mg Chol.; 256mg Sod.; 0g Fiber.

vegetable
main dishes

14

BY NOW, nearly everyone knows that meatless main dishes are not only nutritious but also satisfying. What a change from a decade or two ago! These vegetable-based entrées incorporate every imaginable vegetable in kitchen-tested dishes, including crepes, stuffed peppers, cabbage rolls, phyllo tarts, tzimmes, casseroles, calzones and stews. And in case you didn't get the message already, don't worry about complementing proteins. Even the American Dietetic Association says that a vegetarian diet including a variety of foods supplies ample protein (page 22). So pull out your pots and pans and get cookin'.

Calzones with Sun-Dried Tomatoes and Garlic

makes 6 calzones

Calzones are like pizza suitcases—circles of dough folded over a filling, baked and ready to go.

CRUST

- 1 cup warm water (110°F)
- 1 package active dry yeast
- Pinch sugar
- 3 cups all-purpose flour, plus 1/4 cup or so for kneading
- 1/2 teaspoon salt
- 2 to 3 tablespoons virgin olive oil
- 1 tablespoon cornmeal

FILLING

- 2 or 3 large whole heads of garlic
- 12 sun-dried tomatoes, drained if oil-packed (reserve oil)
- 1/3 cup roughly chopped fresh parsley leaves
- 1 teaspoon virgin olive oil or oil from sun-dried tomatoes
- 1 scallion (green and white parts), minced
- 8 large fresh basil leaves, julienned
- 2 to 4 ounces fontina or bel paese cheese, rind removed and chopped coarsely
- 2 to 4 ounces mozzarella cheese, diced

CRUST: In a small bowl, stir together the water, yeast and sugar. Let sit until bubbly, about 5 to 10 minutes. In a nonmetallic bowl, combine the flour and salt. Stir in the yeast mixture and oil, adding more flour if needed to form a ball. Turn out the dough onto a floured breadboard and knead until smooth and elastic, about 5 minutes. Place the dough in a lightly oiled bowl, turning to coat all sides. Cover with a dishcloth and let rise in a warm spot until doubled in bulk, about 45 minutes. Deflate the dough and divide into 6 portions. Cover and let sit 30 minutes.

FILLING: Preheat the oven to 350°F. Slice off and discard the tops of the garlic heads. Place the garlic on a sheet of foil, drizzle with a few drops of oil if desired, wrap tightly and bake until very soft, about 1 hour. When cool enough to handle, transfer the garlic to a small dish. Set aside. Place the dried tomatoes in a bowl of warm water for 15 minutes, then drain. Thinly slice the tomatoes and place the slices in a small bowl. Combine the parsley, oil and scallion in a separate bowl. Set aside.

ON A FLOURED BREADBOARD, roll out a portion of the dough into a circle about 1/8 inch thick. Spread 1/6 of the scallion mixture on top of the dough, leaving a 1-inch border around the edge. Spread 1/6 of the garlic on top, then add 1/6 of the basil, 1/6 of the fontina or bel paese, 1/6 of the mozzarella and finally 1/6 of the tomatoes. Moisten the edge of the dough (the unoiled part) with a bit of water. Fold the circle in half to enclose the filling; press tightly to seal and to thin the edges. With your fingers, fold 1/2 inch of the thinned-out edge back onto itself and crimp. Repeat with the remaining dough and filling to make 6 calzones. Refrigerate for 1 hour before baking. (At this point, the calzones may be wrapped in plastic and frozen for up to 8 weeks.)

PREHEAT the oven to 450°F. Set a rack on the lowest rung in the oven. Sprinkle a tablespoon of cornmeal over a large baking sheet. Place the calzones on the baking sheet and spray them with a fine mist of water. Bake, spraying with water again about halfway through cooking time, until lightly browned, about 30 to 35 minutes.

TO BAKE FROZEN CALZONES, let them thaw almost completely, preheat the oven to 450°F and proceed as directed.

PER CALZONE:
370 Cal.; 13g Prot.; 9g Fat; 57g Carb.;
17mg Chol.; 317mg Sod.; 4g Fiber.

Eggplant Parmesan

serves 4

With one fourth of the calories and one ninth of the fat of traditional eggplant Parmesan, this dish won't make you feel heavy—or guilty.

| 2 tablespoons red wine
| 1 medium onion, chopped
| 3 large cloves garlic, pressed or minced
| 1 medium bell pepper, chopped
| Freshly ground black pepper to taste
| 4 cups peeled and chopped tomatoes
| 1/2 teaspoon salt, or to taste
| 1 tablespoon minced fresh basil leaves
| 1 teaspoon minced fresh oregano leaves
| 1/2 teaspoon minced fresh thyme leaves
| 1 tablespoon minced fresh parsley
| 1 large eggplant
| Additional salt for salting eggplant
| 1/4 to 1/2 cup water or vegetable stock (page 178)
| 1/2 to 1 cup dry whole-grain bread crumbs
| 3/4 cup part-skim mozzarella cheese, grated coarsely
| 1/4 to 1/2 cup freshly grated Parmesan cheese

HEAT the wine in a large pot, add the onion and cook, stirring, over medium heat for several minutes. Stir in the garlic and bell pepper and cook, stirring, until tender. Add the black pepper and tomatoes, cover and cook over low heat for 5 to 10 minutes. Stir in the salt and simmer gently, uncovered, until the sauce thickens, about 1 hour. Add the fresh herbs and simmer a few minutes longer. Season with additional salt if desired. Remove from heat.

PEEL the eggplant. Cut it crosswise into 1/2-inch slices. Layer the slices in a colander, lightly sprinkling with salt between layers. Cover the eggplant with a plate and set a weight, such as a pot of water, on top. Let sit 30 minutes or longer; rinse eggplant and pat dry.

PREHEAT the oven to 350°F. Spray a large baking sheet with nonstick cooking spray. Dip the eggplant slices in water or vegetable stock and then in bread crumbs to coat. Place on the baking sheet. Bake until the eggplant is tender and the crumbs are crisp, about 30 minutes.

SPRAY the bottom and sides of an 8-inch square baking dish with nonstick cooking spray. Spread a thin layer of sauce on the bottom and arrange half the eggplant slices on top. Sprinkle about 1/3 of the mozzarella over the eggplant. Spread on a thicker layer of sauce than the first one and sprinkle on half of the Parmesan. Repeat layers, beginning with the eggplant and ending with the Parmesan.

BAKE, covered, until heated through, about 30 minutes. Uncover, scatter the remaining mozzarella on top and bake until the cheese is melted and bubbly, about 10 minutes. Remove from your oven and let sit a few minutes before serving.

Variation:

Substitute half as much dried basil, oregano and thyme for fresh herbs; add to the sauté near the end of cooking.

PER SERVING:
225 Cal.; 13g Prot.; 7g Fat; 28g Carb.;
17mg Chol.; 608mg Sod.; 5g Fiber.

Rosemary-Scented Vegetable Phyllo Tart

serves 15

Elegant and sophisticated, this tart makes a showy centerpiece on your buffet.

Two 10-ounce packages chopped frozen spinach, thawed and squeezed dry

1/4 cup fresh rosemary (or 2 tablespoons dried)

1 medium onion, minced

3 cloves garlic, pressed or minced

1/2 to 1 cup crumbled feta cheese

1/2 cup skim milk

1 teaspoon salt, or more to taste

1 teaspoon freshly ground black pepper

1 teaspoon virgin olive oil

1/2 cup white wine

4 medium zucchini, sliced on the diagonal

2 medium onions, sliced and separated into rings

1 pound white button mushrooms, sliced

Olive oil cooking spray or virgin olive oil

One 1-pound package phyllo (see Note)

8 roasted red bell peppers, patted dry and cut into long, thick strips

One 14-ounce jar marinated artichoke hearts, drained and chopped

6 ounces sun-dried tomatoes, reconstituted in hot water and cut into slivers (see Note)

1/4 cup lightly packed fresh basil leaves, slivered

1/2 cup pine nuts, toasted (page 106)

Sprigs of fresh rosemary, for garnish (optional)

PREHEAT the oven to 375°F. In a food processor, purée the spinach, rosemary, onion, garlic, feta, milk, salt and pepper until smooth. If the mixture is too dry to purée, add a bit more milk for desired consistency. Set aside.

IN A LARGE NONSTICK SKILLET, coat the bottom with the oil. Add the wine and heat to a simmer. Cook the zucchini, stirring, for 5 minutes; remove and drain on paper towels. Cook the onions, stirring, for 5 minutes; remove and drain on paper towels. Cook the mushrooms, stirring for 5 minutes; remove and drain on paper towels.

LINE a jelly-roll pan or large deep-dish pizza pan with foil, leaving ends of the foil sticking up beyond edge of pan. Spray the foil with olive oil cooking spray or brush with oil.

TO FORM THE TART CRUST, lay down 1 sheet of phyllo and brush lightly or spray with olive oil. (Keep the rest of the phyllo covered to prevent drying.) Crinkle down the edges of phyllo that extend beyond the pan. Lay down the remaining sheets of phyllo, spraying or brushing each with oil and crinkling down the edges.

SMOOTH the spinach purée mixture over the phyllo crust. Arrange the zucchini, onions, mushrooms, roasted peppers, artichoke hearts and sun-dried tomatoes over the spinach mixture. Bake 15 minutes. If the edges of the crust are browning too quickly, lower the oven temperature to 325°F and bake 5 minutes more. If the crust is just beginning to turn golden, keep the oven temperature at 375°F and bake until the phyllo is golden and crisp and the vegetables are warmed, about 5 minutes more.

SPRINKLE the tart with fresh basil and toasted pine nuts. Tuck rosemary sprigs into the crinkled edges of the crust to garnish. Serve at once.

Notes:

- Phyllo, paper-thin sheets of flaky pastry dough, give a wonderful flavor and a bit of chewiness to dishes. Phyllo needs special handling because it dries out quickly while sitting on your countertop. Keep the yet-to-be-used sheets covered with a damp cloth. You can find phyllo in the frozen section of supermarkets and Greek groceries.

- To reconstitute dried tomatoes, cover them with boiling water and let sit until soft, about 7 to 10 minutes.

> **PER SERVING:**
> 281 Cal.; 11g Prot.; 9g Fat; 37g Carb.;
> 27mg Chol.; 652mg Sod.; 6g Fiber.

Spanokapita

serves 10

This authentic Greek dish is deliciously rich—so rich, in fact, that you may want to think twice before serving yourself seconds.

3 pounds fresh spinach (or four 10-ounce packages frozen spinach, thawed)

Pinch salt

6 tablespoons virgin olive oil

2 large onions, chopped

2 bunches scallions (green and white parts), chopped

1/2 cup chopped fresh parsley

1/2 cup chopped fresh dillweed (or 3 tablespoons dried)

4 eggs

1 1/2 cups crumbled feta cheese

1 cup ricotta or cottage cheese

1/4 cup melted butter

16 sheets of phyllo

IF YOU'RE USING FRESH SPINACH, remove and discard the coarse stems and wash the leaves. Sprinkle the spinach

lightly and evenly with salt, and let sit 10 minutes. Rinse the spinach and squeeze out excess water. Chop and drain in a colander until dry. (If you're using frozen spinach, omit the salt and squeeze the leaves as dry as possible. Place in a colander to drain.)

MEANWHILE, heat 2 tablespoons oil in a skillet and cook the onions and scallions, stirring, until soft but not brown, about 3 minutes. Add the spinach, parsley and dill. Cook, stirring, until the spinach has wilted, about 2 to 3 minutes. Remove from heat, transfer to a bowl and let cool. In a separate bowl, lightly beat the eggs and mix in the cheeses. Combine with the spinach.

PREHEAT the oven to 350°F. Lightly grease a 9 × 13-inch baking pan. Combine remaining 4 tablespoons oil and butter. Remove 8 sheets of phyllo from its package; keep the rest covered in the refrigerator to prevent drying. Center 1 sheet in the baking pan and brush it with the oil-butter mixture. Stack the other 7 sheets one by one on top of the first, brushing each with the oil-butter mixture. (The sheets will overlap the sides of the pan.) Pour in the spinach-egg mixture and spread evenly. Fold the overhanging sides and ends of phyllo over the filling to enclose it. Brush the phyllo with oil-butter mixture. Top with remaining 8 phyllo sheets, brushing each with the oil-butter mixture as you stack them. Tuck the overhanging edges around the inside of the baking pan to seal in the filling. Bake until golden, about 45 minutes. Cut into rectangles and serve.

Helpful hint:

To serve as an appetizer, score the phyllo on the top with a sharp knife into small squares. Once cooked, cut through the scored lines. Serve warm or cold.

> **PER SERVING:**
> 502 Cal.; 20g Prot.; 22g Fat; 60g Carb.;
> 126mg Chol.; 70mg Sod.; 6g Fiber.

Russian Perogies

makes 28

DOUGH

- 3/4 cup unbleached white flour
- 3/4 cup whole-wheat flour
- 1/8 teaspoon cream of tartar
- Dash salt
- 1/2 cup plus 1 tablespoon lukewarm water
- 1 tablespoon vegetable oil
- 1 large potato, steamed, peeled and mashed

FILLING

- 1 large onion, chopped
- 1 cup finely chopped white button mushrooms
- 1 teaspoon virgin olive oil
- Salt and freshly ground black pepper to taste

TOPPING

- 1/2 cup yogurt or nondairy sour cream
- 2 tablespoons bacon-flavored soy bits
- 1 or 2 onions, chopped and sautéed in 1 teaspoon oil

DOUGH: In a large bowl, combine flours, cream of tartar and salt. In a separate bowl, combine the water, oil and 1/4 cup mashed potato. (Reserve the remaining potato for the filling.) Stir the wet mixture into the flour mixture. Knead 5 to 10 minutes on a floured breadboard until smooth. Cover the dough and let rest 30 minutes.

FILLING: Meanwhile, in a skillet, cook the onion and mushrooms in the oil, stirring, over medium heat until lightly browned, about 5 minutes. Transfer to a bowl and combine with the reserved potato. Season with salt and pepper.

TO ASSEMBLE PEROGIES, divide the dough in half. Roll out each half to a 1/8-inch thickness on the floured board. Cut out 3-inch circles with a cookie cutter or a glass dipped in flour. Place a generous teaspoonful of the filling in the center of each circle. Fold in half, and pinch together the edges to seal. Keep the filled perogies between two dishcloths to prevent drying.

COOK the perogies in a large pot of boiling water; be careful not to crowd them. Remove the perogies with a slotted spoon when they float to the surface, about 3 minutes. Transfer to a serving dish. Top with the yogurt or sour cream, soy bits and onions.

> **PER PEROGIE:**
> 49 Cal.; 2g Prot.; 2g Fat; 7g Carb.;
> 1mg Chol.; 17mg Sod.; 0.8g Fiber.

Braised Seitan Roll with Apricots

serves 6

Seitan, pronounced SAY-tahn, is a meatlike food made from gluten flour and seasonings. Here it is formed into a rectangle, filled and rolled up. Although this recipe may seem intimidating at first, it's quite easy to make. (The trickiest part is tying the roll.) You may prepare the seitan several days in advance, then assemble and cook the roll a couple of hours before you serve it. Serve it over a bed of wild or basmati rice.

SEITAN

2 1/2 cups vegetable stock (page 178) (or replace
  1/4 cup with dry red wine if desired)

2 to 4 tablespoons soy sauce

1/4 teaspoon cayenne pepper

1/2 teaspoon garlic powder

About 3 cups gluten flour (available in natural food
  stores)

2 to 3 tablespoons vegetable oil

BRAISING LIQUID

1 large turnip, diced

1 bunch scallions (green and white parts), chopped

4 ounces dried apricots, chopped

3 cups vegetable stock (page 178)

1 1/2 cups dry red wine

3 to 4 tablespoons soy sauce

1 carrot, diced

2 stalks celery, sliced

1 leek, sliced

1 teaspoon black peppercorns

1/2 teaspoon dried thyme

4 to 5 cloves garlic

2 tablespoons cornstarch or arrowroot powder

2 tablespoons water

SEITAN: Combine the stock, soy sauce, cayenne and garlic powder in a large bowl. Stir in about 2 1/2 cups gluten flour. Add the remaining gluten flour a little at a time until the mixture congeals but is pliable and very soft. Roll or pat out the mixture into a rectangle about 1/3 to 1/2 inch thick. Heat the oil in a nonstick skillet and cook the seitan on both sides over medium-low heat until browned and firm, about 15 minutes on each side.

BRAISING LIQUID: Sprinkle the turnip, scallions and apricots on the seitan and roll it up tightly. Wrap a string around the roll to hold it together and tie securely. Place in a large pot with the remaining ingredients except the cornstarch or arrowroot and water. Cover and simmer 45 minutes, occasionally basting the roll (it will expand during cooking). Transfer the roll to a platter and remove the string. Strain the liquid through a colander over a bowl, pressing as much liquid out of the vegetables as possible. Return the liquid to the pot and reheat; discard the vegetables. Dissolve the cornstarch or arrowroot in water and add it to the pot to thicken the stock.

TO SERVE, slice the roll into 1/2-inch-thick slices and place them on a platter or individual plates over a bed of wild rice and pour the thickened stock around the rice.

> **PER SERVING (WITHOUT RICE):**
> 437 Cal.; 19g Prot.; 5g Fat; 30g Carb.;
> 0mg Chol.; 715mg Sod.; 3g Fiber.

Potato Knishes

makes 12

Knishes are flaky pastries filled with mashed potatoes and savory onions.

2 tablespoons oil, butter or margarine,
  or a combination

2 large onions, chopped

4 large baking potatoes

1 egg (or equivalent egg substitute)

Pinch ground nutmeg

Salt and white pepper to taste

12 sheets of phyllo

1/4 cup melted butter or margarine

1/2 cup fresh bread crumbs, toasted (page 106)

HEAT the oil, butter or margarine in a medium skillet and add onions. Lower the heat, and cook, stirring frequently, until browned. Let cool slightly.

MEANWHILE, bake or steam the potatoes until just tender. Peel and mash them or put them through a ricer. (Do not whip the potatoes—some texture is necessary.) Combine the potatoes and onions, and stir in egg or egg substitute and seasonings.

PREHEAT the oven to 375°F. Spray a baking sheet with nonstick cooking spray and set aside. Unroll the phyllo and carefully peel apart 12 sheets. (Return the remaining phyllo to your freezer for another use.) Cover 6 sheets with a damp dishcloth to prevent drying. Brush 1 sheet lightly with the melted butter or margarine. Quickly lay the second sheet on top, and brush with butter or margarine. Continue this process with remaining 4 sheets.

SPRINKLE half of the bread crumbs over the phyllo, then spoon half the potato-onion mixture in a ribbon across the width (short side) about 4 inches in from the edge. Fold this 4-inch edge over to cover the filling, then roll into a cylinder. Carefully transfer the filled roll to the prepared baking sheet. Repeat procedure with the remaining 6 sheets of phyllo, bread crumbs and potato-onion mixture.

WITH A VERY SHARP KNIFE, cut partially through the rolls at 2-inch intervals, leaving the rolls intact and being careful not to separate the slices. Brush the tops very lightly with melted butter or margarine, and bake until golden brown, about 30 to 40 minutes.

> **PER KNISH:**
> 182 Cal.; 3g Prot.; 6g Fat; 28g Carb.;
> 24mg Chol.; 175mg Sod.; 2g Fiber.

Spinach Roulade

serves 6

Festive and flavorful, this roulade—a flattened soufflé that's filled and rolled—belongs on a holiday table or at any special occasion. (Or give yourself a treat and make it on any day when you're not in a rush.)

SOUFFLÉ
- Butter and flour for preparing pan
- 1/4 cup butter
- 1/3 cup all-purpose flour
- 1 3/4 cups milk, warmed
- 1/2 teaspoon salt
- Freshly ground black pepper
- Dash ground nutmeg
- 5 eggs, separated
- 1/2 cup freshly grated Parmesan cheese
- Milk or light cream for brushing

FILLING
- 3 large bunches (about 2 pounds) spinach
- 1 onion, minced
- 2 tablespoons chopped fresh marjoram leaves (or 1 teaspoon dried)
- 1 tablespoon virgin olive oil
- Salt and freshly ground black pepper to taste
- 1 cup grated gruyère cheese

GARNISH
- Red Pepper Sauce (page 480)
- Fresh basil leaves

SOUFFLÉ: Cut a piece of parchment paper about an inch larger than a 10 × 15-inch jelly-roll pan. Lightly butter the pan, then press the paper against it, making creases in the corners so that it fits well. Lightly butter the paper, then dust with flour. Set aside.

PREHEAT the oven to 400°F. Melt the 1/4 cup butter in a saucepan and stir in the flour. Cook over medium heat for 1 minute, then whisk in warm milk. Cook on low heat, stirring frequently, for 10 minutes. Season with salt, pepper and nutmeg. Remove from the heat and whisk a little sauce into the egg yolks to warm them. Gradually whisk the yolk mixture into the sauce. Stir in the Parmesan cheese.

BEAT the egg whites until they form firm peaks. Stir about 1/5 of the egg whites into the sauce to lighten it; then fold in the remainder just until the whites are incorporated. Pour the mixture into the prepared pan and smooth with a spatula. Bake until the soufflé is puffed and lightly browned on top, about 15 minutes. Remove the soufflé from your oven; let cool. (It will flatten as it cools.) Meanwhile, make the filling.

FILLING: Remove the stems from the spinach and wash the leaves. Set aside. Using a 12-inch skillet, cook the onion and marjoram in oil over medium heat, stirring often until lightly browned and soft, about 10 minutes. In several batches, add the spinach leaves with water clinging to the leaves. Season with salt and pepper. Cook just until tender and wilted, then transfer the spinach to a colander. Press out as much liquid as possible. Chop the spinach very finely either by hand or in a food processor, without letting it become purée. Let cool.

TURN OUT the soufflé onto another piece of parchment or waxed paper and remove the paper liner. Sprinkle gruyère cheese over the surface, then spread the spinach mixture evenly on top. Gently but tightly roll up the soufflé, working from a long end to form a roulade. Wrap in plastic wrap and refrigerate until ready to bake.

PREHEAT the oven to 400°F. Brush the roulade with milk or light cream. Bake until hot, about 12 to 15 minutes.

TO SERVE, ladle 3 tablespoons of red pepper sauce on 6 plates, slice the roulade into sixths and set a piece in the middle of each plate. Garnish with basil.

Helpful hints:

- For the best results, bring the eggs to room temperature before preparing the soufflé. If you've forgotten to set them out, cover them with hot water for 5 minutes, then drain.
- You may bake, fill and roll the soufflé the night before you plan to serve it. Wrap it tightly in plastic wrap and refrigerate until ready to use.

> **PER SERVING (WITH SAUCE):**
> 540 Cal.; 28g Prot.; 5g Fat; 29g Carb.;
> 253mg Chol.; 1,140mg Sod.; 8g Fiber.

Jamaican Jerk Skewered Vegetables

serves 4

Jerk is a Jamaican term meaning food that has been barbecued. Serve this dish with rice.

VEGETABLES

8 cherry tomatoes, halved

1 green bell pepper, seeded and cut into 8 pieces

8 large white button mushrooms

8 broccoli florets

1 onion, cut into 8 wedges

MARINADE

- 6 to 8 scallions (green and white parts), diced
- 1 onion, diced
- 1 to 2 Scotch bonnet peppers or jalapeño peppers, seeded and minced
- 3/4 cup soy sauce
- 1/2 cup red wine vinegar
- 1/4 cup vegetable oil
- 1/3 cup brown sugar
- 2 tablespoons chopped fresh thyme leaves (or 1 tablespoon dried)
- 1/2 teaspoon ground cloves
- 1/2 teaspoon ground nutmeg
- 1/2 teaspoon ground allspice or ground cinnamon

VEGETABLES: Thread the vegetables onto 4 barbecue skewers, alternating cherry tomato, bell pepper, mushroom, broccoli and onion. Place the skewers in a casserole dish.

MARINADE: In a food processor fitted with a steel blade, process the marinade ingredients for 15 to 20 seconds. Pour over the skewers and refrigerate for 3 to 4 hours, spooning the marinade over the vegetables occasionally.

PREHEAT the grill until the coals are gray to white. Remove the skewers from the casserole and place them on the grill. Grill until the vegetables are cooked but not burned, about 4 to 5 minutes on each side.

Helpful hint:

Use plastic gloves when removing seeds from the peppers. The peppers can irritate your skin.

PER SERVING:
111 Cal.; 4g Prot.; 4g Fat; 17g Carb.;
0mg Chol.; 282mg Sod.; 3g Fiber.

Mushroom Bourguignonne in a Whole Pumpkin

serves 6

- 5- to 6-pound pumpkin or kabocha squash
- 2 large yellow or red onions, chopped
- 1 to 2 tablespoons water
- 1 pound white button mushrooms, halved
- 1/4 cup unbleached white flour or whole-wheat pastry flour
- 2 to 2 1/2 cups dry red wine
- 1/4 cup soy sauce
- 2 to 3 cubes vegetable bouillon (optional)
- 1/2 teaspoon dried rosemary
- 3 tablespoons dry sherry
- 1 tablespoon honey
- 2 tablespoons balsamic vinegar
- Freshly ground black pepper
- 4 cloves garlic

USING A VERY SHARP KNIFE, carve a 3- to 4-inch zigzagged circle in the top of the pumpkin or squash and remove the top. (If the peel is too thick to cut easily, bake at 350°F for 15 to 20 minutes to soften it.) Remove and discard seeds, and use a large spoon to scrape out the strings.

IN A LARGE SKILLET, sauté the onions in water for a few minutes. Add the mushrooms, cover and simmer for a few minutes, until they have begun to release their juices. Stir in the flour and cook 1 minute. Then add 2 cups red wine and the remaining ingredients, and cook 15 minutes, stirring frequently. Preheat the oven to 350°F. Pour the stew into the pumpkin or squash, place in a large, shallow dish (such as a pie plate) and put the top of the pumpkin on. Bake until the pumpkin is very soft, about 1 hour. While baking, stir the stew a couple of times, adding the remaining 1/2 cup wine if too much liquid evaporates or is absorbed. To serve, spoon out some stew and scrape out some of the pumpkin onto each plate.

PER SERVING:
157 Cal.; 3g Prot.; 0.1g Fat; 19g Carb.;
0mg Chol.; 696mg Sod.; 6g Fiber.

Butternut Squash Casserole

serves 4

- 1 small butternut squash, peeled, seeded and thinly sliced
- 1 small red onion, thinly sliced
- 1/3 cup apple juice
- 2 tablespoons butter or margarine, melted
- 2 tablespoons honey
- 1/8 to 1/4 cup slivered almonds, toasted (page 106)

PREHEAT the oven to 350°F. Combine the squash and onion in a 2-quart baking dish. In a small bowl, blend the apple juice, butter or margarine, and honey. Pour over the squash and top with almonds. Cover and bake until tender, about 40 minutes.

PER SERVING:
182 Cal.; 2g Prot.; 8g Fat; 26g Carb.;
16mg Chol.; 61mg Sod.; 6g Fiber.

Roasted Squash with Fruited Couscous

serves 8

Choose winter squash that have the prettiest, most symmetrical shape, such as acorn or even small round pie pumpkins.

- 1 squash, each about 1 to 2 pounds
- 3/4 cups water, salted if desired
- 2 1/2 cups uncooked couscous
- 1 cup currants
- 2 tablespoons margarine
- 4 tablespoons fat-free margarine spread
- 2 large golden Delicious apples, cored and sliced
- 2 pears, cored and chopped coarsely
- 1/2 cup dried apricots, cut into small pieces
- 1/2 cup golden raisins
- 1/2 cup coarsely chopped walnuts
- 4 tablespoons mild honey
- 1 teaspoon ground cinnamon
- 1/2 teaspoon ground nutmeg
- 1/2 teaspoon mace
- 1/2 teaspoon ground allspice
- 1/2 teaspoon cardamom
- 1/2 teaspoon freshly ground black pepper
- Salt to taste
- Pinch ground cinnamon
- Fresh greens or flowers, for garnish

CUT the top of each squash off to make a handsome lid. Set aside the lids. Cut a thin slice from the bottom of each squash to make it stand firmly. Using a large metal spoon, scoop out and discard the seeds and stringy flesh.

REMOVE the flesh from each to weigh a combined total of about 1 pound, taking some from the lid pieces, if necessary. Cut the scooped-out squash into 1/2-inch cubes. Steam until fork-tender, about 10 minutes. Meanwhile, bring salted water to a rolling boil. Stir in the couscous and currants, cover and remove from the heat. Let sit 10 minutes.

PREHEAT the oven to 325°F. Heat 2 tablespoons margarine in a large skillet, and cook the apples, pears, apricots, raisins and walnuts, stirring, for 5 minutes. Add 2 tablespoons honey, spices except for the pinch of cinnamon, couscous, steamed squash and salt to taste. Cook, stirring gently, for 2 or 3 minutes more. Remove from heat.

IN A SMALL POT, melt the remaining margarine, stir in the remaining honey and a pinch of cinnamon. Generously brush the inside of the squash with the honey mixture and divide the filling equally among them. Replace the squash lids, carefully turn upside down and place on a baking sheet sprayed with nonstick cooking oil. Bake until a fork easily pierces the squash, about 1 hour. Carefully transfer the roasted squash to a large serving platter, remove the lids and cut each squash in half vertically. Garnish the platter with fresh greens or flowers.

> **PER SERVING:**
> 352 Cal.; 7g Prot.; 9g Fat; 59g Carb.;
> 0mg Chol.; 359mg Sod.; 9g Fiber.

Stuffed Pumpkins with Herbs and Bread Crumbs

serves 4

When you bake miniature pumpkins, the rind softens and the flesh sweetens, providing a delicious counterpart to the savory stuffing.

> 4 miniature pumpkins (about 4 to 5 inches in diameter)
> 2 cups cubed rye or whole-wheat bread
> 1/2 cup thinly sliced carrots
> 1 cup diced onion
> 1/2 cup vegetable stock (page 178)
> 1/2 cup diced celery
> 1 teaspoon dried marjoram
> 1 teaspoon dried basil
> 1/2 teaspoon dried oregano
> 1/2 teaspoon freshly ground black pepper
> 1/4 cup minced fresh parsley
> 1 teaspoon virgin olive oil or apple juice

PREHEAT the oven to 325°F. Cut off pumpkin tops and set aside. Scoop out the seeds and membranes. Place the pumpkin shells on a large baking sheet. In a medium bowl, combine the remaining ingredients. Pack the stuffing tightly into the pumpkin cavities. Cover with the reserved tops. Bake until the pumpkin shells are tender, about 45 minutes. Serve hot.

> **PER SERVING:**
> 159 Cal.; 4g Prot.; 2g Fat; 30g Carb.;
> 0mg Chol.; 209mg Sod.; 6g Fiber.

Italian Stuffed Squash

serves 8

1 eggplant, peeled and diced into 1/2-inch cubes

2 tomatoes, diced

2 green bell peppers, diced

1 onion, diced

4 cloves garlic, minced

1 tablespoon dried basil

2 tablespoons virgin olive oil

1 large blue hubbard or banana squash, halved and seeded

1/2 cup grated Parmesan cheese (optional)

PREHEAT the oven to 375°F. Mix together the eggplant, tomatoes, bell peppers, onion, garlic, basil and olive oil. Spoon this mixture into the squash halves and arrange the squash in a baking pan. Bake until the squash is tender when pierced with a fork, about 1 hour; stir the filling ingredients once with a fork during baking. If desired, sprinkle the cheese on the squash halves and bake 10 minutes more. To serve, scoop out pieces of squash and filling with a spoon. Serve in bowls.

> **PER SERVING:**
> 121 Cal.; 3g Prot.; 4g Fat; 20g Carb.;
> 0mg Chol.; 6mg Sod.; 6g Fiber.

Creole Vegetable and Red Bean Jambalaya

serves 4

Here's a nutritious and delicious update of a traditional Creole dish of rice and meat or seafood.

2 tablespoons virgin olive oil

1 green bell pepper, seeded and diced

1 onion, diced

1 tomato, diced

8 to 10 white button mushrooms, sliced

1 cup diced eggplant

1 cup diced chayote or zucchini

1/2 cup diced celery

1 to 2 cloves garlic, minced

2 1/2 cups canned crushed tomatoes

3/4 cup water or vegetable stock (page 178)

1/2 cup chopped okra

8 broccoli florets

1/2 cup cooked red or black beans

1 tablespoon dry red wine

1 tablespoon dried oregano

1 tablespoon minced fresh parsley (or 1 teaspoon dried)

2 teaspoons fresh thyme (or 1 teaspoon dried)

1 to 2 teaspoons red pepper sauce

1/2 teaspoon freshly ground black pepper

1/4 teaspoon white pepper

1/4 teaspoon salt

1/8 teaspoon cayenne pepper

4 cups cooked brown rice

HEAT the oil in a saucepan and cook the bell pepper, onion, tomato, mushrooms, eggplant, chayote or zucchini, celery and garlic, stirring over medium heat until tender-crisp, about 10 to 12 minutes. Lower the heat and stir in the remaining ingredients except rice. Simmer, uncovered, for 15 to 20 minutes, stirring frequently. Serve over rice.

> **PER SERVING:**
> 427 Cal.; 12g Prot.; 10g Fat; 75g Carb.;
> 0mg Chol.; 410mg Sod.; 11g Fiber.

Curried Squash in a Roti

serves 4

Roti is a flatbread, which may be rolled up to hold curries.

DOUGH

- 4 cups all-purpose flour
- 2 teaspoons baking powder
- 1 teaspoon salt
- 1/4 cup vegetable oil
- 1 cup water
- 1 to 2 tablespoons vegetable oil for cooking rotis

FILLING

- 1 to 2 tablespoons vegetable oil
- 2 to 3 cloves garlic, minced
- 1 chili pepper, seeded and minced (optional)
- 1 medium red onion, diced
- 4 cups diced pumpkin, calabasa or butternut squash
- 2 cups water
- 2 tablespoons curry powder
- 1/2 tablespoon ground cumin
- 1 teaspoon dried thyme
- 1 teaspoon ground cloves
- 1/2 teaspoon freshly ground black pepper
- 1/4 teaspoon salt
- One 15-ounce can chickpeas, rinsed

DOUGH: Combine the dry ingredients in a mixing bowl. Gradually mix in the oil and water. Turn out the dough onto your work surface and knead until soft, about 5 minutes. Form into a ball, cover and let sit 15 minutes.

FILLING: Heat the oil in a deep skillet and cook the garlic, chili pepper and onion stirring over medium heat 3 to 4 minutes. Add the squash, water and seasonings, and cook until the squash is soft, about 20 minutes. Add the chickpeas and cook 5 to 10 minutes more, stirring occasionally. Set aside.

DIVIDE the dough into 4 balls. Flatten each ball and roll out into a circle 6 to 8 inches in diameter. Place about 1 cup filling on one side of each circle. Fold the dough over the filling and pinch the edges to seal.

HEAT 1 tablespoon oil or butter in a medium skillet over high heat until it sizzles. Lower the heat to medium and place a filled roti in the skillet. Cook until the crust is golden, about 2 to 3 minutes. Turn the roti with a wide spatula and cook until golden; transfer to a platter. Repeat with the remaining rotis, adding more oil or butter as needed. Serve warm.

Savory Apple Empanada

serves 6

This Spanish tart is sweet and savory. It is delicious served hot out of the oven, at room temperature or chilled.

CRUST

- 3 cups unbleached white flour plus extra flour for rolling dough
- 1 teaspoon salt
- 1/3 cup margarine
- 1/2 cup cold water, or more as needed

FILLING

- 1 tablespoon virgin olive oil
- 1 large Spanish onion, chopped
- 2 red or green bell peppers (or 1 of each), diced
- 6 large ripe tomatoes, broiled and peeled
- 2 cloves garlic, minced
- 2 teaspoons dried thyme
- 1/2 teaspoon salt
- 1/4 teaspoon freshly ground black pepper
- 2 tablespoons minced fresh parsley
- 2 large sweet apples (Delicious or Jonathan), cored, peeled and sliced thinly
- 1 egg white for brushing crust (optional)

CRUST: Mix together the flour and salt. Cut in the margarine until the mixture forms coarse crumbs. With a fork, mix in the water 1 tablespoon at a time to make a stiff dough. Cover with plastic wrap, and let rest at room temperature for 1 hour. Meanwhile, make the filling.

FILLING: Heat the oil in a large, deep-sided skillet over medium heat. Add the onion and cook, stirring, 5 minutes. Add the bell peppers, tomatoes, garlic, thyme, salt and black pepper. Continue to cook over medium heat until the mixture is soft and thick, about 20 minutes. Stir in the parsley.

PREHEAT the oven to 375°F. Divide the pastry dough in half and roll out each half into a circle slightly larger than a 9-inch deep-dish pie pan. Line the dish with one pastry circle. Spread on 1/3 of the vegetable sauce. Top the sauce with 1/3 of the apples. Repeat the layers until all the sauce and apples are used. Cover with the second pastry circle, crimp the edges and brush with egg white. Bake until deep golden brown, about 35 minutes. Serve hot, at room temperature or chilled.

Spanish Tortilla

serves 4

A Spanish *tortilla* is not the flat circle of flour or corn-meal found in Mexican cuisine; instead, it's an omelet made with potatoes. Steaming the potatoes and onions produces a lighter dish than the traditional method of frying them in olive oil.

> 2 pounds potatoes, peeled and sliced thinly
> 2 large Spanish onions, sliced thinly
> 6 large eggs
> 1/2 teaspoon salt
> 1 to 2 teaspoons virgin olive oil

IN A SAUCEPAN fitted with a steamer, steam the potatoes and onions until tender but not mushy, about 10 minutes. Meanwhile, in a bowl, beat the eggs with salt. Fold in the potatoes and onions.

IN A NONSTICK SKILLET, heat the oil. (More oil may be needed for other types of skillets.) Pour in the egg mixture and cook over medium heat. When the bottom becomes crisp, about 5 to 6 minutes, flip the omelet and cook 5 to 6 minutes more. To serve, cut the omelet into wedges. Serve hot, at room temperature or chilled.

Helpful hint:

It's easier to flip the omelet if you slide it onto a plate, then turn it over into the pan.

> ### PER SERVING:
> 274 Cal.; 13g Prot.; 8g Fat; 33g Carb.;
> 320mg Chol.; 376mg Sod.; 5g Fiber.

Mexican Corn Stew

serves 6

> 1 cup dry small red beans
> 1 tablespoon virgin olive oil
> 1 cup chopped onion
> 2 heaping tablespoons minced fresh garlic
> 1/4 cup seeded and diced fresh jalapeño peppers
> 1/2 cup thinly sliced carrots
> 1/2 cup thinly sliced celery
> 2 red bell peppers, seeded and diced
> 3 tablespoons minced fresh cilantro leaves
> 6 cups water or vegetable stock (page 178)
> 3 cups whole-kernel corn (fresh or frozen)
> 2 teaspoons ground cumin
> 2 teaspoons ground coriander
> 1/2 teaspoon cayenne pepper (optional)
> 2 cups crushed no-oil corn tortilla chips (optional)
> Salsa and nonfat yogurt, for garnish (optional)

PLACE the beans in a bowl with water to cover. Let soak overnight; drain. Rinse and set aside. In a large saucepan over medium-high heat, heat the oil and cook the onion and garlic, stirring, until soft, about 3 to 5 minutes. Add the jalapeños, carrots, celery and bell peppers, and continue cooking for 3 minutes, stirring frequently. Add the cilantro, water or stock, corn, cumin, coriander and beans. Cover and cook on low heat until the beans are tender and the stew is thick, about 1 1/2 to 2 hours on your stovetop or 6 to 8 hours in a slow cooker. Add cayenne. Serve in prewarmed bowls. Top with crushed tortilla chips, salsa and nonfat yogurt.

Cuban Corn Tamales

makes 8

Tamales are traditionally made of fried chopped meat, cornmeal dough, peppers and spices and are steamed in corn husks. In this version, cornmeal teams up with corn kernels and onions, and tamale wrapping paper is used to simplify the preparation.

> **2 cups whole-kernel corn (fresh, or frozen and thawed)**
>
> **1/2 cup cold water**
>
> **1 small onion, chopped**
>
> **2 cloves garlic, minced**
>
> **1/2 teaspoon salt**
>
> **1/4 teaspoon freshly ground black pepper**
>
> **2 to 3 tablespoons virgin olive oil**
>
> **1 cup very fine cornmeal**
>
> **8 sheets of tamale wrapping paper**
>
> **Cotton string**

FILL a large pot 3/4 full of water and bring to a boil. Meanwhile, in a blender or food processor, blend the corn kernels and cold water until milky and slightly lumpy. In a skillet, cook the onion, garlic, salt and pepper in the oil, stirring, over medium heat until the onion is translucent, about 5 minutes. Add to the corn mixture and blend. Add the cornmeal a little at a time to the blender and blend until the mixture is creamy.

NEAR ONE OF THE SHORTER ENDS of the tamale wrapping paper, drop 1/4 cup of the mixture. Gently spread out the mixture, leaving an inch of paper above and below. Roll the paper over the mixture and keep rolling until the wrapping paper completely surrounds the tamale. Fold the top end down and the bottom end up. Tie the wrapping paper securely with string. Repeat the process with the remaining tamales. Drop the tamales into the pot of boiling water. Cover and simmer 20 minutes. Unwrap and serve.

Variation:

Add 1/4 cup of chopped green bell peppers, chopped tomatoes or cooked chickpeas while cooking the onions.

Helpful hint:

Make a double batch of tamales and freeze the uncooked ones. For a quick meal, drop the frozen tamales into boiling water, cover the pot and simmer 20 minutes. Unwrap and serve.

Good Shepherd's Pie

serves 4

This recipe lends itself to creativity. If you decide to experiment with different versions of the three components of the dish, use this formula as a guide: For 4 servings, use 4 cups vegetable hash, 1/2 cup gravy and 6 medium potatoes, cooked and mashed.

POTATOES

- 6 medium russet potatoes, peeled and quartered
- 1/2 cup buttermilk, or as needed
- 2 tablespoons freshly grated Parmesan cheese
- Salt and freshly ground black pepper to taste

GRAVY

- 1/2 cup sun-dried tomatoes
- 2/3 cup water
- 2 teaspoons virgin olive oil
- 1 medium onion, chopped
- 1 large green bell pepper, chopped
- 1 small red bell pepper, chopped
- 2 cloves garlic, minced
- 1 teaspoon dried basil
- 1 teaspoon dried oregano
- 1/2 teaspoon ground cumin
- 2 tablespoons soy sauce
- 1/2 cup dry TVP granules (page 72)
- 3/4 cup water

HASH

- 1 teaspoon virgin olive oil
- 1 large onion, chopped
- 2 medium carrots, chopped
- 2 to 4 tablespoons water
- 2 cups cooked lentils
- 2 cloves garlic, minced
- 1/2 teaspoon dried oregano
- 1 tablespoon vegetarian Worcestershire sauce

GARNISHES (OPTIONAL)

- 2 tablespoons grated cheddar cheese
- Paprika

POTATOES: Boil the potatoes in water to cover until easily pierced with a knife, about 15 minutes. Drain and return the potatoes to the pot. Mash and stir in the buttermilk and Parmesan. Season with salt and pepper.

GRAVY: Place the tomatoes in a small pot and cover with 2/3 cup water. Bring to a simmer and cook, covered, until softened, about 5 minutes. Remove the tomatoes and chop, reserving cooking liquid.

IN A MEDIUM SAUCEPAN, heat the oil over medium-high heat. Cook the onion, bell peppers and garlic, stirring until lightly browned, adding the basil, oregano and cumin during cooking. Add the tomatoes, reserved cooking liquid, soy sauce, TVP and 3/4 cup water. Cover and simmer 15 minutes.

HASH: In a large saucepan, heat the oil over medium-high heat. Cook the onion, stirring, 1 minute. Add the carrots and water, and cook, stirring, until the onion is translucent and the carrots are tender, about 8 minutes. Stir in the lentils, garlic, oregano and Worcestershire sauce. Cook 1 or 2 minutes. Remove from the heat.

PREHEAT the oven to 350°F. Lightly butter a 2-quart gratin dish. Spread the hash in the dish, then spoon the gravy over the hash. Spread the mashed potatoes on top. Sprinkle with grated cheese and paprika. Bake until bubbly and fragrant, about 30 minutes.

Variations:

- Substitute potato cooking water for buttermilk in the mashed potatoes. Add a bit of olive oil.
- For a decorative touch, spoon or pipe mashed potatoes around outer edge of the dish, leaving the center open.

> **PER SERVING:**
> 469 Cal.; 21g Prot.; 5g Fat; 84g Carb.;
> 3mg Chol.; 921mg Sod.; 10g Fiber.

Broccoli Casserole

serves 4

1 medium potato, peeled and chopped coarsely

1/2 medium carrot, sliced thickly

1/2 medium onion, chopped coarsely

1 cup water

1 teaspoon salt

One 1-pound package frozen chopped broccoli

1 1/2 cups sliced white button mushrooms

1/4 to 1/2 cup water

4 ounces firm tofu, crumbled

1/2 cup nutritional yeast

1 tablespoon fresh lemon juice

Pinch garlic granules

1 cup uncooked instant brown rice

3/4 cup water

PREHEAT the oven to 350°F. In a small saucepan, bring the potato, carrot, onion, 1 cup water and salt to a boil over medium-high heat. Lower the heat to medium, cover and simmer until the potato and carrot are tender, about 10 minutes. Meanwhile, thaw the frozen broccoli in a colander under hot running water; drain. Cook the mushrooms in the water, stirring, until soft; drain.

POUR the potato mixture into a blender and add the tofu, yeast, lemon juice and garlic. Blend until very smooth and creamy. Pour into a shallow, greased 1 1/2- or 2-quart casserole. Add the broccoli, rice, mushrooms and 3/4 cup water. Stir well and smooth the top of the mixture. Bake until golden and bubbling, about 40 minutes.

Variation:

Instead of frozen broccoli, you may use 1 pound fresh broccoli (tops only), chopped and steamed briefly until tender-crisp, then cooled under cold running water and drained.

> **PER SERVING:**
> 279 Cal.; 16g Prot.; 3g Fat; 46g Carb.;
> 0mg Chol.; 753mg Sod.; 7g Fiber.

Vegetable Casserole with Cornbread Topping

serves 4

VEGETABLES

1 to 2 tablespoons butter or canola oil

1 medium onion, chopped finely

3 cloves garlic, minced

2 large tomatoes, chopped finely

1/2 cup water

1 medium potato, chopped into 1-inch cubes

1 medium sweet potato, chopped into 1-inch cubes

1 cup green beans, cut into 1-inch pieces

1 cup broccoli or cauliflower florets, chopped into 1-inch pieces

Salt and freshly ground black pepper to taste

1/2 cup frozen peas, thawed

CORNBREAD TOPPING

    1 egg

    1 tablespoon sugar

    1/2 cup buttermilk

    1/2 cup cornmeal

    1/2 cup unbleached white flour or whole-wheat
        pastry flour

    1 teaspoon baking powder

    1/2 teaspoon baking soda

    1/4 cup frozen whole-kernel corn, thawed

    1 teaspoon seeded, chopped jalapeño pepper

    1 tablespoon drained and chopped pimiento

VEGETABLES: Heat the butter or oil in a large skillet. Cook the onion and garlic, stirring, until the onion is translucent, about 5 minutes. Add the tomatoes and water, and bring to a boil. Add the potato. Lower the heat, cover and simmer 5 minutes. Add the sweet potato, green beans and broccoli or cauliflower. Simmer, covered, for 5 minutes more. Add the salt and pepper, then the peas. Remove from the heat and keep covered until the topping is ready. (The vegetables are not thoroughly cooked at this stage.)

CORNBREAD TOPPING: Preheat the oven to 425°F. Beat together the egg and sugar in a large bowl until smooth and creamy. Fold in the buttermilk. In a separate bowl, combine the cornmeal, flour, baking powder and baking soda. Add the corn and jalapeño. Add the egg mixture and stir until smooth.

PLACE the vegetables in a lightly oiled 8- or 9-inch square baking pan or a casserole dish. Spread the cornmeal batter in an even layer over the vegetables. Sprinkle the pimiento on top and gently pat into the batter. Bake until a toothpick inserted into the top comes out clean, about 18 to 20 minutes. Serve warm.

Variation:

Topping may be dolloped around the circumference of the baking pan instead of spread evenly.

Note:

You also may add soy sauce or any other seasoning of your choice.

> **PER SERVING:**
> 286 Cal.; 10g Prot.; 5g Fat; 53g Carb.;
> 62mg Chol.; 545mg Sod.; 9g Fiber.

Peppers Stuffed with Vegetables and Rice

serves 6

A classic goes meatless in this saucy version.

FILLING

    1/2 onion, diced

    1 stalk celery, diced

    1 carrot, diced

    1 medium zucchini, diced

    1/4 cup water

    1 teaspoon salt

    2 teaspoons dried basil

    2 teaspoons dried thyme

    2 cups diced tomatoes

    1 cup tomato purée

    4 cups cooked brown rice

    6 bell peppers

SAUCE

- 1 onion, sliced into thin strips
- 1 teaspoon chili powder
- 1/4 teaspoon garlic powder
- 1 1/2 teaspoon ground cumin
- 2 cups tomato purée
- 2 cups tomato juice
- Juice of 1/2 lemon
- 1 cup water
- 1/4 pound white button mushrooms, sliced
- 1 red bell pepper, sliced into thin strips
- 2 scallions (green and white parts), chopped finely

FILLING: In a skillet, cook the onion, celery, carrot and zucchini in the water, stirring. Add the salt, basil and thyme. When the carrot is soft, add the tomatoes and tomato purée. Simmer 5 minutes. Stir in the cooked rice and set aside. Cut the bell peppers in half lengthwise; remove seeds.

SAUCE: Cook the onion with spices in a dry skillet, stirring, for about 5 minutes. Add the tomato purée, tomato juice, lemon juice and water. Simmer over low heat 10 to 15 minutes. Add the remaining ingredients and simmer 5 minutes. Remove from the heat.

PREHEAT the oven to 350°F. Spoon the filling into the pepper halves. Arrange the stuffed peppers in a baking dish and cover with the sauce. Bake 30 minutes.

> **PER SERVING:**
> 280 Cal.; 9g Prot.; 1g Fat; 61g Carb.;
> 0mg Chol.; 764mg Sod.; 12g Fiber.

Garden Vegetable Quiche

serves 4

Quiche usually takes an hour to bake. This flavorful, cholesterol-free microwave version is ready in about half the time.

CRUST

- 2 cups cooked brown rice
- 1 egg white
- 1 tablespoon chopped fresh parsley
- 1/4 teaspoon garlic powder
- 1/4 teaspoon seasoned salt

FILLING

- 1 cup thinly sliced red onion
- 1 cup asparagus tips
- 1/2 cup chopped carrot
- 1 teaspoon margarine
- One 10-ounce carton egg substitute
- 1/3 cup skim milk
- 2 tablespoons all-purpose flour
- 1 tablespoon shredded Parmesan cheese (optional)
- 1/4 teaspoon dried Italian seasoning

CRUST: In a medium mixing bowl, combine the crust ingredients. Mix well. Press the mixture over the bottom and up the sides of a 9-inch pie plate. Microwave at high power until the crust is set, about 1 to 2 minutes, rotating plate twice. Set aside.

FILLING: In a 2-quart casserole dish, combine the vegetables and margarine. Cover. Microwave at high power
until the vegetables are tender-crisp, about 4 to 6 minutes, stirring once or twice. Set aside.

IN A SMALL MIXING BOWL, combine the remaining ingredients. Mix together the egg substitute mixture and the
vegetable mixture. Microwave the egg substitute—and-
vegetable mixture at medium power (50%), uncovered,
until the mixture just begins to set around the edges,
stirring every 2 minutes, for a total of 4 to 6 minutes.

POUR the egg substitute—and-vegetable mixture into the
prepared crust. Microwave at medium power (50%) until
set in the center, about 10 to 12 minutes, rotating the pie
plate 3 or 4 times during cooking. Let sit on your counter
5 minutes before serving.

> **PER SERVING:**
> 252 Cal.; 13g Prot.; 5g Fat; 39g Carb.;
> 0mg Chol.; 316mg Sod.; 4g Fiber.

Sweet and Sour Cabbage Rolls with Sauerkraut

serves 6

This time-honored way to turn a humble head of cabbage into a stick-to-the-ribs delight takes awhile to
make. So prepare it on a day when you can enjoy the
creativity of cooking. If desired, you may make this dish
the day before you plan to serve it.

1 large onion, thinly sliced

2 tablespoons walnut oil or other vegetable oil

1 cup uncooked brown rice

1 1/2 cups vegetable stock (page 178)

2 tablespoons golden raisins

1/4 cup sunflower seeds

1/2 teaspoon ground cinnamon

1 1/2 teaspoons salt

1/2 teaspoon freshly ground black pepper

1 large head cabbage

2 pounds fresh deli-type sauerkraut

One 28-ounce can plum tomatoes (with juices),
    coarsely chopped

One 6-ounce can tomato paste, plus 1 can water

1/4 cup honey or date sugar, or more to taste

FINELY CHOP 1 or 2 onion slices to make about 2 tablespoons. In a saucepan, cook the chopped onion in
1 tablespoon oil, stirring, until translucent and limp.
(Reserve the remaining onion slices.) Mix in the rice,
stock, raisins, seeds, cinnamon, half of the salt and half
of the pepper. Bring to a boil over high heat, lower the
heat, cover and cook until the rice is tender, about
45 minutes.

WHILE the rice mixture is cooking, remove the core from
the cabbage and discard. Place the cabbage in a large
steamer or a deep soup pot and steam until the outer
leaves become limp enough to remove one by one.
(You'll need at least 18 leaves, and more if possible.) Lay
out the leaves on a clean dishcloth to cool. Using a knife,
remove the thick lower portion of the veins. Finely shred
the remaining cabbage and reserve. Drain the sauerkraut, cover with fresh cold water, drain again and
reserve.

IN A CASSEROLE DISH, cook the reserved onion slices in remaining tablespoon of oil, stirring, until limp, about 3 minutes. Add the shredded cabbage, sauerkraut, chopped tomatoes and their juices, tomato paste with water and remaining salt and pepper. Bring the mixture to a boil, stirring constantly. Stir in the honey or date sugar and simmer a few minutes to blend. Taste, and add more honey or date sugar if needed to balance the sour. Remove from the heat.

PREHEAT the oven to 350°F. Fluff the rice mixture to distribute the raisins, sunflower seeds and spices. Place 2 tablespoons of the filling on the lower third of a cabbage leaf. Fold up the lower part of the leaf, then fold over both sides, and roll up. Repeat with the remaining filling and cabbage leaves.

PLACE the rolls seam side down into the casserole dish, pushing them into the sauce. Cover and bake 25 minutes. Spoon the sauce over the rolls and bake 20 minutes more. If desired, continue baking, uncovered, to brown the top. Serve hot.

> **PER SERVING:**
> 350 Cal.; 7g Prot.; 8g Fat; 61g Carb.;
> 0mg Chol.; 1,792mg Sod.; 13g Fiber.

Cabbage Stuffed with Bulgur and Fruit

serves 8

Bulgur, a delicious grain made from wheat that has been hulled and parboiled, replaces ground meat in this rendition of a classic dish. You may make the stuffing and sauce a day or two in advance.

| 1 large head green cabbage

STUFFING
| 1 cup uncooked bulgur
| 2 cups water
| 1 medium onion, chopped finely
| 1 1/2 cups cooked brown or white rice
| 1/3 cup raisins
| 1/4 teaspoon allspice
| 1/4 teaspoon ground cinnamon
| 1/4 teaspoon dried thyme
| 4 cloves garlic, crushed
| Salt and freshly ground black pepper to taste

SAUCE
| 1 cup tomato purée
| 1/4 cup cider vinegar
| 1/4 cup fresh lemon juice
| 1/2 cup dark brown sugar
| 1/2 cup water
| 1/2 cup apricot preserves
| 1/2 cup peach preserves
| 1/2 teaspoon ground ginger
| 1/2 teaspoon ground cinnamon

IN A LARGE POT, bring to boil enough water to cover cabbage. Plunge the cabbage into the water, cover and remove from the heat. Let sit for 20 minutes, drain thoroughly and peel off 8 leaves. Reserve the remaining cabbage for another use.

STUFFING: Combine the bulgur with 2 cups water in a medium saucepan. Bring to a boil, lower heat, cover and simmer 15 to 20 minutes. In a large bowl, mix together the bulgur and remaining stuffing ingredients. Divide the mixture into 8 portions and spoon each portion into the center of a cabbage leaf. Fold up the lower part of the leaf, then fold over both sides and roll up. Place seam side down in a baking dish.

SAUCE: Preheat the oven to 300°F. In a saucepan, combine the sauce ingredients. Cook over medium heat, stirring frequently, until the sauce thickens, about 3 minutes. Pour the sauce over the cabbage rolls and cover the dish with foil. Bake 3 hours, turning the rolls every 30 minutes.

> **PER SERVING:**
> 307 Cal.; 4g Prot.; 0.6g Fat; 74g Carb.;
> 0mg Chol.; 274mg Sod.; 5g Fiber.

Vegetarian Pot Pie

serves 8

Here's the classic vegetarian pot pie.

1/4 to 1/2 cup vegetable stock (page 178) or white wine
1 cup diced onion
1 cup thinly sliced celery
2/3 cup thinly sliced carrots
1 cup diced red bell peppers
2/3 cup sliced frozen green beans
1/3 cup frozen peas
1/3 cup whole-wheat flour
1 cup skim milk or soymilk
2 cups vegetable stock (page 178)
2 tablespoons minced fresh parsley
1 teaspoon salt or low-sodium soy sauce
1/4 teaspoon dried sage
1/2 teaspoon dried thyme
1/4 teaspoon freshly ground black pepper
1/4 teaspoon cayenne pepper
1 recipe Basic Biscuit Crust (page 446)

PREHEAT the oven to 400°F. Coat a 2-quart casserole dish with nonstick cooking spray. In a heavy saucepan over medium-high heat, heat the stock or wine to a simmer and add onion. Cook, stirring, for 3 minutes. Add the celery, carrots, bell peppers, beans and peas. If the mixture begins to dry out, add 1/4 cup more vegetable stock or wine. Cook, stirring, for 3 minutes more.

LOWER the heat and sprinkle the flour over the vegetable mixture; cook, stirring, for 2 minutes. Combine the skim milk or soymilk and 2 cups vegetable stock in a measuring cup. Slowly whisk the liquid mixture into the vegetables. The sauce will start to thicken. Add the parsley, salt or soy sauce, sage, thyme, black pepper and cayenne. Cook, stirring constantly, until the mixture is thickened. Remove from the heat and pour into the prepared casserole dish.

LAY the Basic Biscuit Crust on top. Do not seal the edges. Bake until the crust is golden brown and the filling is bubbling, about 20 to 30 minutes.

> **PER SERVING:**
> 189 Cal.; 6g Prot.; 4g Fat; 31g Carb.;
> 10mg Chol.; 286mg Sod.; 3g Fiber.

Pot Pie with Greens

serves 8

| Nonstick cooking spray
| 2 teaspoons virgin olive oil
| 1/2 cup sliced onion
| 1/4 cup water
| 2 cups cubed red potatoes
| 1/2 cup diced carrots
| 2 medium leeks, halved lengthwise and sliced thinly
| 2 cups coarsley chopped tomatoes
| 2 cups chopped greens: kale, spinach, collard or turnip
| 3 tablespoons minced fresh parsley
| 2 teaspoons nutritional yeast (optional)
| 1 tablespoon low-sodium tamari or soy sauce
| 1 cup cold vegetable stock (page 178) mixed with
| 1 teaspoon cornstarch or arrowroot
| 1 recipe Basic Biscuit Crust (page 446)

PREHEAT the oven to 300°F. Coat a 2-quart casserole dish with nonstick cooking spray. In a saucepan over medium-high heat, heat the oil, add the onion and cook, stirring, until golden. Add the water, potatoes and carrots, and cook 2 minutes, stirring. Add the leeks, tomatoes and greens; cook until the greens wilt, about 3 minutes.

LOWER the heat and add the parsley, nutritional yeast, tamari or soy sauce, and stock mixture. Cook, stirring frequently, until the sauce thickens slightly.

SPOON the mixture into the prepared casserole dish. Lay the Basic Biscuit Crust lightly over the filling. Do not seal the edges. Bake until the crust is lightly browned, about 30 minutes.

> **PER SERVING:**
> 212 Cal.; 5g Prot.; 4g Fat; 39g Carb.;
> 8mg Chol.; 619mg Sod.; 5g Fiber.

Vegetable-Stuffed Potato Kugel

serves 6

The old-fashioned potato kugel (which means "pudding") is made with finely grated raw potatoes and can be quite heavy. Here the texture is lightened considerably by adding fluffy mashed potatoes.

STUFFING

| 2 tablespoons canola oil
| 1 medium onion, sliced thinly
| 1 medium clove garlic, minced
| 1/2 cup shredded carrot
| 1/2 cup shredded parsnip
| 2 stalks celery, chopped finely
| 1/3 cup chopped walnuts
| Salt to taste (optional)
| 1/4 teaspoon freshly ground black pepper

KUGEL

| Butter-flavored cooking spray
| 1 teaspoon fresh lemon juice
| 3 large uncooked potatoes, peeled and diced
| 2 large cooked potatoes, mashed
| 3/4 cup egg substitute
| 1/4 cup matzoh meal
| 1/2 cup reduced-fat margarine
| 1 teaspoon baking powder
| 1 teaspoon salt, or to taste (optional)
| 1/4 teaspoon freshly ground black pepper, or to taste
| Dash cinnamon

STUFFING: In a large nonstick skillet, heat the oil and cook the onion, stirring, over medium-high heat 1 minute; add the garlic and stir for 30 seconds. Stir in the carrot, parsnip and celery, and cook, stirring, until the vegetables are tender-crisp, about 6 to 8 minutes. Stir in the walnuts, salt and pepper.

KUGEL: Preheat the oven to 400°F. Spray a 9 × 13-inch baking pan generously with nonstick cooking spray. Set aside.

IN A FOOD PROCESSOR fitted with a steel blade, purée uncooked potatoes with lemon juice until smooth. Pour into a large mixing bowl. Add the mashed potatoes, egg substitute, matzoh meal, margarine, baking powder, salt, pepper and cinnamon, mixing thoroughly. Pour about half of this mixture into the prepared pan, pushing it into the corners and smoothing it with a wet spatula.

SPREAD the stuffing evenly on top and spoon over the remaining potato mixture. Spray the surface evenly with nonstick cooking spray. Bake until browned, about 1 hour. Cut the kugel into squares and serve hot.

> **PER SERVING:**
> 324 Cal.; 7g Prot.; 23g Fat; 23g Carb.;
> 1mg Chol.; 244mg Sod.; 3g Fiber.

Potato Latkes

serves 4

Latkes are potato pancakes with a distinctive Jewish touch. During the eight days of Chanukah, latkes are especially popular fare in Jewish homes, but they're delicious any time. Top them with applesauce.

| 1 1/2 pounds potatoes, grated
| 2 small onions, minced
| 3 tablespoons cornstarch
| 1 tablespoon finely chopped fresh parsley
| Dash freshly ground black pepper
| 2 tablespoons soy sauce or tamari
| Nonstick cooking spray

MIX all the ingredients in a bowl. Coat a skillet with nonstick cooking spray. Form 3-inch patties and cook over medium heat until crisp on both sides.

> **PER SERVING:**
> 149 Cal.; 7g Prot.; 1g Fat; 33g Carb.;
> 0mg Chol.; 295g Sod.; 4g Fiber.

Tzimmes with Potato Dumplings

s e r v e s 6

Tzimmes is a sweetened dish of stewed vegetables and dried fruit. Here it's simmered with hearty potato dumplings. The dish traditionally is served as part of the last meal before the Yom Kippur fast, but it's also eaten at festive meals throughout the year.

DUMPLINGS

3 large potatoes, peeled and grated finely

1 medium potato, peeled, cooked and mashed

1 tablespoon melted butter or margarine

1/3 cup matzoh meal, or as needed

2 large eggs, beaten (or 1/2 cup egg substitute)

1/2 teaspoon salt

1/4 teaspoon ground cinnamon

Freshly ground pepper to taste

TZIMMES

1 pound carrots, chopped

2 large sweet potatoes, peeled and chopped

8 to 10 pitted prunes (optional)

2 tablespoons brown sugar or maple syrup

1 tablespoon finely minced onion

1/4 teaspoon ground ginger

Pinch of salt

1 1/2 tablespoons cornstarch or arrowroot dissolved in
1 1/2 tablespoons water

DUMPLINGS: To remove excess starch, place the grated potatoes in the center of a dishcloth. Twist it closed and dip in cold water. Then tightly twist the cloth to squeeze out as much liquid as possible.

TRANSFER the potatoes to a large mixing bowl and stir in the remaining dumpling ingredients. If the mixture isn't firm enough to shape, add a little more matzoh meal. Shape into 2 dumplings.

TZIMMES: Place half of the carrots and potatoes, prunes, brown sugar or maple syrup, onion, ginger and salt in a large saucepan. Add the dumplings and top with the remaining vegetables. Add cold water to barely cover. Bring to a boil, lower the heat, cover and barely simmer until the dumplings are cooked and the vegetables are fork-tender, about 1 hour.

UNCOVER, raise the heat and boil until the liquid is reduced by half. Remove from the heat. Transfer the dumplings to a plate. Add the dissolved cornstarch or arrowroot to the saucepan and stir until the liquid is thick and clear, about 1 minute. Slice each dumpling into thirds and serve topped with the tzimmes.

> **PER SERVING:**
> 240 Cal.: 5g Prot.; 4g Fat; 46g Carb.;
> 76mg Chol.; 301mg Sod.; 5g Fiber.

Mexican Lasagna

serves 4

This main dish is a sure hit with your family.

- 1/2 to 1 tablespoon virgin olive oil
- 1 onion, chopped
- 1 to 2 cloves garlic, minced
- 1 green bell pepper, chopped coarsely
- 1 teaspoon ground cumin
- 1 tablespoon chili powder or to taste
- Dash cayenne pepper (optional)
- 1 cup whole-kernel corn (fresh or frozen)
- One 16-ounce can pinto or kidney beans, drained
- 1 cup tomato sauce
- Six 7-inch corn tortillas
- 1 cup low-fat cottage cheese
- 1/2 to 1 cup cheddar cheese

IN A LARGE SKILLET, heat the oil over medium-high heat. Cook the onion, garlic and bell pepper, stirring, until soft, about 5 minutes. Stir in the spices and sauté 1 minute more. Remove from the heat. Mix in the corn, beans and up to 1 cup of tomato sauce.

PLACE 3 tortillas in a 2-quart casserole dish, arranging them to cover the bottom. Spoon in half of the corn-bean mixture and spread 1/2 cup cottage cheese on top. Sprinkle on half of the cheddar. Repeat layers, using up all the ingredients. Microwave, uncovered, on high power until heated through and the cheese is melted, about 10 to 15 minutes. Let sit 5 minutes before serving.

PER SERVING:
424 Cal.; 24g Prot.; 10g Fat; 62g Carb.;
20mg Chol.; 700mg Sod.; 13g Fiber.

Sautéed Spinach, Garlic and Lima Beans

serves 3

Corn on the cob or hearty rye bread complement this dish.

- 1 cup dry large lima beans
- 3 cups water
- 1/2 teaspoon salt
- *Bouquet garni* (or 2 sprigs fresh rosemary, 1 sprig fresh thyme and 2 bay leaves)
- 1 large bunch spinach
- 1 to 2 teaspoons virgin olive oil
- 3 to 5 cloves garlic, minced
- Pinch cayenne pepper
- Dash salt or umeboshi vinegar
- Optional garnishes: wedge of lemon or lime; roasted red bell pepper strips; tomato slices; olives

PLACE the lima beans in a large pot and cover with 3 cups water. Soak at least 4 hours or overnight. Drain and rinse the beans, then drain again. Add salt and fresh water to cover by 1 inch. Bring to a boil, add the *bouquet garni* or fresh herbs, and cover, with the lid ajar. Lower the heat and simmer until the beans are soft, about 45 minutes or longer. (If you're using bay leaves, remove and discard them.) Wash the spinach and remove tough stems. Set aside.

HEAT a skillet over medium-high heat for 30 seconds, add the oil and heat 30 seconds more. Add the garlic and cook, stirring, until golden. Continue cooking until the garlic becomes crisp, about 1 to 2 minutes. Remove the garlic and set aside. Add the cayenne to the skillet. Stir in the spinach, cover and cook until the leaves wilt, about 1 minute. Drain and blot with a dishcloth to remove excess water. Chop the spinach or leave whole. Season with salt or umeboshi vinegar. To serve, mound the spinach on a plate, top with the beans and sprinkle with the roasted garlic. Add garnishes.

> **PER SERVING:**
> 183 Cal.; 14g Prot.; 2g Fat; 31g Carb.;
> 0mg Chol.; 617mg Sod.; 16g Fiber.

Italian-Style Aspic

serves 6

The ingredients of minestrone soup appear in this aspic, which uses agar-agar flakes, not animal-based gelatin, to hold it together. Prepare it the day before you plan to serve it.

2 cups tomato juice
6 tablespoons agar-agar flakes
4 cups vegetable stock (page 178)
1 carrot, diced
1 zucchini, cubed
1 1/2 cups cooked white beans
3 medium tomatoes, sliced thinly
1/2 cup cooked fettuccine
1 tablespoon chopped fresh chives
Celery leaves, endive, fresh basil and fresh marjoram, for garnish

PLACE the tomato juice in a bowl and sprinkle the agar-agar on top. Set aside until the agar-agar softens, about 10 minutes. In a large saucepan, bring the stock to a boil, lower the heat and stir in the carrot and zucchini. Cook until just tender, about 10 minutes. Stir in the beans and the agar-tomato juice mixture. Heat to a simmer. (Do not boil.) Stir occasionally until the agar dissolves. Divide the mixture among 6 deep soup bowls. Let cool at room temperature to set; then refrigerate overnight.

UNMOLD the aspics onto individual plates. Surround with the tomato slices and strands of fettuccine. Sprinkle the chives on top. Decorate with garnishes.

> **PER SERVING:**
> 258 Cal.; 14g Prot.; 3g Fat; 45g Carb.;
> 0mg Chol.; 30mg Sod.; 6g Fiber.

Vegetable-and-Herb Medley

serves 4

This seasoned medley turns ordinary vegetables into a lovely, low-fat supper. Serve it over pasta or rice.

2 small zucchini

1/2 pound eggplant

1/2 pound tomatoes (fresh or canned)

1 medium bell pepper, seeded

1 small red onion

1/4 pound white button mushrooms

1/2 cup water

1 clove garlic, minced

1 tablespoon salt-free tomato paste

1/4 cup chopped fresh parsley

1/4 cup chopped fresh basil leaves

1 teaspoon minced fresh thyme leaves

1/2 teaspoon minced fresh rosemary leaves

Freshly ground black pepper to taste

Splash of balsamic vinegar (optional)

CUT the zucchini, eggplant, tomatoes, bell pepper, onion and mushrooms into 1/2-inch cubes. Place the water in a large, heavy pot over medium heat, and stir in the garlic and tomato paste until blended. Add the vegetables and cook until tender, about 15 minutes. Stir in the herbs and black pepper. Serve warm or cold, with balsamic vinegar.

> **PER SERVING:**
> 75 Cal.; 3g Prot.; 0.7g Fat; 15g Carb.;
> 0mg Chol.; 12mg Sod.; 4g Fiber.

Spinach-Filled Crepes

serves 4

These savory crepes are dressy and delicious.

2 tablespoons virgin olive oil

4 cups quartered white button mushrooms

Salt and freshly ground black pepper to taste

1 large onion, chopped

2 bunches spinach, trimmed and chopped

1 bunch scallions (green and white parts), chopped

1/2 cup chopped fresh parsley

1/2 cup chopped fresh basil leaves or dillweed (optional)

2 tomatoes, chopped

1/4 cup pine nuts (optional)

4 Basic or No-Cholesterol Dinner Crepes (page 441)

1/4 recipe Béchamel Sauce (page 475)

IN A LARGE SKILLET, heat 1 tablespoon oil over high heat, and cook the mushrooms, stirring, until browned. Season with salt and pepper. Remove the mushrooms and set aside.

WIPE the skillet with a paper towel, add another tablespoon oil and cook the onion, covered, over low heat, until tender. Turn up the heat and add the spinach, a little at a time, until all of it fits into the skillet. Add the scallions, parsley and basil or dillweed and cook, stirring, until the vegetables are tender and little liquid remains. Add the chopped tomatoes and cook, stirring, for a few minutes to heat through. Add the reserved mushrooms and pine nuts.

PREHEAT the oven to 350°F. Place 1/8 of the filling on each crepe, roll up and place side by side on a greased baking sheet. Pour the béchamel sauce over the crepes and bake 10 to 15 minutes.

> **PER SERVING (WITH SAUCE):**
> 411 Cal.; 17g Prot.; 19g Fat; 45g Carb.;
> 146mg Chol.; 379mg Sod.; 18g Fiber.

Vegetable-Filled Pouches

serves 4

1 onion, chopped finely

1/4 cup water (or 1 tablespoon oil)

3 cups peeled and chopped potatoes

2 cups peeled and chopped parsnips

2 cups peeled and chopped rutabaga (see Note)

1 carrot, chopped

1/2 cup chopped fresh parsley

Salt and freshly ground black pepper to taste

8 to 10 Basic or No-Cholesterol Dinner Crepes
  (page 441)

Oil for brushing

1/6 recipe Mushroom Sauce (page 477)

IN A SKILLET, cook the onion, stirring, in water or oil until soft; remove from the heat. Meanwhile, in a saucepan fitted with a steamer, steam the potatoes, parsnips, rutabaga and carrot until tender; drain. Mash the vegetables and stir in the onion. Add the parsley, salt and pepper.

PREHEAT the oven to 400°F. Place 1/3 to 1/2 cup of the vegetable mixture in the center of a crepe. Bring the edges up together at the top to form a pouch. Tie loosely with a string. Repeat with the remaining crepes. Place the crepes on a baking sheet, brush them with oil and bake until browned, about 20 minutes. To serve, spoon the mushroom sauce on individual plates and place 1 or 2 pouches on top of the sauce.

Note:

In the same family as the turnip, the often overlooked rutabaga has a delightfully earthy, turniplike flavor. Rutabagas are waxed for commercial sale. Even if they aren't waxed, peel them anyway; the peels are too tough to eat. Eat rutabagas raw or cook them as your recipe directs.

> **PER SERVING (WITH SAUCE):**
> 555 Cal.; 16g Prot.; 13g Fat; 91g Carb.;
> 146mg Chol.; 711mg Sod.; 11g Fiber.

Potato Medley

serves 2

This hearty, flavorful melange is a good source of potassium and vitamin C. Leftovers are great for lunch, or even breakfast.

5 large russet potatoes, cubed

2 cups chopped broccoli

1 tablespoon canola oil

2 cloves garlic, pressed or minced

1 cup frozen peas, thawed

1 red bell pepper, seeded and diced

1 green bell pepper, seeded and diced

2 scallions (green and white parts), minced

1 teaspoon dried oregano or rosemary

1 teaspoon dried basil

Salt and freshly ground black pepper to taste

Cayenne pepper to taste

IN A LARGE POT, boil the potatoes in enough water to cover for 8 minutes. Add the broccoli and cook until the potatoes are just tender, about 4 or 5 minutes more; drain.

HEAT the oil in a large, deep skillet. Add the potatoes, broccoli and the remaining ingredients. Cook, stirring, until the potatoes become slightly creamy and the ingredients are heated through, about 7 minutes. Serve hot.

> **PER SERVING:**
> 385 Cal.; 7g Prot.; 3g Fat; 79g Carb.;
> 0mg Chol.; 64mg Sod.; 11g Fiber.

Chop Suey

serves 4

This version is far lower in fat than its restaurant counterpart. If you're short on time, use a packaged frozen vegetable medley for some of the fresh vegetables. Feel free to omit some vegetables or to use others of your choice.

2/3 cup chopped onion

3 cloves garlic, minced

2 teaspoons grated fresh ginger root

1 tablespoon toasted sesame oil

1/2 cup diagonally cut carrots

1/2 cup diagonally cut celery

2/3 cup sliced white button mushrooms

1 cup sliced bell peppers

2/3 cup coarsely shredded red cabbage

2 cups diagonally cut zucchini

2/3 cup mung bean sprouts

2/3 cup sliced green beans

2/3 cup snow peas

2/3 cup bamboo shoots

2/3 cup sliced water chestnuts

1 cup sliced tomatoes

1 cup water

2 tablespoons low-sodium soy sauce

3 tablespoons arrowroot or cornstarch

3 cups cooked brown rice

COOK the onion, garlic and ginger, stirring, in the oil over medium-high heat. Add the carrots and celery, and cook, stirring, 5 minutes. Add the mushrooms, peppers, cabbage and zucchini, and cook 3 minutes more. Add the bean sprouts, green beans, snow peas, bamboo shoots, water chestnuts and tomatoes, and cook 3 minutes more. Stir together the water, soy sauce and arrowroot or cornstarch; stir gently into the vegetable mixture. Cook until the sauce is thickened and all the vegetables are tender-crisp. Serve over rice.

> **PER SERVING:**
> 329 Cal.; 9g Prot.; 5g Fat; 63g Carb.;
> 0mg Chol.; 158mg Sod.; 13g Fiber.

Chop Suey in the Raw

serves 4

This uncooked meal is a new spin on an ancient dish. It has next to no fat and is resplendent with vitamins and minerals.

- 2 medium heads bok choy
- 2 large heads napa cabbage
- 2 cups broccoli florets
- 1/4 cup minced fresh parsley
- 1/4 cup chopped watercress
- 1/4 cup fresh lime juice
- 3 tablespoons soy sauce
- 3 sheets nori, crumbled (page 78)
- 3 cups red bell pepper strips
- 4 stalks celery, trimmed and chopped
- 1 cup sliced white button mushrooms (optional)
- 1 1/2 cups mung bean sprouts
- Cherry tomatoes, for garnish

CUT off and discard the base ends of each head of bok choy and napa. Shred the bok choy and napa in a food processor, using the medium shredding disk; place in large bowl. Add the broccoli, parsley and watercress. Set aside.

PURÉE the lime juice, soy sauce and nori in a food processor, using the metal "S" blade. Add to the bok choy mixture. Stir in the remaining ingredients except the cherry tomatoes. Mix well and place in a serving bowl. Garnish with a circle of cherry tomatoes.

> **PER SERVING:**
> 217 Cal.; 20g Prot.; 2g Fat; 37g Carb.;
> 0mg Chol.; 875mg Sod.; 16g Fiber.

Carrot-Potato Pancakes

makes 15

Served with a green salad, this delicious variation of potato pancakes makes a light and satisfying supper.

- 1 carrot, grated coarsely
- 1 large russet potato, peeled and grated coarsely
- 1 tablespoon unbleached white flour
- 1 large egg, lightly beaten (or equivalent egg substitute)
- 1 teaspoon dried thyme
- 1/4 teaspoon salt
- 1/4 teaspoon freshly ground black pepper
- Nonstick cooking spray

IN A LARGE BOWL, combine the carrot, potatoes, flour, egg or egg substitute, thyme, salt and pepper. Lightly spray a nonstick skillet with nonstick cooking spray. Drop 1/4-cup amounts of the potato mixture onto the skillet, flattening the pancakes with a spoon if necessary. Fry until lightly browned on one side, about 3 minutes; then fry 3 minutes on the other side. Drain on paper towels. Serve warm.

> **PER PANCAKE:**
> 24 Cal.; 0.8g Prot.; 0.2g Fat; 5g Carb.;
> 11mg Chol.; 42mg Sod.; 0.2g Fiber.

Scattered Sushi with Five Colors

serves 6

Sushi, commonly thought of in the United States as individual portions of raw fish and rice, also may be made in a more casual fashion without fish.

SUSHI RICE

3 cups uncooked short-grain white rice

3 cups water

1/2 cup rice vinegar

1 tablespoon salt

1/3 cup sugar (or 1/4 cup honey)

MUSHROOMS

8 to 10 dried shiitake mushrooms, soaked in water for 3 to 4 hours (or 2 cups sliced white button mushrooms)

1/4 cup water or shiitake stock (from soaking)

2 tablespoons soy sauce

1 tablespoon mirin or dry sherry

1 tablespoon sugar or honey

CARROTS

2 medium carrots, cut into matchsticks

1/2 cup water or shiitake stock

2 tablespoons soy sauce

1 tablespoon mirin or dry sherry

1 tablespoon sugar or honey

PEAS

1 cup green peas (fresh or frozen)

1/4 cup water

1/2 teaspoon salt

1 tablespoon sugar or honey

TOFU

8 ounces firm tofu, cut into matchsticks

1 tablespoon soy sauce

2 tablespoons sugar or honey

1/2 teaspoon salt

Pinch ground turmeric (optional)

NORI

3 to 4 sheets nori (page 78)

RICE: Place the rice and water in a pot and let soak at least 1 hour. (Overnight is okay.) Bring to a boil, cover, lower the heat and simmer 15 minutes. Turn off the heat and let sit 10 minutes.

IN A SMALL SAUCEPAN, combine the rice vinegar with the salt and sugar or honey. Bring to a boil, then remove from the heat. Let cool before using. (This step can be done the day before; if you're short on time, however, simply stir the ingredients to dissolve the salt and sugar.)

TRANSFER the hot rice from the pot to a large bowl. With a large spoon, mix the rice as you pour in the cold vinegar mixture a little at a time. (It is important that the cold vinegar be poured over hot rice, or the vinegar will not be properly absorbed.) Keep the rice covered while you finish the recipe.

MUSHROOMS: Combine all the ingredients in a skillet and simmer over low heat 15 minutes. Drain.

CARROTS: Combine all the ingredients in a saucepan over medium heat and cook until tender. Drain.

PEAS: Combine all the ingredients in a saucepan over medium heat and cook briefly until tender. Drain.

TOFU: Heat all the ingredients in a skillet over medium heat until the tofu absorbs the flavors and turns yellow.

NORI: Briefly pass each nori sheet over an open gas flame or electric burner until crisp. With a pair of scissors, cut each sheet in half, then stack the sheets together. Shred with scissors.

TO ASSEMBLE, place the rice in a large serving dish or on a platter. Arrange the mushrooms, carrots, peas and tofu on top of the rice in separate piles. Mound the nori in the middle. At serving time, toss together all ingredients.

Variation:

For more colors, add sliced radishes, pickled ginger and wasabi (hot mustard).

> **PER SERVING:**
> 389 Cal.; 11g Pro.; 3g Fat; 76g Carb.;
> 0mg Chol.; 1,416mg Sod.; 3g Fiber.

Green Coconut Curry with Vegetables

serves 4

If you prefer a less spicy dish, use the lesser amount of curry paste.

> 1 to 4 tablespoons Green Curry Paste (page 481)
>   (or 1 to 4 tablespoons jalapeño pepper and cilantro)
> 7 ounces coconut milk
> 7 ounces evaporated skim milk
> 1 tablespoon soy sauce
> 1 1/2-inch slice ginger root, peeled and shredded
> 6 to 8 kaffir lime leaves (or zest from 1 lime)
> 4 cups chopped assorted vegetables: zucchini,
>   cauliflower, broccoli or carrots
> 4 cups cooked white rice or noodles
> 10 fresh basil leaves, minced

IN A WOK OR LARGE FRYING PAN bring the curry paste, coconut milk and evaporated skim milk to a simmer. Stir in the soy sauce, ginger, lime leaves or zest and vegetables; simmer until tender, about 5 to 7 minutes. Remove and discard the lime leaves. Serve the curry over rice or noodles. Garnish with basil.

> **PER SERVING:**
> 386 Cal.; 9g Prot.; 10g Fat; 75g Carb.;
> 1mg Chol; 959mg Sod.; 13g Fiber.

Sukiyaki

serves 4

In Japan, this dish is cooked right at the table. You can do the same with an electric skillet or wok. Serve it with individual bowls of rice.

2 tablespoons canola or vegetable oil

1 pound firm tofu, cut into 1/3-inch slices

4 cups whole white button mushrooms (if available, use some shiitake mushrooms as well)

1/2 butternut squash or other winter squash, peeled and cut into 1/3-inch slices

2 zucchini, cut into thick slices

1 cup soy sauce

1/2 cup honey

1/4 cup mirin or dry sherry

1/2 to 1 cup water

6 cups coarsely chopped mustard greens, kale or collard greens

4 bunches scallions (green and white parts), cut into 3-inch lengths

4 cups mung bean sprouts

1 teaspoon grated fresh ginger root

HEAT the oil in a large skillet or wok over medium-high heat and cook the tofu slices on both sides, stirring, until well browned, about 15 to 20 minutes. Slide the tofu to one side of the pan and add the mushrooms, cooking until browned. Push the mushrooms to the side; add the squash and zucchini. Combine the soy sauce with honey, mirin or sherry, and 1/2 cup water; pour over the vegetables, and bring to a boil. Lower the heat and simmer until the squash is tender, about 5 minutes. In separate piles, add as many of the greens, scallions and bean sprouts as will fit. Cook until tender, about 5 minutes more. Stir in the ginger and cook another minute, adding more water (up to the remaining 1/2 cup) as necessary.

TO SERVE, let each diner use chopsticks to remove the tofu and vegetables from the skillet. Add more vegetables as the skillet empties.

> **PER SERVING (WITHOUT RICE):**
> 261 Cal.; 16g Prot.; 12g Fat; 27g Carb.;
> 0mg Chol.; 287mg Sod.; 10g Fiber.

Avial

serves 6

This South Indian curry is packed with vegetables. You may substitute any other vegetables for the ones listed here. Favorites are potatoes, green beans, sweet potatoes, broccoli, eggplant, green plantain and white pumpkin. Serve the curry with rice.

2 large carrots, cut into 1/4-inch rounds

2 medium potatoes, peeled and cut into 1-inch pieces

1/2 cup green beans, cut into 1-inch pieces

2 green chilies, split down the middle (optional)

About 1/2 cup water

1 teaspoon tamarind juice, fresh lemon juice or fresh
    lime juice (see Note)

3 tablespoons grated unsweetened coconut

1/4 teaspoon ground turmeric

4 curry leaves (optional—see Note)

1/4 teaspoon ground cumin (optional)

1/4 teaspoon chili powder (optional)

1/2 cup plain yogurt, at room temperature

Salt to taste

PLACE the vegetables and chilies in a medium saucepan and add water. Cover and cook over medium heat until the vegetables are tender but not mushy, about 15 minutes. Add the tamarind juice, lemon juice or lime juice. Stir in the coconut and spices. Gradually stir the yogurt into the vegetable mixture. Add salt. (Remove the curry leaves before serving.) Serve warm.

Notes:

- Tamarind juice is available in Asian or Indian markets and natural food stores.

- Curry leaves add an aromatic and appetizing touch to Indian dishes. This herb is available fresh or frozen in Asian or Indian markets.

> **PER SERVING:**
> 112 Cal.; 2g Prot.; 4g Fat; 14g Carb.;
> 3mg Chol.; 201mg Sod.; 2g Fiber.

Yellow Curry-and-Pineapple Fried Rice

serves 4

1 medium yellow onion, chopped

4 carrots, julienned

1/4 pound snow peas, trimmed

2 to 5 tablespoons vegetable oil

1 to 2 tablespoons Yellow Curry Paste (page 480)
    (or 1 to 2 tablespoons fresh lemongrass and cilantro)

2 cups cubed fresh pineapple

4 cups cooked white or brown rice

1 cup baby corn

IN A POT of boiling water, partially cook the onion, carrots and snow peas about 3 minutes. Plunge the vegetables into cold water, drain and set aside. In a large skillet, heat the oil. Stir in the curry paste and pineapple, and cook, stirring, 1 minute. Add the rice and stir-fry 5 more minutes. Stir in the baby corn and the cooked vegetables. Cook until hot.

> **PER SERVING:**
> 421 Cal.; 8g Prot.; 8g Fat; 84g Carb.;
> 0mg Chol.; 569mg Sod.; 9g Fiber.

Any-Way-You-Want-It Pizza

makes 2 pizzas • 8 slices each

Vary the toppings to your appetite's desire. The crust is extra-special: Its double rising time creates a wonderful flavor and texture. To keep the fat content low, use just a sprinkling of cheese.

> 2 teaspoons active dry yeast
>
> 1 2/3 cups warm water (110°F)
>
> 4 cups whole-wheat flour
>
> 1/4 teaspoon freshly ground black pepper
>
> 2 teaspoons salt
>
> 3 cups thick tomato sauce
>
> Oil for coating
>
> Optional garnishes: green bell pepper rings;
>   sliced white button mushrooms, onions and olives;
>   pineapple; bits of tofu or tempeh; grated mozzarella
>   or other cheese
>
> 1/4 cup Parmesan cheese

DISSOLVE the yeast in the warm water and set aside until foamy, about 5 to 10 minutes. In a large bowl, mix together the flour, pepper and salt. Make a well in the center, add the dissolved yeast and blend. The dough should be soft. Knead on a breadboard until silky and elastic, about 5 to 10 minutes.

PLACE the dough in an oiled bowl and turn to coat lightly with oil. Cover with a clean dishcloth and let rise in a warm spot for about 1 1/2 hours. Deflate the dough and let it rise again for about 45 minutes.

PRESS the dough flat and divide it in half. Form 2 balls and let rest for 10 minutes, covered with a dishcloth. Grease 2 pizza pans and dust with cornmeal. Using a rolling pin, gently roll each ball into a large circle just a little bigger than a pizza pan.

PREHEAT the oven to 375°F. Transfer the rolled-out dough to the pans. Gently turn up the edges of the dough to form an outer rim. Spread the sauce on top, add garnishes (except cheese) if desired and bake until the crust is browned, about 20 to 25 minutes. Sprinkle cheeses on top if desired and bake until bubbly.

Note:

If you use mushrooms, toss them with olive oil first so they don't shrivel and burn.

> **PER SLICE:**
> 224 Cal.; 13g Prot.; 5g Fat; 35g Carb.;
> 12mg Chol.; 509mg Sod.; 8g Fiber.

Peppery Pizza

serves 4

> 1 recipe Pizza Crust (page 446)
>
> 2 red or yellow bell peppers, sliced into thin strips
>
> 1 tablespoon virgin olive oil
>
> 4 cloves garlic, chopped
>
> 3 medium tomatoes, peeled, seeded and chopped
>   (or 1 cup tomato purée)
>
> 3/4 teaspoon salt
>
> Freshly ground black pepper to taste
>
> 4 ounces grated cheese: mozzarella and/or smoked
>   gruyère, or provolone
>
> 12 pitted black olives, sliced
>
> 1/4 cup grated Parmesan cheese

PREPARE the pizza crust. Preheat oven to 450°F. In a skillet, cook the bell peppers in oil, stirring, until tender, about 10 minutes. Add the garlic and cook 2 minutes more. Stir in the tomatoes or tomato purée, salt and black pepper. Cook over medium heat until the sauce thickens, stirring occasionally. Spread over the pizza crust and top with grated cheese and olives. Bake until the crust begins to brown, about 10 minutes. Remove from your oven and sprinkle with Parmesan. Serve at once.

> **PER SERVING:**
> 424 Cal.; 20g Prot.; 20g Fat; 52g Carb.;
> 20mg Chol.; 1,020mg Sod.; 6g Fiber.

Grilled Vegetable Pizza

serves 4

Ready-made pizza crusts are a great base for any number of interesting vegetable combinations.

- 1 small rutabaga, peeled
- Nonstick cooking spray
- 1 red onion, sliced
- 4 plum tomatoes
- 2 small zucchini, halved lengthwise
- 2 small Japanese eggplants
- 1 large ready-made (prebaked) pizza crust (about 1 pound)
- 2 cloves garlic, minced
- 2 tablespoons grated Parmesan cheese (optional)
- 1 tablespoon minced fresh sage leaves (or 1 teaspoon dried whole leaves)
- Salt and freshly ground black pepper to taste

PREHEAT the broiler. Cut the rutabaga into 1/4-inch slices. In a saucepan fitted with a steamer, steam the rutabaga for 5 minutes. Lightly grease a baking sheet with nonstick cooking spray. Place the rutabaga and other vegetables on the sheet and broil, turning frequently, until fork-tender, glazed and brown. Let cool slightly. Cut the rutabaga into 1/4-inch-thick sticks. Cut the zucchini and eggplants into 1/4-inch-thick slices.

PREHEAT the oven to 500°F. In a small bowl, mash the tomatoes with a fork and spread evenly over the pizza crust. Sprinkle with the garlic and top with the broiled vege-tables. Sprinkle with Parmesan cheese. Bake until the crust is crisp and the vegetables are hot, about 12 minutes. Season with sage, salt and pepper.

Variations:

- Sprinkle the pizza with grated mozzarella or cheddar cheese before adding Parmesan.
- Instead of using a pizza crust, serve grilled vegetables on pita bread. If desired, drizzle with creamy Italian dressing and a touch of tahini.

> **PER SERVING:**
> 332 Cal.; 11g Prot.; 2g Fat; 60g Carb.;
> 0mg Chol.; 934mg Sod.; 8g Fiber.

Pizza with Garlic, Eggplant and Onion

serves 4

1 recipe Pizza Crust (page 446)

1 medium eggplant

1 tablespoon virgin olive oil

3 cloves garlic, chopped

3 medium tomatoes, peeled, seeded and chopped (or 1 cup tomato purée)

3/4 teaspoons salt

1 large red onion, thinly sliced into rings

4 ounces grated fontina, provolone and/or mozzarella cheese

Grated Parmesan cheese (optional)

PREPARE the pizza crust. Preheat oven to 450°F. Slice eggplant into rounds. In a nonstick skillet, cook the eggplant, stirring, in 2 teaspoons oil in 2 or 3 batches until tender, about 5 to 10 minutes per batch. Set aside. Cook the garlic, stirring, briefly in the remaining teaspoon of olive oil. Add the tomatoes and salt, and cook 1 to 2 minutes.

SPREAD the tomato-garlic mixture on the crust, then arrange the eggplant slices on top. Place the onion rings on top. Sprinkle with grated cheese. Bake until the crust begins to brown, about 10 minutes. Sprinkle with Parmesan and serve at once.

> **PER SERVING:**
> 388 Cal.; 18g Prot.; 17g Fat; 46g Carb.;
> 15mg Chol.; 837mg Sod.; 8g Fiber.

Cabbage Toran

serves 4

Most people use cabbage only in coleslaw or in stuffed cabbage. Here's another delicious reason to eat this nutrient-rich vegetable. Serve this dish with rice.

2 tablespoons vegetable oil

1/2 teaspoon mustard seeds

8 cups shredded cabbage

1/4 teaspoon ground turmeric

1/8 teaspoon chili powder (optional)

3 tablespoons shredded unsweetened coconut

Salt to taste

HEAT the oil in a large skillet. Add the mustard seeds. Lower the heat and cover the skillet while the seeds are popping. After the popping has stopped, add the cabbage. Stir well to coat. Cover and simmer 20 minutes. Add the turmeric, chili powder if desired, coconut and salt. Mix well. Cover and simmer 10 minutes more. Serve warm.

Variation:

To make Vegetable Toran, replace the cabbage with 6 cups frozen mixed vegetables. Proceed with recipe.

> **PER SERVING:**
> 198 Cal.; 4g Prot.; 14g Fat; 14g Carb.;
> 0mg Chol.; 91mg Sod.; 8g Fiber.

Potato Ratatouille

serves 4

This dish is delicious served hot on a bed of whole grains or served cold on a plate with mixed salad greens.

> 2 large yellow onions, chopped
>
> 2 cloves garlic, minced
>
> 1/4 cup water
>
> 3 green bell peppers, chopped
>
> 4 zucchini, sliced
>
> 2 large potatoes, peeled and chopped
>
> 4 cups peeled and chopped tomatoes
> (or one 32-ounce can tomatoes)
>
> 1 teaspoon chopped fresh basil leaves
> (or 1/2 teaspoon dried)
>
> 1 teaspoon chopped fresh oregano leaves
> (or 1/2 teaspoon dried)
>
> 2 tablespoons chopped fresh parsley
>
> Freshly ground black pepper to taste

IN A LARGE POT, cook the onions and garlic, stirring, in 1/4 cup water for 3 minutes. Add the remaining ingredients except black pepper, cover and cook over medium heat for 30 minutes, stirring occasionally. Season with black pepper before serving.

> **PER SERVING:**
> 142 Cal.; 4g Prot.; 0.3g Fat; 30g Carb.;
> 0mg Chol.; 21mg Sod.; 6g Fiber.

Savory Squash Stew

serves 4

> 1 onion, diced
>
> 3 cloves garlic, minced
>
> 2 tablespoons vegetable oil
>
> 3 cups peeled, seeded and chopped pumpkin or
> butternut squash
>
> 2 potatoes, peeled and chopped
>
> 2 tablespoons whole-wheat flour
>
> 2 cups vegetable stock (page 178) or water
>
> 2 tablespoons prepared mustard
>
> 3/4 teaspoon ground cinnamon
>
> 2 tablespoons apple cider vinegar
>
> 1 cup frozen peas
>
> 1 cup frozen whole-kernel corn
>
> Salt and freshly ground black pepper to taste

IN A POT, cook the onion and garlic in oil, stirring, until the onion is transparent, about 4 minutes. Add the squash and potatoes. Cook, stirring occasionally, for 5 minutes. Stir in the flour until dissolved. Add the vegetable stock or water, mustard, cinnamon and vinegar, and simmer over medium-low heat, stirring occasionally, until the sauce is thick and the vegetables are tender, about 30 minutes. Add the peas and corn, and cook 5 minutes more. Season with salt and pepper.

Variation:

> Turn this stew into a potpie by baking it in a pie pan
> lined with a biscuit crust.

> **PER SERVING:**
> 261 Cal.; 7g Prot.; 8g Fat; 43g Carb.;
> 0mg Chol.; 402mg Sod.; 10g Fiber.

Mountain Stew

serves 6

| 1 cup uncooked kidney beans
| 2 tablespoons virgin olive oil
| 1 large onion, thinly sliced
| 4 large cloves garlic, minced
| 1 green bell pepper, seeded and chopped coarsely
| 1 cup coarsely chopped green cabbage
| 1/2 cup diced russet potatoes
| One 16-ounce can tomatoes (with liquid)
| 1 tablespoon chili powder, or more to taste
| 1/2 teaspoon ground cumin
| 1/3 cup uncooked brown rice
| 4 cups water or vegetable stock (page 178)
| Salt and freshly ground black pepper to taste
| 1/4 cup grated jalapeño- or pepper-flavored Monterey
| Jack cheese (optional)

PLACE the kidney beans in a large bowl with cold water to cover. Let soak overnight; drain. Rinse and set aside. In a large pot over medium-high heat, heat the oil and cook the onion and garlic, stirring, until the onion is soft, about 3 to 5 minutes. Add the bell pepper, cabbage, potatoes, tomatoes with liquid, chili powder and cumin. Continue cooking, stirring frequently, for 3 minutes. Add the rice, water or stock and the beans. Cover and cook over low heat until the stew is thick and the beans and rice are tender, about 2 hours on your stovetop or 6 hours in a slow cooker. Season with salt and pepper. Top with grated cheese.

> **PER SERVING
> (WITHOUT CHEESE):**
> 356 Cal.; 17g Prot.; 7g Fat; 59g Carb.;
> 0mg Chol.; 155mg Sod.; 15g Fiber.

St. Patrick's Day Stew

serves 4

To get into the spirit of St. Paddy's Day, serve this stew with new potatoes, boiled cabbage and soda bread. (And you don't have to be Irish to enjoy.)

| 1/4 cup water
| 1 large onion, sliced
| 1/2 small cabbage, sliced thinly
| 3 cups cubed winter squash
| 2 parsnips, peeled and sliced
| 1/2 cup rolled oats
| 6 cups water or vegetable stock (page 178)
| 1/2 cup dulse (page 78)
| Salt to taste (optional)
| Freshly ground black pepper to taste (optional)
| Chopped fresh chives, for garnish

HEAT the water in a soup pot and cook the onion and cabbage, stirring, for 3 minutes. Add the squash and cook 2 minutes more. Add the parsnips. Then sprinkle the oats over the vegetables and pour in the water or stock. Cover and simmer over medium heat until the squash is tender, about 20 minutes. Rinse the dulse in a fine strainer (it will shrink greatly) and add to the stew. Season with salt and pepper if desired. Serve hot, garnished with chives.

> **PER SERVING:**
> 219 Cal.; 9g Prot.; 1g Fat; 45g Carb.;
> 0mg Chol.; 287mg Sod.; 6g Fiber.

Indian Vegetable Stew

serves 4

Serve this spicy, hearty stew with basmati rice and a garnish of yogurt and chopped fresh cilantro.

1/2 tablespoon margarine

1 tablespoon safflower oil

2 cloves garlic, minced

1 1/2 tablespoons minced fresh ginger root

1 teaspoon ground cumin

1/2 teaspoon ground coriander

1/4 teaspoon ground cloves

1/2 teaspoon ground cardamom

1/4 teaspoon dry mustard

1/2 teaspoon ground turmeric

1/2 stick cinnamon

1 teaspoon salt

3 cups vegetable stock (page 178)

3 tablespoons fresh lime juice

1 tablespoon honey

3 carrots, sliced diagonally

1 1/2 cups thickly sliced white button mushrooms

2 cups cauliflower florets

1 medium russet potato, diced

IN A LARGE SAUCEPAN, melt the margarine over medium heat and add the oil. Cook the garlic and ginger, stirring, for 1 minute. Add the cumin, coriander, cloves, cardamom, mustard, turmeric, cinnamon and salt. Stir and cook 2 minutes to release the flavors. Add the stock, lime juice and honey, and cook 3 to 4 minutes more. Add the vegetables and cook, covered, until tender, about 25 minutes. Discard the cinnamon stick. Serve warm.

> **PER SERVING:**
> 139 Cal.; 2g Prot.; 4g Fat; 18g Carb.;
> 0mg Chol.; 574mg Sod.; 4g Fiber.

Spicy African Stew

serves 6

6 small potatoes

3 carrots, quartered lengthwise and cut into 2-inch lengths

1 cup green beans, cut diagonally into 2-inch lengths

1 tablespoon vegetable oil

2 teaspoons minced garlic

1 teaspoon freshly grated fresh ginger root

6 scallions (green and white parts), cut diagonally into 2-inch lengths

1 bell pepper, cut into 1/2-inch pieces

1 to 4 hot peppers, cut into 1/4-inch pieces

1 small cabbage, cut into 8 wedges

1 teaspoon turmeric

1 teaspoon freshly ground black pepper

Salt to taste (optional)

PLACE the potatoes in a medium saucepan with salted water to cover. Bring to a boil and cook until the potatoes are almost tender. Add the carrots and beans; boil 5 minutes. Drain and set aside.

IN A SKILLET, heat the oil and cook the garlic, ginger, scallions and peppers, stirring. Gently mix in the potatoes, carrots and beans. Top with the cabbage wedges and sprinkle with the turmeric. Cover and let steam for a few minutes, being careful not to overcook the vegetables.

Stir gently and transfer to a serving dish. Top with black pepper and salt.

> **PER SERVING:**
> 201 Cal.; 5g Prot.; 3g Fat; 40g Carb.;
> 0mg Chol.; 60mg Sod.; 5g Fiber.

Yuca-Vegetable Chili

serves 4

Yuca is somewhat similar to potato. When cooked it becomes slightly sweet and a bit gooey. It's wonderful in this spicy chili.

    1 1/4 pounds yuca, peeled and cut into 1-inch chunks
    1/2 lime
    1 onion, chopped
    3 cloves garlic, minced
    1 jalapeño pepper, seeded and minced
    1/2 red or green bell pepper, seeded and chopped
    2 tablespoons margarine
    One 16-ounce can chickpeas (with liquid)
    6 ripe tomatoes, peeled, seeded and chopped
    2 scallions (green and white parts), chopped
    1 small bunch fresh cilantro, chopped (optional)
    1/2 cup grated cheddar cheese (optional)

PLACE the yuca in a medium saucepan with salted water to cover. Squeeze the juice from the lime and add to the saucepan. Simmer until tender, about 35 to 40 minutes. Meanwhile, in a large saucepan over medium heat, cook the onion, garlic, jalapeño pepper and bell pepper in the margarine. Add the chickpeas with liquid and tomatoes, and cook 3 minutes. Drain the yuca and add to the vegetable mixture. Cook until the flavors are blended, about 10 minutes. Before serving, scatter the scallions, cilantro and cheese over the chili. Serve hot.

> **PER SERVING:**
> 356 Cal.; 8g Prot.; 5g Fat; 68g Carb.;
> 0mg Chol.; 400mg Sod.; 11g Fiber.

15

legumes

LEGUMES—OR BEANS, IF YOU PREFER—ARE A STAPLE in vegetarian cuisine. But they have gotten a bad rep for, ahem, their odoriferous qualities. The truth is, beans have many benefits: Namely, they are a rich source of fiber, protein and other nutrients. By the way, experience proves that the more beans you eat, the better your body digests them. If you're new to eating beans regularly, then start out slowly, increasing the quantity of beans you eat as your body adjusts to your higher fiber intake. This approach has a culinary payoff: Not only do beans come in a variety of shapes and sizes but they also taste great.

Black Beans with Fresh Plums and Bell Peppers

serves 3

Plums lend a wonderfully exotic taste to this savory dish. Serve it hot over rice, or chill it and serve it as a salad.

    4 medium purple plums
    1 1/2 tablespoons unsalted butter or corn oil
    1 large onion, chopped
    1 large red bell pepper, seeded and chopped
    1 large yellow pepper, seeded and chopped
    2 cloves garlic, crushed and minced
    2 whole cloves
    2 teaspoons ground cumin
    1/2 cup minced fresh cilantro leaves
    2 teaspoons fresh lemon juice
    1 teaspoon light honey
    2 cups cooked black beans

FILL a deep pot with water and bring to a boil. Add the plums and boil for 30 seconds to loosen their skins. Remove the plums with a slotted spoon and let cool.

MELT the butter or heat the oil in a large skillet over low heat. Add the onion, bell peppers, garlic, cloves, cumin and cilantro. Cook, stirring often, until the onion softens, about 5 to 10 minutes. Meanwhile, peel the plums, remove the pits and chop the pulp. Add the pulp, lemon juice and honey to the onion-pepper mixture. Add the beans, cover and cook over low heat until the peppers are soft, about 30 minutes, stirring often to prevent sticking. Serve hot or chilled.

> **PER SERVING:**
> 299 Cal.; 10g Prot.; 7g Fat; 48g Carb.;
> 17mg Chol.; 12mg Sod.; 9g Fiber.

Black Bean Medley

serves 4

This simple dish is great served as is or tucked into a whole-wheat tortilla. Serve leftovers topped with salsa for lunch.

    2 large onions
    6 large carrots, diced
    1 cup sliced napa cabbage
    2 teaspoons onion salt
    2 cloves crushed garlic
    1 1/2 teaspoons chili powder
    1/4 teaspoon cayenne pepper (optional)
    1 tablespoon fresh dillweed, rubbed
    1/2 teaspoon freshly ground black pepper
    1 bay leaf (optional)
    9 large scallions (green and white parts), cut into
        1/2-inch pieces
    Two 15-ounce cans black beans, undrained
    2 cups chopped spinach
    5 plum tomatoes, diced
    2 tablespoons red wine vinegar

SLICE the onions into 1-inch strips. Spray a large pot with olive oil cooking spray and place over medium heat. Cook the onions, stirring, until softened, about 2 minutes. Add the carrots, cabbage and seasonings, and cook, stirring, until the carrots soften, about 5 to 10 minutes.

ADD the scallions and cook 10 minutes more. Stir in the black beans, including the liquid, then add the spinach and cook another 5 minutes. Add the tomatoes and cook until they're heated through. Add the vinegar just before serving.

> **PER SERVING:**
> 240 Cal.; 10g Prot.; 0.6g Fat; 48g Carb.;
> 0mg Chol.; 896mg Sod.; 12g Fiber

Barbados Black Bean Cakes with Mango Salsa

serves 4

The vibrantly colored mango salsa makes this Caribbean dish a real show stopper.

MANGO SALSA

- 2 cups peeled, diced mango
- 1/2 cup diced red bell pepper
- 1/4 cup finely diced red onion
- 1 serrano pepper, seeded and minced
- 2 tablespoons coarsely chopped fresh cilantro leaves
- 2 teaspoons minced fresh ginger root
- 1 tablespoon fresh lime juice

BLACK BEAN CAKES

- Two 15-ounce cans black beans, rinsed
- 1/4 cup chopped fresh cilantro leaves
- 1/4 cup finely chopped red onion
- 1 egg white, slightly beaten
- 1 teaspoon ground cumin
- 1 teaspoon minced garlic
- 1/2 teaspoon ground allspice
- 1/8 teaspoon cayenne pepper
- 1/3 cup dry whole-wheat bread crumbs
- Nonstick cooking spray
- 1 tablespoon virgin olive oil
- Fresh chopped cilantro and lime wedges, for garnish (optional)

SALSA: Combine all the salsa ingredients in a bowl. Set aside.

BEAN CAKES: Place the beans in a large bowl and coarsely mash them until they stick together. Add the cilantro, onion, egg white, cumin, garlic, allspice and cayenne. Mix until well blended. Divide the mixture into 8 equal parts. Shape into 1/2-inch-thick patties. Coat the patties with bread crumbs. Spray both sides of the patties with nonstick cooking spray.

HEAT the oil in a skillet over medium-high heat. Add the bean cakes and fry until golden brown on both sides, turning once, about 8 minutes total. Serve warm with the mango salsa. Garnish with cilantro and lime wedges.

> **PER SERVING:**
> 424 Cal.; 19g Prot.; 5g Fat; 75g Carb.;
> 0.1mg Chol.; 81mg Sod.; 13g Fiber.

Spicy Black Bean Cakes

serves 6

Using instant black beans in this dish makes the preparation as quick and easy as can be.

  Nonstick cooking spray

  1 small onion, chopped

  3 cloves garlic, minced

  1 tablespoon water

  3 large scallions (green and white parts), sliced

  One 4-ounce can diced green chilies, with liquid

  4 plum tomatoes, peeled, seeded and diced

  2 tablespoons chunky salsa

  One 7-ounce box instant black beans (available in natural food stores)

  1 cup boiling water

  1 to 3 tablespoons vegetable oil

  Optional garnishes: shredded lettuce, diced tomatoes, shredded cheddar cheese, low-fat sour cream or yogurt, and sliced black olives

LIGHTLY spray a heavy skillet with nonstick cooking spray, and cook the onion and garlic in 1 tablespoon water over medium-high heat, stirring, until the water evaporates and the vegetables begin to brown. Toss in the scallions, chilies with liquid, tomatoes and salsa. Mix well and remove from heat.

ADD the beans and 1 cup boiling water to the skillet. Mix well, scraping the mixture up from the bottom of the skillet. Let sit until the beans have absorbed the liquid and become smooth like refried beans, about 10 minutes. Form into 6 patties.

IN ANOTHER SKILLET, heat the oil over high heat and add the patties. Lower the heat and cook until crisp on one side, turn and cook the other side. Place the patties on individual plates. If desired, add garnishes of choice.

> **PER SERVING:**
> 109 Cal.; 4g Prot.; 2g Fat; 17g Carb.;
> 0mg Chol.; 66mg Sod.; 5g Fiber.

Black Bean-and-Vegetable Hash

serves 2

Made with dehydrated flavorings and instant beans, this dish is simple to make. You even can make it on the trail. Serve it as is or spoon it into pita bread.

  2 1/2 cups water

  1/4 cup dehydrated onion

  2 tablespoons dehydrated garlic

  2 tablespoons dehydrated mixed vegetables (available in a camping supply store)

  Pinch cayenne pepper

  1/2 teaspoon chili powder

  One 7-ounce package instant black beans or instant pinto beans

  1 tablespoon grated Parmesan cheese

BRING the water, onion, garlic and vegetables to a boil. Lower the heat and simmer 2 to 3 minutes. Remove from the heat. Add the remaining ingredients except the cheese. Mix well, cover and let sit 5 minutes. Sprinkle with cheese before serving.

Variation:

Stir cooked instant brown rice (1 1/2 cups rice cooked in 1 1/4 cups water for 5 minutes) into the hash before serving.

> **PER SERVING:**
> 365 Cal.; 24g Prot.; 3g Fat; 64g Carb.;
> 2mg Chol.; 56mg Sod.; 13g Fiber.

Simple Seasoned Black Beans

serves 6

This kid pleaser is big on taste and nutrition.

- 1 1/2 tablespoons virgin olive oil
- 1 cup chopped onions
- 3 cloves garlic, crushed or chopped
- 4 cups cooked black beans (or two 16-ounce cans, rinsed)
- 1/2 cup bean cooking liquid, or vegetable broth or liquid from canned beans
- Juice of 1/2 lemon, or to taste
- 1 teaspoon ground cumin
- Salt and freshly ground black pepper to taste
- 2 cups uncooked quick brown rice or whole-wheat couscous
- Tortilla chips for garnish (optional)

HEAT the oil in a large saucepan. Add the onions and cook, stirring, over medium heat until translucent, about 10 minutes. Add the garlic and cook, stirring, until the onions are golden, about 5 to 10 minutes more. Add the beans and bean liquid and bring to a simmer. Mash about 1/4 of the beans with the back of a wooden spoon to thicken the liquid. Add the lemon juice, cumin, salt and pepper; simmer over very low heat for 15 minutes.

MEANWHILE, prepare the rice or couscous. For brown rice, prepare according to the package directions. For couscous, boil 4 cups water and combine with the couscous in a heat-proof container; cover and let sit for 15 minutes, then fluff with a fork. Serve the bean mixture over the grain. Garnish with tortilla chips.

> **PER SERVING:**
> 326 Cal.; 12g Prot.; 4g Fat; 59g Carb.;
> 0mg Chol.; 182mg Sod.; 7g Fiber.

Chickpea-Couscous Croquettes

serves 6

No eggs are necessary in these savory croquettes. Serve them with Sauce Bourguignonne (page 476), or a tomato sauce of your choice cooked with red wine.

2/3 cup hulled, raw sunflower seeds (optional)

2 cups cooked chickpeas (or two 16-ounce cans, rinsed)

1 cup uncooked couscous

1/2 cup tomato juice

1/2 cup dry red wine

3 tablespoons soy sauce

2 tablespoons Dijon mustard

2 tablespoons red wine vinegar

2 teaspoons dried rosemary

1 teaspoon dried thyme

1/2 teaspoon freshly ground black pepper

3 tablespoons minced fresh parsley

3 or more cloves garlic, pressed or minced

1/2 to 1 tablespoon virgin olive oil

IF YOU'RE USING SUNFLOWER SEEDS, preheat oven to 350°F. Spread the seeds on a baking tray and bake until aromatic, about 5 to 7 minutes. Grind them in a food processor for 30 seconds until coarsely chopped. Add the chickpeas and process until well mixed. (Keep the mixture in the food processor.)

IN A MEDIUM POT, combine the couscous, tomato juice and red wine. Bring to a boil, cover, lower the heat and simmer until the liquid is absorbed. Let sit for 5 minutes.

ADD the couscous mixture to the chickpeas along with the remaining ingredients except the oil. Mix until smooth, stopping the processor once or twice to scrape down the sides.

LIGHTLY OIL your hands. Shape 2 or 3 tablespoons of the mixture into a ball. Repeat with remaining mixture until you have 24 balls. Flatten the balls to form patties about 2 inches wide and 1/2 inch thick.

BRUSH the croquettes with olive oil and place them on a lightly oiled baking tray. Bake for 15 minutes, turn the croquettes over, brush with oil and bake 10 to 12 minutes more.

> **PER CROQUETTE:**
> 48 Cal.; 2g Prot.; 0.8g Fat; 8g Carb.;
> 0mg Chol.; 164mg Sod.; 1g Fiber.

Golden "Chicken" Patties

serves 8

The flavor is similar to chicken, but there's not a morsel of meat in this simple yet satisfying dish. Serve the patties with baked potatoes, cranberry sauce and some greens.

Two 15-ounce cans chickpeas

1 1/2 cups quick oats

1 clove garlic, minced

Salt to taste

Dash freshly ground black pepper

2 to 3 tablespoons vegetable oil

DRAIN the chickpeas and reserve the liquid. In a food processor or blender, process the chickpeas with 1/2 cup reserved liquid. If the purée is dry, add more liquid, a tablespoon at a time, to achieve a smooth, thick paste. Place the chickpea purée in a mixing bowl and add the remaining ingredients except the oil. Mix well, adding additional water or oats as necessary to make a mixture that keeps its shape. Shape into 8 patties. In a heavy skillet, heat the oil and fry the patties until golden brown on each side, about 20 minutes all together.

Variation:

If you like gravy for extra moistness and flavor, try Mushroom Sauce (page 477) or Peanutty Sauce (page 478).

> **PER SERVING:**
> 188 Cal.; 8g Prot.; 6g Fat; 26g Carb.;
> 0mg Chol.; 38mg Sod.; 3g Fiber.

Chickpea Sauté with Garlic and Olives

serves 2

This recipe transforms a humble can of chickpeas into a filling and flavorful meal. It's delicious warm or at room temperature.

1 clove garlic, minced
1/2 red onion, chopped
1/2 tablespoon virgin olive oil
One 16-ounce can chickpeas, rinsed
1/2 teaspoon dried thyme
1/4 cup water
1/4 teaspoon salt
1/4 teaspoon freshly ground black pepper
5 or 6 kalamata olives, pitted and halved

IN A MEDIUM SAUCEPAN, cook the garlic and onion in the olive oil, stirring, over medium heat for 2 minutes. Add the chickpeas and thyme, and cook 1 minute. Add the remaining ingredients and heat through.

Variation:

Substitute kidney beans, adzuki beans or lentils for the chickpeas; use fresh parsley or basil instead of thyme.

> **PER SERVING:**
> 418 Cal.; 18g Prot.; 7g Fat; 67g Carb.;
> 0mg Chol.; 285mg Sod.; 13g Fiber.

Cabbage Rolls with Split Peas and Tomato

serves 8

With the use of a pressure cooker, these filling cabbage rolls are ready in minutes.

| 1 cup dry split peas
| 1 to 1 1/2 cups slightly thinned tomato sauce
| 1 medium tomato, peeled and chopped finely
| 1 medium onion, minced
| 1 clove garlic, minced
| 1/2 teaspoon chopped chipotle pepper
| 1 tablespoon virgin olive oil
| 8 large cabbage leaves
| 1 1/2 cups water

COMBINE the split peas, tomato sauce, tomato, onion, garlic, pepper and oil in your pressure cooker. Bring up to pressure, lower the heat to medium-low and cook 7 minutes. Let the pressure drop naturally.

MEANWHILE, lightly steam the cabbage leaves; drain. Place the split pea mixture in an ovenproof dish. When the pea mixture and the cabbage leaves have cooled slightly, place 1 to 1 1/2 tablespoons of the split pea mixture in the center of each leaf. Roll up and place in the dish. Repeat with the remaining split pea mixture and leaves.

POUR the water into the pressure cooker, insert a metal rack and place the dish on the rack. Bring to pressure and cook 5 minutes. Cool at once by holding the pressure cooker under lukewarm water until the pressure has dropped (or immerse the cooker in a dishpan or sink filled with lukewarm water).

> **PER SERVING:**
> 186 Cal.; 10g Prot.; 4g Fat; 31g Carb.;
> 0mg Chol.; 32mg Sod.; 5g Fiber.

Fruity Stuffed Cabbage

serves 4

| 1 head red cabbage
| 5 teaspoons fresh lemon juice, divided
| 1 tablespoon unsalted butter
| 1 large red onion, chopped
| 4 carrots, chopped
| 1 tablespoon apple cider vinegar
| 1 1/2 cups cottage cheese
| 1 teaspoon low-sodium soy sauce
| 2 teaspoons honey
| 1 cup cooked chickpeas (or one 16-ounce can, rinsed)
| 1 small Granny Smith apple, peeled, cored and diced
| 1/4 cup diced dried apples or raisins
| 1/4 cup water
| Plain yogurt for topping (optional)

BRING a 4-quart pot of water to boil. Meanwhile, peel away and discard the tough outer cabbage leaves. Remove 2 more leaves and chop them well. When the water is boiling, add 3 teaspoons lemon juice and the head of cabbage. Lower the heat and simmer 10 minutes. Remove the cabbage and let cool.

IN A LARGE SKILLET, melt the butter. When it bubbles, add the onion and carrots. Cook, stirring, over very low heat until the onion softens, about 5 minutes. Add the chopped cabbage and stir until it starts to wilt, about 1 minute. Add the vinegar and stir well. Continue to cook, stirring often, until the carrots are cooked and the onion is limp, about 10 minutes. (If the mixture sticks, add water 1 tablespoon at a time, being careful not to let water accumulate in the pan.)

IN A MIXING BOWL, combine the onion mixture, cottage cheese, soy sauce, remaining 2 teaspoons lemon juice, honey, chickpeas, apple and dried fruit. Mix well.

PREHEAT the oven to 425°F. Peel off one cabbage leaf. Place 1/4 of the filling in the center off the leaf. Using your fingers, bend the sides of the leaf over the filling, fold down the top and fold up the bottom to make a package. Place the cabbage roll seam side down in a 9 × 13-inch baking dish. Repeat the procedure until all of the filling is used.

POUR 1/4 cup water in the pan and cover with foil. Bake until the cabbage rolls are heated through, about 20 minutes. Remove the pan from your oven and let sit, covered, for 10 minutes. Serve topped with plain yogurt.

> **PER SERVING:**
> 269 Cal.; 16g Prot.; 7g Fat; 34g Carb.;
> 21mg Chol.; 432mg Sod.; 6g Fiber.

Chickpea-Mushroom Curry

serves 4

Serve this curry with rice or Indian breads. Or spoon the curry over shell-shaped pasta.

> 1 medium onion, chopped
> 1 teaspoon chili powder
> One 1/4-inch piece fresh ginger root, peeled and minced
> 4 curry leaves (optional)
> 2 tablespoons vegetable oil
> 1 teaspoon ground turmeric
> 1 1/2 tablespoons ground coriander
> 1 1/2 cups white button mushrooms, halved
> One 16-ounce can chickpeas, drained
> 1 cup peeled and chopped tomatoes
> Salt to taste

COOK the onion, chili powder, ginger and curry leaves, stirring, in the oil over medium-high heat until the onion is translucent, about 5 minutes. Add the turmeric and coriander, and cook 2 minutes. Lower the heat, add the mushrooms and cook 5 minutes more. Stir in the chickpeas and tomatoes. Cover and cook over low heat until thickened, about 15 minutes. Add salt. Serve hot.

> **PER SERVING:**
> 185 Cal.; 7g Prot.; 9g Fat; 22g Carb.;
> 0mg Chol.; 56mg Sod.; 9g Fiber.

Falafel-Stuffed Wrappers

serves 8

An onion-flavored wrapper encloses a savory chickpea filling in this flavorful dish.

FILLING

2/3 cup dry chickpeas, soaked overnight and drained

1 teaspoon baking soda

1/2 teaspoon salt

1/2 cup finely chopped onion

1/4 cup chopped fresh parsley

2 teaspoons fresh lemon juice

3/4 teaspoon ground cumin

3/4 teaspoon ground coriander

1 clove garlic, minced

1/8 teaspoon cayenne pepper

Dash freshly ground black pepper

2 teaspoons virgin olive oil

2 tomatoes, chopped

SAUCE

1 to 3 cloves garlic, minced

1/4 cup tahini (sesame paste)

1/4 cup cold water

1/4 cup fresh lemon juice

1/4 teaspoon salt

WRAPPERS

1 cup finely chopped onions

1 to 3 tablespoons water

2 teaspoons active dry yeast

1/4 cup warm water (105 to 115°F)

1 teaspoon sugar

2/3 cup whole-wheat flour

2/3 cup unbleached white flour

1/4 teaspoon salt

FILLING: In a food processor or blender, combine the chickpeas, baking soda and salt. Process until the mixture resembles coarse bread crumbs. Transfer to a bowl, and mix in the onion, parsley, lemon juice, cumin, coriander, garlic, cayenne and black pepper.

HEAT 1 teaspoon olive oil in a nonstick skillet over medium heat. Add half of the chickpea mixture; form it into a patty with the back of a spatula. Cook until lightly browned, about 3 minutes. Flip the patty over and break it into pieces. Fry the second side until lightly browned. Remove the pieces from the skillet and transfer to a bowl. Repeat with the remaining 1 teaspoon oil and the chickpea mixture. Add the chopped tomatoes to the bowl.

SAUCE: Process all sauce ingredients in a blender or food processor until smooth. Stir the sauce into the falafel mixture in the bowl. Set aside.

WRAPPERS: Cook the onions in water, stirring, until limp but not browned, about 10 minutes. Meanwhile, sprinkle yeast over warm water in a small bowl. Stir in the sugar. Cover and let sit until foamy, about 10 minutes.

IN A LARGE MIXING BOWL, combine the flours and salt; then stir in the yeast mixture and sautéed onions. Transfer the dough to a floured board and knead until smooth and elastic, about 5 minutes.

HEAT a skillet over medium heat. Divide the dough into 8 pieces. Roll out one of the pieces into an 8-inch circle and cook until lightly browned, about 2 minutes for the first side and 1 minute for the second side. While the wrapper cooks, start rolling out the next piece of dough. Remove the cooked wrapper to a plastic bag to keep it warm, and repeat the procedure with the remaining dough.

PREHEAT the oven to 350°F. Spoon 1/8 of the filling onto the bottom half of a wrapper. Fold up the bottom half of the wrapper to just cover the filling. Fold in the sides and then roll to close. Repeat with the remaining wrappers and filling.

WRAP each one individually in foil and heat for 20 minutes.

Helpful hint:

To cook frozen filled wrappers, bake in a preheated 350°F oven until heated through, about 45 to 55 minutes.

> **PER SERVING:**
> 112 Cal.; 4g Prot.; 3g Fat; 17g Carb.;
> 0mg Chol.; 191mg Sod.; 5g Fiber.

Lentil Curry

serves 4

Lentils are a staple in India, and there are many varieties from which to choose. The brown lentil, an Indian favorite, also is the variety best known by Americans. Serve this dish with rice and Indian breads such as *chapatis,* or serve alone as a tasty vegetarian chili.

- 1 cup uncooked brown lentils
- 7 cups water
- 1 large onion, chopped finely
- 2 tablespoons vegetable oil
- One 2-inch piece fresh ginger root, peeled and chopped
- 2 green chilies, chopped (optional)
- 1 tablespoon coriander powder
- 1 tablespoon curry powder
- 1 teaspoon chili powder, or to taste

COMBINE the lentils and water in a large pot. Bring to a boil, lower the heat and simmer until the lentils are tender but not mushy, about 20 minutes.

MEANWHILE, cook the onion, stirring, in the oil for a few minutes over medium-high heat. Add the ginger and chilies, and cook the mixture until the onion is translucent, about 5 to 10 minutes. Stir in the spices and cook 3 minutes more. Add the onion mixture to the lentils. Cover and simmer 15 minutes more. Serve hot.

> **PER SERVING:**
> 197 Cal.; 9g Prot.; 7g Fat; 25g Carb.;
> 0mg Chol.; 11mg Sod.; 3g Fiber.

Pasta and Chickpeas with Roasted Vegetables

serves 6

Vary the vegetables and pasta shapes as you desire, but include fennel to keep the Mediterranean flavor of this dish.

- 5 red or yellow bell peppers, diced
- 2 fennel bulbs, cored and diced (reserve some minced tops for garnish), see Note
- 1 1/3 cups diced canned tomatoes, drained
- 1 cup chopped fresh basil leaves (or 1 1/2 tablespoons dried)
- Olive oil cooking spray (or 1 tablespoon virgin olive oil)
- 1 1/2 pounds uncooked rotelli or radiatore
- 3 cups cooked chickpeas (or two 15-ounce cans chickpeas, rinsed)
- 1/8 teaspoon cayenne pepper
- 3 tablespoons fresh lemon juice or balsamic vinegar
- 1/2 cup grated Parmesan cheese
- Salt and freshly ground black pepper to taste

PREHEAT the broiler. Mix the peppers, fennel bulbs and some of the tops, tomatoes and basil in a bowl; spread the vegetables evenly over a large baking pan. Generously spray or drizzle the vegetables with half of the oil. Broil until the vegetables soften and blacken slightly, stirring occasionally, about 15 minutes. While the vegetables broil, prepare the pasta according to the package directions; drain.

COMBINE the chickpeas, cayenne and lemon juice or vinegar in a large serving bowl. Toss the broiled vegetables, hot pasta and cheese with the chickpea mixture. Season with salt and pepper. Spray or drizzle with remaining oil and sprinkle with reserved minced fennel tops.

Note:

Choose crisp white bulbs of fennel with bright green tops. To prepare, remove any dry or damaged sections. Wash and dry the bulbs, and trim the stalks. Dice as directed.

> **PER SERVING:**
> 351 Cal.; 14g Prot.; 7g Fat; 56g Carb.;
> 8mg Chol.; 193mg Sod.; 8g Fiber.

Pinto Beans with Marinated Seitan over Lettuce

serves 8

Seitan is a meaty food made from high-gluten flour. You can buy it at natural food stores.

> 1 pound seitan, julienned
>
> 1/4 cup tamari or soy sauce
>
> 1/4 cup virgin olive oil
>
> 1/3 cup fresh lime juice
>
> 1 large clove garlic, minced
>
> 1 teaspoon salt, or to taste
>
> 1/2 teaspoon freshly ground black pepper, or to taste
>
> 1/2 teaspoon ground cumin
>
> 12 cups finely shredded lettuce
>
> Two 16-ounce cans pinto or light red kidney beans, rinsed
>
> 1 large red bell pepper, julienned
>
> 1/4 cup fresh cilantro leaves or fresh parsley, for garnish (optional)

IN A LARGE SKILLET, combine the seitan and tamari or soy sauce. Heat to a simmer and cook, stirring frequently, until the liquid is absorbed. Remove from the heat and let cool.

IN A LARGE BOWL, combine the oil, lime juice, garlic, salt, pepper and cumin. Mix well. Stir in the cooked seitan. Marinate for at least 15 minutes. (Or, cover and refrigerate overnight. Remove the marinated seitan from your refrigerator at least 1 hour before assembling the rest of the dish.)

TO ASSEMBLE, place the lettuce in a large serving bowl, spread the seitan mixture on top, add the beans and red bell pepper. Toss lightly. Garnish with cilantro or fresh parsley.

PER SERVING:
295 Cal.; 19g Prot.; 8g Fat; 50g Carb.;
0mg Chol.; 1,053mg Sod.; 7g Fiber.

Pinto Beans with Vegetables and Red Wine

serves 4

1 large onion, chopped

1/4 cup water

1 large carrot, sliced in half-rounds

1 large potato, cubed

1 cup water

3 tablespoons tomato paste

1 teaspoon dried thyme

2 bay leaves

1 1/2 cups dry red wine

4 cups cooked pinto beans

2 cloves garlic, pressed or minced

1 teaspoon salt (omit if beans are salted)

1/2 pound white button mushrooms, sliced

IN A LARGE POT, cook the onion, stirring, in 1/4 cup water. Stir in the carrot, potato, 1 cup water, tomato paste, thyme and bay leaves. Bring to a boil and simmer briskly until the potato and carrot are cooked, about 20 minutes. (Add extra water if necessary to keep the vegetables covered.) Near the end of cooking time, add the wine, beans, garlic and salt. Return to a boil, lower the heat and simmer, uncovered, 10 minutes more. Remove the bay leaves.

MEANWHILE, spray a small skillet with nonstick cooking spray, and cook the mushrooms, stirring, over low heat. Combine with the beans and serve.

PER SERVING:
381 Cal.; 17g Prot.; 1g Fat; 64g Carb.;
0mg Chol.; 379mg Sod.; 22g Fiber.

Navy Beans and Rotini in Herbed Tomato Sauce

serves 5

3/4 pound uncooked rotini

2 tablespoons virgin olive oil

3 cloves garlic, slivered (or to taste)

3 plum tomatoes (or 1 large tomato), chopped

2 cups low-sodium tomato sauce

1/4 cup water

3 sprigs fresh parsley, chopped

2 teaspoons dried oregano

2 teaspoons dried basil

2 cups broccoli florets

2 cups cooked navy beans (or one 16-ounce can navy beans, rinsed)

1/4 cup slivered black olives

Salt and freshly ground black pepper to taste

Chopped fresh parsley, for garnish

PREPARE the rotini according to the package directions; drain. In a large pot, heat the oil and cook the garlic, stirring, until lightly browned. Stir in the tomatoes. Add the tomato sauce, water, parsley, oregano and basil. Cook, uncovered, over medium heat, mashing the tomatoes with a spoon. When the sauce thickens (about 8 minutes), add the broccoli. Simmer, covered, until the broccoli is tender but still crunchy, about 5 minutes.

STIR in the beans and olives. Simmer, covered, until heated through. Add the rotini, salt and pepper. Garnish with parsley.

PER SERVING:
488 Cal.; 21g Prot.; 9g Fat; 85g Carb.; 0mg Chol.; 306mg Sod.; 16g Fiber.

Hoppin' John

serves 6

This Southern dish is traditionally served over rice on New Year's Day to bring good luck during the new year.

- 1 1/4 cups dry black-eyed peas
- 4 cups fresh water
- 1 1/2 cups chopped onion
- 1 clove garlic, minced
- 1 bay leaf
- 1/2 teaspoon freshly ground black pepper
- 1/4 teaspoon cayenne pepper
- 8 ounces tempeh
- 1 tablespoon low-sodium soy sauce
- Salt to taste

SOAK the peas overnight in a large pot of water. (Or boil them for 2 minutes, cover and let stand 1 hour.) Drain, then cover with 4 cups fresh water and bring to a boil. Add the onion, garlic, bay leaf, black pepper and cayenne. Bring to a boil, cover and simmer 1 hour, stirring occasionally.

BRUSH the tempeh on both sides with soy sauce; set aside for 5 minutes. Coarsely chop the tempeh and add to the peas. Simmer another hour, stirring frequently. Remove and discard the bay leaf. Mash the peas slightly to make a sauce. Stir in salt.

PER SERVING:
165 Cal.; 12g Prot.; 3g Fat; 22g Carb.; 0mg Chol.; 193mg Sod.; 5g Fiber.

Spice-Fried Bombay Beans

serves 6

Enhance the flavor of Indian spices in this dish with Pineapple-Mango Chutney (page 482).

- 3/4 cup dry yellow split peas
- 2 cups hot (not boiling) water
- 1 large tomato, chopped finely
- 1 teaspoon fresh lemon juice
- 1 tablespoon vegetable oil
- 1 teaspoon black mustard seeds
- 1/4 teaspoon fenugreek seeds
- 2 teaspoons chopped garlic
- 3 to 4 cups Brussels sprouts, trimmed
- 1/4 pound fresh green beans, cut into 1-inch pieces
- 2 tablespoons chopped fresh cilantro leaves

PLACE the peas and hot water in a 2-quart casserole dish. Cover and microwave at high power until boiling, about 5 minutes. Stir well, then cook at medium power (50%) until quite tender, about 25 minutes. Let sit, covered, for 5 minutes.

IN A BLENDER or food processor, purée the tomato with lemon juice. Set aside. Combine the oil, mustard seeds and fenugreek seeds in a large glass container and cook, uncovered, at high power for 1 minute. Add the garlic and cook 1 minute more. Add the Brussels sprouts and beans, and stir to coat with the oil and spices. Add the tomato purée, cover and cook at high power until the vegetables are just tender, about 6 to 8 minutes, stirring once. Add the peas, cover and cook 2 minutes more. Let sit, covered, for 2 minutes. Stir in the cilantro.

> **PER SERVING:**
> 153 Cal.; 8g Prot.; 4g Fat; 26g Carb.;
> 0mg Chol.; 30mg Sod.; 9g Fiber.

Better than Meatloaf

serves 6

You may customize this recipe to satisfy your particular craving. Simply ask your mother or another relative for his or her meatloaf recipe, then substitute the spices in the recipe for the spices listed here.

2 cups dry lentils

1 bay leaf

8 cups water

1 cup uncooked fine bulgur

1 cup soft whole-wheat bread crumbs

1 egg, beaten

1 tablespoon ketchup

1 medium onion, chopped

1 clove garlic, crushed

1 teaspoon crumbled dried thyme

2 teaspoons crumbled dried oregano

1 teaspoon crumbled dried tarragon

Salt and freshly ground black pepper to taste

3 tablespoons tomato paste or tomato sauce

COMBINE the lentils and bay leaf in a large pot with 6 cups water. Bring to a boil, lower the heat, cover and simmer until the lentils are soft and the water has been absorbed, about 45 minutes.

COMBINE the bulgur and 2 cups water in a medium saucepan. Bring to a boil, lower the heat, cover and simmer for about 15 minutes. Preheat the oven to 350°F. Transfer the lentils to a large mixing bowl. Add the bulgur and remaining ingredients except the tomato paste or sauce. Mix with your hands until thoroughly combined. Pat the mixture into a 5 × 9-inch loaf pan. Bake until firm but not dry, about 40 minutes. During the last 5 minutes of baking, brush the top with tomato paste or sauce. Let cool 15 minutes. Cut into slices and serve warm.

> **PER SERVING:**
> 302 Cal.; 18g Prot.; 2g Fat; 54g Carb.;
> 36mg Chol.; 273mg Sod.; 9g Fiber.

Nutty Lentil Loaf

serves 4

This one-dish meal is perfect to take along on day hikes or to eat at home.

| 1 cup dry lentils
| 3 cups water
| 1/2 cup chopped onion
| 2 cloves garlic, minced
| 1 tablespoon vegetable oil
| 2/3 cup chopped carrot
| 1/3 cup chopped celery
| 2 eggs, lightly beaten
| 2 tablespoons whole-wheat flour
| 3/4 cup unsalted raw cashews, chopped
| 1/4 cup raisins
| 1 teaspoon dried thyme

IN A MEDIUM SAUCEPAN, cook the lentils in the water until soft, about 45 minutes. Set aside. Cook the onion and garlic in the oil, stirring, until the onion is translucent. Add the carrots and celery. Simmer, covered, until the carrots are tender, about 10 to 15 minutes. Let cool.

PREHEAT the oven to 350°F. In a large bowl, mix together the lentils, vegetable mixture and remaining ingredients. Spoon into an oiled loaf pan. Bake until firm, about 45 minutes. Serve warm. (Or let the loaf cool and wrap it in foil for transport. On the trail, slice and serve loaf as is, or use the slices in sandwiches.)

> **PER SERVING:**
> 338 Cal.; 18g Prot.; 11g Fat; 45g Carb.;
> 107mg Chol.; 70mg Sod.; 9g Fiber.

Lentil Burgers

makes 12

You can make these delicious, low-fat burgers from scratch in less than an hour, or enjoy them in almost no time from the freezer. Serve the burgers on buns with your favorite trimmings.

| 1 cup dry lentils
| 2 1/2 cups water
| 1 bay leaf
| 1/2 cup diced onion
| 1/2 cup diced celery
| 1 tablespoon vegetable oil
| 1 tablespoon chopped fresh tarragon
| 2 teaspoons chopped fresh marjoram
| 1 teaspoon ground cumin
| 1/2 teaspoon dark sesame oil
| 1/2 teaspoon fresh lemon juice
| 1/2 teaspoon salt
| 1/4 teaspoon freshly ground black pepper
| 3/4 cup rolled oats
| 3/4 cup dry bread crumbs

IN A MEDIUM SAUCEPAN, simmer the lentils in water with the bay leaf until the lentil skins split easily, about 45 minutes. Meanwhile, cook the onion and celery in the oil, stirring, until soft, about 5 minutes. Remove from the heat and stir in the remaining ingredients except the oats and bread crumbs. Process the oats in a blender or food processor until finely ground. Combine the oats and bread crumbs with the lentil mixture. Shape the mixture into 12 patties while it's still warm. (You may freeze the patties at this point.)

PREHEAT the oven to 400°F. Bake the patties on a non-stick baking sheet or a sheet lightly coated with nonstick cooking spray until the patties are lightly browned, about 15 minutes.

> **PER BURGER:**
> 69 Cal.; 3g Prot.; 2g Fat; 10g Carb.;
> 0mg Chol.; 166mg Sod.; 4g Fiber.

Lentil-Chickpea Sauté with Apple and Curry

serves 6

Accompany this spicy main dish with a small salad or a side dish of plain yogurt.

- 1 cup uncooked lentils
- One 16-ounce can chickpeas, rinsed
- 1 small red onion, diced
- 1 clove garlic, minced
- 1 1/2 tablespoons vegetable oil
- 1 tablespoon curry powder
- 1 teaspoon minced fresh ginger root
- 1/4 teaspoon cayenne pepper (optional)
- 4 teaspoons soy sauce
- 1/3 cup golden raisins
- 1 cup water
- 1 Rome beauty apple, cored and chopped
- 2 tablespoons chopped fresh cilantro leaves
- 4 cups cooked brown rice

IN A MEDIUM SAUCEPAN, cook the lentils in water to cover over medium heat until tender, about 25 minutes; drain. Stir in the chickpeas and set aside. In a large saucepan, cook the onion and garlic in the oil, stirring, over medium-high heat for 3 minutes. Add the curry, ginger and cayenne, and cook 1 minute. Add the lentil-chickpea mixture and cook, stirring, 1 minute more. Stir in the soy sauce, raisins and water, and cook 15 minutes, stirring often. Add the apple during the last 3 minutes of cooking. Just before serving, sprinkle with cilantro. Serve over rice.

> **PER SERVING:**
> 416 Cal.; 16g Prot.; 6g Fat; 77g Carb.;
> 0mg Chol.; 246mg Sod.; 10g Fiber.

Black Bean Flautas

makes 12

- Two 16-ounce cans black beans (including bean liquid)
- 2 teaspoons chili powder
- 1/2 teaspoon ground cumin
- 1 clove garlic, minced
- 1 bay leaf
- Twelve 6-inch flour tortillas
- 6 scallions (green and white parts), minced
- 2 tomatoes, chopped
- 1 cup grated cheddar cheese or soy cheese
- Salsa, sour cream or yogurt for dipping (optional)

IN A MEDIUM SAUCEPAN, combine the beans, bean liquid, chili powder, cumin, garlic and bay leaf. Simmer over low heat for 10 minutes. Remove the bay leaf. Drain the bean mixture, reserving the liquid. Mash the beans, adding liquid as needed for desired consistency.

PREHEAT the oven to 400°F. Fill the tortillas with 1 or 2 heaping tablespoons of the bean mixture and top with the scallions, tomatoes and cheese. Roll up each filled tortilla into a tube shape and place them in a 9 × 13-inch baking pan, seam side down. Bake until lightly browned, about 15 minutes. Use any leftover bean mix for dipping. Or dip the flautas in salsa, sour cream or yogurt.

Variation:

Substitute one 16-ounce can vegetarian refried beans for the mashed black beans and spices. Spread on tortillas and proceed with recipe.

> **PER FLAUTA (WITHOUT SALSA, SOUR CREAM OR YOGURT):**
> 83 Cal.; 5g Prot.; 3g Fat; 8g Carb.;
> 10mg Chol.; 65mg Sod.; 4g Fiber.

Catalan Garbanzos

serves 6

This flavorful dish is popular in Barcelona, where it is often served in wide soup plates and eaten as a light main course. Garbanzos is another word for chickpeas.

1 1/2 cups dry chickpeas
6 cups fresh water
2 tablespoons virgin olive oil
4 cloves garlic, minced or pressed
1 green bell pepper, diced
4 large ripe tomatoes, peeled and chopped
Small pinch nutmeg
Small pinch ground cinnamon
1/4 teaspoon dried thyme
1/2 teaspoon salt
1/4 teaspoon freshly ground black pepper

SOAK the chickpeas overnight in water to cover; drain. In a large pot, bring the chickpeas and 6 cups fresh water to a boil. Lower the heat, simmer 3 hours, drain and set aside.

IN A SKILLET, heat the oil over high heat. Add the garlic, bell pepper, tomatoes, nutmeg, cinnamon, thyme, salt and black pepper. Cook, stirring, 3 minutes. Lower the heat, cover and simmer 10 minutes. Preheat oven to 325°F. Place the chickpeas in a baking dish and top with the tomato mixture. Cover and bake 1 1/2 hours, stirring each half hour.

Helpful hint:

You may substitute 3 cups canned chickpeas for the dry chickpeas.

> **PER SERVING:**
> 201 Cal.; 8g Prot.; 7g Fat; 27g Carb.;
> 0mg Chol.; 191mg Sod.; 7g Fiber.

Bean-and-Rice Burritos

serves 6

Here's an untraditional way of serving burritos: Tortillas are filled with beans, rice, onions and olives, covered with tomato sauce and baked. Garnish with chopped scallions.

SAUCE

- 2 cups salt-free tomato sauce
- 3 cups water
- 1/4 teaspoon garlic powder
- 1/2 teaspoon onion powder
- 3 tablespoons chili powder
- 4 tablespoons cornstarch or arrowroot

CASSEROLE

- 3 cups mashed pinto beans
- 2 cups cooked brown rice
- 1 cup sautéed, chopped scallions (cooked in 1 teaspoon oil over medium-high heat for 5 minutes)
- 1/2 cup chopped black olives
- 12 whole-wheat tortillas

SAUCE: In a saucepan, combine all the sauce ingredients and cook, stirring constantly, until the mixture boils and thickens, about 7 minutes.

CASSEROLE: Preheat the oven to 350°F. Place the casserole ingredients in separate bowls. To assemble the casserole, spread 1 cup sauce in the bottom of a casserole dish. Fill each tortilla with a mixture of the beans, rice, scallions and olives. Roll up the tortillas and place seam side down in the casserole dish. Pour the remaining sauce over the rolled-up tortillas. Cover and bake 30 minutes.

> **PER SERVING:**
> 402 Cal.; 14g Prot.; 5g Fat; 79g Carb.;
> 0mg Chol.; 557mg Sod.; 16g Fiber.

Southwestern Tacos

makes 24

In this lower-fat version of tacos, the tortillas are baked, not deep-fried. If you're short on time, use packaged soft corn or flour tortillas.

FILLING

- 4 cups dry pinto beans
- 6 cups dry TVP granules (page 72)
- 5 cups boiling water
- 4 large onions, minced
- 1/4 to 1/2 cup water
- 12 cups vegetable stock (page 178)
- 4 tablespoons chili powder
- 8 cloves garlic, minced
- 2 1/2 tablespoons ground cumin
- 2 1/2 tablespoons dried oregano
- 2 1/2 tablespoons dried basil
- Salt to taste
- 24 taco shells

TOPPINGS

- 16 cups shredded iceberg lettuce
- 3 pints mild salsa
- 2 cups low-fat or nondairy sour cream or yogurt
- 2 to 3 cups grated cheddar cheese or soy cheese (optional)
- 2 to 3 cups mashed or sliced avocado mixed with a little fresh lemon juice (optional)

FILLING: Soak the beans overnight in water to cover; drain. Rinse and set aside. In a large bowl, mix the TVP with boiling water. Stir and let sit for 5 to 10 minutes. Meanwhile, in a large skillet, cook the onions by stirring them over high heat, adding 1 to 2 tablespoons of water from time to time to keep them from sticking. As the onions brown, add enough water to dissolve the brown residue on the bottom of the pan, mixing it into the onions, until they are browned and soft.

IN A LARGE POT, combine the onions, beans, TVP and remaining ingredients except the salt and taco shells. Bring to a boil, lower the heat, cover and simmer until the beans are tender, about 2 hours. Add salt to taste.

TO SERVE, set out a basket of taco shells and a large bowl of the filling. Use smaller bowls for the shredded lettuce, salsa, sour cream or yogurt, and any other desired toppings.

Variation:

In place of the TVP use 4 pounds tofu that has been frozen, thawed and squeezed to remove all possible water and crumbled.

> **PER TACO:**
> 405 Cal.; 22g Prot.; 8g Fat; 60g Carb.;
> 0mg Chol.; 972mg Sod.; 8g Fiber.

Black Bean Quesadillas

serves 4

Depending on your choice of cheese and beans, you can really get creative with this Tex-Mex-inspired "sandwich." This version uses jack cheese and black beans, but sharp cheddar with scarlet runner beans, and mozzarella with anasazi beans are two more unusual favorites. Sprouted-wheat and whole-wheat tortillas are available at natural food stores.

One 15-ounce can black beans, rinsed

1/4 cup chopped green or red tomato

3 tablespoons chopped fresh cilantro leaves

12 black olives, pitted and sliced thinly

Eight 6-inch sprouted-wheat tortillas or whole-wheat tortillas

4 ounces shredded jalapeño jack cheese or soy cheese

32 spinach leaves (about 10 ounces), stemmed and shredded finely

1/4 cup hot salsa

MASH the beans in a large bowl. Stir in the tomato, cilantro and olives. Spread the bean mixture evenly onto 4 tortillas. Sprinkle with the cheese, spinach and salsa. Top with the remaining tortillas.

PREHEAT the oven to 350°F. Place the filled tortillas on an ungreased baking sheet and bake until the cheese melts, about 12 minutes. Or cook them on a cast-iron griddle over medium heat, turning once, until the cheese melts. Cut into wedges and serve hot.

> **PER SERVING:**
> 443 Cal.; 21g Prot.; 14g Fat; 56g Carb.;
> 25mg Chol.; 646mg Sod.; 8g Fiber.

GARNISH

> 3 to 4 cups spinach leaves, stems removed
>
> 2 tablespoons yogurt cheese, yogurt or soy yogurt
>
> 4 to 6 lemon wedges
>
> Freshly ground black pepper
>
> 1 tablespoon chopped fresh parsley or fresh cilantro leaves

STEW: Cover the lentils with hot water and let sit. Warm the oil in a soup pot over medium-low heat, and cook the onions and spices, stirring, for 8 minutes. Remove 1/3 of the onion mixture and reserve it for garnish. Add the rice to the onions in the soup pot, and cook 1 minute to coat the grains. Drain the lentils and add to the onion-rice mixture along with the water, bay leaves, salt and pepper. Simmer, covered, until the rice and lentils are tender, about 30 to 45 minutes. Add the chickpeas and heat until warmed through. Discard the bay leaves.

GARNISH: Steam the spinach, chop coarsely and stir into lentils. Ladle the stew into bowls and top with a spoonful of yogurt cheese or yogurt. Add the reserved onions, lemons, pepper and parsley or cilantro.

Variation:

> Instead of onions, substitute diced, chopped tomatoes as part of the garnish.

> **PER SERVING:**
> 473 Cal.; 20g Prot.; 11g Fat; 71g Carb.;
> 0mg Chol.; 914mg Sod.; 9g Fiber.

Red Kidney Bean Stew

serves 4

Beans, potatoes and carrots mingle in a thick, spicy sauce.

> 3 1/2 cups cooked kidney beans (or two 16-ounce cans red kidney beans)
>
> 1 cup bean cooking liquid (or liquid from can plus water to make 1 cup)
>
> 1 teaspoon vegetable oil plus 1/4 cup water
>
> 2 small onions, chopped finely
>
> 3 cloves garlic, minced
>
> 1 teaspoon curry powder
>
> 1 tomato, chopped
>
> 2 medium potatoes, cooked and cubed
>
> 2 carrots, cut in 1/2-inch cubes and steamed
>
> 1 tablespoon chopped fresh parsley, for garnish

IN A BLENDER, purée 1 cup beans with 1 cup bean liquid until smooth. Set aside. Place the remaining 2 1/2 cups beans in a separate bowl.

IN A LARGE SAUCEPAN, heat the oil and water, and cook the onions and garlic, stirring, until the onions are translucent. Add the curry powder and stir. Add the tomato and reserved bean purée. Simmer, covered, about 10 minutes. Add the potatoes and carrots and simmer 5 minutes. Add the reserved beans and simmer 5 minutes more. Garnish with parsley.

> **PER SERVING:**
> 340 Cal.; 16g Prot.; 8g Fat; 53g Carb.;
> 0mg Chol.; 35mg Sod.; 21g Fiber.

Saffron-Flavored Stew
à la Marseilles

serves 4

1 cup dry navy beans or small lima beans

3 cups water

Bouquet garni (see Note) with orange peel
  (1 × 2-inch piece)

1 teaspoon virgin olive oil

1 onion, diced

2 medium leeks, diced

1 carrot, diced

2 to 3 stalks celery, diced

1 to 2 small new potatoes, diced (optional)

3 to 4 cloves garlic

1/2 teaspoon dried thyme

1/2 teaspoon dried basil

1/2 teaspoon white pepper

1 teaspoon ground fennel seed

Pinch salt

1/4 teaspoon saffron

2 cups fresh water or vegetable stock (page 178)

2 large tomatoes, peeled, seeded and chopped

PLACE the beans in a pot with the water. Bring to a boil, lower the heat and simmer 5 minutes. Cover, remove from the heat and let soak at least 20 minutes. Make the *bouquet garni*, adding orange peel to the *garni's* basic ingredients. Set aside.

DRAIN and rinse the beans, and return them to the soup pot. Add water to cover and the bouquet garni. Bring the beans to a boil, lower heat and simmer until the beans are soft, about 45 minutes. Remove the bouquet garni.

IN A SKILLET, heat the oil. Add the onion, leeks, carrot, celery, potatoes and garlic. Cook, stirring, for 3 to 5 minutes. Stir in the herbs, pepper, fennel, salt and saffron. Add the fresh water or stock. Stir the beans into the vegetable mixture and add the tomatoes. Bring to a simmer, and cook 10 to 15 minutes. Serve hot.

Note:

To make a basic *bouquet garni*, place 3 bay leaves, 12 peppercorns, 10 to 12 parsley stems, 1 sprig fresh thyme (or 1 teaspoon dried) and 2 to 3 whole cloves of garlic in the center of a 12-inch square of cheesecloth, then tie the ends together.

> **PER SERVING:**
> 238 Cal.; 14g Prot.; 2g Fat; 42g Carb.;
> 0 Chol.; 111mg Sod.; 17g Fiber.

Three-Bean Chili

serves 6

Delicious and dramatic, this dish—with its many vegetables—is a mosaic of colors.

1 orange bell pepper, seeded

1 red bell pepper, seeded

1 yellow bell pepper, seeded

2 medium bulbs fennel

1 tablespoon virgin olive oil

1/4 teaspoon cayenne pepper

1 tablespoon coriander seeds

1 tablespoon cumin seeds

1 teaspoon dried oregano

2 tablespoons chili powder

3 medium tomatoes, peeled and chopped (or one 16-ounce can diced tomatoes)

1 1/2 cups cut green beans

1 3/4 cups cooked kidney beans

1 3/4 cups cooked black beans

1 3/4 cups cooked white beans

Water or tomato juice as needed

Salt and freshly ground black pepper to taste

1/2 cup chopped fresh cilantro leaves or fresh parsley

Shredded cheese or yogurt, for garnish (optional)

CUT the bell peppers into 1/2-inch squares. Remove the tops from the fennel bulbs, cut out the core with a small knife and finely chop. Set aside.

WARM the oil, cayenne, coriander and cumin in a heavy 4-quart saucepan over medium heat. Fry until the seasonings darken slightly. Add the bell peppers, fennel, oregano and chili powder, and cook, stirring, for 5 minutes. Stir in the tomatoes and all the beans, and bring to a boil. Lower the heat and simmer 30 minutes, adding water or tomato juice as needed if too much liquid evaporates. Season with salt and black pepper, and stir in the cilantro or parsley. Serve in shallow bowls, garnished with shredded cheese or yogurt.

> **PER SERVING:**
> 286 Cal.: 14g Prot.: 3g Fat; 50g Carb.:
> 0mg Chol.: 380mg Sod.: 11g Fiber.

grains

16

HERE'S A POP QUIZ: NAME THREE GRAINS. You have ten seconds. Time's up! We bet you said "rice." But how about barley, bulgur, couscous, quinoa and kasha? And that's not all. Ancient grains such as teff and amaranth are being rediscovered by cooks. If you listed corn or wheat, you're technically right—they are grains—but the recipes that follow emphasize the staples of the vegetarian diet that include rice (but not corn or wheat) and many more less-known grains. These grains may be new to you, but they have found homes in many regions, such as the Middle East, Africa, the former Soviet nations and the Andes. And it's no wonder grains are basic to nearly every cuisine: They're low in fat and rich in vitamins B and E, various minerals and fiber. You can use them to make pilafs, burgers, fillings for crepes, and croquettes, to name a few dishes. The fun is in the discovering, so expect many delicious returns.

287

Wild Rice Crepes

serves 4

3/4 cup uncooked wild rice

2 3/4 cups vegetable stock (page 178)

1/4 onion, chopped finely

2 stalks celery, sliced thinly

2 tablespoons vegetable oil

3/4 onion, chopped coarsely

1 1/4 cups sliced white button mushrooms

1/2 cup oyster mushrooms, separated into small clumps
   (or an additional 1/2 cup white button mushrooms)

5 to 6 shiitake mushrooms (or dried shiitakes reconstituted in warm water), cut into quarters or eighths

1 large tomato, chopped

1/2 teaspoon dried sage

1 tablespoon soy sauce

Salt and freshly ground black pepper to taste

8 to 12 Basic or No-Cholesterol Dinner Crepes
   (page 441)

PLACE the rice, stock and finely chopped onion in a
saucepan; bring to a boil over high heat. Lower the heat,
cover and cook until the rice is tender and all liquid is
absorbed, about 1 hour.

MEANWHILE, cook the celery in the oil, stirring, until tender. Add the coarsely chopped onion and mushrooms,
and cook, stirring, until the vegetables are soft. Stir in
the cooked rice, tomato, sage, soy sauce, salt and pepper, and cook 10 to 15 minutes more.

PREHEAT the oven to 350°F. Fill the crepes with the rice
mixture. Roll up and place in a single layer in a baking
dish. Heat for 10 minutes.

Variation:

If desired, top the heated crepes with your favorite
sauce. A good bet is Almond Sauce (page 475).

> **PER SERVING:**
> 468 Cal.; 16g Prot.; 17g Fat; 65g Carb.;
> 146mg Chol.; 666mg Sod.; 9g Fiber.

Brown Rice-and-Cheese Croquettes

makes 12

Traditionally deep-fried, croquettes may be made
lighter. The solution is easy: Bake them.

1 cup uncooked short-grain brown rice

2 1/2 cups vegetable stock (page 178) or water

1/2 cup freshly grated Parmesan cheese

1 egg white, lightly beaten

2 tablespoons whole-wheat flour

Twelve 1/2-inch cubes mozzarella cheese

1 cup dry whole-wheat bread crumbs

IN A SAUCEPAN, bring the rice and stock or water to a boil.
Lower the heat, cover and cook until the rice is soft and
all the liquid is absorbed, about 45 to 60 minutes. Cool.
Mix in the Parmesan cheese, egg white and flour.

PREHEAT the oven to 400°F. Form the rice mixture into
2-inch balls; place a mozzarella cube at the center of
each. Spread bread crumbs on a plate and roll the croquettes in them. Bake the croquettes in a lightly greased
baking pan for 30 minutes, turning the croquettes once
midway through.

Jolof Rice

serves 8

Jolof rice is named for the Wolof people in West Africa. This dish is rich and spicy, but can easily be adjusted to your taste. Serve it with Banana Condiment (page 488) on the side.

1 cup dry black-eyed peas

3 quarts water

2 medium eggplants

1 teaspoon salt

1 1/2 tablespoons canola oil

2 large onions, chopped

3 tablespoons chopped ginger root

2 jalapeño peppers, roasted, stems and seeds removed, chopped

2 cloves garlic, minced

1 green bell pepper, chopped

4 large tomatoes, chopped

1 1/2 tablespoons tomato paste

2 teaspoons cayenne pepper

2 teaspoons curry powder

Hot pepper sauce to taste (optional)

1 pound carrots, chopped

1 1/2 cups uncooked long-grain brown rice

1/2 pound green beans, cut in thirds

IN A LARGE POT, soak the peas overnight in 1 quart water. Drain. Add 2 quarts fresh water to the peas and simmer 15 minutes. Drain and reserve the cooking water. Slice the eggplants into rounds about 1/2 inch thick and place in a colander. Sprinkle with salt and let drain 5 minutes.

HEAT the oil in an ovenproof saucepan or casserole. Add the eggplant, 1 tablespoon chopped onion, 1 tablespoon chopped ginger, 1 chopped jalapeño, 1 clove garlic and the bell pepper. Cook, stirring, until the eggplant is browned, about 5 minutes. Remove the eggplant from the saucepan or casserole and set aside. Add the remaining onion, ginger, jalapeño, garlic, bean liquid, tomatoes, tomato paste, cayenne, curry powder and hot pepper sauce. Simmer 10 minutes. Add the peas, carrots and rice. Simmer 5 minutes more. Add the green beans and browned eggplant. Simmer 15 minutes. Meanwhile, preheat the oven to 400°F. Cover the saucepan or casserole, and bake 25 to 30 minutes.

Steamed Rice with Mixed Vegetables

serves 8

Feel free to substitute other seasonal vegetables as desired.

3 cups uncooked brown rice

5 cups vegetable stock (preferably made from kombu and shiitake mushrooms; see page 178)

2 tablespoons sake or dry sherry

1/4 cup soy sauce

1/2 pound white button mushrooms, sliced

2 carrots, cut into thin sticks 1-inch long

1 1/3 cups frozen green peas

IN A LARGE POT, combine the rice and stock. Stir in the sake or sherry and soy sauce. Place the vegetables on top of the rice. Bring to a boil, cover, lower the heat and simmer 45 to 50 minutes. Remove from the heat and let sit 10 minutes. Before serving, fluff the mixture lightly with a fork to distribute vegetables. Serve warm.

PER SERVING:
289 Cal.; 8g Prot.; 1g Fat; 61g Carb.;
0mg Chol.; 551mg Sod.; 4g Fiber.

Fried Rice

serves 12

This dish is traditionally made with eggs, but you may omit them and still have a perfectly satisfying meal.

2 to 4 tablespoons peanut oil

2 onions, chopped

2 cloves garlic, minced

1/2 to 3 teaspoons sambal or cayenne pepper

2 teaspoons ground coriander

1 teaspoon ground cumin

1 to 2 cups mung bean sprouts

4 cups cooked brown rice, cooled

2 tablespoons *kecap manis* (see Note), or 2 tablespoons soy sauce plus 1 tablespoon brown sugar

2 eggs, scrambled or fried (optional)

HEAT the oil in a wok or large skillet. Cook the onions, garlic, sambal or cayenne, coriander and cumin, stirring, until the onions are soft. Add the bean sprouts and cook, stirring, 2 to 3 minutes more. Add the rice, a little at a time, and cook, stirring, until the rice is thoroughly heated, about 5 to 10 minutes. Stir in the *kecap manis* and eggs. Serve warm.

Note:

Kecap manis is a sweet-salty seasoning found in Asian markets and gourmet food stores.

PER SERVING (WITHOUT EGGS):
108 Cal.; 3g Prot.; 3g Fat; 19g Carb.;
0mg Chol.; 173mg Sod.; 2g Fiber.

Paella Vegetariana

serves 6

Paella, a popular Spanish one-pot meal, traditionally contains saffron-scented rice with bits of chicken, sausage, shellfish and vegetables. In this version, pre-seasoned soyfoods stand in for the meat and seafood—with delicious results.

8 ounces flavored tofu or tofu sausage

6 ounces seasoned tempeh, thawed

1/4 cup vegetable oil

2 tablespoons virgin olive oil

2 to 3 tablespoons minced garlic

1 red bell pepper, diced

1 large onion, diced

1 large carrot, diced

1 teaspoon paprika

1/2 teaspoon fennel seeds (optional)

1 teaspoon ground cumin

1/2 teaspoon salt

1/2 teaspoon freshly ground black pepper

1/4 teaspoon cayenne pepper (optional)

1/4 teaspoon crushed saffron

2 cups uncooked basmati or other white rice, rinsed

3 1/2 cups boiling water

2 bay leaves

1 cup fresh or frozen peas

1 cup fresh or frozen whole-kernel corn (optional)

Cherry tomatoes, quartered, for garnish

Chopped fresh parsley or fresh cilantro leaves and sliced black olives, for garnish (optional)

SLICE the tofu or tofu sausage and tempeh into bite-sized pieces. In a large skillet, heat the vegetable oil over medium-high heat until hot but not smoking. Add half of the tofu and tempeh, and fry until golden brown, about 10 to 15 minutes. Remove and drain on a paper towel. Fry the remaining tofu and tempeh, adding more oil if needed. Drain and set aside.

HEAT 1 tablespoon olive oil in a pot over medium-high heat. Add 1 tablespoon garlic and cook, stirring, until golden, about 1 minute. Add the diced bell pepper and cook, stirring, with the garlic until fragrant, about 1 to 2 minutes. Remove from the pot and set aside.

ADD the remaining tablespoon of olive oil to the pot. Stir in the remaining 1 to 2 tablespoons garlic, onion and carrot, and cook, stirring, 2 minutes. Add the paprika, fennel, cumin, salt, black pepper, cayenne and saffron. Stir 30 seconds. Mix in the rice, then add boiling water, bay leaves, tofu and tempeh. Stir well. Cover the pot, lower the heat and simmer 12 to 15 minutes. When the liquid has been absorbed, remove the pot from the heat. Add the cooked peppers, peas and corn to the top of the rice, replace the lid and let sit 5 minutes. Remove the lid and fluff the paella with a fork. Remove and discard the bay leaves.

TRANSFER the paella to a serving tray. Garnish with cherry tomatoes. Sprinkle with parsley or cilantro and olives.

> **PER SERVING:**
> 486 Cal.; 15g Prot.; 19g Fat; 63g Carb.;
> 0mg Chol.; 216mg Sod.; 5g Fiber.

Mushrooms with Wild Rice

serves 4

Four different types of mushrooms appear in this colorful dish. If you can't find fresh shiitake mushrooms, you may substitute dried mushrooms reconstituted in water.

RICE

- 1 cup uncooked wild rice
- 3 cups water
- 1 tablespoon low-sodium soy sauce
- 1/4 cup minced scallions (green and white parts)

MUSHROOMS

- 1 medium yellow onion, chopped
- 2 stalks celery, chopped
- 1/4 cup water
- 1/2 pound white button mushrooms, sliced
- 8 fresh shiitake mushrooms, chopped
- 1/2 to 3/4 cup chopped oyster mushrooms
- 1/4 cup trimmed enoki mushrooms
- 12 snow peas, quartered
- 1/2 red bell pepper, diced
- 2 tablespoons low-sodium soy sauce
- 1/2 teaspoon dried sage
- 1/4 teaspoon poultry seasoning
- Freshly ground black pepper to taste

RICE: Place the rice, water, soy sauce and scallions in a saucepan. Bring to a boil. Lower the heat, cover and cook over medium heat until the liquid has evaporated and the rice is tender, about 1 hour. Set aside.

MUSHROOMS: Place the onion, celery and water in a large saucepan. Cook and stir for several minutes, until the vegetables soften slightly. Add the button, shiitake and oyster mushrooms. Cook, stirring occasionally, for 10 minutes. Gently stir in the cooked rice, enoki mushrooms, snow peas, bell pepper and seasonings. Cook over low heat 15 minutes more.

> **PER SERVING:**
> 152 Cal.; 6g Prot.; 0.1g Fat; 31g Carb.;
> 0mg Chol.; 829mg Sod.; 3g Fiber.

Herb-and-Mushroom Rice Casserole

serves 6

This dish tastes best when served piping hot with a generous dollop of yogurt on the top.

- 2 cups uncooked white rice
- 4 1/2 cups vegetable stock (page 178)
- 1 tablespoon butter or margarine
- 3 tablespoons virgin olive oil
- 5 scallions (green and white parts), chopped finely
- 1 teaspoon minced garlic
- 1/4 teaspoon cayenne pepper
- 1/2 teaspoon dried oregano
- 1/4 teaspoon freshly ground black pepper
- 1 medium bunch fresh parsley, stems removed and minced
- 4 cups finely chopped white button mushrooms
- 2 medium bunches dillweed, stems removed and minced

IN A MEDIUM SAUCEPAN, combine the rice with 3 cups vegetable stock. Add the butter or margarine. Bring to a boil, lower the heat, cover and simmer until the rice is tender, about 20 minutes.

MEANWHILE, in a large skillet, heat the oil over medium heat. Cook the scallions and garlic, stirring, until the scallions are limp, about 5 minutes. Add the cayenne, oregano and black pepper, and cook 1 minute more. Add the parsley, mushrooms and dill, and cook until the mushrooms are soft, about 5 to 10 minutes.

PREHEAT the oven to 350°F. Combine the rice with the vegetable mixture in a 2 1/2-quart casserole dish. Pour the remaining 1 1/2 cups of vegetable stock over the entire dish. Bake, uncovered, for 30 minutes.

> **PER SERVING:**
> 315 Cal.; 5g Prot.; 9g Fat; 52g Carb.;
> 5mg Chol.; 7mg Sod.; 4g Fiber.

Saffron Risotto Timbales with Grilled Tomato Sauce

serves 6

Risotto is an Italian rice dish made with arborio, a medium-grain white rice that becomes very creamy when cooked. In this version, the risotto—a pretty yellow with the addition of saffron—is packed into small cups or ramekins and dished out in individual servings called timbales.

SAUCE

- 2 pounds plum tomatoes
- 1 tablespoon virgin olive oil or vegetable oil
- 1/2 small onion, diced finely
- Salt and freshly ground black pepper to taste
- Sugar to taste (optional)

RISOTTO

- 4 to 5 1/2 cups vegetable stock (page 178)
- 3 tablespoons butter
- 1/2 cup finely diced onion
- 1/4 teaspoon saffron threads
- 1/4 teaspoon ground turmeric
- 1 1/2 cups uncooked arborio rice
- 1/2 cup white wine
- 1/2 cup grated Parmesan cheese
- 3 tablespoons chopped chives
- 2 tablespoons finely chopped fresh Italian flat-leaf parsley
- 2 tablespoons finely chopped fresh marjoram or basil leaves
- Salt and freshly ground black pepper to taste
- 2 tablespoons chopped opal basil leaves, for garnish (optional)

SAUCE: Grill the tomatoes over a preheated grill, or broil them in a foil-lined pan under the broiler. Turn frequently with a pair of tongs, until the skin is blistered and charred in places. Remove from the heat. If desired, scrape off the crispier, more blackened pieces of skin. Then purée the tomatoes, including the skin. Set aside.

IN A MEDIUM SAUCEPAN, heat the oil over medium-high heat. Add the onion and cook, stirring, until translucent, about 8 minutes. Add the puréed tomatoes and cook over medium heat until the sauce thickens slightly, about 10 minutes. Season with salt, pepper and a teaspoon or 2 of sugar to correct the acidity if the tomatoes are very tart. Set aside.

RISOTTO: Preheat the oven to 350°F. Bring the stock to a simmer in a medium saucepan. Meanwhile, melt the butter in a 3- to 4-quart oven-proof saucepan with a lid. Add the onion, saffron and turmeric to the melted butter. Cook over medium heat, stirring frequently, until the onion softens, about 2 minutes. Add the rice and stir. Add the wine and continue cooking and stirring until the wine has been completely absorbed. Remove from the heat.

STIR in 2 cups of the heated stock. Cover and place in the oven. After 10 minutes, remove the pan, stir, and add another 2 cups of stock. Return the pan to the oven for 10 minutes more, then place the pan over medium heat on the stovetop.

TASTE the rice. If it's not done, add more stock in half-cup increments, stirring constantly until the rice is tender but still a little chewy. At the end, stir in the Parmesan, chives, parsley and marjoram or basil. Season with salt and pepper.

LADLE the rice mixture into 6 lightly oiled cups or ramekins and gently pack it down. Let sit a few minutes, then invert the ramekins onto a metal spatula and carefully slide them onto 6 plates. Ring each with 1/3 cup tomato sauce and garnish with basil.

> **PER SERVING
> (WITH 1/3 CUP SAUCE):**
> 383 Cal.: 8g Prot.: 11g Fat: 50g Carb.:
> 22mg Chol.: 903mg Sod.: 3g Fiber.

Asparagus Risotto with Mushrooms and Sun-Dried Tomatoes

serves 6

This dish is comfort food gone gourmet. The delicate flavors of fresh vegetables and basil are a delicious complement to the rich creaminess of arborio rice.

- 1 tablespoon virgin olive oil
- 1 large onion, diced
- 1 large leek, halved and sliced thinly
- 1 tablespoon finely minced garlic
- 2 cups uncooked arborio rice
- 1/4 teaspoon freshly ground black pepper
- 8 cups vegetable stock (page 178)
- 12 sun-dried tomatoes, sliced thinly on the diagonal
- 1 cup asparagus, sliced thinly on the diagonal
- 1 1/2 cups sliced white button mushrooms
- 1/2 cup coarsely chopped fresh basil leaves
- 1/4 cup grated Parmesan cheese (optional)

IN A LARGE SAUCEPAN over medium heat, heat the olive oil over medium-high heat. Cook the onion, leek and garlic, stirring, for 3 minutes. Add the rice and pepper, and cook 5 minutes more.

IN A SEPARATE POT, heat the vegetable stock to nearly boiling, then remove from heat. Add 7 cups stock and the sun-dried tomatoes to the rice mixture. Bring the rice mixture to a boil, lower the heat and simmer 12 minutes, stirring often.

MEANWHILE, after the rice mixture has cooked 5 minutes, steam the asparagus, mushrooms and basil until the asparagus is tender-crisp, about 5 minutes. Add to the rice mixture along with the remaining 1 cup vegetable stock. Mix well and simmer until the mixture is creamy and the rice is just done, about 5 minutes more. Stir in the Parmesan just before serving.

> **PER SERVING:**
> 344 Cal.; 9g Prot.; 3g Fat; 68g Carb.;
> 0mg Chol.; 94mg Sod.; 3g Fiber.

Raspberry-Borscht Risotto

serves 2

Here's an elegant presentation of rice, raspberries and, yes, beets.

2 medium beets, peeled and quartered

2 carrots, chopped

1 large onion, quartered

1 bay leaf

1 cup fresh orange juice

3 cups water

1 tablespoon unsalted butter

1 small white onion, chopped finely

1 cup crushed fresh raspberries

2/3 cup uncooked arborio rice

1 tablespoon sour cream or light sour cream

1/2 teaspoon finely grated lemon or orange zest

IN A LARGE SAUCEPAN, combine the beets, carrots, onion, bay leaf, orange juice and water. Bring to a boil, cover and simmer 1 hour. Strain the broth into another saucepan and keep it warm over low heat. Discard all the vegetables except the beets. Dice a beet and set it aside. In a food processor, purée the other beet and add it to the broth.

IN THE LARGE SAUCEPAN, melt the butter over medium heat. Add the chopped onion and cook, stirring, until translucent, about 7 minutes. Add the diced beet and raspberries, and stir well. Add rice and stir to blend. Pour in enough hot beet broth to cover the rice by about an inch. Continue cooking and stirring until the liquid is absorbed, about 4 minutes. Add more broth, again to cover by about an inch, and stir until absorbed. Continue adding broth and stirring until the rice is plump and soft in the center. No liquid should be left on the surface of the rice, and the texture should be thick like oatmeal. This process should take about 30 minutes. (You'll probably have broth left over.) Stir in the sour cream and grated lemon or orange zest. Serve at once.

> **PER SERVING:**
> 502 Cal.; 8g Prot.; 8g Fat; 96g Carb.;
> 20mg Chol.; 126mg Sod.; 12g Fiber.

Indian-Style Risotto

serves 6

This traditional dish is ready in short order if you use an untraditional cooking method: pressure cooking.

 1 tablespoon *ghee* (clarified butter used especially in
    Indian cooking) or corn oil

 1 jalapeño pepper, minced

 1 teaspoon cumin seeds

 1/8 teaspoon asafetida (optional)

 1 cup uncooked split yellow mung beans

 1 1/2 cups uncooked basmati rice or other
    long-grain rice

 1 small cauliflower, cut into florets

 6 cups water

 1/2 teaspoon ground turmeric

 1 1/2 teaspoons salt, or to taste

 1/2 cup frozen peas

 Freshly ground black pepper to taste

 1/4 cup chopped fresh cilantro leaves

HEAT 1/2 tablespoon *ghee* or oil in a pressure cooker. Add the jalapeño and cumin; fry until the seeds begin to darken. Add the asafetida; fry 5 seconds. Add the beans, rice and cauliflower, and cook 2 minutes.

STIR in 4 1/2 cups water, turmeric and 3/4 teaspoon salt. Lock the lid in place and bring to pressure over high heat. Lower the heat slightly, but maintain the pressure; cook 6 minutes. Reduce the pressure by the quick-release method and remove the lid.

GENTLY STIR in the remaining 1 1/2 cups water and 3/4 teaspoon salt. Add the peas and black pepper. Place the cooker over medium heat for 1 minute. Stir in the cilantro. Drizzle the risotto with the remaining 1/2 tablespoon *ghee* or oil. Serve at once.

Helpful hint:

To cook this dish in a saucepan, cook the ingredients as instructed in the first paragraph. Then add 4 1/2 cups water, turmeric and salt, and bring to a boil. Lower the heat, cover and simmer, stirring frequently, until the beans and rice are tender and the liquid is absorbed, about 30 to 45 minutes. (Add more water if necessary.) Stir in the peas, black pepper and cilantro. Cover and steam 1 minute more. Drizzle with the remaining 1/2 tablespoon *ghee* or oil.

> **PER SERVING:**
> 228 Cal.; 7g Prot.; 3g Fat; 43g Carb.;
> 0mg Chol.; 596mg Sod.; 5g Fiber.

Summer Vegetable Risotto

serves 4

Risotto requires a lot of attention on the stovetop; a microwave cuts down on the work significantly.

    1 tablespoon margarine
    3/4 cup chopped green bell pepper
    3/4 cup chopped red bell pepper
    1 cup sliced fresh white button mushrooms
    1/4 cup sliced scallions (green and white parts)
    1 clove garlic, minced
    1/2 cup water
    One 14 1/2-ounce can vegetable broth (or 1 3/4 cups
        vegetable stock, page 178)
    1 cup uncooked arborio rice
    2 tablespoons sherry (optional)
    Pinch or more ground saffron
    1/4 cup grated Parmesan cheese
    2 cups shredded fresh spinach leaves
    1 medium tomato, seeded and chopped

IN A 2-QUART CASSEROLE DISH, combine the margarine, bell peppers, mushrooms, scallions and garlic. Cover. Microwave at high power until the vegetables are tender-crisp, about 4 to 6 minutes, stirring once. Stir in the water, broth, rice, sherry and saffron. Microwave at high power, uncovered, until the liquid is almost absorbed, about 14 to 16 minutes, stirring frequently. Stir in the Parmesan, spinach and tomato. Serve at once.

PER SERVING:
188 Cal.; 6g Prot.; 4g Fat; 30g Carb.;
4mg Chol.; 181mg Sod.; 4g Fiber.

Vegetables and Spanish Rice

serves 4

This dish isn't your run-of-the-mill Spanish rice. It's flavorful without being too spicy, and it's pleasing to the eye as well.

    1 cup uncooked white rice
    2 cups cold water
    2 tablespoons virgin olive oil
    1 small onion, chopped
    1/3 cup chopped red bell pepper
    1/2 teaspoon saffron
    3 tablespoons tomato paste
    1/4 cup peas (shelled fresh or frozen)

PLACE the rice in a medium saucepan and cover with cold water. Bring to a boil, cover, lower the heat and simmer 15 minutes, stirring occasionally to keep the rice from sticking.

MEANWHILE, heat the oil in a saucepan over medium heat and cook the onion, pepper and saffron, stirring, until the onion is translucent, about 5 to 10 minutes. Add the tomato paste and stir until smooth. Add the peas, stir briefly and remove from the heat. Mix the vegetable mixture into the rice and cook, stirring occasionally, until the rice is light and fluffy, about 10 minutes.

PER SERVING:
257 Cal.; 4g Prot.; 7g Fat; 43g Carb.;
0mg Chol.; 19mg Sod.; 3g Fiber.

Basmati Rice and Kale Gratin

serves 8

This fragrant, creamy gratin provides a whopping 522 milligrams of calcium per serving.

- 2 cups vegetable stock (page 178)
- 1 cup diced red bell pepper
- 1 cup whole-kernel corn
- 1 1/4 cups uncooked basmati rice
- 1 teaspoon dried thyme
- 4 pounds kale or mixed greens
- 1 1/4 cups part-skim ricotta cheese
- 2/3 cup grated Parmesan cheese
- 1/2 teaspoon salt
- Freshly ground black pepper to taste
- 1/2 cup fresh bread crumbs
- Olive oil cooking spray

COMBINE the stock, bell pepper, corn, rice and thyme in a saucepan. Bring to a boil, lower the heat, cover and simmer until the rice is tender, about 15 minutes. Set aside.

PREHEAT the oven to 400°F. Wash (but do not dry) the kale or greens, and trim and discard the stems. Place the kale or greens in a large pot, cover and cook over medium-high heat until it wilts, about 5 minutes. (The water on the leaves is sufficient to steam the greens.) Drain and coarsely chop. Fluff the rice mixture with a fork.

IN A LARGE BOWL, combine the cooked kale, the rice mixture, ricotta, half of the Parmesan, salt and black pepper. Place in an oiled, 2-quart gratin dish. Sprinkle with the remaining Parmesan and bread crumbs, and spray well with oil. Bake until golden and bubbling, about 30 minutes.

PER SERVING:
308 Cal.; 15g Prot.; 6g Fat; 46g Carb.;
17mg Chol.; 424mg Sod.; 15g Fiber.

Red Beans with Saffron Rice Pilaf

serves 6

BEANS
- 1 tablespoon virgin olive oil
- 1 teaspoon cumin seeds
- 1/2 teaspoon coriander
- 1/4 teaspoon asafetida (or 1 clove garlic, chopped)
- Two 15-ounce cans red beans, rinsed
- 1 1/2 cups vegetable stock (page 178) or water

RICE
- 1/4 teaspoon saffron
- 2 cups water
- 1/2 teaspoon salt
- 1 cup basmati rice or millet
- 1 cup whole-kernel corn
- 1 red bell pepper, seeded and diced
- 1 zucchini, diced
- 1 cup small broccoli florets
- 3 tablespoons chopped fresh cilantro leaves, for garnish

BEANS: In a large skillet, heat 1/2 tablespoon oil over medium-low heat. Add the cumin, coriander and asafetida or garlic; cook until the seeds darken slightly. Add the beans and vegetable stock or water, and cook, stirring occasionally, until the stock thickens, about 15 minutes. Cover and keep warm.

RICE: Toast the saffron in a heavy saucepan over medium-low heat until it crisps, no more than 30 seconds. Using a spoon, crush the saffron to a powder. Add the water and salt, and bring to a boil. Stir in the rice or millet, corn, pepper, zucchini and broccoli. Cover and simmer over low heat until the liquid is absorbed, about 15 minutes. Remove from the heat. After 5 minutes, fluff the mixture with a fork.

TO SERVE, divide the rice and beans among 6 plates. Drizzle with the remaining oil and garnish with cilantro.

PER SERVING:
286 Cal.; 10g Prot.; 3g Fat; 54g Carb.;
0mg Chol.; 687mg Sod.; 11g Fiber.

Kasha Pilaf with Vegetables

serves 4

Kasha, or toasted buckwheat, is a Russian favorite. Here, it is combined with three colorful vegetables: sweet potatoes, corn and peas.

1 1/2 tablespoons vegetable oil
1/2 medium onion, chopped finely
1 1/2 cups uncooked kasha
1 egg, beaten lightly
2 1/2 cups boiling water
1 medium sweet potato, peeled and cubed
1/2 cup frozen whole-kernel corn
1/2 cup frozen peas

IN A SMALL SKILLET, heat the oil over medium heat. Cook the onion, stirring, until it browns, about 5 minutes. Remove from the heat and set aside. Place the kasha in an ungreased skillet over medium-low heat. Toast, stirring often, until the kasha becomes slightly darker, about 3 to 5 minutes. Add the egg and stir quickly to coat the grains. Add the water at once but do not stir. Add the sweet potato, corn and peas. Lower the heat and simmer, covered, until the water is absorbed, the kasha is puffy and the sweet potato is tender, about 20 to 25 minutes. Top with the cooked onions.

PER SERVING:
330 Cal.; 10g Prot.; 8g Fat; 58g Carb.;
53mg Chol.; 38mg Sod.; 7g Fiber.

Couscous Pilaf with Saffron Cream

serves 4

PILAF

- 1 tablespoon virgin olive oil
- 1/2 teaspoon coriander seeds
- 2/3 cup diced red bell pepper
- 1/4 teaspoon cayenne pepper
- 1/4 teaspoon ground cinnamon
- 3 cups water or vegetable stock (page 178)
- 1 1/2 cups uncooked couscous
- Salt and freshly ground black pepper to taste
- 4 tablespoons chopped fresh mint leaves
  (or 2 tablespoons chopped fresh thyme leaves)

SAFFRON CREAM

- 1/2 cup neufchâtel cheese or light cream cheese
- 1/3 cup low-fat yogurt
- Pinch saffron threads, crushed

PILAF: Heat the oil in a saucepan over medium heat. Add the coriander seeds and fry until toasted. Stir in the bell pepper, cayenne and cinnamon, and cook, stirring, until barely tender, about 4 minutes. Pour in the water or stock, and bring to a boil. Stir in the couscous, cover and remove from heat. Let sit 10 to 15 minutes.

CHECK the couscous. It is ready when the grains swell and the liquid is absorbed. If any liquid remains, return the pan to low, heat briefly and cook until absorbed. Season with salt, pepper and mint or thyme.

SAFFRON CREAM: Combine the cheese, yogurt and saffron in a blender or food processor. Blend until creamy. Serve on the side.

> **PER SERVING (WITH 1 TABLESPOON CREAM):**
> 141 Cal.; 5g Prot.; 5g Fat; 21g Carb.;
> 8mg Chol.; 219mg Sod.; 3g Fiber.

Quinoa Pilaf with Almonds and Raisins

serves 6

PILAF

- 2 medium carrots, diced into 1/2-inch cubes
- 1/2 to 1 tablespoon canola oil
- 1/2 medium onion, thinly sliced
- 1/4 teaspoon ground turmeric
- 3 cups water
- 1 1/2 cups uncooked quinoa
- 1/2 green bell pepper, chopped
- 2 tablespoons slivered almonds
- 2 tablespoons golden raisins
- 1/2 cup frozen peas, thawed
- Toasted pistachios, for garnish (page 106)

CROUTONS (OPTIONAL)

- 1/2 to 1 tablespoon virgin olive oil
- 2 large cloves garlic, pressed or minced
- 1 slice whole-wheat bread, cut into 1-inch cubes

PILAF: Steam the carrots for 5 to 8 minutes. (They need not be completely cooked.) Heat the oil in a large skillet over medium heat. Add the onion and stir, cooking, until translucent, about 5 minutes. Stir in the turmeric. Add the water and bring to a boil. Add the quinoa, stirring to push it under the water. Place the bell pepper, almonds and raisins on top. Cover and simmer until all the water is absorbed and the quinoa is light and fluffy, about 25 to 30 minutes. Add the peas to the quinoa during the last 5 minutes of cooking and fluff with a fork.

CROUTONS: Preheat the oven to 425°F. Heat the oil and garlic in a small pan until simmering. Brush the olive oil onto the bread cubes, patting the garlic bits on top. Bake until brown on top, about 6 to 9 minutes. Place the quinoa in a serving dish. Garnish with pistachios and garlic croutons.

PER SERVING:
122 Cal.; 4g Prot.; 4g Fat; 19g Carb.;
0mg Chol.; 22mg Sod.; 3g Fiber.

Middle Eastern Rice with Lentils

serves 4

- 1/2 medium onion, chopped
- 1 tablespoon vegetable oil
- 1 cup uncooked brown rice
- 1 tablespoon low-sodium tomato paste
- 2 1/2 cups water
- 1/4 teaspoon ground cinnamon
- 1/4 cup dry lentils
- 1 teaspoon salt
- 1/2 cup raisins
- 1/2 cup pine nuts, toasted (page 106)
- Additional water if needed

IN A LARGE SAUCEPAN, cook the onion in oil, stirring, until soft, over medium heat. Add the rice and stir for several minutes. Combine the tomato paste with the water and cinnamon. Add to the rice along with the lentils. Bring to a boil, cover and lower the heat. Simmer for 30 minutes.

PREHEAT the oven to 350°F. Stir the salt, raisins and pine nuts into the rice mixture. The mixture should be a little watery; add 1/4 cup water if it is dry. Place the mixture in a greased 2 1/2-quart baking dish. Cover and bake for 20 to 30 minutes.

PER SERVING:
341 Cal.; 8g Prot.; 9g Fat; 60g Carb.;
0mg Chol.; 522mg Sod.; 6g Fiber.

Teff Cakes with Groundnut Sauce

serves 4

Teff is the grain used for *injera*, the traditional Ethiopian flatbread. These cakes are a spin on the traditional use of teff.

GROUNDNUT SAUCE

- 1 small onion, diced
- 1 tablespoon peanut oil
- 1 medium tomato, sliced thinly
- 2 jalapeño peppers, roasted, seeded and minced
- 2 tablespoons peanut butter
- 1 cup boiling water
- 2 teaspoons arrowroot or cornstarch
- 1/4 teaspoon freshly ground black pepper

CAKES

- 1/2 cup uncooked teff
- 3 1/2 cups water
- 3/4 cup chopped onion
- 1 jalapeño pepper, seeded and diced
- 1 cup whole-wheat pastry flour
- 1 tablespoon sesame oil

GROUNDNUT SAUCE: In a skillet, cook the onion, stirring, in the oil over medium heat. Add the tomato and jalapeños and cook until soft, about 10 minutes. In a bowl, stir the peanut butter, water, and arrowroot or cornstarch into a smooth paste. Add the peanut paste to the tomato mixture. Sprinkle with black pepper.

CAKES: Place the teff and 2 cups water in a medium saucepan. Bring to a boil, cover and lower the heat. Simmer, stirring occasionally, until the water is absorbed, about 15 minutes. Stir in the onion, jalapeño, flour and the remaining 1 1/2 cups water to make a batter.

GREASE a hot skillet with oil. For each cake, pour 1/4 cup batter onto the skillet. Fry until the cakes are browned on both sides. Warm the groundnut sauce. Drizzle 1/4 cup sauce over the cakes.

Note:

Groundnut sauce tastes great over greens and other vegetables.

> **PER SERVING:**
> 218 Cal.; 6g Prot.; 6g Fat; 34g Carb.;
> 0mg Chol.; 127mg Sod.; 6g Fiber.

17

pasta

PASTA COMES IN SO MANY SHAPES AND SIZES, and may be enhanced with endless fillings and sauces: You could eat pasta every day of the year and never repeat the same dish twice. This selection of recipes reflects the amazing versatility of such a simple food. Most of the recipes are low in fat, and several of them are low-fat remakes of their traditional versions. We've included two recipes for fresh pasta dough; one contains eggs and the other does not. Fresh pasta takes some effort to prepare, but try to find an uneventful day to make it. You'll taste the difference.

Fettuccine Alfredo

serves 4

This lightened-up version has only 5 grams of fat in a serving. Traditional fettuccine Alfredo weighs in with an extravagant 46 grams of fat per portion.

1 pound uncooked fettuccine

1/2 cup nonfat cottage cheese

1/2 cup evaporated skim milk

1/2 teaspoon arrowroot powder or rice flour

Salt and freshly ground black pepper to taste

1 teaspoon garlic powder (optional)

1 teaspoon onion powder (optional)

2 teaspoons minced fresh parsley

Grated Parmesan cheese, for garnish

PREPARE the fettuccine according to the package directions; drain. Meanwhile, purée the cottage cheese, skim milk, arrowroot or rice flour, salt, pepper and garlic and onion powders in a blender until smooth. Transfer the mixture to a large skillet, add the parsley and warm over medium-low heat for 10 minutes. Do not let the sauce boil. Remove from the heat and pour over the hot pasta. Sprinkle with Parmesan.

Variations:

- Use tomato or spinach fettuccine, and garnish with sun-dried tomatoes and chopped fresh basil leaves.
- While you're warming the sauce, lightly steam 1 cup broccoli florets until tender-crisp, about 3 to 4 minutes. Toss with the sauce and hot noodles.
- While you're warming the sauce, cook 3/4 cup sliced white button mushrooms in 2 tablespoons red wine, stirring, over medium-high heat for 5 to 10 minutes. Toss with the sauce and hot noodles.

> **PER SERVING:**
> 452 Cal.; 19g Prot.; 5g Fat; 80g Carb.;
> 104mg Chol.; 424mg Sod.; 0.4g Fiber.

Creamy Spinach Lasagna

serves 6

TOMATO SAUCE

1/2 tablespoon virgin olive oil

1 small onion, minced

2 cloves garlic, minced

1 teaspoon dried oregano

1/2 teaspoon salt

1/4 teaspoon freshly ground black pepper

Two 28-ounce cans plum tomatoes

1/2 cup chopped fresh Italian flat-leaf parsley

BÉCHAMEL SAUCE

1 tablespoon margarine

1 tablespoon unbleached white flour

1 cup skim milk

Salt and freshly ground black pepper to taste

FILLING

12 ounces fresh spinach, stems removed

2 cups low-fat ricotta cheese

1/2 cup egg substitute (or 2 eggs), beaten

2 cloves garlic, minced

1/2 cup grated Parmesan cheese (optional)

Salt and freshly ground black pepper to taste

1 pound lasagna noodles, cooked firm and drained

1 to 2 cups grated mozzarella

TOMATO SAUCE: In a large saucepan, heat the oil over medium heat. Cook the onion and garlic, stirring, 3 minutes. Add the oregano, salt, pepper and tomatoes. Cook over medium heat until thickened, about 45 minutes. (With the back of a wooden spoon, mash the tomatoes as they cook.) Add the parsley and set aside.

BÉCHAMEL SAUCE: In a small saucepan, melt the margarine over medium heat. Whisk in the flour and cook 30 seconds. Slowly add the milk, whisking and cooking until thickened, about 10 minutes. Add salt and pepper. Set aside.

FILLING: In a large saucepan fitted with a steamer, steam the spinach over medium heat until wilted. Drain, squeeze out any excess water and chop coarsely. Transfer to a medium bowl. Add the ricotta, egg substitute or eggs, garlic, Parmesan, salt and pepper. Mix well and set aside.

PREHEAT the oven to 350°F. Spray a 9 × 13-inch baking pan with nonstick cooking spray. Spread half of the béchamel sauce over the bottom of the pan. Layer 1/4 of the noodles over the sauce, overlapping them slightly. Spread half of the tomato sauce over the noodles and top with half of the mozzarella. Put down another 1/4 of the noodles and spread with half of the spinach mixture. Continue with the noodles, tomato sauce, mozzarella, noodles and spinach mixture. Spread the remaining béchamel sauce over the top. Cover with foil and bake for 20 minutes. Remove foil and continue baking until bubbly, about 15 minutes more.

> **PER SERVING:**
> 437 Cal.; 22g Prot.; 12g Fat; 55g Carb.;
> 38mg Chol.; 1,021mg Sod.; 8g Fiber.

Ravioli with Mixed Greens

serves 6

This dish is traditionally served with a light sauce of butter and fresh sage or other herbs.

4 cups (about 5 ounces) lightly packed spinach leaves

2 cups lightly packed broccoli rabe leaves

1/4 teaspoon ground nutmeg

1/4 cup grated Parmesan cheese (optional)

1/4 teaspoon salt, or to taste

1 recipe Fresh Pasta Dough (page 326)

RINSE the greens, but don't dry them. In a saucepan fitted with a steamer, steam the greens until wilted, about 5 minutes. When the greens have cooled, squeeze out the water and chop finely. Transfer the greens to a bowl. Mix with the nutmeg, Parmesan and salt.

WITH A PASTA MACHINE or rolling pin, roll an egg-sized ball of the fresh pasta dough into a rectangle or circle as thinly as possible; cut it into strips about 2 × 12 inches. Place 1 strip on a floured surface and dot it with teaspoonfuls of the greens mixture about 1 inch apart from each other. Place a second strip of pasta on top. Press down around the portions of the filling, then cut the filled pasta into squares with a knife or pastry crimper.

Press the edges together a second time to be sure they stick. Transfer the ravioli to a floured plate. Repeat with the remaining dough and filling. Boil the ravioli in a pot of salted water for only 2 minutes. Drain and add the sauce of your choice.

Variation:

In place of broccoli rabe, use other types of greens. Just don't exceed a 1:2 ratio of bitter green (such as collard or mustard greens) to nonbitter greens (such as spinach).

Note:

If you have a ravioli attachment for your pasta machine, or other ravioli maker, follow the manufacturer's directions.

> **PER SERVING WITHOUT SAUCE:**
> 268 Cal.; 12g Prot.; 4g Fat; 46g Carb.;
> 110mg Chol.; 164mg Sod.; 4g Fiber.

Herb and Walnut Ravioli

serves 6

1 cup walnuts

3 cups lightly packed fresh basil leaves

3 cups lightly packed fresh Italian flat-leaf parsley

1/4 teaspoon salt, or to taste

Fresh Pasta Dough (page 326)

TOAST the walnuts in a 350°F oven for 8 minutes. Meanwhile, rinse the basil and parsley and pat dry. Discard the stems and chop the herbs very finely until they almost form a paste. (This step may be done with a mortar and pestle or a food processor.) Chop the nuts by hand into small crumbs and mix them with the herbs. Season with salt.

WITH A PASTA MACHINE or rolling pin, roll an egg-sized ball of the fresh pasta dough into a rectangle or circle as thinly as possible; cut into strips about 2 × 12 inches. Place 1 strip on a floured surface, and dot it with teaspoonfuls of filling about 1 inch apart from each other. Place a second strip of pasta on top. Press down around the portions of the filling, then cut into squares with a knife or pastry crimper. Press the edges together a second time to be sure they stick. Transfer the ravioli to a floured plate. Repeat with the remaining dough and filling. Boil the ravioli in a large pot of salted water for only 2 minutes. Drain and add the sauce of your choice.

Note:

If you have a ravioli attachment for your pasta machine or other ravioli maker, follow the manufacturer's directions.

> **PER SERVING WITHOUT SAUCE:**
> 411 Cal.; 15g Prot.; 9g Fat; 54g Carb.;
> 110mg Chol.; 139mg Sod.; 4g Fiber.

Pumpkin-Filled Ravioli in Herbed Cream Sauce

serves 6

This ravioli is untraditional to be sure: Wonton wrappers—not pasta—enclose the naturally sweet filling.

RAVIOLI

> 1 cup canned pumpkin or homemade pumpkin purée
>
> 1 cup cooked and mashed sweet potato
>
> Pinch nutmeg
>
> Dash salt
>
> 1/4 teaspoon white pepper, or to taste
>
> 72 wonton wrappers

SAUCE

> One 4-ounce package neufchâtel cheese or light cream cheese, at room temperature
>
> 1/2 cup plain low-fat yogurt
>
> 1/2 cup skim milk
>
> 1 tablespoon unbleached white flour
>
> 1 teaspoon minced fresh thyme leaves (or 1/4 teaspoon dried thyme)
>
> 1/4 teaspoon salt
>
> White pepper to taste
>
> 1/4 to 1/2 cup freshly grated Parmesan cheese (optional)

RAVIOLI: In a bowl, combine all the ingredients except the wonton wrappers. Place a wonton wrapper on your lightly floured work surface. Mound 1 tablespoon filling in the center, and wet the edges of the wrapper with a little water. Place a second wrapper over the first, pressing down around the filling to expel any air. Seal the edges and trim the excess dough around the filling with a sharp knife or a decorative cookie cutter. Transfer the ravioli to a dry towel. Repeat the process with the remaining wontons. Turn over the ravioli occasionally to let them dry slightly.

BRING a large pot of salted water to a gentle boil. Cook the ravioli in batches of 8 to 12 until they rise to the surface and are tender, about 2 minutes. Do not let the water boil vigorously. Transfer the cooked ravioli to a dishcloth. Cover and keep warm.

SAUCE: Mash together the softened cheese, yogurt and milk in a small saucepan; whisk in the flour. Stir over low heat until very smooth. Do not let the sauce boil. Stir in the herbs, salt and pepper. Remove from the heat.

TO SERVE, divide the ravioli among 6 individual plates and top with the sauce and a sprinkling of Parmesan.

> **PER SERVING:**
> 394 Cal.; 18g Prot.; 6g Fat; 65g Carb.;
> 18mg Chol.; 299mg Sod.; 13g Fiber.

Italian Brochettes with Angel-Hair Pasta

serves 6

BROCHETTES

2 to 3 small Japanese eggplants

1 zucchini

1 yellow crookneck or butternut squash

1 other soft-skinned squash, such as yellow summer
   squash

1/2 pound white button mushrooms

1 red bell pepper

1 yellow bell pepper

2 small red onions

1 bulb fennel

1/2 pound cherry tomatoes

MARINADE

1/2 bunch fresh thyme leaves

Pinch cayenne pepper

Grated zest of 1 lemon

1/2 to 1 teaspoon salt (optional)

1/2 to 1 teaspoon freshly ground black pepper
   (optional)

9 to 10 cloves garlic

Juice of 2 lemons

1/4 to 1/2 cup vegetable broth or virgin olive oil

PASTA

1/2 to 1 cup tomato sauce

1 pound uncooked angel-hair pasta

BROCHETTES: Cut the eggplant and squash into pieces no more than 1/4 inch thick. Cut the mushrooms in half and bell peppers into strips. Quarter the onions, trimming the root ends but leaving the bottoms intact, removing the papery skins only if they're dirty. Trim the outer leaves of the fennel and take a paper-thin slice off the root end to remove any dirt. Leave the base intact. Slice the fennel into 8 thin wedges. (Any loose leaves may be skewered individually.) Place the cut vegetables and cherry tomatoes in a large bowl.

MARINADE: Strip the thyme leaves from the stems, reserving stems for grilling. In a food processor, blend the thyme leaves, cayenne, zest, salt and pepper. While the machine is running, add the garlic. Stop the machine and add the lemon juice. Turn on the machine and add the vegetable broth or olive oil in a slow stream through the feed tube. Process 1 minute. Pour the marinade over the cut vegetables. For the best flavor, let marinate 15 minutes.

PREPARE the grill, and cover to build an intense heat. Skewer the vegetables, alternating for color. (Reserve the leftover marinade.) Toss the thyme stems onto the heat shield or coals. Place the brochettes on the hot grill. Cover and let smoke 5 minutes. Uncover, turn the brochettes and continue cooking until the vegetables are tender, about 3 to 5 minutes more.

PASTA: Meanwhile, drain the reserved marinade into a small, nonreactive saucepan. Add the tomato sauce and simmer. Prepare the pasta according to the package directions; drain. Return the pasta to the pot. Pour the sauce over the pasta and toss to coat. Serve with the grilled vegetables.

Variation:

Instead of pasta, substitute thick slices of sourdough bread that have been brushed with marinade and lightly grilled.

PER SERVING:
314 Cal.; 14g Prot.; 3g Fat; 58g Carb.;
0mg Chol.; 240mg Sod.; 8g Fiber.

Macaroni and Cheese

serves 6

This dish has 4 grams of fat in a serving. Compare that to the hefty 32 grams of fat per portion in the traditional version.

- Nonstick cooking spray
- 3/4 teaspoon canola oil
- 1 tablespoon water
- 1/8 cup unbleached white flour
- Pinch cayenne pepper
- 1/2 teaspoon dry mustard
- 1 1/2 cups skim milk, heated
- Salt and freshly ground black pepper to taste
- 1/2 cup shredded reduced-fat cheddar cheese
- 1/4 cup shredded reduced-fat Swiss cheese
- 3 1/2 cups cooked elbow macaroni
- 1 tablespoon toasted whole-wheat bread crumbs (page 106)

PREHEAT the oven to 350°F. Lightly coat a 1 1/2-quart casserole with nonstick cooking spray; set aside. In a large saucepan over medium heat, heat the oil and water until bubbling. Stir in the flour, cayenne and mustard. Cook, stirring frequently, for 3 minutes. (The sauce may lump at this stage.) Add the heated milk, a little at a time, whisking constantly. (It will take 5 to 7 minutes to add the milk. The sauce should continue to bubble as you add the milk; otherwise you're adding it too quickly.) If necessary, after all of the milk is added, cook the sauce until it is the consistency of thick cream, about 2 to 4 minutes more. Season with salt and pepper. Remove from the heat and stir in 1/4 cup cheddar and all of the Swiss cheese.

POUR the macaroni into the prepared casserole, top with the sauce and toss well. Sprinkle the remaining 1/4 cup cheddar and bread crumbs on top. Bake until lightly browned and bubbly, about 30 minutes.

> **PER SERVING:**
> 180 Cal.; 10g Prot.; 4g Fat; 25g Carb.;
> 12mg Chol.; 198mg Sod.; 1g Fiber.

Cheesy Confetti Macaroni

serves 4

- 1 1/2 cups uncooked elbow macaroni
- 1/2 cup grated carrot
- 1/2 cup grated yellow summer squash
- 1 tablespoon chopped fresh parsley
- Oil for baking dish
- 1/2 cup low-fat milk
- 1/2 cup grated low-fat cheddar cheese
- 1 teaspoon arrowroot powder
- 1/2 teaspoon dry mustard powder
- 1/2 teaspoon paprika

PREPARE the macaroni according to the package directions; drain. In a bowl, combine the macaroni with the carrot, squash and parsley. Set aside.

PREHEAT the oven to 350°F. Lightly oil a 1 1/2-quart baking dish. In a saucepan, whisk together the milk, cheese, arrowroot, mustard powder and paprika. Place the pan over medium-high heat and cook, stirring, until the cheese melts and the mixture begins to thicken slightly. Pour over the macaroni and mix well. Spoon the mixture into the prepared baking dish and bake until lightly browned and set, about 40 minutes.

> **PER SERVING:**
> 226 Cal.; 10g Prot.; 6g Fat; 34g Carb.;
> 17mg Chol.; 109mg Sod.; 2g Fiber.

Straw and Hay Pasta

serves 4

Ribbons of green and yellow pasta (the straw and hay) are studded with chunks of tomato and dressed in garlicky olive oil. If you can't find flavorful fresh tomatoes, opt for canned.

> 1 cup coarsely chopped fresh tomatoes (or two
>   28-ounce cans stewed tomatoes, drained and
>   chopped coarsely)
> 1 1/2 to 2 tablespoons virgin olive oil
> 1 to 2 cloves garlic, pressed or minced
> Dash cayenne pepper
> 1/2 teaspoon salt
> 5 ounces fresh spinach fettuccine
> 5 ounces fresh yellow fettuccine
> 1/4 cup packed fresh basil leaves, slivered
>   (or 1 tablespoon dried basil)

PLACE the tomatoes in a large serving bowl. In a skillet over very low heat, warm the oil, garlic, cayenne and salt. When the garlic begins to sizzle, remove the skillet from the heat and let sit 10 minutes. (Do not let the garlic brown or it will taste bitter.) Pour the spice mixture over the tomatoes.

PREPARE the spinach and yellow fettuccine according to the package directions until *al dente*; drain. Gently

toss with the tomato mixture. Sprinkle with basil and toss again.

> **PER SERVING**
> 163 Cal.; 6g Prot.; 6g Fat; 23g Carb.;
> 62mg Chol.; 332mg Sod.; 6g Fiber.

Rasta Pasta

serves 4

This Jamaican-inspired dish calls for a number of ingredients—most of which are probably in your kitchen—and the results are well worth the measuring and mixing.

> 8 ounces uncooked linguine or angel-hair pasta

SAUCE

> 2 tablespoons butter or margarine
> 1 small onion, diced
> 2 cloves garlic, minced
> 2 tablespoons minced fresh ginger root
> 1 chili pepper, seeded and minced
> 2 cups diced pumpkin, calabasa, butternut or acorn
>   squash
> 1 cup water or vegetable stock (page 178)
> 1 cup canned coconut milk
> 1 teaspoon ground coriander
> 1 teaspoon ground cumin
> 1 tablespoon fresh thyme leaves (or 1/2 tablespoon
>   dried thyme)
> 1/2 teaspoon white pepper
> 1 teaspoon ground allspice
> 1/2 teaspoon salt

VEGETABLES

- 2 tablespoons butter or margarine
- 2 bell peppers, seeded and chopped
- 8 to 12 white button mushrooms, chopped
- 1 small zucchini, chopped
- 1/2 cup whole-kernel corn
- 8 to 12 broccoli florets

PREPARE the pasta according to the package directions; drain. Set aside.

SAUCE: Melt the butter or margarine in a saucepan over medium heat; cook the onion, garlic, ginger and chili pepper, stirring, for 4 to 5 minutes. Add the squash and water or stock to the pan and cook until the squash is tender, about 15 to 20 minutes. Add the coconut milk and seasonings, and simmer 4 to 5 minutes. Place the mixture in a food processor fitted with a steel blade and process until the sauce is smooth, about 15 seconds.

VEGETABLES: In a large skillet, melt the butter or margarine, and cook the bell peppers, mushrooms and zucchini, stirring, for 4 to 5 minutes over medium heat. Add the corn and broccoli, and cook 2 minutes more. Pour the sauce into the skillet and stir gently. Bring the mixture to a simmer and cook for about 1 minute. Stir in the pasta and cook until steaming, about 1 to 2 minutes. Serve hot.

PER SERVING:
469 Cal.; 11g Prot.; 24g Fat; 5g Carb.;
31mg Chol.; 409mg Sod.; 8g Fiber.

Pesto Primavera

serves 4

Basil lovers rejoice: This twist on pasta primavera is packed with flavor. The dish is on the table in minutes too.

- 2 cups fresh broccoli florets
- 1/2 medium red bell pepper, seeded and cut into thin strips
- 1 cup sliced white button mushrooms
- 1/2 cup thin carrot strips ($2 \times 1/4$-inch strips)
- 1 cup sliced zucchini
- 2 tablespoons water
- 8 ounces uncooked fettuccine
- 1 cup packed fresh basil leaves
- 1/4 cup oil-free Italian dressing
- 1 to 2 cloves fresh garlic, cut in half
- 2 tablespoons virgin olive oil
- 1 tablespoon shredded Parmesan cheese
- 1/4 teaspoon grated lemon peel (optional)

IN A 2-QUART CASSEROLE DISH, combine the vegetables and water. Cover. Microwave at high power until the vegetables are tender-crisp, about 6 to 8 minutes, stirring once. Drain and set aside.

PREPARE the fettuccine according to the package directions; drain. Cover to keep warm. Set aside. Place the remaining ingredients in a blender or food processor. Process until smooth to make the pesto. Spoon the pesto over the fettuccine. Toss to coat. Arrange the fettuccine on a serving platter. Top it with the vegetable mixture. Serve at once.

Variation:

Instead of using a microwave, steam the vegetables in a saucepan fitted with a steaming basket until tender-crisp.

> **PER SERVING:**
> 310 Cal.; 10g Prot.; 7g Fat; 50g Carb.;
> 1mg Chol.; 84mg Sod.; 5g Fiber.

Rice Noodles with Ginger and Snow Peas

serves 3

In this beautiful dish, nearly transparent noodles mingle with shimmering snow peas and shredded carrots.

8 ounces uncooked rice noodles

Hot water for soaking or cooking

1 1/2 to 3 tablespoons vegetable oil

1 tablespoon grated fresh ginger root

3 cloves garlic, minced

3 scallions (green and white parts), sliced thinly

1 fresh green chili, seeded and chopped

Up to 1/2 cup finely shredded carrots

20 snow peas, trimmed

1/2 teaspoon salt

Dash sesame oil (optional)

Dash hot chili oil (optional)

Chopped fresh cilantro leaves or fresh parsley,
   for garnish

SOAK or prepare the rice noodles according to the package directions. Drain and set aside. Heat the oil in a skillet over medium-high heat, and cook the ginger and garlic, stirring, for 1 to 2 minutes. Add the scallions, chili, carrots and snow peas. Cook, stirring, for 2 minutes. Stir in the salt.

ADD the noodles and toss to coat. Remove from the heat. Stir in the sesame and chili oil. Garnish with cilantro or parsley. Serve at once.

> **PER SERVING:**
> 363 Cal.; 9g Prot.; 9g Fat; 62g Carb.;
> 0mg Chol.; 374mg Sod.; 3g Fiber.

Chinese-Style Pasta

serves 2

This flavorful pasta dish has an Eastern flair. Accompany it with brightly colored sautéed vegetables.

3 tablespoons low-sodium soy sauce

2 teaspoons dark sesame oil

2 teaspoons white wine vinegar or rice vinegar

1/4 teaspoon garlic powder

8 to 12 ounces uncooked vermicelli pasta

MIX together the soy sauce, oil, vinegar and garlic powder. Set aside.

PREPARE the pasta according to the package directions; drain. Transfer the pasta to a serving dish. Pour the dressing over the pasta. Toss and serve at once.

> **PER SERVING:**
> 352 Cal.; 10g Prot.; 7g Fat; 65g Carb.;
> 0mg Chol.; 385mg Sod.; 1g Fiber

Ma Po Noodles

serves 4

If you like spicy, tomato-garlic dishes, you'll love this variation of Ma Po Tofu, a Chinese classic.

- 1/2 cup vegetable stock (page 178)
- 1/3 cup hoisin sauce
- 1 tablespoon rice wine or dry sherry
- 1/3 cup ketchup
- 1/2 teaspoon hot pepper sauce
- 1 pound uncooked Chinese egg noodles (fresh or dried) or other egg noodles
- 1 tablespoon sesame oil
- 1 tablespoon vegetable oil
- 3 cloves garlic, minced
- 1 pound firm tofu, cut into 1/2-inch cubes
- 2 cups mung bean sprouts
- 1 tablespoon cornstarch dissolved in 2 tablespoons water
- 2 scallions (green and white parts), slivered, for garnish

IN A SMALL BOWL, combine the stock, hoisin sauce, rice wine or sherry, ketchup and hot pepper sauce. Set aside.

PREPARE the noodles according to the package directions. Drain, rinse under cold water and drain again. Gently toss with the sesame oil and place on a serving platter. Set aside.

HEAT a wok or large frying pan until hot over medium-high heat. Add the vegetable oil, swirling to coat the sides. Add the garlic and cook, stirring, until fragrant, about 5 seconds. Add the tofu and cook, stirring, 2 minutes. Stir in the reserved sauce and cook 1 minute. Add the bean sprouts and cook 1 minute more. Add the dissolved cornstarch and stir until the sauce boil and thickens. Pour the mixture over the noodles. Garnish with scallions.

> **PER SERVING:**
> 401 Cal.; 16g Prot.; 11g Fat; 60g Carb.;
> 67mg Chol.; 187mg Sod.; 3g Fiber.

Pad Thai

serves 4

Pad Thai shows up on just about every Thai restaurant menu. In Thailand, street vendors sell this aromatic dish in a variety of versions to hungry passers-by.

- 2 quarts water
- 8 to 10 ounces uncooked dried flat-sided rice noodles
- 1/4 cup white vinegar
- 3 tablespoons tomato paste
- 3 tablespoons water
- 2 tablespoons sugar
- 1 to 2 tablespoons vegetable oil
- 2 cloves garlic, minced
- 1 fresh green chili, seeded and minced
- 2 eggs (optional)
- 1 cup mung bean sprouts
- 1/3 cup chopped unsalted dry-roasted peanuts (optional)
- Lime wedges and sliced scallions, for garnish

BRING 2 quarts water to a boil; remove from the heat. Soak the noodles in the hot water for 20 minutes. Drain and set aside.

IN A BOWL, blend the vinegar, tomato paste, water and sugar. In a frying pan, heat the oil and stir-fry garlic and chili on medium heat for 3 minutes. Stir in the tomato-vinegar mixture and make a well in the center of the pan.

CRACK in the eggs, and cook until almost set, about 2 minutes; then stir quickly into the sauce. Continue to simmer the sauce on low heat until very thick, about 4 to 5 minutes. Stir the reserved noodles into the sauce. Remove from the heat.

TO SERVE, place the noodles and sauce on one end of a large serving plate. On the other end, place a pile of bean sprouts and peanuts. Garnish the plate with lime wedges and scallions. Let diners help themselves to noodles, bean sprouts, peanuts and garnishes.

> **PER SERVING:**
> 343 Cal.; 4g Prot.; 12g Fat; 48g Carb.;
> 0mg Chol.; 952mg Sod.; 2g Fiber.

Indonesian Fried Noodles

serves 12

- 1 pound uncooked soba noodles or any other Asian noodles
- 2 to 4 tablespoons peanut oil
- 1 onion, finely chopped
- 3 cloves garlic, minced
- One 1/2-inch piece ginger root, peeled and grated
- 2 leeks (or 6 scallions, green and white parts), chopped
- 1 to 2 cups snow peas
- 1 to 2 cups mung bean sprouts
- 3 tablespoons *kecap manis* (or 3 tablespoons soy sauce plus 1 1/2 tablespoons brown sugar)
- 1 to 3 teaspoons sambal or cayenne pepper
- 2 eggs, scrambled (optional)
- 1 pound firm tofu, drained and cubed (optional)

PREPARE the noodles according to the package directions; drain and set aside. In a wok or large skillet, heat the oil and add the onion, garlic and ginger; stir-fry until the onion is limp. Stir in the leeks or scallions, snow peas and bean sprouts, and cook until tender-crisp. Then stir in the noodles, *kecap manis,* and sambal or cayenne. Add the eggs or tofu. Mix thoroughly until heated through, about 5 minutes.

**PER SERVING
(WITHOUT EGGS AND TOFU):**
169 Cal.; 5g Prot.; 4g Fat; 29g Carb.;
0mg Chol.; 260mg Sod.; 2g Fiber.

Noodles in Coconut Gravy

serves 3

GRAVY

- 2 tablespoons grated fresh ginger root
- 2 cloves garlic, minced
- 2 stalks lemongrass (white part only), made into a paste with 2 teaspoons water (see Note)
- 1 tablespoon finely ground almonds
- 1/4 teaspoon ground turmeric
- 1 1/2 to 3 tablespoons vegetable oil
- 1 medium onion, minced finely
- 3/4 cup coconut milk

NOODLES

- 8 ounces uncooked rice noodles or spaghetti
- 3/4 cup mung bean sprouts, blanched (see Note)
- 3/4 cup tofu cubes, sautéed (optional—see Note)
- Chili slivers, pineapple slices and lime or lemon wedges, for garnish

GRAVY: Combine the ginger, garlic, lemongrass paste, almonds and turmeric in a small bowl; set aside. Heat the oil in a skillet. Cook the onion over low heat, stirring, until well-cooked but not burned, about 15 minutes. Stir in the ginger-garlic mixture, and cook, stirring, for a minute. Gradually add the coconut milk; cook, stirring constantly, until the sauce thickens, about 15 minutes. Cover and remove from the heat.

NOODLES: Prepare the rice noodles or spaghetti according to the package directions; drain. Divide the noodles and bean sprouts among 3 or 4 plates. Add the tofu. Spoon the coconut gravy on top of each plate. Garnish with chili slivers, pineapple slices and lime or lemon wedges. Serve at once.

Notes:

- To make lemongrass paste, coarsely chop the stalk and pound it in a mortar and pestle with 2 teaspoons water until smooth. Or mash the lemongrass on a cutting board with the back of a spoon, then place it in a bowl and mix with 2 teaspoons water.

- To blanch bean sprouts, dip in boiling water for 30 seconds, then rinse in cold water and drain.

- Sauté the tofu before adding to the plates. To sauté, heat 1 to 2 teaspoons vegetable oil in a medium skillet over medium heat. Gently add the tofu. Cook, stirring, until golden, about 15 minutes, being careful not to break up the cubes.

PER SERVING:
472 Cal.; 11g Prot.; 21g Fat; 61g Carb.;
0mg Chol.; 11mg Sod.; 4g Fiber.

Potato and Fennel Cappelletti

serves 6

These delicious little parcels resemble miniature tricorner hats.

    1 bulb fennel
    2 medium potatoes, peeled
    1 small white onion
    1/2 teaspoon salt, or to taste
    1 recipe Fresh Pasta Dough (page 326)

TRIM the stems from fennel bulb, reserving the feathery greens. Cut the bulb into 8 pieces. Quarter the potatoes and onion. Place the fennel, potatoes and onion in a soup pot with enough cold water to cover. Cover the pot, bring to a boil, lower the heat, and simmer until the vegetables can be pierced easily with a fork, about 25 to 30 minutes.

DRAIN the vegetables and let cool slightly. Transfer them to a large bowl and mash with a fork. Chop the fennel greens and add to the mixture. Add salt.

WITH A PASTA MACHINE or rolling pin, roll an egg-sized ball of the fresh pasta dough into a rectangle or circle and cut into strips about 2 inches wide and 12 inches long. Place 1 strip on a floured surface, and cut it into rectangles about 2 × 1 1/2 inches. Place 1/2 teaspoon of the filling about 1/2 inch from the short end of each rectangle. Fold the rectangle in half and press the edges together. Then pick up the rectangle with your index finger and thumb, holding the folded edge up. Pull the 2 folded corners together around your index finger and press them together to seal then flip up the rim. Transfer the cappelletti to a floured plate. Repeat with the remaining dough and filling. Boil the cappelletti in a large pot of salted water for only 2 minutes. Drain and add the sauce of your choice.

> **PER SERVING WITHOUT SAUCE:**
> 279 Cal.; 11g Prot.; 4g Fat; 51g Carb.;
> 110mg Chol.; 216mg Sod.; 2g Fiber.

Acorn Squash Tortellini

serves 6

Tortellini are circles of pasta formed into rings. An acorn squash filling lends a distinctly American taste to this dish.

    1 acorn squash
    1/4 teaspoon ground nutmeg
    1/4 teaspoon ground cinnamon
    1/4 teaspoon honey
    1 recipe Fresh Pasta Dough (page 326)

PREHEAT the oven to 400°F. Slice the squash in half lengthwise. Remove the seeds and strings, and place the squash halves cut side down on a lightly oiled baking dish. Bake until tender, about 45 minutes. Remove the squash from your oven. Let cool. Scoop out the flesh into a bowl. With a fork, mash the squash with the nutmeg, cinnamon and honey.

WITH A PASTA MACHINE or rolling pin, roll out a sheet of the fresh pasta dough as thinly as possible. Use a cookie cutter or juice glass to cut the dough into circles about

2 1/2 inches in diameter. Place 1/2 teaspoon of the filling about 1/2 inch from the edge of each circle. Fold the circle in half and press the edges together. Pick up the half circle with your index finger and thumb, holding the folded edge up. Pull the 2 corners together around your index finger. Press the corners together to seal, then turn up the rim to meet the sealed corners. Transfer the tortellini to a floured plate. Repeat with the remaining dough and filling. Boil the tortellini in a large pot of salted water for only 2 minutes. Drain and add the sauce of your choice.

> **PER SERVING WITHOUT SAUCE:**
> 277 Cal.; 11g Prot.; 4g Fat; 50g Carb.;
> 110mg Chol.; 38mg Sod.; 4g Fiber.

Carrot and Leek Tortellacci

serves 6

Tortellacci are pasta packets that hold twice as much filling as tortellini.

10 small carrots

4 leeks, trimmed

1 shallot, minced

2 teaspoons virgin olive oil

1/2 teaspoon salt

1 recipe Fresh Pasta Dough (page 326)

CHOP the carrots and leeks into matchsticks 1-inch by 1/4-inch. In a skillet, cook the carrots, leeks and shallot in the oil, stirring, over low heat for 2 minutes. Increase the heat to medium, add enough water to cover, and braise until the vegetables are tender, about 15 minutes. Stir occasionally and add water as needed to keep the skillet becoming dry. Drain the vegetables in a colander. Let cool.

WITH A PASTA MACHINE or rolling pin, roll out a sheet of the fresh pasta dough as thinly as possible. Use a cookie cutter or juice glass to cut the dough into circles about 2 1/2 inches in diameter. Place a teaspoon of the filling in the center of half of the pasta circles. Top each with a second circle and seal the edges. Transfer the tortellacci to a floured plate. Repeat with the remaining dough and filling. Boil the pasta in a large pot of salted water for only 2 minutes. Drain and add the sauce of your choice.

Variation:

Instead of adding a sauce, boil and serve tortellacci in vegetable broth.

> **PER SERVING WITHOUT SAUCE:**
> 367 Cal.; 12g Prot.; 5g Fat; 67g Carb.;
> 110mg Chol.; 272mg Sod.; 7g Fiber.

Stuffed Shells

serves 6

SAUCE

12 medium fresh tomatoes, peeled (or one 28-ounce
  can whole, peeled tomatoes)

2 cloves garlic

1/2 tablespoon virgin olive oil

Salt and freshly ground black pepper to taste

FILLING AND PASTA

2 cups part-skim ricotta cheese

1/3 cup grated Parmesan cheese

1 cup diced low-fat mozzarella cheese

1/3 cup chopped fresh Italian flat-leaf parsley

Pinch ground nutmeg

1 recipe Fresh Pasta Dough (page 326)
  (or 12 ounces large pasta shells)

SAUCE: If you're using fresh tomatoes, remove and discard the seeds, and chop the tomatoes coarsely. If you're using canned tomatoes, chop them finely and reserve the liquid. In a saucepan, cook the garlic in the oil, stirring, for 1 minute over medium-high heat, then add the tomatoes and tomato liquid. Simmer, uncovered, over low heat, stirring occasionally, about 30 to 45 minutes. Season with salt and pepper.

FILLING AND PASTA: Preheat the oven to 350°F. Combine the cheeses, parsley and nutmeg in a bowl and mix well. Set aside. If you're using the fresh pasta dough, roll out the dough slightly thicker than for small stuffed pasta and cut into 5-inch squares. Boil the shells in a large pot of salted water until *al dente*, about 2 minutes. Meanwhile, spread a little bit of sauce on the bottom of a 9 × 13-inch baking pan. When the pasta is done, drain and let cool slightly. Place a square of pasta in your palm and spoon in the filling. Fold the pasta over slightly without sealing the filling and tuck the stuffed shell into a corner of the pan. Repeat with the remaining squares and filling until the pan is full and all the ingredients used up. (This placement will keep the dough in a "shell" shape.) Spread the remaining sauce on top, cover with foil and bake 30 minutes.

IF YOU'RE USING DRY SHELLS, prepare them according to the package directions until *al dente*; drain. Let cool slightly. Spread a little bit of sauce on the bottom of a 9 × 13-inch baking pan. Fill the shells with the filling, placing them in the pan. Spread the remaining sauce on top, cover the pan with foil and bake 30 minutes.

> **PER SERVING:**
> 412 Cal.; 23g Prot.; 12g Fat; 53g Carb.;
> 138mg Chol.; 394mg Sod.; 3g Fiber.

Potato Gnocchi

serves 6

This traditional Italian dish is comfort food at its best. Serve it plain or with tomato sauce.

1 pound potatoes

1 large egg

1 tablespoon butter

1 teaspoon salt

1 3/4 cups flour, plus extra for kneading

Extra butter (optional)

1/3 cup grated Parmesan cheese (optional)

LIGHTLY BUTTER a 9 × 13-inch baking dish; set aside. Cut the unpeeled potatoes into 1-inch chunks and boil in water to cover until very soft, about 20 minutes. Meanwhile, fill a large saucepan with water, cover and place over medium-high heat.

DRAIN the cooked potatoes and transfer to a food processor fitted with a steel blade. Process the potatoes, egg, butter and salt until very smooth and creamy. Transfer to a medium bowl. Add flour 1/4 cup at a time to the potato mixture, mixing well with a wooden spoon after each addition. Turn out the dough onto your floured work surface and gently knead for a few minutes, adding more flour as necessary to prevent stickiness.

BREAK off a fist-sized piece of the dough, dip in the flour and roll with your hands into a rope about 1 inch in diameter. Cut the rope into 1-inch pieces; set aside. Repeat with the remaining dough. You should end up with about 48 pieces of dough. (It is Italian tradition to press the pieces with the tines of a fork for both decorative reasons and because it helps the sauce cling better to the gnocchi.)

WHEN the water reaches a boil, lower the heat to a simmer and add as many gnocchi as you can fit without crowding. Partially cover and let simmer 40 minutes. Remove the gnocchi with a slotted spoon, place in the buttered dish and add the next batch of gnocchi to the simmering water. Repeat the process.

PREHEAT the oven to 300°F (or preheat broiler). Drizzle a little melted butter over the gnocchi and sprinkle liberally with Parmesan. Bake until lightly browned, about 30 minutes (or broil for 5 minutes). Serve at once.

PER SERVING:
213 Cal.; 6g Prot.; 3g Fat; 41g Carb.; 41mg Chol.; 389mg Sod.; 2g Fiber.

Artichoke Cannelloni with Lemon Béchamel

serves 6

The savory flavor of artichokes fills these pasta tubes. Prepare the béchamel at the last minute, because it becomes lumpy if it sits.

- 24 baby artichokes (or 24 canned artichoke hearts—see Note)
- 2 lemons
- 1 recipe Fresh Pasta Dough (page 326) (or 8 ounces uncooked cannelloni)
- 1 to 1 1/2 cups diced low-fat mozzarella cheese (8 to 12 ounces)
- 1/2 teaspoon salt
- 1 cups skim milk or soymilk
- 2 tablespoons butter or margarine
- 1 1/2 tablespoons flour

IF YOU'RE USING FRESH ARTICHOKES, fill a large bowl with cold water and squeeze the juice of 1/2 lemon into it. Reserve both lemon halves. Peel away any hard green leaves from each artichoke and slice off the top of each stem. Cut away the yellow leaves as close to the base as possible, then skin the base and the stem, removing the tough, green outside layer. Remove the fuzzy "choke" (center part) with the tip of a knife and discard it. Cut each artichoke in half and rub the squeezed lemon half over all surfaces, then drop the artichokes into the bowl of water. When all the artichokes are trimmed, drain and rinse them; then place them in a pan with enough water to cover. Simmer, covered, over medium heat until tender, about 12 minutes. Drain and set aside. If you're using canned artichoke hearts, drain and set aside.

IF YOU'RE USING FRESH PASTA DOUGH, roll out the dough to about 1/8-inch thickness; cut into rectangles 5 inches by 8 inches. Cook the fresh or dry pasta in a large pot of boiling salted water until *al dente* (only a few minutes for fresh pasta). Meanwhile, dice the artichokes and combine with the diced mozzarella. Add salt.

PEEL the rind from the uncut lemon, being careful to keep it in one or two large pieces; set aside. Juice this lemon and the remaining 1/2 lemon; set aside the juice. When the artichoke mixture and pasta are ready, pour the milk into a small pot and add the lemon rind. Heat until the milk begins to bubble; then remove the lemon rind and remove the pot from the heat. In a separate pan, melt the butter or margarine over low heat and whisk in the flour, 1 teaspoon at a time, stirring constantly. When all the flour has been added, continue to cook and stir constantly for 2 minutes. Remove from the heat and slowly add hot milk, stirring constantly. Add the reserved lemon juice. Over low heat, cook and stir until the sauce thickens slightly, about 2 minutes.

PREHEAT the oven to 400°F. Spread a little sauce on the bottom of a 9 × 13-inch baking pan. If you're using fresh pasta, roll each rectangle around a portion of the artichoke mixture and place the cannelloni in the baking pan; if you're using uncooked cannelloni, prepare the pasta according to the package directions; drain and let cool. Stuff each piece with the artichoke mixture and place in the pan. Spread the remaining sauce over the top. Cover the pan with foil and bake 15 minutes.

Note:

Choose canned artichoke hearts that are not marinated in spices.

> ### PER SERVING:
> 466 Cal.; 21g Prot.; 11g Fat; 71g Carb.;
> 131mg Chol.; 531mg Sod.; 10g Fiber.

Goat Cheese and Radicchio Agnolotti

serves 6

Radicchio is a reddish-hued variety of greens that's sautéed before it's placed in these half-moon pasta packets.

- 2 heads radicchio
- 2 cloves garlic, minced
- 1 tablespoon virgin olive oil
- 6 ounces low-fat goat cheese
- 1 recipe Fresh Pasta Dough (page 326)

WASH and dry the radicchio. Discard the thick white stems and shred the reddish leaves. Cook the garlic in the oil in a large skillet, stirring, over low heat for 1 minute. Add the radicchio and cook until wilted, about 3 to 5 minutes, stirring constantly. Mash the radicchio and cheese together.

WITH A PASTA MACHINE or rolling pin, roll out a sheet of fresh pasta dough as thinly as possible. Use a cookie cutter or juice glass to cut the dough into circles about 2 1/2 inches in diameter. Place 3/4 teaspoon of the filling about 1/2 inch from the edge of each circle. Fold the circle in half and seal the edges. Transfer the agnolotti to a floured plate. Repeat with the remaining dough and filling. Boil the agnolotti in a large pot of salted water for only 2 minutes. Drain and add the sauce of your choice.

> ### PER SERVING WITHOUT SAUCE:
> 357 Cal.; 13g Prot.; 13g Fat; 45g Carb.;
> 135mg Chol.; 155mg Sod.; 2g Fiber.

Cheesy Pasta Wedges with Vegetable Sauce

serves 6

Start this recipe the day before you plan to serve it because you need to refrigerate the pasta for at least eight hours.

PASTA WEDGES

- 8 ounces uncooked angel-hair pasta (or 3 cups cooked pasta of choice)
- 3 tablespoons minced fresh parsley or shredded fresh basil leaves
- 1 tablespoon virgin olive oil
- Salt and freshly ground black pepper to taste
- 2 tablespoons grated Parmesan cheese (optional)

SAUCE

- 2 teaspoons virgin olive oil
- 1/2 tablespoon cracked coriander seed
- 1/2 teaspoon fennel seed
- 1/4 cup chopped fresh dill or fresh parsley
- 1 1/2 cups chopped fennel bulb, trimmed
- 1 1/2 cups chopped celery
- 1 1/2 cups chopped carrot
- 1 1/2 cups chopped parsnips
- 1 1/2 cups chopped red bell pepper
- 4 cups water
- 2 cups diced tomatoes or tomato sauce
- Salt to taste
- 1/4 teaspoon freshly ground black pepper
- 2 tablespoons chopped fresh cilantro leaves or shredded fresh basil leaves

PASTA WEDGES: Prepare the pasta according to the package directions; drain. In a medium bowl, toss the pasta with parsley or basil, 1/2 tablespoon oil, salt and pepper. Line a 9-inch round cake or pie pan with plastic wrap. Distribute the pasta evenly on top of plastic wrap. Cover with a second sheet of the plastic wrap and nestle a second cake or pie pan over the pasta. Place a weight (such as a can) on the top pan. Refrigerate the pasta at least 8 hours.

SAUCE: Warm the oil in a large saucepan. Stir in the seeds and toast them over medium-high heat. Add the dill or parsley, fennel, celery, carrot, parsnips and bell pepper. Cook, stirring, until the vegetables are slightly soft, about 5 minutes. Add the water and cook over medium heat for 20 minutes. Stir in the tomatoes or tomato sauce and cook another 10 minutes. Continue cooking if you desire a thicker sauce. Season with salt and pepper.

WARM the pasta to room temperature. Cut into 6 wedges. Place the wedges on a nonstick or oiled baking tray. Drizzle the remaining 1/2 tablespoon olive oil over the wedges and sprinkle them with the Parmesan. Broil until lightly browned, about 4 minutes.

TO SERVE, place a pasta wedge in a shallow soup bowl and sprinkle with cilantro or basil. Pour some vegetable sauce around the pasta wedge. Repeat with the remaining wedges and sauce.

> **PER SERVING:**
> 157 Cal.; 4g Prot.; 4g Fat; 26g Carb.;
> 0mg Chol.; 76mg Sod.; 7g Fiber.

Pasta Cacciatore

serves 4

For absolutely delicious results, select a bouillon with a delicate vegetable flavor rather than a "beefy" one.

> 2 medium or large yellow onions, quartered
>
> 1 pound carrots
>
> 3/4 pound celery stalks
>
> 2 to 3 tablespoons virgin olive oil
>
> 1/2 teaspoon reduced-sodium salt
>
> 2 vegetable bouillon cubes, dissolved in 1/2 cup boiling water
>
> 6 tablespoons tomato paste
>
> 1 3/4 to 2 cups dry sherry
>
> Salt and freshly ground black pepper to taste
>
> 1 recipe Fresh Pasta Dough (page 326), cut into 1/4-inch widths (or 12 ounces uncooked whole-wheat fettuccine)
>
> Grated Romano cheese (optional)

FINELY chop the onions; set aside. Cut each carrot into 4 to 6 strips, then slice. Cut each celery stalk into 2 strips, then slice.

IN A LARGE SAUCEPAN, heat the oil over medium heat. Add the onions and cook, stirring, until limp and transparent. Add the carrots and celery, and cook, stirring, until tender-crisp, about 8 to 10 minutes. Stir in the reduced-sodium salt, dissolved bouillon, tomato paste and 1 cup sherry. Cover and simmer 10 minutes. Stir in the remaining sherry, and simmer 10 minutes more. Add the salt and pepper.

PREPARE the fresh pasta dough according to the recipe directions, or prepare uncooked pasta according to the package directions and drain. Transfer to a platter and top with the sauce. Serve with Romano cheese.

> **PER SERVING:**
> 499 Cal.; 13g Prot.; 8g Fat; 77g Carb.;
> 0mg Chol.; 448mg Sod.; 10g Fiber.

Pasta with Roasted Carrot Sauce

serves 2

Roasting the vegetables for this low-fat pasta sauce gives them a sweet, smoky flavor.

> 6 carrots, sliced
>
> 1 onion, chopped
>
> 1 tablespoon virgin olive oil
>
> 2 cloves garlic, minced
>
> 1/2 pound uncooked pasta
>
> 1 cup vegetable broth

PREHEAT the oven to 350°F. Combine the carrots, onion, olive oil and garlic in a small bowl, then spread them out on a baking sheet. Bake until golden and tender, stirring twice, about 45 minutes. Meanwhile, prepare the pasta according to the package directions; drain. Purée the roasted vegetables with broth in a food processor or blender. Toss with the hot pasta. Serve at once.

> **PER SERVING:**
> 491 Cal.; 14g Prot.; 9g Fat; 89g Carb.;
> 0mg Chol.; 78mg Sod.; 15g Fiber.

Noodle-Currant Latkes

serves 5

A slightly sweet noodle pudding called lukshen kugel is traditional in many Jewish homes. This recipe borrows the cooking technique traditionally used for potato pancakes (latkes) to turn this kugel into a crispy noodle pancake. Top it with applesauce and sour cream.

> One 8-ounce package thin egg noodles
>
> 2 eggs, beaten (or 1/2 cup egg substitute)
>
> 1/2 cup currants
>
> 1 tablespoon all-purpose flour
>
> 1 teaspoon ground cinnamon
>
> 2 tablespoons brown sugar
>
> 1/4 teaspoon salt
>
> Nonstick cooking spray

PREPARE the noodles according to the package directions until *al dente*; drain. In a large mixing bowl, mix together the noodles, eggs or egg substitute, currants, flour, cinnamon, brown sugar and salt; set aside.

SPRAY a large, nonstick skillet with nonstick cooking spray. Place over high heat for 30 seconds. Lower the heat to medium and drop the noodle mixture by heaping tablespoons into the skillet, flattening each mound into a pancake with the back of the spoon. Fry the latkes until browned and crisp, about 4 minutes on each side. Keep them warm in a 200°F oven until ready to serve.

> **PER SERVING:**
> 153 Cal.; 5g Prot.; 2g Fat; 27g Carb.;
> 80mg Chol.; 133mg Sod.; 1g Fiber.

Farfalle with Carrot, Sage and Scallion

serves 3

This recipe seems too simple to be downright delicious, but with its pretty bow-tie noodles and mixture of slightly sweet and snappy flavors, expect it.

> 1/2 pound uncooked farfalle
>
> 1 teaspoon virgin olive oil
>
> 2 to 3 tablespoons unsalted butter
>
> 3 medium carrots, julienned
>
> 9 scallions (green and white parts), cut diagonally into 1 1/2-inch pieces
>
> 40 fresh sage leaves, stems removed
>
> Salt and freshly ground black pepper to taste
>
> Juice from 1/2 lemon
>
> 3 tablespoons freshly grated Monterey Jack cheese (optional)

PREPARE the pasta according to the package directions; drain. Meanwhile, heat a large skillet over medium-high heat. Add the oil and 1 1/2 tablespoons butter. When the oil and butter are sizzling, add the carrots and cook, stirring, until soft and golden, about 7 minutes. Add the scallions and sage leaves, and cook, stirring, until the sage begins to crisp and the scallions are brown, about 7 minutes. Lower the heat, add salt and pepper, and cover to keep warm.

RETURN the pasta to the cooking pot. Add the lemon juice and remaining 1/2 to 1 1/2 tablespoons butter. Toss lightly. Divide the pasta evenly among 3 serving bowls and top each serving with the vegetable mixture. Sprinkle with cheese.

Bean Pasta Primavera

serves 6

This purée of beans and roasted peppers dresses up pasta. And it's a calcium winner, too, with 273 milligrams of this mineral per serving.

SAUCE

2 1/2 cups cooked white beans

1 1/4 cups vegetable stock (page 178)

2 roasted red bell peppers (page 106), peeled and seeded (or a 7-ounce jar roasted red peppers, drained)

1 1/2 tablespoons chopped fresh tarragon leaves (or 1 teaspoon dried)

1 tablespoon chopped fresh thyme leaves (or 1 teaspoon dried)

1 1/2 tablespoons chopped fresh marjoram leaves (or 1 teaspoon dried)

Pinch cayenne pepper or paprika

1/2 teaspoon salt

Freshly ground black pepper to taste

PASTA

1 pound uncooked spinach spaghetti, udon noodles or whole-wheat pasta

2 pounds broccoli

1 pound asparagus

3 large yellow or red peppers, seeded

3 bunches spinach, trimmed and torn

1/2 cup fresh basil leaves, shredded

1 1/2 tablespoons poppy seeds

Salt and freshly ground black pepper to taste

8 oil-packed sun-dried tomatoes, drained and slivered

SAUCE: In a food processor, process 1 1/2 cups beans, stock and roasted peppers until smooth and creamy. Fold in the herbs, and season with the cayenne or paprika, salt and pepper. Set aside.

PASTA: Prepare the pasta according to the package directions; drain. Meanwhile, remove the broccoli florets from the stalks and cut into small, bite-sized pieces. Peel the broccoli stalks and cut diagonally into 1/4-inch-thick slices. Cut the asparagus stalks diagonally into 1 inch-long slices. Cut the bell peppers into long slivers. Steam the broccoli, asparagus and peppers until tender-crisp, about 10 minutes; set aside. Steam the spinach for 3 to 4 minutes. Cool, press out excess liquid and chop coarsely.

PLACE the pasta in a large warmed bowl. Add the sauce, vegetables, basil, poppy seeds and the remaining 1 cup white beans. Toss gently to mix. Season with salt and pepper. Garnish with sun-dried tomatoes.

Mexicana Corn Pasta

serves 6

Pinto beans and peppers in a spicy sauce top corn pasta to make an unusual and delicious dish.

| 1 cup canned tomato purée
| 1 medium red onion, chopped
| 2 garlic cloves, minced
| 2 large roasted red bell peppers, chopped
| 1 roasted pasilla chili pepper, chopped (or 1 tablespoon chopped canned jalapeño chilies)
| 2 teaspoons ground cumin
| 2 teaspoons ground oregano
| 2 teaspoons chili powder
| Cayenne pepper to taste
| Juice of 1/2 lemon
| 1 1/2 cups pinto or kidney beans
| 1 cup whole-kernel corn
| 1/3 cup sour cream or plain yogurt
| 1/2 cup coarsely grated cheddar cheese
| 14 ounces uncooked corn pasta
| Fresh cilantro leaves, minced
| 12 flour tortillas (optional)

IN A LARGE SKILLET, gently simmer the tomato purée. Add the onion and garlic, and simmer until the onion softens. Stir in the red peppers and pasilla or jalapeño peppers, cumin, oregano, chili powder, cayenne and lemon juice. Add the beans and corn.

ADD a heaping spoonful of the bean mixture to the sour cream or yogurt, then stir the mixture back into the skillet. Add the grated cheese and blend well.

PREPARE the corn pasta according to the package directions; drain. Top the cooked pasta with the bean-cheese mixture, and sprinkle with cilantro. Serve at once, accompanied by the flour tortillas.

> **PER SERVING:**
> 408 Cal.; 16g Prot.; 6g Fat; 71g Carb.;
> 15mg Chol.; 84mg Sod.; 7g Fiber.

Fresh No-Cholesterol Pasta Dough

serves 8

This eggless pasta contains semolina, which helps it retain its shape.

| 1 cup whole-wheat flour (see Note)
| 1 cup plus 2 to 3 tablespoons white semolina
| 1/2 to 3/4 cup water
| Additional semolina for flouring
| 1 teaspoon salt (optional)

USING A FOOD PROCESSOR, with the metal "S" blade in place, add the whole-wheat flour and 1 cup semolina to the work bowl, pulsing on and off to mix. With the machine running, dribble in the water until the dough forms a ball. Process for about 40 seconds. Stop the machine and feel the dough; it should be firm yet elastic.

ADD as much of the additional 2 to 3 tablespoons of the semolina to the dough as possible. If the dough breaks apart, add a little water and process into a ball again.

TRANSFER the dough to your work surface. Flour it with additional semolina, divide it into quarters and flour it again. Flatten one piece of the dough with your hand. (Cover the other quarters with plastic wrap to prevent them from drying.) Flour again and pass it through the roller mechanism of a hand-crank pasta machine at the first setting. Then rub the semolina onto both sides, fold the dough into thirds and pass it through the second setting. Cut the resulting piece in half vertically. Then flour each half well and pass through the third setting. Repeat and pass through the fourth setting.

HANG the sheets of dough on a pasta rack or on the back of a chair covered with a dishcloth. Let the dough dry, about 15 minutes or slightly longer, depending on the humidity. When it's dry, flour the dough on both sides and cut it into 1/4-inch ribbons using the noodle-cutting mechanism of your pasta machine (or leave the dough in sheets for lasagna). Repeat the process with the remaining quarters of dough.

TO COOK, bring the water to a boil in a large pot. Add the pasta and salt, and cook only until the water returns to a boil, 2 to 4 minutes; drain. (Do not overcook.) Serve the pasta or use it in a recipe.

Variation:

To make fresh spinach pasta, use 3/4 cup whole-wheat flour, 3/4 cup white semolina and 8 ounces fresh spinach (washed and stemmed but not dried). Using the metal "S" blade, process these ingredients together, then add 1 to 3 tablespoons water. Form the dough into a ball, work in 3 to 5 additional tablespoons of semolina, and make the pasta as instructed above.

Note:

Choose a hard, finely ground whole-wheat flour. Do not use pastry flour or coarsely ground flour.

> **PER SERVING:**
> 113 Cal.; 5g Prot.; 0.7g Fat; 24g Carb.;
> 0mg Chol.; 1mg Sod.; 0.4g Fiber.

Fresh Pasta Dough

serves 6

Making pasta dough may seem complicated, but with a little practice, it's a breeze. Besides, store-bought pasta can't compare in taste or texture. You may make fresh pasta dough by hand or with the help of a food processor.

> About 3 cups unbleached white flour (see Note)
> 4 eggs (or 1 cup egg substitute or 1 cup hot water—see Note)

BY HAND: Pour the flour onto a flat surface, making a mound. Make a well in the center. Crack the eggs into the well and break up the yolks with a fork. (Or pour in egg substitute or hot water.) With your fingers, begin drawing in a little bit of flour at a time and mixing it with eggs or water. When the mixture forms a paste, draw in all the flour. Mix well and begin kneading. Knead until the dough is a soft, firm ball, about 8 minutes. Wrap the dough in a damp dishcloth.

IN A FOOD PROCESSOR: Insert the metal blade in the processor, pour in 1 1/2 cups flour and crack 2 eggs on top (or start the processor and pour in half of the egg substitute or hot water through the feeding tube.) Process until the dough forms a ball on top of the blades and cleans the sides of the bowl, about 1 minute. Then process 2 more minutes to knead it. Remove the dough and wrap it in a damp dishcloth. Repeat with the remaining flour and eggs (or egg substitute and hot water).

TO SHAPE: Remove a piece of dough appropriate for the recipe you are making (an egg-sized piece for ravioli or cappelletti; a larger piece for tortellini, tortellacci, cannelloni, agnolotti or shells). Keep the remaining dough covered with a dishcloth. Roll out the dough with a pasta machine or a rolling pin until it is almost translucent. (When using a pasta machine, pass a floured piece of dough through the first setting, flour again and pass through the second setting, and continue this process ending with the thinnest setting.) Cut into shapes needed for the dish you are making and add the filling if necessary. Try to use up as much of the rolled-out pasta as possible the first time. (You may collect the trimmings and roll them again, but rolling too many times toughens the dough.) Repeat with the remaining dough.

TO COOK: Bring a large pot of water to a rolling boil and add a pinch of salt. Add the fresh pasta and stir gently. It will begin bobbing to the surface after 1 to 2 minutes, indicating that it's almost ready. Stir and cook another 30 seconds or until it tastes done. Pasta should be served *al dente*, or slightly firm to the tooth. Do not let fresh pasta overcook.

Notes:

- The amount of flour you will need can vary greatly, depending on the size of your eggs, the batch your flour comes from and even the weather. If the dough is wet or sticks to your hands rather than forming a soft ball, add 1 teaspoon of flour at a time, kneading between additions, until the dough reaches the right consistency. If the dough is dry and crumbly, add 1 teaspoon of water at a time, kneading between additions, until it reaches the right consistency.

- If you use water instead of eggs or egg substitute, the water should be hot from the tap, not boiling. This version is somewhat stickier than the egg or egg-substitute methods, so be extra attentive to flouring the rolling pin, work surface and your hands.

PER SERVING:
248 Cal.; 10g Prot.; 4g Fat; 43g Carb.;
110mg Chol.; 36mg Sod.; 2g Fiber.

18

soy-based dishes

WHEN MANY PEOPLE THINK "VEGETARIAN," the word *tofu* often comes to mind. Tofu—or soybean curd, if you prefer—became popular in the United States in the 1970s, about the same time that many young people said they didn't trust anyone over thirty. Now that they're in their middle years and are rediscovering the vegetarian choice (primarily for health reasons), a few facts about tofu have come to light. Namely, tofu and most other soy-foods are high in fat. In fact, about half of the calories in tofu come from fat, although none from saturated fats. (Some tofu makers have developed fat-reduced tofu in recent years.) Before you decide to skip these recipes, keep in mind that tofu traditionally serves as a secondary food, boosting the protein and calcium contents of an entrée. When tofu is predominant, serve several side dishes to lower the overall fat profile of the menu. Tofu also has the flexibility to take on the flavor of the dish it's in. And it can be sautéed, crumbled or frozen and thawed (to achieve a meaty texture).

Neatloaf

serves 6

This loaf has a meaty flavor and is much lower in fat, cholesterol and sodium than meatloaf. The next day, have neatloaf sandwiches with your favorite trimmings.

    2 cups ground seitan
    12 ounces firm tofu, drained and crumbled
    1 slice bread, torn into crumbs
    2 eggs, slightly beaten (optional)
    1/4 teaspoon ground cloves
    1/8 teaspoon grated nutmeg
    3/4 teaspoon freshly ground black pepper
    3/4 teaspoon salt
    1 tablespoon soy sauce
    1 tablespoon vegetarian Worcestershire sauce (or additional soy sauce)
    2 tablespoons oil
    1/2 cup minced celery
    1 onion, diced
    1 carrot, diced
    1/4 cup chopped fresh parsley

PREHEAT the oven to 350°F. Mash together the seitan, tofu, bread crumbs, eggs and seasonings. Set aside. Heat the oil in a skillet and cook the celery, onion and carrot, stirring, until soft. Stir in the parsley and remove from the heat. Add the vegetables to the tofu mixture and mix well. Shape into a loaf, place in an oiled 9 × 5-inch loaf pan and bake, uncovered, until well browned, about 1 hour.

> **PER SERVING:**
> 140 Cal.; 11g Prot.; 8g Fat; 8g Carb.;
> 0mg Chol.; 674mg Sod.; 1g Fiber.

Oven-Crisp Tofu Sticks with Ketchup Sauce

serves 6

Most kids love this dish because it's a finger food with a ketchup sauce. For extra flavor, use herb-flavored tofu.

KETCHUP SAUCE
    3/4 cup water
    1/4 cup tomato paste
    2 tablespoons maple syrup
    2 tablespoons fresh lemon juice
    1/2 teaspoon puréed fresh ginger root
    1 tablespoon minced fresh parsley
    Cayenne pepper to taste
    Salt to taste

TOFU STICKS
    24 ounces firm or extra-firm tofu (water-packed, not aseptic or silken), drained
    1/3 cup fine cracker crumbs
    2 tablespoons cornmeal
    1 1/2 tablespoons salt-free all-purpose seasoning
    1/2 teaspoon ground chipotle pepper or chili powder
    1/4 teaspoon salt
    Olive oil cooking spray or mesquite oil cooking spray

KETCHUP SAUCE: Whisk together the water, tomato paste, maple syrup, lemon juice and ginger in a small pan. Bring to a boil, stirring constantly, and cook 1 minute. Let cool. Add the parsley and season with cayenne and salt.

TOFU STICKS: Preheat the oven to 375°F. Drain the tofu and wrap in paper towels for 10 to 15 minutes. In a shallow bowl, mix together the cracker crumbs, cornmeal, seasoning, ground chipotle or chili powder, and salt. Set aside. Spray a large wire cooling rack with oil. Cut each block of tofu into 12 sticks about 3 inches long and 3/4 inch thick. Dredge each stick in the crumb mixture and place the sticks on the wire rack. Spray them with oil. Bake until crisp and brown, about 35 to 45 minutes. Serve the tofu sticks warm, with the ketchup sauce drizzled on top or served on the side.

> **PER SERVING:**
> 253 Cal.; 17g Prot.; 11g Fat; 21g Carb.;
> 0mg Chol.; 84mg Sod.; 1g Fiber.

Tofu with Key West Barbecue Sauce

serves 4

Each region of the South lays claim to possessing the definitive barbecue sauce. This one comes from the Florida Keys.

TOFU

- 1 pound extra-firm tofu
- 2 tablespoons unbleached white flour
- 2 tablespoons cornmeal
- 1 1/2 teaspoons poultry seasoning
- 2 teaspoons nutritional yeast
- 1/2 teaspoon salt (optional)
- 1/4 teaspoon freshly ground black pepper
- 2 tablespoons prepared yellow mustard
- 4 tablespoons canola or peanut oil

SAUCE

- 1/2 cup ketchup
- 1/3 to 1/2 cup sugar or honey
- 2 tablespoons fresh lime juice
- 2 cloves garlic, minced
- 1 small onion, minced
- 4 tablespoons vegetarian Worcestershire sauce
- 1 teaspoon hot pepper sauce

TOFU: Cut the tofu on the short end into 1/4-inch slices. Drain on a dishcloth for 30 minutes. On a plate, mix together the flour, cornmeal, poultry seasoning, nutritional yeast, salt, and pepper. Brush the drained tofu on both sides with mustard, then roll in the cornmeal mixture. Set aside.

HEAT 1 tablespoon oil in a heavy skillet over medium heat. carefully place four slices of tofu in the skillet, without crowding, and cook, stirring, until golden brown. Drain on paper towels. Keep warm in a slow oven while you cook the remaining tofu in the remaining oil.

SAUCE: In a heavy, medium saucepan, combine all the ingredients. Bring to a boil, lower the heat and simmer 20 to 30 minutes. To serve, pour the sauce over the tofu.

> **PER SERVING
> WITH 1 TABLESPOON SAUCE:**
> 344 Cal.; 17g Prot.; 22g Fat; 15g Carb.;
> 0mg Chol.; 205mg Sod.; 2g Fiber.

Pacific Rim Brochettes

serves 4

These brochettes taste best if the tofu is marinated for 4 to 6 hours.

TOFU AND MARINADE

- 1 pound extra-firm tofu, drained
- 1 stalk fresh lemongrass (or 1 teaspoon grated lemon zest)
- 1/2 bunch fresh mint leaves, chopped
- 5 cloves garlic
- 1 serrano pepper, seeded and minced
- 2 tablespoons chopped fresh cilantro stems
- 2 tablespoons chopped fresh ginger root
- 3 scallions (green and white parts), chopped
- 1 to 2 teaspoons peanut butter (optional)
- 2 tablespoons brown sugar
- 1 to 2 tablespoons coconut milk (optional)
- Juice of 1 lime
- 1/4 cup liquid tamarind (see Note) or 1/4 cup nonfat yogurt
- 2 tablespoons low-sodium soy sauce

BROCHETTES

- 6 to 8 scallions (green and white parts)
- 2 medium tomatoes, cut into eighths
- 6 to 8 small jalapeño peppers (optional)
- 1/4 to 1/2 pound snow peas
- 1/4 to 1/2 pound white button mushrooms
- Fresh cilantro leaves, for garnish

TOFU AND MARINADE: Gently press the tofu between dish towels to remove excess moisture. Slice the tofu into pieces about 2 × 1 × 1/2 inch. Then cut each chunk in half crosswise. Set aside. (If desired, you may bake the tofu on a lightly oiled baking sheet at this point for 30 minutes at 350°F. Then turn and bake until lightly browned and crisp, about 10 to 15 minutes more. Set aside.)

SLICE off and discard all but the bottom 3 inches of the lemongrass root. With a mallet or rolling pin, pound the lemongrass stalk to release aromatic oils. In a food processor, combine the stalk with mint, garlic, serrano pepper, cilantro, ginger and scallions. Pulse on and off for 30 seconds. Add the remaining ingredients and process 1 minute. Transfer to a shallow plastic or glass container. Add the tofu pieces and cover. Marinate 4 to 6 hours.

BROCHETTES: Prepare the grill. Cut the scallions into 2-inch pieces. Place the vegetables and the tofu on skewers, alternating for color. (Snow peas should be grouped in threes so they don't cook too quickly.) Place the skewers on the hot grill and brush with the remaining marinade. Grill, turning once, until the vegetables are tender, about 5 to 10 minutes. Place on a serving platter and garnish with cilantro.

Note:

Used in Indian cooking, tamarinds are fruits from the tamarind tree. Sold in Indian groceries in a jellylike, concentrate form, tamarinds also are sometimes sold dried and may be added to vegetable, bean and other dishes to lend a piquant, sour flavor.

> **PER SERVING:**
> 258 Cal.; 18g Prot.; 9g Fat; 26g Carb.;
> 0mg Chol.; 333mg Sod.; 5g Fiber.

Tandoori Tofu Brochettes

serves 4

TOFU AND MARINADE

- 1 pound extra-firm tofu
- 3 scallions (green and white parts)
- 1 tablespoon minced fresh ginger root
- 3 cloves garlic
- 1 to 2 tablespoons brown sugar
- 1 tablespoon low-sodium soy sauce
- Pinch saffron dissolved in 1/2 cup boiling water
- 1/2 cup nonfat yogurt or soy yogurt
- 2 tablespoons chili powder
- 2 tablespoons paprika
- 1 tablespoon *garam masala* (optional)
- Salt and freshly ground black pepper to taste

BROCHETTES

- 4 to 6 small red onions, unpeeled
- 1/4 to 1/2 pound white button mushrooms
- 1 pint cherry tomatoes
- 1 green bell pepper, seeded and sliced
- Fresh cilantro leaves and lemon wedges, for garnish

TOFU AND MARINADE: Gently press the tofu between dish-cloths to remove excess moisture. Slice the tofu into large pieces, about 2 × 1 × 1/2 inch. Then cut each chunk in half crosswise. Set aside. (If desired, you may bake the tofu on a lightly oiled baking sheet at 350°F for 30 minutes. Then turn and bake until the tofu is lightly browned and crisp, about 10 to 15 minutes more. Set aside.)

PLACE the scallions and ginger in a food processor, and process briefly. With the machine running, drop in the garlic cloves, one at a time. Process for 30 seconds. Add the remaining ingredients and process for 1 minute. Transfer the marinade to a plastic or glass container.

BROCHETTES: Place the onions, mushrooms and the tofu in the marinade; cover and refrigerate overnight.

PREPARE the grill. Quarter the onions and remove their outer skins. Skewer the onions, mushrooms, tomatoes, green pepper and tofu, alternating for color. Place the skewers on the hot grill and brush with the remaining marinade. Cover the grill and let the vegetables smoke for 5 minutes without opening the lid. Then turn the skewers and cook until the vegetables are tender, about 3 to 5 minutes more. Place the skewers on a serving platter and garnish with cilantro leaves and lemon wedges.

> **PER SERVING:**
> 322 Cal.; 21g Prot.; 9g Fat; 36g Carb.;
> 1mg Chol.; 514mg Sod.; 5g Fiber.

Peppers Stuffed with Rice, Tofu and Fruit

serves 4

The usual stuffed peppers made with ground beef have about twice the fat of this slimmed-down version.

| 4 green bell peppers
| 1 cup uncooked brown rice
| 2 cups water
| 1/4 cup port wine
| 1/2 cup finely diced firm tofu
| 1/2 cup dried cherries, dried cranberries or currants
| 1/4 to 1/2 cup pine nuts or chopped nuts (such as pecans, walnuts or almonds)
| 3 to 5 tablespoons freshly grated Parmesan cheese
| 1 teaspoon salt
| 1 teaspoon freshly ground black pepper

Cut off the tops of the peppers and remove the seeds and membranes. Place the peppers in a shallow glass baking dish with 1/2 inch of water. Microwave on high power until the peppers are barely tender, about 3 to 4 minutes. Set aside to cool. (Or steam the peppers on your stovetop until barely tender, about 5 minutes.)

IN A SAUCEPAN, combine the rice and water. Cover, bring to a boil, then lower the heat and simmer until the rice is tender, about 50 minutes. Meanwhile, in a small skillet, heat the wine to a simmer over medium-low heat and add the tofu; simmer until the wine is absorbed or evaporated, about 8 minutes.

PREHEAT the oven to 350°F. In a mixing bowl, stir together the hot rice, dried fruit, nuts, Parmesan, salt, pepper and tofu. Stuff the peppers, pressing the filling into the cavities. Bake until the filling is hot and the peppers are tender, about 15 minutes.

> **PER SERVING:**
> 320 Cal.; 13g Prot.; 9g Fat; 42g Carb.;
> 3mg Chol.; 611mg Sod.; 5g Fiber.

Roasted Tofu and Okra with Dipping Sauce

serves 4

Tofu, blackstrap molasses, okra and sesame seeds combine to make this dish a calcium bonanza (692 milligrams of calcium per serving).

TOFU

| 1 1/2 pounds extra-firm tofu
| 1/3 cup blackstrap molasses
| 1/3 cup prepared mustard, preferably stone-ground
| 1/2 teaspoon salt
| 1/2 teaspoon seasoned pepper (such as lemon or garlic)

OKRA

| 1 1/2 pounds small okra, rinsed and patted dry
| Olive oil cooking spray or virgin olive oil for brushing
| 1 tablespoon ground coriander
| 1 teaspoon ground cumin
| 1 teaspoon curry powder
| Salt to taste (optional)

DIPPING SAUCE

> 3 tablespoons tahini (sesame paste)
>
> 1 tablespoon sugar or molasses
>
> 1 tablespoon chopped stalks of fresh lemongrass
> (or 1 1/2 tablespoons dried lemongrass or
> 1/3 teaspoon lemon or lime zest)
>
> 1/4 teaspoon cayenne pepper
>
> 1 teaspoon curry powder
>
> 1 cup water
>
> 1/4 cup tomato sauce
>
> 1 tablespoon sesame seeds, toasted (page 106)

TOFU: Cut the tofu crosswise into eight 3/4-inch-thick slabs, then cut in half lengthwise to yield 16 pieces. Put the tofu between 2 dishcloths and place a cutting board on top. Let sit about 10 minutes. Combine the molasses and mustard in a baking dish. Mix in salt and pepper. Place the tofu in the marinade and turn to coat on all sides. Cover and marinate in the refrigerator for at least 1 hour.

OKRA: Cut off and discard the okra stems, and transfer the okra to 2 baking sheets. Spray or brush well with oil; sprinkle with spices and salt. Toss to coat and set aside.

DIPPING SAUCE: Combine the sauce ingredients in a small saucepan. Cook over very low heat, stirring frequently, until slightly thickened, about 5 minutes. Set aside.

TO COOK, if you're using a charcoal grill, oil the grill. Place the tofu and okra over medium-hot coals and grill, covered, for 10 to 20 minutes, turning once. (If you're using an oven, preheat to 500°F; roast the okra on a baking sheet and place the tofu on an oiled cooking rack resting over a baking sheet until the tofu is browned and okra is tender, about 15 to 25 minutes.) Arrange the tofu and okra on a platter with the dipping sauce.

> **PER SERVING**
> **(WITH 1 TABLESPOON SAUCE):**
> 406 Cal.; 28g Prot.; 14g Fat; 37g Carb.;
> 0mg Chol.; 478mg Sod.; 5g Fiber.

Scrambled Tofu with Tortillas

serves 6

Full of lively flavors, this Hispanic-style recipe may become one of your family's favorite tofu dishes.

> 1 tablespoon virgin olive oil
>
> 1 medium onion, chopped finely
>
> 6 corn tortillas, torn or cut into 1-inch pieces
>
> 3 plum tomatoes, diced
>
> 1 pound firm tofu, drained and diced
>
> One 14-ounce can crushed tomatoes or tomato purée
>
> 1/2 teaspoon ground cumin
>
> 1/2 teaspoon dried oregano
>
> Salt to taste
>
> 1 cup grated cheddar cheese or cheddar-style soy
> cheese (optional)
>
> Prepared salsa (optional)

HEAT the oil in a large skillet. Add the onion and cook, stirring, until lightly golden. Add the remaining ingredients except the cheese and salsa, cover and cook over medium heat for 10 minutes. Sprinkle with the grated cheese, cover and cook over low heat 5 minutes more. Serve as is or top with the salsa.

> **PER SERVING:**
> 219 Cal.; 13g Prot.; 9g Fat; 20g Carb.;
> 0mg Chol.; 198mg Sod.; 3g Fiber.

Baked Vegetable Frittata

serves 6

This tofu-based frittata is like a crustless quiche: fancy, flavorful and relatively low in fat.

- 1 onion, chopped
- 1 leek, sliced
- 8 ounces white button mushrooms, sliced
- 3 1/2 cups chopped fresh spinach (about 5 ounces)
- 1 pound firm or regular tofu
- 1/2 cup soymilk or low-fat milk
- 1/2 teaspoon nutritional yeast
- 1/2 teaspoon grated nutmeg
- 2 tablespoons arrowroot powder or cornstarch
- Pinch ground turmeric (optional)
- Salt and freshly ground black pepper to taste
- 1 tomato, sliced
- Mushroom slices, for garnish (optional)
- 1/2 teaspoon dried basil

COOK the onion and leek, stirring, in a heavy skillet with a little water until the onion is translucent. Add the mushrooms and cook, stirring, until the vegetables are tender. Add the spinach and cook until just wilted.

PREHEAT the oven to 350°F. In a food processor or blender, purée the tofu, soymilk or milk, nutritional yeast, nutmeg, arrowroot or cornstarch, and turmeric. Combine with the cooked vegetables. Season with salt and pepper. Pour into 6 lightly oiled individual soufflé dishes or a 9-inch quiche dish or round glass dish.

Decorate the top with the sliced tomatoes and a few extra slices of mushrooms. Sprinkle with basil. Bake until the frittata has risen slightly and is golden brown and firm to the touch, about 40 minutes. (If baked in a single pan, let cool 10 minutes before cutting into wedges like a pie.)

> **PER SERVING:**
> 170 Cal.; 13g Prot.; 6g Fat; 14G Carb.;
> 0mg Chol.; 227mg Sod.; 4g Fiber.

Brunswick Stew

serves 16

Thick and rich in flavor, this updated Southern classic is perfect for feeding a crowd.

TOFU
- 1 tablespoon canola oil
- 1/3 cup low-sodium soy sauce
- 2 tablespoons water
- 2 cloves garlic, minced
- 1 small piece fresh ginger root, peeled and minced
- 1 tablespoon sugar
- 1 pound extra-firm tofu
- 8 ounces tempeh, diced
- 8 ounces seitan, diced

STEW

- 2 stalks celery (with leaves), chopped
- 1 large onion, chopped finely
- 2 quarts water or vegetable stock (page 178)
- One 10-ounce package frozen baby lima beans
- One 10-ounce package frozen green peas
- One 16-ounce can whole-kernel corn
- One 28-ounce can chopped tomatoes (with juices)
- 2 large potatoes, peeled and diced
- 3 tablespoons low-sodium soy sauce
- 1 tablespoon liquid smoke, or to taste (optional)
- 1 teaspoon ground allspice
- 1/2 teaspoon hot pepper sauce, or to taste
- 1 teaspoon freshly ground black pepper
- 1 tablespoon prepared yellow mustard
- 3 tablespoons vegetarian Worcestershire sauce

TOFU: In a large, heavy soup pot, combine the oil, soy sauce, water, garlic, ginger and sugar, and bring to a simmer. Crumble the tofu into the sauce and cook, stirring, over medium-high heat until the liquid has evaporated and the tofu is browned. Add the tempeh and seitan; cook, stirring, until browned, about 5 minutes.

STEW: Add the remaining ingredients to the tofu mixture. Bring to a boil and lower the heat to a simmer. Cook, uncovered, until the stew is thick, about 45 minutes. (If the stew looks dry, add 1/2 to 1 cup water and simmer 10 minutes more.)

PER SERVING:
176 Cal.; 11g Prot.; 4g Fat; 21g Carb.;
0mg Chol.; 568mg Sod.; 5g Fiber.

Mexican Salad with Tofu and Tomatoes

serves 4

- 4 corn tortillas
- 1 pound firm tofu, drained and crumbled
- 1 tablespoon chili powder
- 1 teaspoon ground cumin
- 1 tablespoon ground coriander
- 1/4 teaspoon salt (optional)
- 2 teaspoons vegetable oil
- 6 cups shredded romaine lettuce
- 4 medium tomatoes, quartered
- 1/2 cup shredded low-fat Monterey Jack or soy cheese (optional)
- 4 tablespoons sour cream (optional)

PREHEAT the oven to 350°F. Place the tortillas on a dry cookie sheet and bake until crisp, about 15 minutes. Crumble into small pieces; set aside. In a skillet, cook the tofu, chili powder, cumin, coriander and salt in the oil, stirring, until the mixture is dry, about 5 minutes. Remove from the heat and cover.

ARRANGE the lettuce on 4 plates and sprinkle with the crumbled tortilla chips. Spoon the tofu mixture on top, add the tomato wedges and top with cheese and sour cream.

PER SERVING:
201 Cal.; 12g Prot.; 8g Fat; 23g Carb.;
0mg Chol.; 46mg Sod.; 4g Fiber.

Jambalaya with Tempeh

serves 6

Tempeh and TVP (textured vegetable protein; available in natural food stores) take the place of meat in this Creole dish.

- 2 cups chopped plum tomatoes
- 1 cup dry white wine
- 2 tablespoons virgin olive oil
- 1 medium onion, diced
- 1 stalk celery, sliced
- 1 green or red bell pepper, diced
- 3 cloves garlic, minced
- 1 1/2 cups vegetable stock (page 178)
- 2 cups prepared TVP (1 cup dry TVP reconstituted in 1 cup boiling water)
- 12 ounces tempeh, cut into bite-sized chunks
- 1 cup uncooked brown rice
- 1/2 teaspoon dried thyme
- 1/2 teaspoon dried sage
- 1/2 teaspoon dried marjoram
- 1 teaspoon salt
- Freshly ground black pepper to taste
- 1/2 cup chopped fresh parsley
- Dash hot pepper sauce
- Parsley sprigs, for garnish

Marinate the tomatoes in the wine for 1 hour. Meanwhile, in a large pot, heat the oil over low heat. Cook the onion, celery, bell pepper and garlic, stirring, until the onion is translucent, about 15 minutes. Stir in the vegetable stock and bring to a boil. Add the remaining ingredients (including the marinated tomatoes and marinade) except the garnish. Add water, if necessary, to cover the ingredients in the pot. Bring to a boil, lower the heat and simmer until the rice is tender and the water is absorbed, about 50 minutes, stirring occasionally. Fluff with a fork. Garnish with parsley sprigs.

> **PER SERVING:**
> 398 Cal.; 23g Prot.; 12g Fat; 38g Carb.;
> 0mg Chol.; 376mg Sod.; 6g Fiber.

Tempeh Paprikas

serves 6

- 2 tablespoons toasted sesame oil
- 2 large onions, chopped
- 2 tablespoons paprika
- 2 cups vegetable stock (page 178) or water
- 2 tablespoons dark miso
- 1 pound tempeh, cut into 32 triangles
- 1 teaspoon soy sauce
- 1 tablespoon apple cider vinegar
- 4 tablespoons tahini (sesame paste)
- Chopped scallions or fresh parsley, for garnish

Heat the oil in a large skillet over medium heat, and cook the onions and paprika, stirring, until the onions are golden, about 10 minutes. Bring 1 1/2 cups stock or water and the miso to a boil. Add the tempeh, lower the heat and simmer 30 to 45 minutes.

BLEND the soy sauce, vinegar and tahini with the remaining 1/2 cup stock or water. Add this mixture to the skillet, stirring as it thickens. Do not let it boil. Garnish with scallions or parsley.

Mushroom Stroganoff with Tempeh and Tofu

serves 6

This dish demands your undivided attention—if you overheat it, the sauce will separate irreparably. If you don't mind a few extra calories, splurge on real sour cream; it has a distinctly wonderful flavor.

I pound pasta of your choice

2 tablespoons unsalted butter or canola oil

I large white onion, sliced thinly

I clove garlic, crushed

2 1/3 cups sliced meaty mushrooms, such as shiitake or oyster mushrooms

2 1/3 cups sliced white button mushrooms

8 ounces tempeh, sliced into 1/2-inch-thick strips

2 cups low-fat sour cream or soy substitute

I cup soft tofu

2 tablespoons soy sauce

I tablespoon dry sherry

I teaspoon dry mustard

2 teaspoons dried dillweed, crumbled

Dash paprika

PREPARE the pasta according to the package directions; drain and keep warm. Heat the butter or oil in a large skillet. Cook the onion and garlic until soft and translucent. Add the mushrooms and tempeh, and continue to cook, stirring, until the mushrooms are completely soft. Remove from the heat.

IN A BLENDER or food processor, combine the sour cream or soy substitute, tofu, soy sauce, sherry and mustard. Process until smooth. Transfer the mixture to the top of a double boiler. Stir in the mushroom mixture and heat until warmed. Do not overheat. Stir in the dill and paprika. Pour the stroganoff over the pasta. Serve at once.

Note:

If you can't find meaty mushrooms, substitute white button mushrooms.

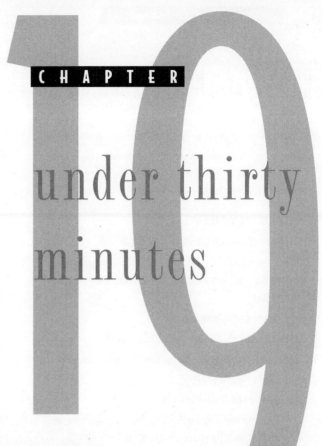

under thirty minutes

SURE, YOU CAN MAKE A SANDWICH, prepare a box of macaroni and cheese or toss a salad with odds and ends from your refrigerator in less than 30 minutes and call it dinner. But none of these options—or many other quick attempts at dinner—is truly satisfying. They seem thrown together without much thought, and taste might suffer. In this selection of satisfying main dishes, none take more than 30 minutes to prepare from start to finish. The recipes run the gamut from ethnic specialties to pasta dishes to vegetable sautés. Serve them with one of your favorite side dishes and some bread or a grain, and you won't leave the table hungry.

Rutabagas, Chickpeas and Greens

serves 4

Rutabagas—root vegetables with lots of complex carbohydrates and a flavor similar to turnips—team up
with noodles, vegetables and seasonings.

> 1 rutabaga, peeled and chopped
>
> 2 tablespoons virgin olive oil
>
> 1/4 pound mixed mild greens (such as spinach, red leaf
> lettuce and napa cabbage), torn into bite-sized
> pieces
>
> 2 cloves garlic, minced
>
> 1 teaspoon chopped hot red chili pepper
>
> 2 cups cooked chickpeas (or one 15-ounce can
> chickpeas, rinsed)
>
> 1 tablespoon fresh lemon juice
>
> 1/2 pound uncooked pasta, preferably a short pasta
> such as farfalle (bow-tie noodles)
>
> Salt to taste

IN A SKILLET, cook the rutabaga in the oil, stirring, over
medium heat for 5 minutes. Lower the heat, and add the
greens, garlic, chili pepper and chickpeas. Cover and
cook 5 minutes, stirring occasionally. Stir in the juice.
Meanwhile, prepare the pasta according to the package
directions. Toss with the vegetable mixture and add salt.

> **PER SERVING:**
> 309 Cal.; 12g Prot.; 8g Fat; 45g Carb.;
> 0mg Chol.; 62mg Sod.; 11g Fiber.

Vegetable Sauté with Tomato Sauce

serves 4

Serve this sauté over packaged quick brown rice or
leftover brown rice.

> 1 onion, chopped
>
> 1 clove garlic, crushed
>
> 1 potato, peeled and chunked
>
> 1 carrot, sliced
>
> 1 stalk celery, sliced
>
> 1 zucchini, chunked
>
> 1/4 pound white button mushrooms, cut in half
>
> 2 cups low-sodium tomato sauce
>
> 1 tablespoon chopped parsley
>
> 1/2 teaspoon paprika
>
> 1/2 teaspoon chili powder
>
> 1/2 teaspoon dried basil
>
> 1/4 teaspoon dry mustard
>
> 1/4 teaspoon ground cumin
>
> Dash freshly ground black pepper

COOK the onion, garlic, potato, carrot and celery in a
small amount of water for 10 minutes. Add the remaining
ingredients and cook until all the vegetables are just tender. Serve hot.

> **PER SERVING (WITHOUT RICE):**
> 98 Cal.; 3g Prot.; 0.4g Fat; 22g Carb.;
> 0mg Chol.; 48mg Sod.; 4g Fiber.

Pasta in Southwestern Sauce

serves 2

This not-too-spicy pasta dish is especially appealing if you use fresh pasta in various flavors, such as spinach, artichoke and beet.

1/4 cup dry sherry

1 teaspoon virgin olive oil

1 tablespoon minced fresh garlic

1/4 cup minced shallots

4 oil-packed sun-dried tomatoes, drained and chopped coarsely

2 tablespoons finely chopped pickled whole jalapeño peppers

2 large ripe tomatoes, seeded and chopped coarsely (or 1 1/2 cups chopped, canned plum tomatoes)

1/2 pound fresh pasta of choice

2 tablespoons chopped fresh basil leaves

2 tablespoons chopped fresh parsley

IN A HEAVY SKILLET over medium-high heat, heat the sherry and oil to bubbling; add the garlic and shallots. Cook, stirring, for 3 minutes; add the sun-dried tomatoes, jalapeño pepper and ripe or canned tomatoes. Lower the heat to low and cook, stirring occasionally, for 15 to 20 minutes.

WHILE the tomato-pepper sauce is simmering, bring a large pot of water to a boil and cook the pasta until tender, about 3 to 5 minutes, stirring frequently to prevent sticking; drain and rinse briefly in hot water. Drain again. Place the pasta in the skillet. Sprinkle basil and parsley on top. Toss with the sauce and serve.

PER SERVING:
282 Cal.; 8g Prot.; 2g Fat; 45g Carb.;
0mg Chol.; 155mg Sod.; 1g Fiber.

Carrot and Tofu Scramble

serves 4

Even people who dislike tofu usually love it when it's prepared this way. Serve it with rice.

2 tablespoons oil

1 pound carrots, grated

1 pound extra-firm tofu, drained and crumbled

1/3 cup soy sauce

1/3 cup sesame seeds (optional)

1 teaspoon dark sesame oil

IN A SKILLET, heat the oil over medium heat and cook the carrots, stirring, for 15 minutes. Add the tofu and cook, stirring, until the carrots are soft, about 5 minutes more. Add the soy sauce and sesame seeds. Cook 1 minute more. Stir in the sesame oil. Serve hot.

PER SERVING (WITHOUT RICE):
203 Cal.; 12g Prot.; 13g Fat; 16g Carb.;
0mg Chol.; 1,417mg Sod.; 4g Fiber.

Peanut Butter Spirals

serves 8

Kids love this mild, easy-to-make dish. Add a little hot chili oil or red pepper sauce to the adults' portions. The dish tastes great the next day eaten cold or reheated in a microwave or on a stovetop. The sauce also is delicious over rice and steamed vegetables.

12 ounces uncooked spiral pasta

2/3 cup no-salt, no-sugar peanut butter

3/4 cup water

3 to 4 tablespoons soy sauce

2 tablespoons mild vinegar

1 scallion (green and white parts), chopped coarsely

1 tablespoon honey or rice syrup

1/2 teaspoon ground ginger

1/2 teaspoon chili powder

1 1/2 cups frozen green peas, thawed

PREPARE the pasta according to the package directions; drain. Meanwhile, combine all the remaining ingredients except the peas in a food processor or blender and process until smooth. Transfer the pasta to a large serving bowl. Add the peas and sauce, stirring to combine. Serve warm.

Helpful hint:

The sauce thickens as it sits. Mix in more water if it sits too long before serving.

> ### PER SERVING:
> 224 Cal.; 9g Prot.; 11g Fat; 22g Carb.;
> 0mg Chol.; 259mg Sod.; 4g Fiber.

Hot and Spicy Noodles with Vegetables

serves 4

When you have a craving for fatty fried rice, try this low-fat recipe made with rice noodles, which come in many types, such as angel hair and fettuccine. They require only soaking in hot water to cook them.

1 teaspoon peanut oil

1/4 cup rice wine or mirin

2 tablespoons grated fresh ginger root

2 cloves garlic, minced

1 cup thinly sliced carrots

1 cup thinly peeled and sliced broccoli stems

1 cup thinly sliced green cabbage

2 scallions (green and white parts), sliced diagonally

1/4 cup water

2 teaspoons dark sesame oil

1/2 to 1 teaspoon cayenne pepper

1 tablespoon honey

1 teaspoon hoisin sauce (optional)

4 cups cooked rice noodles (about 16 ounces)

Low-sodium soy sauce to taste

IN A WOK or skillet over medium-high heat, heat the peanut oil and rice wine or mirin until bubbling. Add the ginger, garlic, carrots and broccoli. Stir-fry until the carrots soften slightly, about 5 minutes. Add the cabbage and scallions, cover and cook 3 minutes. With a slotted spoon, remove the vegetables to a platter; set aside.

ADD THE WATER, sesame oil, cayenne, honey and hoisin sauce to the wok or skillet and heat until bubbling. Add the noodles and stir-fry until heated through. Stir in the vegetables. Add soy sauce to taste.

Variation:

If you can't find Chinese rice noodles, substitute any variety of wide noodle.

> **PER SERVING:**
> 269 Cal.; 9g Prot.; 4g Fat; 45g Carb.;
> 0mg Chol.; 420mg Sod.; 3g Fiber.

Pasta with Dill and Tomatoes

serves 4

> 1 pound uncooked fusilli pasta
> 4 medium tomatoes, chopped
> 4 cloves garlic, minced
> 2 to 4 tablespoons virgin olive oil
> 3/4 cup grated Parmesan cheese (optional)
> 1 teaspoon salt
> 1 teaspoon freshly ground black pepper
> 1/4 cup chopped fresh dillweed

PREPARE the pasta according to the package directions; drain. Transfer the pasta to a serving bowl. Add the remaining ingredients and toss well. Serve warm or cold.

Variations:

- Substitute fresh chives, basil, thyme or cilantro for the dill.

- Substitute cooked broccoli, beans, white button mushrooms or squash for the tomato, or replace the tomato with sun-dried tomatoes.

> **PER SERVING:**
> 218 Cal.; 5g Prot.; 7g Fat; 33g Carb.;
> 0mg Chol.; 547mg Sod.; 3g Fiber.

Supreme Green Spaghetti

serves 4

This nutrient-packed vegetable sauce is a change from the usual tomato sauce served over spaghetti.

> 8 ounces uncooked spaghetti or other pasta
> 1 pound frozen chopped spinach or broccoli
> 1/2 cup skim milk
> 1 clove garlic, crushed
> 1 tablespoon butter, melted
> Salt to taste
> 4 teaspoons grated Parmesan cheese (optional)

PREPARE the pasta according to the package directions; drain. Meanwhile, microwave the frozen spinach or broccoli to thaw and cook, about 4 minutes on high power (or steam until just cooked). Transfer to a blender and add the milk, garlic, butter and salt. Purée. Pour the sauce over the hot pasta. Toss and sprinkle with Parmesan.

> **PER SERVING:**
> 242 Cal.; 9g Prot.; 4g Fat; 44g Carb.;
> 1mg Chol.; 184mg Sod.; 7g Fiber.

Classic Minestrone

page 161

Photo by Bob Skalkowski

page 165

Russian Bean-and-Potato Soup

Angel Hair Pasta with Eggplant Sauce

page 478

Photo by Bob Skalkowski

page 280

Bean-and-Rice Burritos

Photo by Bob Skalkowski

**Middle Eastern
Rice with
Lentils**

page 301

page 275

Hoppin' John